The Writer's Workshop

The Writer's Workshop

John F. Parker

Addison-Wesley Publishers

Don Mills, Ontario • Reading, Massachusetts
Menlo Park, California • London • Amsterdam • Sydney

Research: Barbara-Anne Eddy and Mary Parker
Design: Pronk & Associates
Editorial: Evlyn Windross, Phyllis Schwartz, Norma Jamieson,
     Ed Peck and Margaret MacDonald
Illustration: Paul McCusker, Graham Bardell, John Bianchi

The author also wishes to acknowledge the contributions of
    the students and teachers of various pilot projects
    his colleagues, Bob Read and Arne Lund
    his researchers, Barbara-Anne Eddy and Mary Parker
    and Tony Vander Woude and the staff of Addison-Wesley
    (Canada) Limited.

Canadian Cataloguing in Publication Data
Parker, John F. (John Frederick), 1933-
    The writer's workshop

Includes index.

ISBN 0-201-05724-7

1. English language — Composition and exercises.
2. English language — Rhetoric.   3. English
language — Grammar — 1950-   I. Eddy, Barbara-
Anne.   II. Parker, Mary.   III. Title.

PE1408.P37   808'.042   C82-094626-5

ISBN 0-201-05724-7

Printed in Canada

  B C D E F — BP — 86 85 84 83

to Bobbi

Table of Contents

Laboratory Section **385**

PREFACE

Are the following statements true or false?

Writers have a "special talent."
Writers always know what they are going to say before they sit down to write.
Writers have the ability to turn out a perfect product at one sitting.
Writers do their best writing working alone, in quiet surroundings.
All writers follow the same procedures when they write.

Most writers and teachers of writing would say that the above statements are false.[1] Recent studies have established several facts about the writing process. First, the major difference between good writers and other people is that good writers write – a great deal. Second, most good writers do not sit down and turn out perfect products in one sitting. Their work is the product of a process that involves an initial willingness to experiment and make mistakes, the ability to learn from their mistakes, frequent discussion and comments from other people; and, above all, repeated revision of their material.

While there is no magic formula that will automatically produce good writers, any student can become a better writer by going through the same process in a variety of meaningful writing assignments. This is the basic premise of *The Writer's Workshop.*

The Writer's Workshop will help you to develop your own writing process in several ways:

a) by providing a series of writing assignments, with strategies to assist you at each stage of the writing process;
b) by encouraging you to write for a real purpose to a specific audience;
c) by encouraging revision and offering suggestions for you and your fellow students to help each other in this process;
d) by providing an activity section, with exercises and games to help you and a partner improve writing skills and techniques, as required;
e) by providing an individualized-learning laboratory section, with sentence combining activities to help you express yourself in a variety of ways;
f) by encouraging you to approach the writing process positively;
g) by offering opportunities for you to become an independent, confident writer.

1. Smith, Frank. "Myths of Writing," *Language Arts*, October 1981.

A Brief Look at the Writing Process

The writing process involves four general steps. As you examine these steps, however, realize that you do not necessarily move from Step One to Step Two to Step Three, ending up very comfortably at Step Four. Writers often backtrack, leap forward, and backtrack again. But a knowledge of the steps will help you to develop *your* personal writing process.

Step One   Prewriting

The writing process begins with the generation of ideas. *The Writer's Workshop* provides you with specific prewriting suggestions for every assignment, but here are some general prewriting activities that you can use. You might:

a) develop an idea that you have been thinking about (the *think/write* method),
b) brainstorm a topic by talking with other people (the *talk/write* method),
c) read until an idea of your own comes (the *read/write* method),
d) simply write until an idea comes (the *write/write* method), or
e) be told what to write about (the *assign/write* method).

At some point during the prewriting stage, you should begin to control and limit your piece of writing according to four main writing variables: topic, format, purpose, and audience. (The writing variables are explained thoroughly in Activity 1.) Once you have specified your writing variables, you will then be able to draft your assignment from a solid foundation.

Step Two   Drafting

The drafting stage of the writing process involves the composing of your assignment, shaping and organizing it so that it communicates exactly what you want to say.

At this stage of the process, you will be considering the selection and organization of your information, your sentence structure, and your word choice.

The Writer's Workshop provides specific suggestions for drafting each assignment, as well as models of student and professional writing at the end of the assignment. In addition, you can refer to the Activities and Labs when you require help with a specific technique or sentence structure.

As you compose, you will probably make many changes, perhaps even writing several drafts, before you proceed to Step Three.

Step Three   Revision

Revision and evaluation is an ongoing process for every writer. In fact, most writers revise their work many times before and after they show it to others.

Although you can and should revise your work by yourself, modern research has shown that receiving feedback from your peers is even more beneficial. Although at first you may be reluctant to show your fellow students your writing, you will soon discover that this kind of sharing can create a happy working situation; not only will you learn a great deal from your fellow students, but you will be able to share with them what you know.

Appendix B offers suggestions for evaluating or revising your own work, or the work of your fellow students. A check list of questions to consider at this stage of the process is also included in the Appendix.

Step Four   Polishing

Once you are satisfied with the content and general organization of your work, you should polish it by proofreading and editing for specific errors in spelling, punctuation, and word usage. This is discussed in detail in Appendices B and C, where there is also a check list of items to consider in polishing your assignments.

When you have polished your paper, it is ready to be presented to your intended reader.

What the writing process should have helped you accomplish is a publishable paper with an appropriate title. *Publishable* simply means that, in your opinion, your work is ready to be given to a final reader. If this reader finds any difficulty in understanding what you have written, the writing process on that particular piece is not over, and you may have to take more time to bring it to the publishable stage.

The Contents of *The Writer's Workshop*

The Writer's Workshop has three sections: Assignments, Activities, and Labs. You are not expected to complete everything in this textbook in a single term, so you should become familiar with its contents to see what portions of it can best fulfil your needs. As you go through the textbook, you may find parts that — for you — are too easy, too difficult, or inappropriate. In consultation with your teacher, you both can decide on the parts that are appropriate and challenging, and that both of you believe can help you become a better writer.

The Assignment Section

The *Assignment Section* is designed for you to complete with the assistance of your teacher/editor and peers. In this section you can become involved in many real-life projects, all with strategies to shape your writing at each stage of the writing process. Since writing for the sake of writing often produces bad results, every assignment should be written for a real audience and a real purpose.

The assignments can be followed sequentially, or grouped in one of the ways found on page 5. You should, though, begin with Assignment One where you can learn to go through the steps of the writing process in an actual assignment.

The Activity Section

The *Activity Section* is designed for work with a partner: a fellow student at school or a friend or relative at home. Most of it deals with specific techniques that will improve your writing. Occasionally an activity will culminate in a special writing assignment that you can do for your partner.

You can work on the activities in any order as well as completing only those portions of an activity that you require to help you refine a particular writing technique or eliminate a bothersome problem. You are encouraged, however, to begin with the first few activities, which deal with the fundamentals and philosophies of the writing process.

The Laboratory Section

The *Laboratory Section* is designed for individualized learning; you can work on this section by yourself, at home or at school. Basically, the exercises in the labs will help you improve your sentence structure through the use of sentence combining. Suggested answers are provided for all sentence work so that you can check your answers yourself.

You are encouraged to begin with the first two labs as they introduce the sentence patterns and terminology you will need for the rest of the Laboratory Section.

The Writer's Workshop also contains Appendices and an Index. You will have many opportunities to refer to the material in both.

Special Interest Programs

Academic

Goal: counsellor, lawyer, librarian, minister, psychologist, social worker, and other jobs requiring a university degree.
Assignments 1, 4, 8, 6, 20, 11, 9, 10, 12, 2, 5

Commercial

Goal: accountant, banker, bookkeeper, computer operator, data programmer, investment broker, receptionist, real estate agent, secretary, travel agent, and other business-oriented jobs.
Assignments 1, 15, 14, 18, 4, 7, 16, 19, 6, 13

Arts

Goal: actor, announcer, dancer, designer, film maker, journalist, musician, painter, publicist, sculptor, writer, and other creative jobs.
Assignments 1, 7, 2, 3, 17, 20, 9, 10, 13, 4, 6

General Interest

Goal: athlete, cab driver, farmer, fisherman, policeman, rancher, sailor, sales-person, soldier, steward/stewardess, telephone operator, waiter/waitress, and similar jobs requiring specific training.
Assignments 1, 2, 4, 14, 15, 17, 18, 19, 20, 9, 7

Science

Goal: biologist, chemist, dentist, dietitian, doctor, nurse, optometrist, phar-macist, physicist, physiotherapist, veterinarian, and other science-related jobs.
Assignments 1, 3, 4, 6, 14, 8, 11, 12, 13, 9, 18, 19

Technical/ Vocational

Goal: carpenter, chef, contractor, electrician, hairdresser, mechanic, plumber, and other jobs requiring a trade-school degree.
Assignments 1, 14, 2, 15, 5, 3, 4, 19, 16, 6, 11, 13

Home Use

If you are not a student and are interested in improving your written English, work with a friend or relative beginning with the following assignments:
Assignments 1, 17, 18, 15, 14, 20, 19, 16, 2, 4, 6

If you have difficulty with written English, begin to work in one of the following areas *before* you move into your interest program
Weak Writers
Assignments 1, 14, 13, 17, 18, 20, 2, 3, 4, 5, 6, 11
English as a Second Language
Assignments 1, 17, 15, 14, 2, 18, 3, 4, 5, 6, 11

Assignment Section

About the Assignments

Introduction

Assignments in this section are designed to meet a variety of needs, interests, and levels of ability. Select those that are useful and interesting to you.

Each assignment consists of an introduction and specific suggestions on the various steps of the writing process. Each is also accompanied by models written by students, teachers, and professionals so that you can see what a finished assignment looks like. You are encouraged to read these models before, during, and after you do your own piece of writing.
Each assignment:

a) stresses prewriting, drafting, revising, and polishing;
b) promotes peer/editor and teacher/editor feedback;
c) encourages you to think about your audience, purpose, topic, and format (the writing variables) *before* you write;
d) recommends that you always write honestly, thoroughly, and emphatically;
e) suggests that you present your final piece of writing to its intended reader.

You should begin with the first assignment, which introduces you to the writing process. For subsequent assignments, consult your teacher/editor so that you can both decide which of the programs on page 5 best serves your needs.

How to set up an Assignment

Following is a student model. Notice how it is set up. You should use the suggestions below when you hand in your work to be peer or teacher edited.

a) On a *separate* piece of paper, include the assignment number, a list of the writing variables, and your name. This information will assist your editors in their feedback sessions; the information would *not* be presented to your intended reader.
b) The piece of writing itself should be double-spaced with margins on the right and left. The space is particularly helpful during the revision process, so that your editors or you have room to write any additions, instructions, or suggestions for a further rewrite.
c) The final piece of writing should be carefully positioned on the paper in order to represent an impressive, polished copy to your intended reader.

d) Most assignments should have a title. Some assignments such as reports and research essays may require a title page, table of contents, or bibliography. In all cases, present your writing neatly; your readers will appreciate the care you have taken.

```
ASSIGNMENT 4                              Carol Klassen

TOPIC:    accepting criticism
AUDIENCE: my peer group
PURPOSE:  to help them accept criticism
FORMAT:   expository paragraph
```

Your Creation

Writing and expressing a part of yourself is a great joy, but to request and accept criticism of something so personal is one of the most difficult things you may have to experience. Imagine taking your newborn baby to a family gathering for inspection, where your experienced aunt (a mother of eight) states that his face is still blue, his nose is rather flat, his ears stick out, and his head has an odd shape. Your English teacher, who has conceived and given birth to many essays, may remind you of this learned aunt as she scrutinizes your essay and points out that your introduction is wordy, that your third sentence has a comma splice, and that your dangling modifier and split infinitive are not acceptable. Your inability to sever yourself from your conception in order to accept her criticism may force you to defend your creation by protesting that the sweat and labour involved in writing an essay is in itself worthy of recognition and congratulations. But think again. Your teacher is not your aunt. She does take into account the labour you have put into your creation; she does recognize the worth of your efforts. When you recognize that your teacher is not a fault-finder, you will be able to accept criticism, question what you disagree with, and appreciate the joys of revision.

Assignment **1** An Introductory Assignment

Introduction

Because the best way of learning how to do something is to actually do it, you can best learn about the writing process by working through this assignment. Remember these points as you work:

1. Because the point of this assignment is to become familiar with the writing process, concentrate on each part of the process rather than on the finished product.
2. Plan to complete the assignment in a specific period of time. If you are doing this in your classroom, your teacher will perhaps set a time limit for each step; if you are doing it at home, you should set up your own time limits.
3. Be prepared to try new things. By working through the steps of this assignment, you may recognize that you are on the way to discovering your voice as a writer.
4. Relax. Research has shown that a knowledge of the writing process makes writing easier and more interesting.

Assignment

Write a 125-word piece about some memorable place or time in your childhood.

Prewriting Suggestions

As you begin this assignment, and start thinking about your childhood, you have already begun the writing process. During this "prewriting" time, concentrate on generating or inventing ideas.
1. The possibilities of topics for this assignment are infinite and the methods for choosing one are many. To discover a topic for this assignment quickly, you may want to focus your attention on childhood places and times that were safe or frightening. To help you think more systematically, draw two columns. Label one "Safe" and the other "Frightening." Now, jot down places and times from your childhood, putting them in the appropriate column.

Safe	Frightening
anywhere in my bedroom	the time I collected hawk eggs
beside the wood stove	when a gobbler chased me
in my mother's arms	my first day of school
listening to the radio	when wolves tried to claw
	down our door

2. After you have written down as many places and times as you can remember, decide which of these was the most safe or the most frightening. This will be your *topic* for the assignment. Think about the topic and its importance to you. What would you like to convey to your reader about the topic? By thinking about the reasons for wanting to write about a particular place or time, you will discover your *purpose* for writing the assignment, and your *main claim* or thesis.

3. List as many details (supporting evidence) as you can about your topic, using all your senses to recall it: sight, sound, smell, taste, touch. Do not be concerned about the order of your list; prewriting is just for you.

When wolves tried to claw down our door

dead of winter
they were hungry
my mother had a shotgun
my father was not home
I sat on mother's knee
gun felt cold
could feel my mother's heartbeat
we could hear wolves clawing
   on door
next day we saw claw marks
wolves didn't get in
we were scared
I felt protected
we could see our breaths

4. If you have plenty of supporting evidence, you are nearly ready to draft your paper. However, you have two more writing variables to consider.

Who is going to read your assignment? You should know who your *audience* will be so that you can consider how you will recreate your experiences for your reader. Think how differently you would write to a fellow classmate, a teacher, a psychiatrist, or your mother. (Your writing teacher may indicate a specific audience for your introductory assignment.)

You should also consider the *format* of this assignment. Because you are doing this assignment to familiarize yourself with the writing process, feel free to write a paragraph, essay, or letter. The only restriction is that your piece of writing should be short: not much more than 125 words.

5. State your writing variables before you draft your piece of writing. Something like this will do:

> **Topic:** the safest place when the wolves appeared
> **Audience:** my writing teacher
> **Purpose:** to share a childhood experience
> **Format:** a paragraph

Drafting Suggestions

Writing is a means of discovery as well as a means of communication. Perhaps you have already found that writing a letter or a diary entry clarified a problem.

As you write your first draft for this assignment, you may find that more significant ideas emerge. If you discover a new insight or approach to your topic, use it as the basis for another piece of writing, and begin the process again.

1. Present your central idea at the beginning of your paper in a clear way so that your audience will appreciate and understand what you are going to write about.

2. Think about how you are going to develop your central idea. You would not want to compose your draft following the random method of collecting supporting evidence that you used during prewriting.

There are many methods of organization (comparison/contrast, chronological order, cause and effect, general to particular, and so on); perhaps for this assignment you might use climactic (order of importance) or spatial (order of position).

As you write, present details to help your reader see what you saw, feel what you felt, or share the thoughts that you had.

3. Conclude your piece by summing up your central idea in a way that you think will interest your reader.

4. Write a relatively clean, double-spaced copy of your assignment, with an appropriate title, in preparation for a revision session. The following is an example of a final draft model. As you read it, think about what you would say to the writer to help him revise his paragraph.

ASSIGNMENT 1   John Jamieson

TOPIC: the safest place when the wolves appeared
AUDIENCE: my writing teacher
PURPOSE: to share a childhood experience
FORMAT: a paragraph

A Safe Place When Wolves Appeared

The safest place you could be was in our farm house in Northern
Manitoba on my mother's knee. It was especially safe during winter
time when the wolves were outside our front door, clawing to get in.
Between the door and I were my mothers arms and the shotgun which she
held. No wolf ever managed to claw it's way into our kitchen-cum-living
room. I don't know what would have happened if one had got in. My
father was away logging. And now, years later, sitting here in a
classroom, I wonder if my mother would have know what to do if a wolf
had sprung into our home.

But she gave me a sense of security and it is this feeling that has
stayed with me to this day.

Revising Suggestions   This part of the writing process deals with editing your final draft. Although you should always revise your own work, listening to the opinions of others will help you a great deal. Ask your friends, relatives, or fellow students to help you prepare your assignment for its intended reader. During such a feedback session, they should make sure that your assignment has been written and organized so that its overall meaning is clear, and its overall purpose has been fulfilled. If your editors suggest that you reform your assignment, you should be prepared to add, delete, move, or change significant parts of your writing.

During the revising process, you should not worry about whether a word is spelled correctly or a punctuation mark is in the right place. These are, of course, important, and your editors may bring them to your attention. However, at this time you should concentrate on larger issues, such as making sure that your main claim is clear and worth while, that your development is complete and easy to follow, and that your readers can understand what you have said. You can attend to minor editing in the Polishing Suggestions.

For future assignments, you and your peer/editors should use the suggestions in Appendix B. For this assignment, though, use the following suggestions as a basis for a feedback session so that you can talk about each other's papers.

1. You or your editors should check your writing variables against your draft.

  a) Are your topic and main claim clear?

  b) Does your paper fulfil its purpose?

  c) Have you kept your reader in mind throughout your entire paper?

  d) Have you followed the conventions of the format that you have chosen?

2. Now they should edit your assignment more specifically by using this check list:

  a) What do they like best about the paper?

  b) What do they like least? What do they think can be done about it?

  c) Is anything unclear?

  d) Should further details be added?

  e) Should anything be left out?

  f) Should anything be rearranged?

  g) Are there any problems with "mechanics": spelling, punctuation, or sentence structure?

  h) Do the sentences flow logically from one to the other?

  i) Are there enough connecting or transitional words to keep the reader on track?

  j) Is the title interesting?

3. Remember, the responsibility to accept or reject what your peer/editors suggest is always yours.

4. What follows is the result of a peer feedback session. Do you agree with the comments?

Assignment 1   John Jamieson

TOPIC: the safest place when the wolves appeared
AUDIENCE: my writing teacher
PURPOSE: to share a childhood experience
FORMAT: a paragraph

good topic!

A Safe Place When Wolves Appeared   *needs a shorter title*

① *to*
The safest place ~~you could~~ be was in our farm house in Northern   *lower case*

Manitoba on my mother's knee. It was especially safe during winter

~~time~~ when the wolves were outside our front door, clawing to get in.

me
Between the door and I were my mothers arms and the shotgun which she

its
held. No wolf ever managed to claw ~~it's~~ way into our kitchen-cum-living

transpose
room. I don't know what would have happened if one had got in. (My

② ③   *good*
father was away logging.) And now, years later, sitting here in a   *contrast*

n
classroom, I wonder if my mother would have know what to do if a wolf

had sprung into our home. *continue paragraph*

(But she gave me a sense of security and it is this feeling that has

stayed with me to this day.   *good conclusion*

① *don't bring "you" into it*
② *leave out-seems unimportant*
③ *can you start a sentence with "and" and "but"?*

Polishing Suggestions

In this part of the process, concentrate on proofreading and minor editing: check your spelling, grammar, punctuation, word choice, and sentence structure.

This is the last opportunity for you to make sure that your writing says what you want to say in the way you want to say it. Your writing is an extension of you; it reflects your personality. To give a high-quality paper to your reader may mean that you must do a great deal of careful editing, using a dictionary, a thesaurus, and a handbook. Finally, make sure the assignment that you submit is neat and legible.

For future assignments, refer to Appendix C for suggestions on polishing.

Model

As you read this paragraph, can you tell how much help the writer accepted from his peer/editors?

Keep in mind that your paper should be about the same length.

Wolves

For me, the safest place in our farmhouse in northern Manitoba was on my mother's knee. It was especially safe during winter when the wolves were outside our front door, clawing to get in. Between the door and me were my mother's arms and the shotgun which she held. No wolf ever managed to claw its way into our kitchen-cum-living room. I don't know what would have happened if one had got in. And now, years later, sitting here in my comfortable, sophisticated classroom, I wonder if my mother would have known what to do if a wolf had sprung into our home. But she gave me a sense of security and that feeling has stayed with me to this day.

Assignment 2 Narrative Paragraph

Introduction

There are many times when you will want to tell or retell a good story. Narration is, therefore, a format that you will use frequently.

A narrative may be imaginary, or it may be based on a real experience. In both cases, however, a narrative is an account of events, told so that the reader shares the experience.

Assignment

In a narrative paragraph of not more than 200 words, tell about an incident that has happened to you.

Prewriting Suggestions

1. For your first narrative paragraph, choose an amusing, exciting, frightening, or significant experience that you remember well. The key to good narrative writing is bringing the incident to life for your reader through the use of convincing detail. For this reason, it is generally easier to write a successful narrative about something that you have experienced.

2. Do not choose a long, involved incident; remember that you are limited to only 200 words.

3. You may want to choose an incident that involves conflict – a struggle against something or someone. Conflict does not necessarily mean a physical struggle. (Your reader is not looking for the "Gunfight at the O.K. Corral.") The struggle can be with another person, with nature, with society, or even with yourself.

It is quite possible for a particular incident to have more than one conflict; for example, your story may involve an argument with a relative (conflict with another person), may be set in a snowstorm (conflict with nature), and may also deal with an incident where you try to control your anger (conflict with yourself).

4. If you are having difficulty thinking of a topic, consider one of the following:
   a) your proudest, happiest, or saddest moment
   b) a triumph or failure
   c) your funniest or most embarrassing mistake
   d) a "first": first date, first dance, first job interview
   e) a disaster: fire, accident, flood, storm

f) an argument with a friend or relative

g) a difficult decision

h) a time you defied authority

5.   Before you draft your narrative, establish a definite purpose and audience. If your short narration is part of a larger piece of work, such as a letter, specify the format.

List your writing variables like this:

Topic: my driving test

Audience: a close friend

Purpose: to relate how I failed my test

Format: a letter (which includes a narrative paragraph)

Drafting Suggestions

1.   Your story should have a beginning, a middle, and an end. Your *beginning* should capture your reader's interest. Which of these opening sentences would encourage you to continue reading?

I was sure the customs officer could see my heart pounding in my chest as she opened my suitcase.

"The Fonz" raised his thumbs, the band started to play, then I saw her coming towards me from across the room.

"He's dead!" she kept screaming. "Your pet frog is dead!"

Your *middle* should relate events in the order in which they happened – chronological order. Details in the description of the action should "bring the events to life" for your reader.

Your *ending* should satisfy the reader's expectations. He or she must not feel that your story has been a waste of time, or merely a trick. Which of these endings would you find unsatisfactory?

I counted my cash. I had enough.

I waited impatiently for my mother's answer. Finally it came. Yes.

...cautiously I placed one foot ahead of the other. A stone fell, plummeting to the base of the canyon far below. My foot slipped. I fell. Down, I plunged. Suddenly I awoke. Safe and sound in my own bed.

2.   Your story should contain, as close to the end as possible, a *climax*. (The climax has been called the highest point of excitement, the decisive moment, and the turning point of the plot.)

Create suspense by delaying the climax. You can do this by using dialogue or description. Make sure that your description or dialogue contributes to the plot or you may lose your story line – and your reader.

When you get nearer to your climax, shorter sentences will usually add to the reader's excitement.

3.   Use action, reaction, and dialogue to help your reader experience the incident. Describe physical and facial expressions so that your reader can see

your subject's emotional reactions, and introduce some actual words that were spoken during the incident. *Showing* what happened is much more effective than *telling*. Notice the difference between showing and telling in the following two passages:

Telling
Mr. Morehouse shouted angrily at the customs agent. He didn't understand why he should be charged more than twenty-five cents for his pets. The rates were clearly printed in the rate book.

Showing
"But, you everlasting stupid idiot!" shouted Mr. Morehouse madly, shaking a printed book beneath the agent's nose. "Can't you read it here – in your own plain printed rates? Pets, domestic, twenty-five cents each." He threw the book on the counter in disgust. "What more do you want? Aren't they pets? Aren't they domestic?"

from *Pigs Is Pigs*

4. If you want to "stretch" the truth to make your story better (a quite acceptable practice among writers of narration), use detail to keep your writing credible. Your narration must sound believable.

Revising Suggestions

When you or your peers edit your short narration, apply the check list from Appendix B as well as the following specific questions:

1. Is your story interesting? If not, consider these questions:
  a) Is there conflict?
  b) Is the first sentence interesting?
  c) Is there a climax?
  d) Is there suspense?
  e) Is the final sentence satisfying?

2. Is your story believable? If not, would dialogue or description help to bring the story to life?

3. Is the sequence of events clear?
  a) Have you kept strictly to the story? (If there are any details that do not contribute directly to the narrative, they should be eliminated.)
  b) Have you told all the important things?
  c) Have you told the story in the same order as it actually happened (chronological order)?

4. Is the point of view consistent and clear? These ideas should help in evaluating consistency:

Person
"I" stories help the reader to believe the incident actually happened to the writer. Remember to be consistent: do not switch to the "you" or "he/she"

point of view. In another narrative paragraph you can write a story from a "you" or "he/she" point of view.

Tense
Because you will be retelling an event that took place in the past, you should use the past tense. Do not suddenly shift into present or future tenses.

Voice
Use active voice rather than passive voice for narration. *My car crashed into the post* is stronger than *The post was crashed into by my car.*

Polishing Suggestions

When you are satisfied with the overall content and organization of your short narration, proofread it for spelling, grammar, word usage, and punctuation. See Appendix C for specific suggestions.

Models

Fun and Games

by Conall Barr, student

Sy, the manager of the H. R. MacMillan Planetarium, became an enemy to my friends and me while we were growing up. Things we thought of as fun and games, such as frightening an elderly couple almost to death by taking the places of dummies in a display and sitting up as they approached, were malicious mischief to Sy. Time after time he caught us sneaking around, and time after time he ordered us to leave and warned us never to return. Walking out, our heads hanging low, our hands drooping in our pockets, and our feet kicking any small object that obstructed our path, we headed away from our favourite play area. Our melancholy lasted no longer than two days, for sneaking back into the planetarium, we found a new adventure. Creeping about the place, trying not to let Sy see us, we looked like spies in a war movie, and felt like them too. Sy soon caught on to our games when he started to receive complaints of strange giggling and animal noises coming from behind the theatre screen. Finally, after he had personally kicked us out and advised every member of the staff to throw us out on sight, we admitted defeat and moved on to greener pastures at the Maritime Museum.

My Aunt

by Linda Danielson, student

Mar. 11

Dear Jennie.

I'm sorry to have taken so long between letters, but school and band concerts have kept me too busy to write. Our band has been working extra hard, hoping to be chosen to go to Peterborough for the national concert band finals.

In your last letter you mentioned that you had visited Madame Tussaud's wax museum while you were in London, and how realistic the wax figures were. That reminded me of something that happened to my aunt when we were in Victoria.

My aunt had recently arrived in Canada from Holland and my family was showing her the sights. She had only been to Canada a couple of times before, and had a very limited English vocabulary. While we were visiting the wax museum, we became concerned about the time. My aunt strutted up to a lady to ask the time. After repeating her question and receiving no answer, she went to shake the lady to get her attention. When she turned around with an embarrassed look on her face, my aunt saw my family laughing because we had all done the same thing on the previous visit. She had been "talking" to a wax figure!

I have to dash off to rehearsal now. Give my love to the rest of your family, especially Mike!

Love, Linda

Shopping

by Shirley Friesen, student

Only three years old, I am fascinated by this place. The ceilings are as high as the sky and the aisles are wider than the street near my house. I cling to mommy's coattails so that she won't get lost as I walk along, admiring all the packages that line the shelves. When she stops for a moment, I let go of her to pick up a particularly intriguing cereal box. When I look up, to my horror, she is lost! I race up and down the aisles screaming her name at the top of my lungs: "Mommy!" Out of breath, I stop running, and a smiling lady with snowy white shoes approaches me, then gently taking my hand, she guides me to a room at the back of the store. The friendly lady sets me down, gives me some candy, and assures me that someone will find my mother in no time. After polishing off the last candy, I start thinking about mother again. It seems like hours now since we've been apart! No sooner have I finished that thought than the door swings open and there she is. I am so relieved I cry all the way home. You can be sure it will be a long time before I take my mother to the supermarket again!

Trapped

by Bob Klettke, student

Completely dark. Can't move backward; can't see forward. Stuck. A cloud of unhealthy anxiety disperses through the cave, searching for and finding my cramped, immobile body, forcing a rush of adrenalin into my pulsing arteries. My heart beats faster, stronger; my breath quickens, deepens; and my eyes widen, still blind. I search through the muddled maze of my mind looking for answers. None. Yelling provides a safe, if temporary, escape from this tomb of darkness. Screaming uses up the adrenalin, allowing a false calm to follow. A brief calm. Hard, harsh walls slowly move in, squeezing the air from my weakening body. My one free hand, battered and bloody, flails helplessly at the unseen, but solid walls in front of me. No freedom. My mind stalls. Too many questions with no answers. I pass out. Maybe seconds, minutes, or hours. Later I wake up and nothing has changed. Still stuck. Completely dark. Trapped.

Skalbania

by Peter Newman

"I'll never forget coming from a hockey meeting with Skalbania and arriving in Toronto on the same plane," recalls Johnny F. Bassett, the Toronto entrepreneur. "He had this briefcase with him, and we stopped somewhere on the way into town. I asked Nelson, 'Where are you going? We've got a meeting at Carling's and they're waiting for us.'

"He said, 'I'll just be a minute.'

"He came out in about seven minutes, and I asked him what he'd done.

" 'Just bought a piece of property,' he said.

"A few minutes later, Skalbania stops the cab again, and when I wanted to know where he was going now, he replied, 'I'll be back in a minute.'

"He came back out, and I asked what he'd done.

" 'Just sold it,' he said and told me he'd made a million bucks. The poor cab driver – I don't think he'll ever get over it."

Analysis

Fun and Games

1. What do you find out about the student author? Which sentences help you to answer?

2. What is your opinion of the sentence beginning "Walking out..."?

My Aunt

1. The student writer has placed her narrative paragraph within a letter. For it she uses a chronological order rather than starting at a high point in the action of her narrative. Do you think she is right to use this structure?

2. Did you find the climax surprising or did you find it unsatisfying?

3. Besides the verb "strutted," what other words give you an impression of the aunt?

4. You assume that the writer was present during the incident. How could she have let the reader know that she was definitely there?

5. Do you find any wordiness in the paragraph?

Shopping

1. The student author assumes a persona of herself at three. She does so for two reasons: to show a child's point of view of a supermarket and to show a child's interpretation of being lost. In doing so, she has a great deal of satiric fun. Can you find some examples of irony?

2. Are there any words that do not fit her three-year-old persona?

Trapped

1. This narrative paragraph calls for an interpretation by the reader. Is the student writer literally or figuratively trapped? Do you think this event is based on truth?

2. Regardless of whether it is true or not, it has the feeling of truth. Do you feel the author's helplessness and terror?

3. What is the effect of the many non-sentence fragments?

4. Which of your senses were stimulated?

Skalbania

1. "Skalbania" has been excerpted from Peter Newman's *The Acquisitors*. What makes the piece effective?

2. How would indirect speech change the tone?

3. Where is the conflict in the piece?

Before you leave this assignment, you might like to read a few master narrators. Go to the library and pick up a narrative essay by George Orwell, Aldous Huxley, Pierre Berton, or Robertson Davies.

Assignment **3** Descriptive Paragraph

Introduction

Description has been called "a picture in words." In writing description, you re-create a scene or person by putting in words what you have experienced through your senses.

Even though you may find little occasion to write a purely descriptive paragraph, there will be many opportunities to include descriptive elements in all other types of writing.

GARFIELD   By Jim Davis

©1979 United Feature Syndicate, Inc.

Assignment

In a descriptive paragraph of no more than 150 words, create a "word picture" of a person, place, or thing.

Prewriting Suggestions

1. Make a list of people, places, or things that you remember vividly. Your list may include everything from a specific object to an entire scene. For example:
    a) the face of a friend or relative (or your own face)
    b) something seen in a store that you would like to own
    c) your room at home
    d) a building or home that you find interesting
    e) the main street in your city or town
    f) a crowd scene at a football stadium

2. Choose one subject from your list and begin to experiment with some of these techniques:
    a) List words and phrases that describe the sights, sounds, smells, and tastes that you associate with your subject. To what sense or senses does the subject appeal most?
    b) If the subject of your piece were sitting as a still life for a painter, what feature would the artist highlight? Why? How can you highlight the feature in your writing?
    c) Use analogies or comparisons. How is your subject like a watermelon, a mouse, a sharp knife, a cushion, or some other object?
    d) Determine where you are in relation to your subject. Are you looking at your subject directly? Are you above it or below it? Are you moving through the scene like a television camera, or looking at it through a pair of binoculars?
    e) How would you describe your subject to your mother? a Martian? your best friend?

3. Consider your purpose and audience in selecting your descriptive detail. You may not, for example, describe your girl friend or boy friend to your parents in the same way you would describe her or him to a friend.

   Also, decide on the format for your short description. Will it be a separate paragraph specifically for your writing teacher, or part of a chemistry report, a friendly letter, or an autobiography?

4. After you have experimented with your topic, you should consider your purpose and audience for this assignment. Make a list of writing variables similar to one of these:

   Topic: a girl/boy I just met (I think I'm in love)
   Audience: a close friend
   Purpose: to describe her/him to my friend
   Format: a letter (which includes a descriptive paragraph)
   or
   Topic: a painting from the Emily Carr exhibit
   Audience: my art class
   Purpose: to describe it to the class
   Format: a report (which includes a descriptive paragraph)

Drafting Suggestions

1. Consider the overall impression that you wish to create, and select your descriptive details accordingly. Do you want your reader to like your subject? Dislike it? Be frightened? Amused? The good writer of description does not use *every* detail: he or she *selects* details to evoke a certain reaction from the reader.

Choose words with connotations or associations that will create the overall impression you are striving for. The word "slender," for example, will create a different impression from the word "scrawny," although both mean "thin."

2. To organize the description of a scene, start at a focal point and proceed in a logical direction, perhaps from top to bottom, or from near to far, or build to a climax in some other way. Do not jump indiscriminately from one area to another.

3. Carefully choose words that will appeal to your reader's senses. What words in the following sentences allow the reader to see, hear, or smell the subject?

The bawling, red-faced infant howled for attention.
Discarded running shoes, sweaty clothing, and forgotten lunches fouled the air.

4. A metaphor can breathe new life into the most mundane subject.

Raking furiously, the gardener raised the cherry blossom petals in miniature snow flurries.
The mums twitter over their young like sparrows nesting at nightfall.

Occasionally, a writer will use an extended metaphor or analogy; every detail suggests a comparison between the subject and something else. (See "The Living Sea" in the Models.)

Revising Suggestions

When you have completed your final draft, judge your description according to the standards in the first part of Appendix B or use one of the peer-feedback methods in the last part of Appendix B. In addition, consider the following specific items:

1. What overall mood or impression does the paragraph create? Do the words create the picture that you want your reader to see?

2. How many senses are involved in the description? Which ones are used most effectively? Which additional ones could have been used?

3. Which emotions are involved in the writing? Which ones are used most effectively? Which additional ones could have been used?

4. Do the words add to the total effect of the description? Should any words be added, deleted, or substituted? Should you add a more precise word, cut out a detail that takes the focus from your subject, or change ineffectual words (*it, this, that, these, those*) for stronger words? Are there unnecessary descriptive words, such as *actually, really, quite, kind of?*

5. Do the sentences have variety, emphasis, and appropriateness?

6. Is the piece of description appropriate for its intended purpose and intended audience?

Polishing Suggestions

When you have completed your description, and just before your intended reader sees it, read it, then close your eyes. Do the words paint the exact picture that you want your audience to see? Do they bring to mind the sounds, smells, tastes, and tactile sensations that you want your audience to imagine? Appendix C may help to make your writing more distinctly yours.

Models

Drifting Home
by Pierre Berton

Craggy rocks, plumed with evergreens, rise from the water. Around the next corner, the river passes under clay banks three hundred feet high. Mixed in with the dark spruces are the bleached trunks of birches and the olive greens of aspen poplars, many of them notched by the teeth of beaver. At times we seem to be plunging directly through the dark forest, the river no more than sixty feet wide and shaded by the trees; at others the channel broadens into flat meadows; then again, the high, eroded banks return, pocked by swallows' nests and marked by mud slides. We will come upon these clay cliffs again and again as we drift north.

The Living Sea
by M. Boyle, student

Beneath the weathered wharf, the water swelled, throbbed, and breathed. In cavernous breaths the wharf was pushed upwards, held there for a tense moment, then lowered to its resting position as water was expelled from beneath. Inhale, exhale. A breath, a sigh. Over and over again, an unseen belly drew in the water and expanded in voluminous balloon form, only to deflate gently in the end. Old Man Sea was alive and well and living beneath the wharf.

Moving In

by Chris Moffat, student

Finally the packing boxes are empty. Worn and beaten by the long, hard journey, they sit in a corner of the porch, waiting for a garbage truck to arrive and put them out of their misery. The belongings that lived inside those boxes are now unpacked and strewn across the floor of the room that is to be mine. Plain and square, it does not feel like my room. Its four walls, painted white, have no character, just cold emptiness. Familiar bits of junk gladly liberated from the boxes seem so out of place, so foreign to this bland room. Nothing lives here; not even ants creep along the floor. Even plants are absent from the window sill, so how can I be expected to survive? The absence of colour haunts me. How can I even try to sleep, knowing those four blank walls loom above, staring down at me, waiting for me to claim them? Tomorrow morning I have a huge task before me – to make this place my home!

The Locker Room

by David Brand, student

The locker room is unique. Bodies are everywhere. Dirty bodies. Aching bodies. Stinking bodies. Filthy clothes are strewn on the floor like rags. Sweat saturates the air. Curses, boasts, and threats fly across the room. Injuries are bandaged and massaged to the grunts and groans of the wounded. Emotions drown in the showers.

Watson

With head and tail saluting the sun, Watson is off on his morning stroll. His rich, sable brown coat glistens with each controlled movement. Everyone takes notice. Throughout the tour of his domain Watson is well aware of his audience, for nothing escapes his alert, golden eyes. As I watch him strutting homeward, his inspection complete, I can't help thinking that from the tip of his nose to the tip of his tail, Watson is a sophisticate.

Analysis

Drifting Home

1. This paragraph by Pierre Berton is from the book of the same name. What distinctive characteristics do you notice in Berton's style?
2. What word picture do you like best?
3. Can you tell the location of the river he is describing? How?

The Living Sea

1. What analogy is used by the student writer of this paragraph? Does it work?
2. Are the non-sentence fragments used effectively?
3. Could phrases like "voluminous balloon form" have been expressed differently?
4. To what sense does the description appeal most?

Moving In

1. What impression of the room do you get from this description?
2. To what senses does the writer appeal?
3. What do you think of the writer's metaphors?
4. Besides describing things, what else does this paragraph do?

The Locker Room

1. To which senses does this student writer appeal?
2. What makes the use of fragments appropriate for the subject?
3. Do you think the metaphor in the last sentence works?

Watson

1. Who, or what, do you think Watson is?
2. What one word would you use to describe Watson? What details in the description add to this impression?

Assignment 4 Expository Paragraph

Introduction

Exposition involves the presentation of information, opinions, or ideas. As a student, you will probably be using exposition more often than narration or description. You will often find yourself having to explain something, whether it's a chemistry experiment, an historical event, an insight into a short story, or your opinion on a particular topic.

So that you will not confuse pure exposition with narration and description, remember that narration tells a story, description describes something, while exposition explains or persuades. Notice the difference:

> **Narration:** Last night I got lost in the snow.
> **Description:** Under a microscope, a snowflake looks like a glittering gem.
> **Exposition** (to explain): When the temperature is less than 0° Celsius, water vapour in the air turns to snow.
> **Exposition** (to persuade): Snowball fights on school grounds should be banned.

(If you do not see the differences among these, do Exercise Four of Activity 1 before you do this assignment.)

Assignment

In an expository paragraph of not more than 200 words, either explain something you know very well to your reader or try to persuade your reader to adopt your point of view on a topic that you feel is important.

Prewriting Suggestions

1. Choose a topic that is in your range of experience or that can be easily researched. Good exposition relies on supporting material based on personal experience *or* knowledge.

2. Once you have chosen a topic, narrow it down to a particular main claim. For example, here is a breakdown on the general topic of "education."

Education
↓
high school
↓
graduation
↓
Every high-school student should graduate.

Here are some general topics for you to examine. What particular main claims do they suggest to you?

a) freedom   c) weather   e) transportation
b) religion   d) travel   f) communication

3. As you narrow your chosen topic, you may come up with several main claims; for example, here are some others on the general topic of "education":
a) No one should be compelled to go to school.
b) Boys and girls should be able to take the same courses.
c) A high-school diploma increases the choices available to you when you leave school.

Can you think of more?

4. There are four specific things to consider when you choose a main claim:

a) *Choose a main claim suitable for a paragraph.*

Your topic of interest might fill volumes rather than a single paragraph, or it might be so limited that a single sentence will say all that can be said about it. So, make sure your main claim takes only a single paragraph to explain thoroughly.

b) *Choose a main claim about which you can write accurately.*

If you write about something which you do not know well, or about which you are unable to gather accurate information, your reader will soon discover your lack of expertise on your chosen subject.

c) *Choose a main claim which you consider original.*

The problem of choosing an original claim is made more difficult by the fact that what may be original to you may be hackneyed or worn-out to your reader. By writing about something that affects you personally, however, you ensure a degree of originality.

d) *Choose a main claim of importance to you.*

If you are enthusiastic about your main claim, you will have a much better chance of stirring your reader's enthusiasm. Besides, you will find that you can say a great deal about your main claim. Your problem will be what to leave out, not what to include – a very comfortable position for a writer. Being able to include specific details which are important to you will help to prevent your writing from being vague.

5. If you are having difficulty finding a main claim, examine the following controversial statements. Choose one with which you agree or disagree. Would the statement make a good subject for your persuasive paragraph?

a) No one should be allowed a driver's licence before the age of eighteen.
b) Girls should not hitch-hike.
c) French should be taught from kindergarten to grade twelve.
d) Children of separated parents are happier than children of fighting parents.
e) An untidy room indicates an untidy mind.
f) Sports teams in high school should include both girls and boys.
g) Women cause fewer car accidents than men.
h) All high-school graduates should know how to type.

6. Once you have settled on your main claim, decide on the writing variables of purpose and audience for your expository paragraph. If you write for a *real* reason to a *real* audience, the process of writing will no longer be just an exercise to keep you busy. Write for members of a club you belong to, for the purpose of convincing them to take a particular kind of action; write for the readers of your local newspaper, informing them of the history of a local landmark. Present a case to anyone over anything that you feel strongly about.

When you decide on your purpose and audience, you will also want to establish your format. Your paragraph can be designed to be part of a larger piece of writing – for example, a letter or an essay – or it can be written as a self-contained paragraph especially for this assignment. Your statement of writing variables should make clear which format you are using.

7. End your prewriting process by listing the specific writing variables:

> **Topic:** advantages of a high-school diploma
> **Audience:** students who are thinking about quitting school before graduating
> **Purpose:** to persuade students to graduate from high school
> **Format:** self-contained expository paragraph

Drafting Suggestions

1. For your first expository paragraph, you are encouraged to follow *basic paragraph structure*, as follows:

Introduction and Main Claim

Your first few sentences should tell your reader your main claim and your attitude toward it. In some cases, your introduction and main claim can be combined in one sentence. In other cases, your introductory sentence will capture your reader's attention and the following sentence will state your main claim. Ways to begin a piece of writing are discussed in more detail in Activity 4.

Which of the following provides a good way of introducing a paragraph?
a) Is grade twelve worth it? What is the use of spending another year in classrooms with teachers and books when one could be making one's way in the world?
b) Racquetball is one of North America's fastest growing sports.
c) There are probably half a dozen ways to bring Lake Erie back to life. To me, the most important one is to stop the dumping of chemicals now.
d) I am going to explain what I think would eliminate wars.

Development

The next step in drafting your paragraph is its development. You must back up your main claim through the use of supporting evidence in order to make your paragraph convincing. Decide which types of support to use (facts, examples, or reasons). Notice how one main idea might be supported through the use of different types of evidence.

Facts

Racquetball is one of North America's fastest growing sports. In 1970, there were only two racquetball clubs in all of Canada. By 1980, this figure had grown to 10,000.

Reasons

Racquetball is one of North America's fastest growing sports. And for good reason. It's fun, it's easy to learn, and it's one of the best ways to all-round fitness.

Illustration Through Narration

Racquetball is one of North America's fastest growing sports. Five years ago, I'd never heard the word. But then one of my neighbours introduced me to the game.

There are several methods of organizing your supporting evidence (chronological order, cause and effect, comparisons and contrasts, restatements, and so on). Writers sometimes use a combination of methods. To see how various main claims have been organized, read the models at the end of this assignment and the many examples in Activity 2.

Whatever method(s) you use, you must solidly support your main claim. If you have not used enough supporting detail, or if your examples or illustrations do not relate to your main claim, your reader will be confused. Try putting your paragraph away for a few days. Coming back to it with a fresh outlook, you may see gaps, inconsistencies, or contradictions.

Conclusion

Finally, you should summarize your main claim in a memorable way. Besides a summation, you might end with a question. This allows your reader to take a more active part in your presentation.

2. In summary, while you draft your paragraph, you should do the following:

a) Consider the parts of Basic Paragraph Structure: introduction, main claim, development, conclusion.
b) Know your purpose for writing. You should be aware of exactly what you are trying to do.
c) Keep your audience in mind throughout.
d) Know which types of supporting evidence you are collecting and which distinctive method of organization you are using.

3. Read the following draft of the paragraph entitled "Graduation." It will reappear in the Revising Suggestions so that you can see the writing process at work. Can you identify the Basic Paragraph Structure?

Graduation

Is grade twelve worth it? What is the use of spending another year in classrooms with teachers and books when one could be making one's way in the world? What is it about a high-school diploma that would make me do all that work? One of the most important things you can learn in grade twelve is how much a higher education can help you. If you finish getting there, you can take a long look at the choices you can make: to go to university, to go to a community college, to go to a trade school, to get a job, or just bum around for a while before making up your mind. If you decide that high school is as far in the academic world as you want to go, you will at least be able to answer all those job ads that say "Only high school graduates need apply."

Revising Suggestions

When you or your peers edit your paragraph, apply the check list from Appendix B as well as the following specific questions:
1. Is the main claim clear?
2. Is it clear whether the writer is trying to inform, persuade, or do both?
3. Is there sufficient evidence to support the main claim?
4. Is it clear which method of organization has been used?
5. Do the sentences flow smoothly and logically from one to another?
6. Is there anything that you would omit in the paragraph because it does not support the main claim? Is there anything that you would add because something seems to be needed?

7. Is any statement in the paragraph unclear?

8. Is there any problem with point of view?

9. Do you see any errors, such as spelling, grammar, punctuation, sentence structure, and so on?

10. What follows is an example of the results of a peer editing session of the paragraph, "Graduation." Note the comments.

Graduation *title is too general*

lower case

Is ~~G~~rade ~~T~~welve worth it? What is the use of spending another year in classrooms with teachers and books when ~~one~~ *you ①* could be making ~~one's~~ *your* way in the world? What is it about a high-school diploma that would make ~~me~~ *you ②* do all that work? <u>One of the most important things you can learn in grade twelve is how much a higher education can help you.</u> *③* If you finish <u>getting there</u>, you *vague* can take a long look at the choices you can make: to go to university, to go to a community college, to go to a trade school, to get a job, or just <u>bum around</u> for a while before making up my *slang* mind. If you decide that high school is as far in the academic *good point!* world as you want to go, you will at least be able to answer all those job ads that say "Only high-school graduates need apply." *④*

① *point of view shifts from "one" to "you"*
② *questions are a good introduction – should you answer?*
③ *main claim is not clear*
④ *paragraph seems incomplete – could you summarize main claim to conclude?*

---

11. Read the following revised product, noting the changes that the student made as a result of his/her peer feedback session.

Why Graduate?

Is grade twelve worth it? Is there any point in spending another year in the classroom when you could be making your way in the world? The answer to both questions is *yes*. One of the most important advantages of earning a high-school diploma is the many choices available to you: to go to university, community college, or trade school; to find a job; or to travel for awhile before deciding what you want to do with your future. If you decide that high school is as far in the academic world as you want to go, you will at least be able to answer all those job ads that say "Only high-school graduates need apply." If you decide to travel for awhile, your choices will still be open when you return. Leaving high school in the last year is like leaving your own birthday party before opening your presents. Give yourself the best chance to succeed in later life – stay in school and graduate.

Note particularly the following:
 a) The main claim – a high-school diploma increases the choices available to you when you leave school – is now clearly stated.
 b) The problems with shifting point of view ("one," "me," "you") have been corrected.
 c) All irrelevant material has been eliminated.
 d) The conclusion summarizes the writer's point of view by introducing a comparison (birthday party) and ending with a strong, challenging sentence.

Polishing Suggestions

When you are satisfied with the overall content and organization of your expository paragraph, proofread it for spelling, grammar, word usage, and punctuation. See Appendix C for specific suggestions.

Models

Big Men in Small Planes

Bush pilots, more than any other group of people, opened up northern Canada. They showed the uses to which small planes could be put in ferrying people and supplies into the North. These resourceful pilots used lakes as runways, equipping their planes with pontoons in the summer and skis in the winter. Through their pioneering work, bush pilots such as Grant MacConachie brought areas of the North that once were accessible only by dog team or canoe into contact with the rest of Canada. In fact, the bush pilots helped to bring Canada together.

A Shredded Wheat Breakfast

Feb. 21

Dear Rick,

Never say I don't keep my promises. You've been nagging me for months about how I prepared the shredded wheat you had the last time you stayed here with our family.

I am finally going to divulge my no-fuss secret of a piping hot Shredded Wheat breakfast. The key elements are steam and an egg flipper. Once you have created a source of steam (a boiling kettle is fine), the Shredded Wheat biscuit is placed on the egg flipper and given a sauna instead of a bath. A few moments of holding it in the steam flow will reward you, the breakfast connoisseur, with a delicacy that only Nabisco is capable of processing. Flip the biscuit into a bowl, cover with milk, sugar, and bananas, and even Captain Crunch couldn't refuse it.

Good Luck,
Jackie

Smokers Beware

by Tracey Rockwell, student

To the Editor:

I want to let my fellow students know about how bad a habit smoking is.

Smoking is possibly the most disgusting habit a person could engage in. Not only is it dangerous to the smoker's health, but it is even worse for the affected non-smoker. The second-hand smoke that enters the air from the burning end of a cigarette is more damaging than the smoke being inhaled. Often a smoker will ignore the fact that he or she is polluting the air with this deadly substance simply because for so long this has been accepted as normal behaviour. Rather, it is an inconsiderate invasion of the right that everyone should have to breathe air without fear of being damaged in some way. Fortunately, the population of smokers is gradually decreasing. Someday, with any luck, they will be of such a minority as not to do unnecessary damage to non-smokers.

I would like to suggest that the students urge their parents to have smoking banned in all public places.

Sincerely,
Tracy Rockwell

Racquetball Mania

Who says exercise can't be fun? Racquetball provides more exercise and more fun than any other court game. A game of racquetball every three or four days may be exactly what the doctor ordered for those who feel out of sorts or depressed. Faster than handball, slower than squash, racquetball is easier to learn than both. Most beginning players need no more than one lesson. From then on, they'll be able to play, exercise, and have fun perfecting their technique. After only a few games, most players find themselves starting to play the corners, take a ball off the back wall, slam one from the back wall to the front; in fact, there's nothing they won't try. Enthusiasts say that racquetball takes minutes to learn, but a lifetime to perfect. Why not try it?

Daydreams

by Wun Yue Au, student

Do you ever get frustrated? And have you ever wondered what to do when work piles up at a greater rate than you can manage or when successive failures weary your body and soul? Here is an easy answer – daydream. Take a short rest and allow your oppressed mind to wander freely. In stretching itself, the mind can fly to a comforting asylum, to cure its wound by relaxation and flights of fancy. Then, with renewed energy and confidence, all the pressure of everyday work or unpleasant experiences will seem small in comparison to the profound meanings of your fantasies. After daydreaming, you are once again your optimistic, delighted, happy self. Besides, daydreams can help you enrich yourself. With your mind travelling freely, new ideas take shape which carry you beyond your limited scope of experience – you become brighter and more flexible. Under sensible control, then, daydreaming contributes to your mental and physical health. To be certain, daydreaming, if handled deftly, wastes no time at all.

The Arms Race

by Charles Saramo, student

Most people don't realize that the arms race between the U.S. and the U.S.S.R. could affect our lives dreadfully. There is nothing that can change our lives so drastically and so quickly as nuclear war. I think that every country should press for immediate nuclear disarmament. Why does the United States need enough ICBMs (Intercontinental Ballistic Missiles) to kill everyone on earth sixteen times? Isn't once enough? Why can't the money spent to increase the nuclear arsenal be put to better uses: to help develop third-world countries or expand the space program? Nuclear war is senseless genocide. I can understand the need for defence on security, but tanks, submarines, aircraft carriers, attack helicopters, and planes which can launch radar homing missiles from 126 miles away are defence enough. Nuclear weapons have but one use and that is to exterminate every human on this planet. Why would we want to kill ourselves? Total nuclear disarmament has to become a reality before something goes dreadfully wrong.

Analysis

Big Men in Small Planes

1. This is a purely informative paragraph. Is all the information relevant to the main claim?

2. Under what conditions would you write this kind of paragraph?

3. What is its method of organization?

A Shredded Wheat Breakfast

The student writer is merely explaining how she prepares a special breakfast in a letter to a Shredded-Wheat-loving friend; the way she informs her reader may convince him to follow the "sauna" method. In what way does she organize her directions?

Smokers Beware

1. Here you have a letter to the editor of a student newspaper. The writer supports her main claim by providing examples of the dangers of smoking. Are there enough examples to convince you?
2. Does her argument seem reasonable?
3. If you are a dedicated smoker, you might write a rebuttal.

Racquetball Mania

1. A self-contained expository paragraph, "Racquetball Mania" tries to persuade the reader of the benefits of playing racquetball. The details are placed in order of importance, from beginning the game as therapy to becoming an expert player. Are all the details relevant?
2. Has anything been left out?
3. What is the effect of beginning and ending with questions?

Daydreams

1. The student writer, who wrote the paragraph for a humanities class, supports her main claim by providing reasons for daydreaming. Does she convince you?
2. Are there other reasons she could have mentioned?
3. You might write a paragraph pointing out the harmful effects of daydreaming.

The Arms Race

1. This paragraph, intended to be part of a persuasive essay, is by a student who is obviously appalled by the nuclear build-up. Do the many questions he asks provide sufficient support to his argument?
2. What is the effect of his double use of "dreadfully"?
3. Perhaps a problem exists in the paragraph because he does not seem to have a specific audience. Can you suggest any ways he could have corrected this? As well, how could he have encouraged his reader to take direct action?

Assignment 5 Narrative Essay

Introduction

You have learned that a narrative is an account of events. Longer narratives are built on a series of events: actual, imaginary, or a blend of both.

Do not confuse the format of a narrative with that of a short story. A short story is fictitious (even when based on facts), not necessarily chronological, and uses literary elements (Assignment 10). Short stories usually emphasize character, plot, setting, and theme in more depth than narrative essays. The narrative relates the events of an incident in chronological order (as it actually happened), although some do include flash-back information. The writer controls the content of a short story, whereas the content of a narrative controls the writer.

In the hands of many professional writers, however, the narrative essay has become as creative and exciting as any novel or short story. Before you begin your long narration, take time to read, strictly for pleasure, the models at the end of this assignment.

Assignment

Write a first- or third-person narrative essay of not fewer than 300 and not more than 1000 words.

Prewriting Suggestions

1. If you have not done Assignment 2 (short narration), or if you have forgotten the details it contains, you should look over the suggestions there. Many apply to this assignment.

2. Choose an incident that involves conflict – a struggle against something or someone. Conflict does not necessarily mean a physical struggle; the struggle can be with another person, with nature, with society, or even with yourself.

3. Narratives may be written in the first person (*I*) or third person (*he* or *she*). Here is a prewriting activity that may result in a suitable topic for a first-person narrative essay.

On a piece of paper jot down answers to these questions:

a) In what true-life situation have I really wanted something?

b) What prevented me from having it?
c) What was the nature of the conflict?
d) Whom or what did it involve?
e) How long did it take me to get what I desired?

4. Here is a prewriting activity that may result in a suitable topic for a third-person narrative essay.

On a piece of paper jot down answers to these questions:

a) Whom do I know who always seems to be involved in some kind of conflict?
b) Which conflict most intrigued me?
c) Who was involved in the conflict?
d) What was the nature of the conflict?
e) How was it resolved?
f) Was there anything that nearly prevented it from being resolved?
g) How long did the conflict last? Who won?

5. Create a list of writing variables before you proceed. Something like one of these will help you:

> **Topic:** how I damaged my father's car
> **Audience:** my father
> **Purpose:** to tell him exactly what happened to his car
> **Format:** narrative essay
>
> or
>
> **Topic:** my first Canadian high-school dance
> **Audience:** my friends in Hong Kong
> **Purpose:** to tell what goes on at a Canadian high-school dance
> **Format:** a letter (which includes a narrative essay)

Drafting Suggestions

1. Use dialogue to help tell your story. As narratives are often improved by the use of dialogue, you are encouraged to include it in your work. The only rule about dialogue is to make sure it sounds real – so match the talk to the person.

Here is where slang, colloquialisms, and so on can be legitimately used in writing. But practise artistic economy. Rather than repeating everything your character would say, select only what you think is necessary in order to suggest a particular characteristic or further the development of your story.

Also, be careful with strings of "he said," "you said," "she said," as well as exaggerated expressions such as "she cooed" and "they squealed." Once the speakers have been established and their style of speech made distinctive, it is possible to present their dialogue without speech tags.

Make sure that your dialogue contributes to the plot or you may lose your story line – and your reader.

2. Use description to help tell your story. Use description in the same way as dialogue: to help create a more real situation. When you introduce a "word picture," involving the senses, you place the reader *in* your story. But make sure that your description contributes to the plot or you will confuse your reader.

3. Longer narratives often build to a climax – the point of highest excitement. Using shorter paragraphs prior to a climax can create the same suspenseful feeling that shorter sentences do in narrative paragraphs. You may, however, be better off with several terse sentences in a longer paragraph. At any rate, experiment. Dialogue and description can also be used to delay the climax, and thereby create excitement and suspense.

4. Paragraph your narrative so that your audience will be able to read it easily. There is no hard and fast rule about paragraphing for any piece of writing, but perhaps these ideas may help you in determining the number and length of your paragraphs. At the very least, they should help you focus on the structure of your essay.

a) Narrative essay paragraphs are generally shorter than those of an expository essay, but unless you can justify their use, paragraphs of only one or two sentences should be avoided.

b) Excessively long paragraphs may be filled with too many details and not allow the reader time to reflect. Correct this problem by removing nonessential details. Overly long paragraphs might also include more than one idea. The solution to this problem is simple: divide the paragraph.

c) Ideally, paragraphs should develop a single idea fully and completely and end with another idea, suggestion, or hint of the next paragraph to entice the reader to push on. A new paragraph often requires some kind of transitional device to link it to the previous paragraph.

d) When you use dialogue, include a new paragraph for each speaker. Even though many modern writers do not use this method, you should use the traditional paragraphing style for your first narrative essay.

5. Because narrative essays are longer than narrative paragraphs, you will have to be concerned with variety:

a) Your word choice should be original. Do not repeat similar word patterns or single words unless you want a particular effect.

b) Create vivid imagery. Your task is to make sure your reader *sees* what happens in your narrative. Figurative comparisons, expressive verbs, and exact nouns all help. Long lists of descriptive words do not often help.

Which sentence does the better job of painting a word picture?

She was heartbroken, sobbing, and tearful as she came and stood in front of me.

She dissolved before me.

c) Sentences should not all be of a uniform length or structure. Capable narrative essayists strive to create the same movement in their sentences that is in the action they are describing. If you are describing a runaway car on a canyon highway, one long sweeping sentence may be more effective than several jerky ones. What kinds of sentences would you include in a narrative essay about a hockey game?

6. Work for a consistent point of view not only in person but also in style. Once you have established from whose viewpoint or in whose voice the events of the narrative are being told, you should maintain that viewpoint. (Read about using a persona in Activities 1 and 19.) Also, once you have established a direct or ironic tone for your narrative, you should be consistent. If you must shift point of view, prepare your reader for the shift.

Revising Suggestions

When you have completed your final draft, judge your narrative essay according to the standards in Appendix B or use one of the peer feedback methods from Appendix B. In addition, consider the following specific items to help revise your long narration.

1. What are some of the distinguishing features of your essay?

a) Have you a unique style which makes your writing different from everyone else's?
b) Which sentences are particularly effective?
c) Which paragraph is the best?
d) To which senses have you most appealed?

2. The items that appear in the Revising Suggestions in Assignment 2 apply directly to the narrative essay. Use those suggestions and questions to edit your essay.

3. Because this is a longer selection, carefully consider your paragraphing and transitions.

4. Delete anything from your essay that does not move your plot forward. The art of selection is a major asset to a good writer.

5. Short cuts can be confusing. Remember you must assume that you are at the scene of the story. You can see everything. Your reader *sees* only what you tell him/her. Does your essay need any more details?

6. Is it clear why the narrative has been written? Are the subject matter, sentence structure, word choice, and style appropriate for the audience?

Polishing Suggestions

When you have completed the revision of your long narration, continue the process with careful proofreading. In preparing your essay for your final reader, give it your personal stamp of approval. Appendix C will help you polish your essay.

Models

Scaredy Cat

by Patricia Davies, student

In my childhood days, the most frightening place in the world for me was in my home – the basement. Nooks and crannies abounded in the basement where a "bogey man" could hide, waiting and watching from the cool, dark corners of the room, just longing to catch me alone.

Typical of an old-fashioned cellar, the basement had a low ceiling; a bulb hanging at the end of the room was the only illumination. Shadows from haunted, old furniture played havoc with my mind, making my imagination run wild. A door to the right of the main room led to a small, dim laundry room and workshop.

One day, my eldest sister asked me to run downstairs and fetch some clean dish towels, as she was busy tidying the kitchen. (Personally, I think that the basement frightened *her*, too!)

"Well, I'm kind of busy right now," I replied, as I sat at the table, twiddling my thumbs.

"Oh, come on, don't be so lazy. Unless, of course, you're afraid of the bogey man!" she said gleefully. "Hey, you guys … ."

To avoid weeks of harassment from my younger sisters, I hurriedly assured her that I would be happy to get the towels, and bounced down the stairs to the basement.

The gloomy, quiet atmosphere seemed to close in on me, as I cautiously stepped into the room. My footsteps echoed loudly – along with my heart – as I walked slowly across the floor. The laundry room door whined protestingly, a warning of my presence to all who lurked in the shadows.

The shelves of clean laundry remained hidden by a black curtain. Taking a ragged, deep breath, I drew the curtain to one side, and a pair of evil green eyes glared malevolently from within the deep, dark recesses of the cupboard. A coronary arrest threatened to overtake me, as the cat shot over my shoulder and through the open window like a bullet.

I crawled upstairs, a nervous wreck, and told my sister of my fright, swearing emphatically that I would never, ever go downstairs alone again. She was extremely sympathetic.

"Oh, but you've forgotten the tea towels!"

Hmphf, sympathetic indeed!

Upon Hearing Myself Read...

by Chris Moffat, student

Today I felt brave. I walked into my room, tape-recorder in hand, resolved that today would be the day to listen to the best piece of writing I have. I thought, "It can't be terrible; I mean, all I have to do is sit here and read this poem into this tape-recorder and play it back. Then I'll write a little paragraph and stick it in my journal. Simple!" So I set up the microphone, plugged it all in, and *voilà!*, there it was. The dreaded thing sat there grinning at me, daring me to try and make my poetry really come alive.

I had heard my voice on tape before, but it had sounded foreign somehow, not the way I imagined I would sound. Well, I had to do it, so I pressed the "record" button, determined to make this piece good. I read my poem with all the feeling I could possibly feel, with the fear of listening to it hanging over my head. After I finished, I quickly rewound the tape and checked to see if there was anyone within hearing range by yelling "Hello?" Then I pressed "Play."

The first time I listened was terrible. I was so critical of my voice and expression I sat for about half an hour trying to change my voice. I then ran the tape once more just listening to it as if I was another person.

Now I'm sitting here, thinking as objectively as possible about what I heard. My conclusion is that my piece wasn't bad. Improvements could be made, but all in all, it was O.K. Maybe I could even call the recording a useful experience, but I'll have to listen a few more times to feel optimistic about it!

Excerpt from *Never Cry Wolf*

by Farley Mowat

Quite by accident I had pitched my tent within ten yards of one of the major paths used by the wolves when they were going to, or coming from, their hunting grounds to the westward; and only a few hours after I had taken up residence one of the wolves came back from a trip and discovered me and my tent. He was at the end of a hard night's work and was clearly tired and anxious to go home to bed. He came over a small rise fifty yards from me with his head down, his eyes half-closed, and a preoccupied air about him. Far from being the preternaturally alert and suspicious beast of fiction, this wolf was so self-engrossed that he came straight on to within fifteen yards of me, and might have gone right past the tent without seeing it at all, had I not banged my elbow against the teakettle, making a resounding clank. The wolf's head came up and his eyes opened wide, but he did not stop or falter in his pace. One brief, sidelong glance was all he vouchsafed to me as he continued on his way.

It was true that I wanted to be inconspicuous, but I felt uncomfortable at being so totally ignored. Nevertheless, during the two weeks which followed, one or more wolves used the track past my tent almost every night – and never, except on one memorable occasion, did they evince the slightest interest in me.

By the time this happened I had learned a good deal about my wolfish neighbors, and one of the facts which had emerged was that they were not nomadic roamers, as is almost universally believed, but were settled beasts and the possessors of a large permanent estate with very definite boundaries.

The territory owned by my wolf family comprised more than a hundred square miles, bounded on one side by a river but otherwise not delimited by geographical features. Nevertheless there *were* boundaries, clearly indicated in wolfish fashion.

Anyone who has observed a dog doing his neighborhood rounds and leaving his personal mark on each convenient post will have already guessed how the wolves marked out *their* property. Once a week, more or less, the clan made the rounds of the family lands and freshened up the boundary markers – a sort of lupine beating of the bounds. This careful attention to property rights was perhaps made necessary by the presence of two other wolf families whose lands abutted on ours, although I never discovered any evidence of bickering or disagreements between the owners of the various adjoining estates. I suspect, therefore, that it was more of a ritual activity.

In any event, once I had become aware of the strong feeling of property rights which existed amongst the wolves, I decided to use this knowledge to make them at least recognize my existence. One evening, after they had gone off for their regular nightly hunt, I staked out a property claim of my own, embracing perhaps three acres, with the tent at the middle, and *including a hundred-yard long section of the wolves' path.*

Staking the land turned out to be rather more difficult than I had anticipated. In order to ensure that my claim would not be overlooked, I felt obliged to make a property mark on stones, clumps of moss, and patches of vegetation at intervals of not more than fifteen feet around the circumference of my claim. This took most of the night and required frequent returns to the tent to consume copious quantities of tea; but before dawn brought the hunters home the task was done, and I retired, somewhat exhausted, to observe results.

I had not long to wait. At 0814 hours, according to my wolf log, the leading male of the clan appeared over the ridge behind me, padding homeward with his usual air of preoccupation. As usual he did not deign to glance at the tent; but when he reached the point where my property line intersected the trail, he stopped as abruptly as if he had run into an invisible wall. He was only fifty yards from me and with my binoculars I could see his expression very clearly.

His attitude of fatigue vanished and was replaced by a look of bewilderment. Cautiously he extended his nose and sniffed at one of my marked bushes. He did not seem to know what to make of it or what to do about it. After a minute of complete indecision he backed away a few yards and sat down. And then, finally, he looked directly at the tent and at me. It was a long, thoughtful, considering sort of look.

Having achieved my object – that of forcing at least one of the wolves to take cognizance of my existence – I now began to wonder if, in my ignorance, I had transgressed some unknown wolf law of major importance and would have to pay for my temerity. I found myself regretting the absence of a weapon as the look I was getting became longer, yet more thoughtful, and still more intent.

I began to grow decidedly fidgety, for I dislike staring matches, and in this particular case I was up against a master, whose yellow glare seemed to become more baleful as I attempted to stare him down.

The situation was becoming intolerable. In an effort to break the impasse I loudly cleared my throat and turned my back on the wolf (for a tenth of a second) to indicate as clearly as possible that I found his continued scrutiny impolite, if not actually offensive.

He appeared to take the hint. Getting to this feet he had another sniff at my marker, and then he seemed to make up his mind. Briskly, and with an air of decision, he turned his attention away from me and began a systematic tour of the area I had staked out as my own. As he came to each boundary marker he sniffed it once or twice, then carefully placed *his* mark on the outside of each clump of grass or stone. As I watched I saw where I, in my ignorance, had erred. He made his mark with such economy that he was able to complete the entire circuit without having to reload once, or, to change the simile slightly, he did it all on one tank of fuel.

The task completed – and it had taken him no longer than fifteen minutes – he rejoined the path at the point where it left my property and trotted off towards his home – leaving me with a good deal to occupy my thoughts.

Analysis

Scaredy Cat

1. This student author writes of a frightening experience she had as a child. Although she does not assume a persona of a child, she does often write from a child's perspective. Which words and sentences are childlike? Which are more mature? Do you find these two approaches inconsistent? Would the essay have been more effective if she used a child's persona?

2. Notice the irony in the title, "Scaredy Cat." Can you find any other examples of irony?

3. What does the use of dialogue and description contribute to the narrative? Do you think the dialogue is realistic?

Upon Hearing Myself Read ...

1. The subject of this student writer's essay deals with an experiment. How does the structure of his essay reflect the idea of experimenting? As you read, are you concerned about his discoveries? Are you satisfied with the results of his experiment?

2. There is very little action in the essay. Is there enough to make clear what he is doing? Where is the conflict?

3. Who is the audience? How does this affect his writing?

Excerpt from *Never Cry Wolf*

1. As this is an excerpt from Farley Mowat's best-selling book, it does not have a formal introduction. Are you given enough information to be clear about the setting and the characters?

2. For what purpose does Mowat relate this particular incident?

3. Mowat sometimes uses humour to convey his serious message about wolves. For instance, he does not say directly how the wolves and he marked their territories. Can you find other examples of humour? Are they effective?

4. Why do you think he uses words like "vouchsafe," "evince," and "lupine"?

5. If you enjoyed this excerpt, you might enjoy reading Mowat's entire narrative.

Assignment **6** Persuasive Essay

Introduction

Persuasion is the art of getting others to agree with you; therefore, your task in writing a persuasive essay is to convince your audience that your point of view is correct (or at least reasonable). Changing someone's beliefs is a difficult task; you may have to be satisfied if he or she says, "Maybe you're right. I never thought of it quite that way."

ON THE OTHER HAND, MOOSE, I CAN QUOTE NO SCIENTIFIC PRECEDENT THAT PROVES DAISIES AREN'T PRETTY!

Assignment

In 500–700 words, present your point of view on a topic you feel strongly about.

Prewriting Suggestions

Begin the prewriting suggestions by reading the models and analyses at the end of this assignment.

1. Use the same steps as outlined in the prewriting suggestions for Assignment 4 to find a topic for this assignment. A persuasive paragraph can quite easily be turned into a persuasive essay through the use of further supporting details: facts, incidents, reasons, and so on. You may wish, therefore, to look over some of your shorter expositions to see if one of them contains the basis for a good argument.

2. In your statement of writing variables, clearly specify your main claim and purpose. If *you* are not clear on your point of view, your reader will likely be confused as well.

Your statement of purpose should be like one of the following:

a) to persuade our coach that Smithson High consistently beats us because of the superior conditioning of their team

b) to convince our principal that the new computer report cards are not as good as the old personal ones

c) to convince my boy friend that he is destroying our relationship through his lack of consideration.

Notice that the statement of purpose includes the phrase "to persuade" or "to convince," rather than the phrase "to inform" or "to explain."

3. Carefully consider the beliefs of your readers or audience. By putting yourself in their position, and attempting to understand their beliefs, you will more easily be able to provide the reasons and evidence that will change their minds.

4. Once you have recorded your writing variables, begin to gather facts or evidence to support your main claim. Consider the quality of your supporting evidence. Facts, illustrations and reasons are more convincing than unsupported generalizations or name-calling. Quotations from authorities or experts who support your argument will help to convince your reader.

Examples with which the reader can identify will help him or her understand your point of view. Humour is also an effective device for winning your reader's sympathy or for demolishing an opposing point of view.

5. Generally, the more evidence you produce, the more convincing you will be. However, your paper must also be readable, so organize all the support you have gathered into workable sections. Outline three to five of the most convincing reasons for your argument. Under each reason, list the supporting facts or examples that you will use to convince your reader.

Drafting Suggestions

1. For this assignment, you should use Basic Essay Structure, an extension of Basic Paragraph Structure, discussed in Assignment 4. By carefully examining the essay, "The High Price of Soft-Sell," one of the models in this assignment, you will not only see Basic Essay Structure in action but you will also see a good example of a persuasive essay.

2. Place your introduction and main claim in the first paragraph of your essay. Keep your purpose for writing in mind as you draft your opening statements. The following example clearly presents the writer's topic and point of view.

Everyone joins in condemning the "word from our sponsor," but how do we reconcile this general attitude with the fact that we see commercials every day which are witty and entertaining?

3. In the development portion of your essay, you must convince your reader of your opinion. To gain your audience's support, you should provide a great deal of supporting evidence (facts, reasons, examples, and so on). Whereas in a single paragraph you are encouraged to use only one or two types of supporting evidence, in an essay you can use a variety of means of support.

The same is true of methods of organization (chronological order, cause/ effect, comparison, analogy, and so on): you may use a combination of methods to develop your essay. (Types of supporting evidence and methods of organization are illustrated in Activity 2.)

One method of organization is to develop each new example, reason, or incident that supports your argument in a paragraph of its own, reserving the best example for last. By logically organizing your essay in this kind of climactic order, you will produce a more convincing paper. If your reader can follow the organization of your essay, he or she is more likely to follow the logic of your argument.

4. Do not forget to look at the opposing viewpoint. Although you do not need to produce a solid argument against yourself, you should not ignore the fact that one exists. It's a good idea to start with the opposing opinion, presenting it honestly and fairly. Then you can dash it to pieces (in a thoroughly honest and fair way, of course).

5. The conclusion of your essay may either have a paragraph of its own or be contained at the end of the last developmental paragraph.

Revising Suggestions

Once you and your peers have decided on the method of feedback (Appendix B), you should consider these specific questions:

1. Is the main claim clearly stated?

2. Is the main claim adequately supported with facts, incidents, reasons, and so on?

3. Is the organization logical? Do you know which method of organization was used for each paragraph? Does one paragraph lead to another? Is the overall method of organization for the entire essay clear? Is it obvious that an outline has been followed?

4. Is any part of the essay unclear? What can be done to clarify it?

5. Has the audience been considered? Are there any points mentioned on which the writer and audience agree? Has the audience been treated fairly?

6. Will your audience be convinced of your opinion? If not, why?

Polishing Suggestions

When you are satisfied with the overall content and organization of your persuasive essay, proofread it for spelling, grammar, word usage, and punctuation. Also make sure that your essay is an honest account of your opinions. Make sure you have taken your audience into consideration throughout your essay. See Appendix C for specific suggestions.

Models

The **title** attracts your attention with its play on high/low and soft/hard. Does the title tell you anything about the subject of the essay? Does it make you want to read the essay? Is it appropriate?

The essay follows Basic Essay Structure. The **introduction** captures the reader's attention immediately because everyone has an opinion about TV advertising. The final question provides the writer's main claim and intrigues the reader as well. He is going to say something good about commercials. We want to read on to find out why.

The **development** contains three paragraphs (the essay is an example of the often maligned Five-Paragraph Essay.) In the second paragraph, the writer hooks the reader with a question, then provides three detailed examples. Do you agree that the examples support the thesis of this paragraph; that is, "the quality of some commercials far surpasses the programmes they interrupt"? The end suitably sums up the paragraph. Do you think the paragraph could stand on its own?

The High Price of Soft-Sell

by Ken MacMillan

We've all been told many times that television advertising is bad, that it is mindless and repetitive, that it appeals unabashedly to the materialism in our nature, and that it uses half-truths and clever distortions to sell us products and services we don't need. Each of us, moreover, has personally been irritated and offended by commercials of the mindless "ring around the collar" variety which grate on our nerves and offend our intelligence. Everyone joins in condemning the "word from our sponsor," but how do we reconcile this general attitude with the fact that we see commercials every day which are witty and entertaining?

Isn't it true that there are commercials which far surpass in quality the programmes they interrupt? Think, for instance, of the Bell Telephone commercials with their superbly photographed scenes of people enjoying simple pleasures together while the sound track carries a nostalgic song like "Heart of my Heart" or "You'll Never Know." The actual message, that we should use long distance more to get in touch with old friends far away, is very quietly stated at the end. Or again, remember the aftershave commercial which parodies the old movie cliché: "thanks, I needed that," to suggest how fresh and awake we will feel after using the product. In both these cases, the commercial message is largely implied rather than blatantly stated. A different type is the "Coke has life" commercial with its lively montage of people working and playing hard and quenching their thirst with icy bottles of Coke. Sentiment, humour, excitement are used effectively in these three examples of advertising at its most attractive.

The first sentence of the third paragraph is not only linked to the previous paragraph; it also hooks the reader again. How? After presenting examples of two bad commercials, the writer asks a series of questions. What are your answers to the questions? He ends with an effective sentence fragment which certainly sums up the thesis of this paragraph: "all commercials are dangerous." What would you have to change to make this paragraph stand on its own?

Commercials like this, however, present a particular kind of danger to us all. It is easy to dismiss a commercial of the Ultrabrite level or of some local car dealer reading strained witticisms from the aptly named idiot cards. They affront our intelligence so flagrantly that we are in no danger of being seduced by their pleadings. But how do we react when the commercial message is presented with such wit that it is entertaining? Do we even think of the implications behind the messages? Do we think that in these inflationary days Bell should perhaps not be encouraging us to spend even more money on useless long distance calls? Do we really believe that a slap in the face with a handful of scented alcohol really makes us feel fresh? Or do we consider what a bottle of sugared soft drink does to our diets not to mention our teeth? Probably not.

The first sentence of the fourth paragraph lets the reader know that this paragraph is the most important of the essay. How? The writer organizes this paragraph by a combination of methods. Which sentence or sentences contain details, examples, and facts as supporting evidence? He ends with a question which confronts the reader and sums up the thesis of the paragraph: the morality of advertising. Can this paragraph stand on its own?

Advertising confronts us with the contemporary discrepancy between morality and proficiency. We have the tendency today to praise anything well done even if the thing is not worth doing. Our heroes are quarterbacks who have the ultimately useless skill of throwing a football further than anyone else. So our advertising agencies pay large sums of money to imaginative men and women to make art subservient to commerce. It is not surprising that commercials are skillful when more money is spent on creating a thirty second commercial than on making the thirty minute programme it interrupts; we have to ask if we are not suffering from a confusion of values here. Perhaps we should ask if human virtues are any longer virtues when applied to a bad end. Is intelligence, in the mad scientist or the mad ad man, something to be praised when its effect is destructive or corrupting?

The **conclusion** sums up the thesis of the entire essay: resist the commercial announcement. Notice that the word "good" in the last line contrasts well with the word "bad" in the first line of the introduction. The essay is well tied together.

What is disturbing about TV advertising, then, is not that it is so bad; rather, what should worry us is that it is so *good*. Its glossy, polished competence presents us with a meretricious beauty. We need to be able to make a clear distinction between what is said and how it is being said. We need to resist the Siren call of "good" advertising.

Two Cities

by Henry Still

There are two dreams about the city of tomorrow.

One is a nightmare.

It goes this way:

A traveler takes a supersonic jet to Chicago, but loses an hour waiting in the traffic pattern for turns to take off and land. Once he arrives, at a jet-port fifty miles from the city, he loses another three hours while his taxicab or limousine crawls through bumper-to-bumper traffic in smog so thick the car windows cannot be rolled down. The journey may be made only with the aid of radar and super fog-piercing headlights though the time of day is high noon.

In the city no one walks outside because machines monopolize all space not taken up by roving gangs of unemployed hoodlums who make their living by looting unbarricaded buildings and victimizing the occasional careless pedestrian. If the pedestrian were not killed by one or the other of these, the noise and smog would do the job within a short time.

Buildings have no windows. Shops no longer face the street. Flowers and trees are nonexistent except in the distant mountains and even there the stunted growth tells the tale of smog polluting the earth. Residents of this nightmare city are fearful of strangers and have no time to meet and chat with a new person. They use all their energies working, commuting, and visiting the doctor or psychiatrist.

The visiting businessman hurries from his taxicab into the air-conditioned hotel which furnishes piped-in oxygen to its first-class rooms and walking-carpet hallways for those who wish to move without using their weakened legs. Once in his room, the visitor is informed by a wall television set of what he already knows – the air outside is too contaminated for breathing, although there is some chance that it may be freshened in the evening by a northwesterly breeze.

The tired businessman picks up the telephone to conduct his business, and decides next time it will be easier to do it that way from his own home town. *This* city, he concludes, is dead.

It requires little imagination to visualize this nightmare of the future.

If you live in any one of the major urban centers of our nation, look around you. It's happening there now, and will reach the critical stage long before the end of the century unless we prevent it.

There is, however, that other dream.

Here the ramjet lands without delay and within minutes the traveler is whisked by underground tube car to a level beneath his hotel. There he rides the elevator up to his room, which had been assigned by automatic check-in during his brief journey from the rocket port. Gazing out a clean window, the

Chicago visitor notices that the sky is bright and clear. Feeling the urge for a brisk walk before beginning his sales rounds, he rides the elevator back down to street level and steps outside. There is no rush and roar of automobile traffic, no clatter and sparks from the elevated railway, only a muted murmur of vibration under his feet; all vehicular traffic has been banished to subterranean levels. The cacophony of Michigan Avenue has given way to a pleasant mall lined with trees where pedestrians hold a muted pace in resonance with a spring noon. A scent of flowers fills the air. There are no fumes or coal soot because all utilities, too, have been buried underground. The fetid breath of a huge working city is now funneled through deep tubes to central areas where the air is scrubbed of contaminants before it is exhausted to the atmosphere above. In this city, utility lines, transportation networks, and even many buildings have been placed under the earth where they may serve man without imposing their existence upon him.

The two dreams of what our metropolitan areas may become by the end of the century are equally possible. One may come true if we make it happen; the other will come true automatically if we do nothing or continue our current inept fumbling.

I Would Rather Be Fat

by Barbara Kaiser, student

I am usually content with my figure and weight, but every time I open a magazine, have coffee and cake with company, or go to a party, I am told that I ought to be concerned about it. I protest that I am unable to read a magazine, as I lie leisurely on the couch with my fingers playing in a box of chocolates, without a beautiful, slim – not to say skinny – finger pointing at me from a glossy journal page, reminding me that there are fifty calories in each bite.

I dream of going to a *Konditorei*, having a hot chocolate with a mountain of whipped cream, and a second mountain of cream covering a cake. But whoever I am with will be remarking on its enormous amount of calories. Why can't I have a whole bag of potato chips or a pizza for myself without somebody telling me what it will do to my waistline? Don't these well-meaning friends realize how many moments of pure joy they are taking out of my life?

The key to a longer life is promised with slimness, which is a worthy claim. But, when I shop at the supermarket and watch rosy-cheeked, happy-looking women heap yet another bucket of ice cream onto their shopping carts, I cannot help but see their anticipated joy for the next meal. Then I see the scrawny-looking lady in front of the cottage cheese. I would rather have sixty years of contentment, looking a bit on the plump side and happily satisfying my appetite than seventy years of miserable calorie counting.

Admittedly, the lean woman has her grand moment as she enters a garment shop, walking towards her size rack with a quick, assured step. She then picks out whatever pleases her eye, tries it on, and walks out, ever so elegant in her slimness. But these rare moments of triumph surely do not compensate for the hours spent suffering in a restaurant later that day. While she picks at a salad, her plump neighbour, on the other hand, has the most glorious fight with the escargot scissors. When the "cherries jubilee" is served, the chubby woman forgets the morning in the shop, when she held in her breath and tummy, struggling into a dress one size too small.

Petite physiques are almost required for the successful woman today. Slimness is drilled into our consciousness day after day by TV, radio, magazines, and films. In the supermarkets, rows of "diet this" and "diet that" show the importance of weight control.

For centuries the most admired women were buxom. Some of the greatest paintings are of the full-bodied women of past times. Let us retrieve this shapely ideal and free women to be joyful epicures again.

Smoking in Public Places

by Meldon Ellis, student

The issue of smoking in public has become of increasing concern to the nonsmoking citizens of our country. Living in a free country, we as citizens have individual rights. On this issue, the nonsmoker unequivocally deserves the right to be free from the annoyance of cigarette smoke in public places. The smoker, of course, has the right to decide whether or not he or she smokes. However, this right should definitely not extend to the point of causing irritation to others. When smoking in public infringes upon a nonsmoker's right to inhale clean air, when it causes the nonsmoker to cough or suffer adverse physiological effects, then we have reached a point when it must be regulated by law.

Generally, when we think of the potential health hazards surrounding smoking, we think in terms of dangers for the smoker as opposed to dangers for the nonsmoking public. Indeed, most of the information we receive on the topic tends to reinforce our thinking. Recently, however, the public health authorities have directed their concern towards the detrimental effects of tobacco smoke to nonsmokers. The Canadian Medical Association announced that at least thirteen percent of our population is sensitive to cigarette smoke. Though this figure includes persons with emphysema, asthma, bronchitis, hay fever, and heart disease, the average nonsmoker is also subject to reactions from cigarette smoke. These reactions range from eye irritation, coughing, and nasal symptoms, to headaches and even dizziness. According to the Canadian Lung Association, sidestream smoke, the smoke that is exhaled, contains twice as much nicotine as the mainstream smoke inhaled by the smoker. Conclusive evidence to date suggests that sidestream smoke contains three times as much benzopyrene (a cancer-causing agent), and up to fifty times more ammonia than mainstream smoke.

The question about enacting legislation to govern nonsmokers' rights has become a civil rights issue. On one side of the argument we have the smokers, who champion that regulating this area of personal choice threatens the individual freedom this country was built upon. Unsurprisingly, this side receives support from the cigarette company executives, who maintain that in opening ourselves to this type of legislation, we are in effect leaving ourselves wide open to increased government restriction in every area of our lives. The nonsmokers, diametrically opposed to this view, simply feel that when in public places they should be afforded the right to inhale clean air without the hindrance of tobacco smoke.

If this issue could be resolved effectively through mutual respect and common courtesy, I could see no reason for government legislation. But, in concluding, I must state that an individual's right to smoke ends when the smoke of his cigarette reaches the nose of another person in a public place, who might suffer irritating or distressful consequences.

Analysis

Two Cities

1. Although there are some similarities mentioned, Henry Still uses the contrast method to discuss his nightmare and dream cities. Can you find three examples of the features of each city that he includes as supporting evidence in his contrast?

2. He describes the nightmare city first, then the dream city. What would be the effect if the order were reversed?

3. He describes the nightmare city in seven paragraphs and the dream city in one. Why? What is the effect?

4. He uses the AAA/BBB method of contrast rather than the ABABAB method (see Activity 2). Would the latter method have been effective for his subject matter?

5. This essay does not follow Basic Essay Structure. Unlike "The High Price of Soft-Sell," it has no introduction. It simply begins with his main claim: "There are two dreams about the city of tomorrow." The final paragraph contains a restatement of his main claim but with a clearly persuasive argument in the form of a threat: "One may come true if we make it happen; the other will come true automatically if we do nothing or continue our current inept fumbling." In other words, it is within our power to choose the city that future generations will inhabit. Which aspects in the essay are present today in a city in which you live or that you live near?

I Would Rather Be Fat

1. The student writer has taken a brave stand; she advocates being fat in a world where "thin is in." Does she persuade successfully?

2. She provides a series of narrative examples as supporting evidence, contrasting the thin image from the media with a fat reality. Is there another way this theme could be organized?

3. In the main, she writes from a first-person point of view. Do you think this approach is more effective than using the more academic third person?

4. You might enjoy writing an essay about the value of being slender.

Smoking in Public Places

1. Which sentence in the first paragraph contains the writer's main claim?

2. The student writer has collected facts from a number of authorities. How has he incorporated the facts into his work? Do you think he should have used footnotes? What would have been the effect with footnotes?

3. What methods of organization does he use within each paragraph and for the essay as a whole?

4. What precisely is he trying to persuade his audience to do?

5. Compare this essay to the paragraph "Smokers Beware" (Assignment 4). Do you see how an expository paragraph can be expanded into an essay?

Assignment 7 Autobiography

Introduction

Writing an autobiographical piece can be one of the most fascinating of your assignments. Everyone, in one way or another, wants someone to know who he or she is, and judging from the proliferation of autobiographies on the best-seller lists, a large audience is often eager to find out.

You do not have to write an entire book (or, as John Diefenbaker did, three books) for this assignment; a short essay will suffice.

Assignment

Using a specific point of view, write your autobiography in a 300- to 500-word essay.

Prewriting Suggestions

1. Decide to whom you want to tell something about yourself, what you want to tell, and why you want to tell it. List your writing variables before you begin. For example:

Topic: my background and accomplishments
Audience: the student body
Purpose: to introduce myself and convince other students to vote for me in the upcoming election
Format: a speech (which includes my autobiography)

Rather than telling everything about yourself from your birth to the present, select your information according to your purpose and audience.

2. Attempt to find a thread, an organizational tool, to keep your autobiography unified and concise. This "thread" may be a generalization about your life, or a quality or characteristic that you want to emphasize.

As you read the following autobiographical material, locate the "thread" that is introduced to give each one coherence.

I was the only girl I ever knew who could hang by her toes from the exercise bar in our upstairs front sunporch. It was about my only accomplishment. And I always realized it wasn't important. It wasn't like being able to ripple "Barcarolle" over the piano or daub unlikely streaks of green into a pastel portrait. There was no real future in toe-hanging. Unless, of course, you planned to make a career of testing crash helmets. And there were times when it seemed I might have to settle for just that.

from Confessions of a Toe-Hanger

I was born in Fort Macleod, Alberta, in the foothills of the Canadian Rockies – an area of extreme temperatures and mirages. When I was two feet off the ground I collected broken glass and cats. When I was three feet off the ground I made drawings of animals and forest fires. When I was four feet off the ground I discovered boys and bicycles. When I was five feet I began to dance to rock'n'roll and sing the top ten and bawdy service songs around campfires and someone turned me on to Lambert Hendricks and Ross and Miles Davis and later Bob Dylan. Through these vertical spurts there was briefly the church choir, grade one piano, bowling, art college, the twist, marriage, runs in the nylons and always romance – extremes in temperatures and mirages.

Joni Mitchell

3. In order to find the appropriate thread, you must do a bit of stocktaking of your life to date. Make a list of questions such as the following to discover a pattern in your life that might serve as a unifying device.

a) What are your three best characteristics? Your three worst?
b) What people or events have been significant in your life? Why?
c) Of what accomplishments are you proud?
d) What are your goals and ambitions?

This activity can be done on your own, but it might be better to work with one other person.

4. When you have completed the above prewriting activity, list events that illustrate the generalization or characteristic that you want to emphasize. Under each event, jot down details. Make sure you include the similarities and differences between the recurring events. For example:

I am outspoken	
Gets me into trouble.	Gets me out of trouble.
embarrassed mom's guests	saved the family from a fire
sent to principal	chosen class president
got a black eye	won a court case

Drafting Suggestions

1. Besides using your "thread" to give your autobiography unity, you should plan exactly how you are going to organize your writing. Refer to one of the methods of organization (chronological, climactic) in Activity 2.

2. Maintain a consistent tone and style in your writing. Attempt a few practice drafts until you find the particular style which suits you and the events that you wish to include.

3. Notice the various ways of saying the same thing. Each is given a label to distinguish it from the others.

A straightforward style
I was born in Regina on July 15, 1964.

A colloquial style
I showed up in Regina on July 15, 1964.

A breezy style
With sweat dripping off its beak, the stork dropped me in the middle of the Prairies on July 15, 1964.

A lecturing style
My nativity occurred in the capital of Saskatchewan on the fifteenth day of July in the year nineteen hundred and sixty-four.

An ironic style
The highlight of my parents' life was my birth on July 15, 1964; they've never got over it.

A comic style
It was marvellous the way everyone turned out for my birth on July 15, 1964. Even my mother was there.

Revising Suggestions

When you have completed your final draft, judge your autobiography according to the standards in Appendix B. Then, with your peers, decide on one method of feedback from Appendix B. Use the following specific questions to help your revision process.

1. What feature of the autobiography is the most revealing? What is the most important thing the audience will learn about you?

2. What is the thread which runs through the autobiography?

3. In what style is the autobiography written?

4. What kind of organization do you follow: chronological, climactic, decreasing importance, increasing importance, smaller to bigger, bigger to smaller, bad to good, good to bad, and so forth?
5. Should any words, sentences, or paragraphs in the autobiography be omitted?
6. Should anything be added?
7. Does the autobiography fit its purpose and audience?

Polishing Suggestions

Before you submit your autobiography to your audience, use the check list in Appendix C to proofread your selection.

Models

Memories

by John Parker

I was born during the Depression to poor but loving Manitoba farmers who specialized in growing rocks. Piles of white rocks towering amid our spindly wheatfields is one of my most vivid memories of growing up in the thirties.

Since the nearest school was seventeen miles from our farm and the only way there was by horse and buggy, I spent my time on more important jobs – raiding crows' nests and trapping gophers for their precious tails. Think of the thrill that comes to a seven year old when he hands in fifty-three gophers' tails to a government agent and receives $1.06 in cash. My first pay check.

With the outbreak of World War II, my world changed; I thought it had crashed. My father joined the army and was sent to Europe; my mother, my young sister, and I moved to Arden, a small Manitoba town, and I started school. I sometimes wonder that it took a war to get me educated. At any rate, my mother decided that education and I should become acquainted, so at eight years of age, my carefree days ended. During the next few years, as my family moved around Manitoba and then to Vancouver, I attended fourteen different schools, ranging from a tiny country school with eight grades in one room to a large, sterile city high school. Always a little behind everyone else, I remembered my early education as both frightening and downright difficult.

At the end of grade nine, just when I was beginning to enjoy school, I was forced to leave and help support my family. I spent a frustrating year getting my hands stuck between print rollers and cutting the tops off my fingernails with a paper cutter. My boss and I discovered I was not mechanically inclined. As I despaired, a friend told me about night school and how it could change my life. So at the end of each day, I scrubbed off the ink, bandaged my fingers, and attended King Edward. I took grades 10, 11, and 12, managing by some miracle to graduate in one year.

After a year at college, I became a teacher. I'll never forget my first day of teaching. Nervous, nineteen, and totally dehydrated, I needed a drink of water before I walked into my grade-six class. Never be the first to drink from a drinking fountain after the summer holidays. I'm sure my delightful group of twelve year olds wondered why their teacher was drenched from his head to his shoes. But from that day I knew I had found my niche. I can't think of a single unhappy day that I have had in a classroom. I moved up the teaching ladder to the College level, while at the same time obtaining a Bachelor of Arts in English and Drama at UBC and a Master's Degree at the University of Washington.

Besides teaching, I've always been a dabbler in theatre – first as an amateur, then as a professional. After seven years as an Artistic Director of two Vancouver theatre companies, I moved to London, England so that I could work as a professional actor in films and television as well as on stage. In 1977 my wife, daughter, and three sons all agreed to join me there.

After nearly three years in the world of British theatre, I returned to education with good memories, no regrets, and lots of enthusiasm for my current project, *The Writer's Workshop*.

Foot Loose

by Gino Nasato, student

I am a foot. I was pulled kicking from warm security on August 16, 1957. It was not so much the cold that startled me that fateful morning, as my realization that I was forever attached to a stumbling lout named Gino Nasato. Still, life was grand during the early months; Gino simply lay on his back and played baby. At the age of eight months, though, our peaceful co-existence was shattered when the lout started to walk. Oh, to describe the pain of those early years brings back horrid memories. I was kicked, I was bumped, I was stubbed, and I was stomped. Self-preservation in mind, I fought back with a vengeance. For the first ten years I tripped him as often as possible. The knees and the elbows hated me for the pain I inflicted, and his poor mother despised me for the clothes she was always mending. Through the high-school years I was continually abused. If I wasn't being butted painfully against a soccer ball, I was risking toes and heels with daring slides into second base. My only hope was that Gino would get a soft desk job after graduating. I hoped in vain.

First, it was logging and those dastardly spiked boots. Tired of logging,

Gino went to sea, where hard, slippery, cold steel decks awaited me. I still lose my footing when I think of how that ship rolled. In his twenty-first year, Gino decided to go to Europe. The dreams I had – visions of pretty painted toes, French music and Gino sitting in cafés, resting me on stools. Oh, the naïveté of a foot! That beggar shuffled me through Paris subways, blistered me in Athens' midday heat, and hobbled me on cobbled streets in Amsterdam. My only respite came when we hit the beaches of Greece. For two glorious months I was in Dr. Scholl's heaven: cool wet sand to leave my autograph in and sparkling surf to soak my calluses. But, alas, it wasn't to last; Gino wound up in Vancouver.

It was about this time that I felt my toes had been stepped on long enough. I formulated a plan with the ankle, and during one of Gino's efforts to kick up his heels, we twisted severely. I was tickled pink when the doctor prescribed one month of total rest, with me kept in an elevated position. Finally, after twenty-three years, I was put on the pedestal I rightfully deserved. With some guidance from me, Gino has finally recognized the prominent role I play in his life. He's now back studying at school, which gives me plenty of time to relax. In fact, things have been going so well lately, I'm thinking of passing on my secrets to other downtrodden feet. I might even start a revolution. After all, just think of all the foot soldiers I could recruit!

Analysis

Memories

1. You, the reader of *The Writer's Workshop*, are obviously the intended audience for this autobiography. What is your feeling about knowing something of the person who is trying to improve your writing? Are there things left unsaid that you feel you would like to know?
2. The style of the essay is basically direct, but it does contain satire. Can you find examples of each style?
3. Does the connecting thread, "education," help you to read?

Foot Loose

1. This is a witty and wonderful example of a student autobiography using a persona. Does it tell you everything you want to know about Gino?
2. Why do you think the author chose to use this persona? If you were to use a part of your body as a persona, which part would it be?
3. Can you pick out examples of irony in the piece?

Assignment 8 Biography

Introduction   You will probably find writing a biography much easier than writing an auto-biography. We seem to be better observers of others than revealers of ourselves.

This assignment is informal; in other words, you are not obliged to use research, footnotes, or a bibliography. The research essay is handled in Assignments 11 and 12.

Assignment

In a 300- to 500-word essay, write a biography of someone you know well.

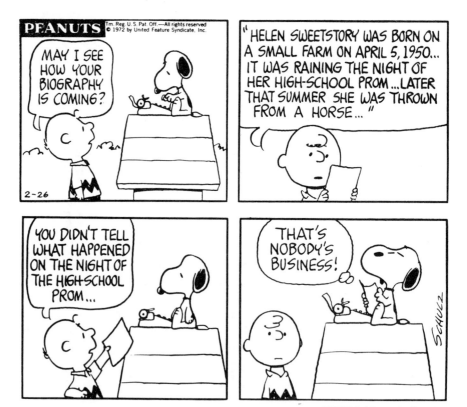

Prewriting Suggestions

1. As this is to be an informal biography, decide who will be your subject. Mother, father, or sibling? Grandparent? Boy friend, girl friend? You may know a great deal about a particular athlete, movie star, or other celebrity. The choice of subject is yours.

2. Before you begin, create a purpose for writing the biography. Sorry, but "Because I have to write it," is not a good enough reason. The statement of purpose should take into account not only your subject but also your audience. Read these statements of purpose:

a) I intend to write a newspaper article for our school paper to introduce a friend who is running for the student council.

b) I must present an oral introduction of a speaker at a student assembly so that the students and teachers will know a little about her before she speaks.

c) I have been invited to a roast for a friend of mine where I have to give a humorous speech to all the guests. I must make them laugh by telling them some funny stories about my friend's life.

d) I am going to write a "Who's Who" about my activity partner and post it on the bulletin board for everyone to read. I will write in the style of the published *Who's Who.*

Use your imagination as you think of your purpose and your reader.

3. Keep your purpose and audience in mind as you gather information for your biography. In some cases, your audience will be concerned with factual details about your subject; in others, they will want to get to know him or her in a more personal sense.

4. You may wish to choose a major characteristic of your subject and base your biography on that particular quality. If you cannot think of a major quality, perhaps you have not chosen the correct subject for this assignment. You should certainly know a great deal about your subject and see distinctive features in your subject's life.

If you are having difficulty determining a major characteristic, make up a few questions and interview your subject. Here are some examples of questions you can ask:

a) What do you think is your best characteristic?

b) What is your worst?

c) What makes you happiest?

d) Which countries have you visited?

e) How many times have you moved?

f) What are you proudest of in your life?

g) (If your subject is running for office) What would you do if elected?

5. You may want to do some reading or talk to others about your subject (with permission, of course) before proceeding.

Drafting Suggestions

1. Use the Drafting Suggestions in Assignment 7 to help you draft this assignment.

2. You can describe your subject directly, by simply telling your readers about him or her; or indirectly, by relating things he or she did, said, or what others said about your subject. A combination of methods is often effective.

3. Normally, a biography is organized in chronological order, although you may wish to use some other pattern: comparison/contrast, cause/effect, generalizations supported by details, and so on.

Revising Suggestions

When you have completed your final draft, judge your biography yourself according to the standards in Appendix B. Then, use Appendix B to help you and your peers choose a method for a feedback session. The following specific suggestions should help:

1. Does the information in your biography satisfy the needs of your intended audience?

2. Are your subject's major qualities or accomplishments easily recognized?

3. Does your subject seem "real" to your readers? If not, would the inclusion of dialogue or anecdotes help?

4. Have you avoided the use of overworked adjectives, such as "nice," in describing your subject?

Polishing Suggestions

Use Appendix C to help you proofread your biography.

Models

The Terror of Oxted

Whenever I hear the word Grandmother I always presume I should visualize a plump little old lady who lives in the background of the family and pops out occasionally to dispense doses of wise advice and home-made cookies. However, if this idea of a grandmother is the right one then I would have a hard time explaining Nana. Nana is my paternal grandmother; a petite English woman, reserved and genteel in the true British tradition, but one whose apparent gentility is a well-learned façade covering a dynamic, determined, wilfulness.

Before I even start to describe my personal experiences with Nana, perhaps I could mention what I know of her past. She was an orphan; so by the age of thirteen she was working as a barmaid. (Those circumstances still bothered her at the age of sixty, as was evidenced by the solemnity on her face when she spoke of those times.) Eventually she met Gramps, and saw in him an attractive, independent, up-and-coming businessman. They were married, and eight months later celebrated the birth of their first child. Gramps continued to make a living, and Nana continued to live life. Throughout my childhood I would receive a yearly postcard from Nana depicting such exotic places as Morocco and Majorca, although Gramps was never persuaded to leave Oxted or Godstone.

I more or less met Nana for the first time when I was fifteen and my father took my sister and me "home" for the summer holidays. Surrounded as I was by so much that was new, Nana was just a vague figure; someone who showered us with treacle tarts and plums and who demonstrated deep concern that we should meet more young people. My next encounter with Nana did not take place until the event of my grandfather's death three years later. Nana had suffered a deep loss and I went back to England as the emissary of the Canadian contingent of the family. I was to console Nana, to care for her needs, to watch for her welfare and possibly bring her back to Canada. It was assumed that I would stay with her during this stressful time. However, these plans up-ended on us when Nana promptly wrote to say that she 'didn't want the added expense or responsibility of my staying with her' – an assertion that was made with as much British tact as an assertive person can summon. Still I wasn't going to be denied my trip to England so I went and was welcomed into my cousin Pam's household. From Pam I learnt a great deal more about Nana. I was deluged with tales of Nana's outrageous escapades and scandalous behaviour. She would run about Oxted telling such unfamiliar folk as the greengrocer all about things which ought best be kept within the family. Everywhere she went she kept up a constant stream of amicable chatter about anything and everything and nothing. The people of the village soon fell into the pattern that most people fell into with Nana, of agreeing approximately every seven minutes and otherwise continuing with their business.

Nana's bereavement seemed not to affect her at all. After Gramp's death Nana was the beneficiary of a fair sum of money. But did she store it away to provide comfort and income in her twilight years? No. Much to Pam's disgust she ran amuck like a child in a candy store. The beautiful garden behind 20 Paddock Way received a Gazebo on a swivel base so that it could be turned to face the sun at any time of day. New pink garage doors were installed, though, as Pam chidingly said, "There was absolutely nothing wrong with the old ones." Appearance was of top importance to Nana. Her pastel-coloured clothes were always trim, tailored, and expensive, she never missed an appointment with her chiropodist, and her hair was always neatly coiffed and the barest shade of blue thanks to weekly appointments with the beauty salon.

Her social life, too, seemed to blossom with her bereavement. More and more neighbours were obliged to attend Nana's Tea Parties; if the invitation was not accepted, Nana would stay and chat to make up for time that would otherwise be missed. I was frequently the guest star at these affairs. As the grown-up grand daughter from Canada, I would be shown off and my life story told to one and all.

There we would be: Dr. and Mrs. Cockerill, Nana, and I assembled around a tea table in the Gazebo. I was on a rigorous diet at the time and could only watch the food beckoning me as the small-talk circulated. Having discussed the size of roses that year Nana would ask them for the umpteenth time if she had mentioned that her grandaughter was visiting from Canada. They would feel obliged to ask my opinion of England, now that I was back, and I would suddenly find myself the focus of attention just as I had finally given in and stuffed both cheeks with cucumber sandwiches. I did manage to reply, though rather inelegantly, that I liked the country. Nana would consider this unseemly episode for a moment and then decide that it hadn't happened. "Did you know," she would say, "that Mrs. Ellis' daughter is back from Belgium?" and the three of them, tea cups poised, would discuss the impact of this on Oxted while I devoured as delicately as I could.

Nana knew no laws, at least not the ones that didn't appeal to her. She couldn't be bothered with such trivial things as lines dividing the road into lanes. She would go careening through the countryside at a remarkable speed with the nose of her 'Daf' headed precisely down the middle of the road. After all, that was where a car should be: the middle of a road. Heaven help the car that saw her coming from the opposite direction, but God help her passengers, who gripped the edges of their seats and stared ahead with glazed eyes. All this time Nana would be chatting merrily away, keeping up a one-sided conversation while looking directly at her passenger and audience who could only respond with muttered prayers. Pam often stormed about Nana's being a public health hazard and stated that she should be banned from the road. But we all knew that that would destroy her. She could never give up her car.

On one occasion though, Nana's interference and will-fulness proved to be opportune. Over the last month I had seen several doctors about stomach pains and each one in turn seemed reluctant to do anything for me. I was beginning to get quite desperate when finally Nana was notified (or gained notification). She took it upon herself to sort everything out and sent her own doctor round to see me on the spot. From that point on everything was accomplished with amazing speed. Dr. Cockerill had me admitted to Redhill Hospital within the hour. The Hospital arranged to operate immediately and the surgeons' annoyance at having been routed out at midnight on a Sunday turned to embarrassment when they discovered a gangrenous cyst. The cyst had been completely hidden and the diagnosis was impossible without costly surgery. What motivated Dr. Cockerill to have me admitted was not a certainty that surgery was needed but a deep fear that there was no other way to get Nana off his back. During visiting hours the next day Nana swept into the ward emanating the belief that she could handle the whole world just as usual. But on this occasion I viewed her with slightly less amusement and a little more respect. To some she may be the terror of Oxted but to me she's a fine old lady.

An Interview with John Milton (1608–1674)

by Chantal Phillips, student

John Milton was one of the most exceptional men of the seventeenth century. His academic excellence, which arose from the diligence of his scholarly days and from his European travels, as well as from his lively career as author of many pamphlets, poems, books, and letters, attests to his intelligence and greatness of mind. The fact that he is still studied by high-school students three hundred years after his death is, unfortunately, more a deterrent to discovering his wit and humour than a help. Studying for this interview, however, has led me to an understanding that Milton was an exceptional man as well as an enjoyable one.

ME: Thank you for coming Mr. Milton. I have conjured up this image of you to answer some questions on your works and your life. Are you willing to allow my readers to know about you?

MILTON: Certainly. I always enjoy talking about myself, as it is the subject I know most about.

ME: You were always a lively youth, used to your own tutors and a freedom of study that let you become learned in many subjects by the age of fifteen. When you were sixteen you entered Christ's College, Cambridge. How did you react to the situation there?

MILTON: Before Cambridge I had gone to St. Paul's school from the age of twelve until I was fifteen. I always preferred having the freedom of a private tutor, but the resources at the school and my studies in Sallust, Horace, Virgil, and the New Testament,[1] kept me very busy. I enjoyed the atmosphere of the school and all my schoolmates.

When I got to Cambridge, however, composing all those trivial declamations became more of a bore. I felt I was being dragged from my studies. I disagreed with my tutor so much that I was rusticated. But I have to admit that my

---

[1] *Encyclopedia of World Biography*, 1973 ed., s.v. "Milton," by J. Max Patrick.

university career wasn't only study. I also filled my time with walks, plays, girls, and, most of all, my friends, especially Charles Diodati. I wrote some lovely poems in those days. Nothing that was a test of my true intellect, though.

ME: From what I've read, your life in the country when you returned to your family home for five years was a complete renunciation of your more carefree days at university....

MILTON: To a certain extent it was in reaction to a belief that I have held all my life, a belief that I was appointed for some great work which could only come to me as the outgrowth of a life of austerity.[2] The renunciation of my carefree days, as you call it, gave me time to study....

ME: I believe most of your biographers refer to this as your "Horton Period."

MILTON: Yes, that's correct. I left university for Horton and spent my time studying and enjoying the pastoral scenery around me. God has instilled into me, if into anyone, a vehement love of the beautiful. I used the natural setting often to express moods I felt in my poetry.

But, it's not quite true to say I completely gave up my social life to study. I lived at Horton but I continued to be involved in the cultural life of London. I wrote "Comus" and my poem "On Shakespeare" while at Horton.

ME: In 1634 "Comus" was performed at Ludlow Castle. It marks the beginning of your concentration on temptation themes.[3] The villain in this musical comedy makes a very good argument in favour of seduction. In "Lycidas" you even suggest the idea that if God allows the young to die, why not give in to temptation, "sport with Amaryllis in the shade" while you have time?

MILTON: Yes, but I end that particular poem by stating that "laborious days are wasted": eternal life lies ahead, does it not? As for being concerned with temptation themes, I'm not sure. I never looked at it like that. The times forced many people to re-evaluate their ideas on temptation; certainly I myself tried to convince many that what I said in "Lycidas" holds true.

ME: That reminds me of your involvement in the Puritan movement. Somehow your love of life, music, women, society – none of these reconciles with the bleak Puritan outlook on the world as it should be.

MILTON: I suggest to you that the Puritans were not trying to enslave people by shackling them with rules and regulations and social codes of austerity; quite the contrary. We were trying to free the people of England from the

---

[2]Leon Amiel, ed., *The Complete Poetical Works of John Milton* (New York: Universal Classics), p. xi.

[3]Patrick, p. 424.

tyranny of royalty. All men have the right to break contracts they make with rulers....

ME: I agree with the Puritan cause, but what I was trying to illustrate was that you have two definite sides to your personality. Your social side seems to have been overshadowed in your later years by that of the dedicated scholar who continually read and produced great works.

MILTON: Thank you for the compliment. Certainly my blindness, my deteriorating health, and the return of the monarchy all led me to a more reclusive life. They also gave me the opportunity to write my greatest and most challenging work, *Paradise Lost*.

ME: *Paradise Lost* certainly is a masterpiece, and I'll end with a question on it. When I studied this work in school, we related it to the politics of the age, and I noticed a few jabs at Roman Catholicism in it as well. Did you mean *Paradise Lost* to be a satire of the political situation of the times?

MILTON: No, I did not. That is the most interesting part of watching people criticize your works. *Paradise Lost* was mainly derived from my imagination, and of course I was inspired by the Bible. It was not, however, meant to be taken as a satire. I must admit I did insert those pokes at the Roman Catholics but that is all. I felt it to be my life's work, and an effort to convey God's wisdom and providence to my fellowman.[4]

ME: Thank you very much, Mr. Milton.

---

[4]Patrick, p. 425.

Bibliography

Amiel, Leon, ed. *The Complete Poetical Works of John Milton*. New York: Universal Classics.

Encyclopedia of World Biography, 1973 ed. S.v. "Milton," by J. Max Patrick.

Hughes, Merrit. *John Milton: Paradise Lost*. Indianapolis: Bobbs-Merrill Co., 1962.

Inglis, Reway, et al. *Adventures in English Literature*. Toronto: W. J. Gage and Co., 1952.

Joni Mitchell

by Ritchie Yorke

Joni Mitchell, that wistful girl from the Canadian prairies, has become a composer and lyricist of world stature. Her songs can be heard in a dozen different languages in fifty countries. Judy Collins sold a million copies of the poignant Joni Mitchell love ballad, "Both Sides Now." Miss Collins has since gone on record as saying: "I sing Joni's songs because I like them immensely. There doesn't seem to be anyone quite as good. Her lyrics are exquisite and it all fits together."

Joni Mitchell now lives, a golden goddess, in Laurel Canyon, California. She is one of west coast folk's elite – respected and often loved by her contemporaries, admired and emulated by thousands of young girls with long, brown hair and a guitar.

But not all her songs are about the sunny haven she has built in California. She writes of things and people she knew while young, growing up in Saskatoon. "Michael from Mountains," one of her best-loved ballads, was dedicated to her grade seven teacher, Mr. Kratzman. "Most of my songs are written from personal experiences. The Michael in 'Michael from Mountains' is a real person. He was a child-man always showing you his treasures, like a boy.

"Mr. Kratzman taught me how to write about the simple things in life, things that I knew about – like gathering tadpoles in an empty mayonnaise jar after the rain. I still remember playing dress-up in the attic of the house in Saskatoon with trunks of old clothes in a world of make believe."

Joni Mitchell is now into a second era of composing. Her first was often lonely and loveless, like an old person without a friend. Now she's more intent on bringing people up.

"I do a lot of night writing," she once told Larry LeBlanc, a Canadian free-lance writer. "I need solitude to write. I used to be able to write under almost any condition but not anymore. I have to go inside myself so far, to search through a theme. Writing is more than simply arranging a pleasant combination of sounds.

"When I write a new song, I take it and play it for my friends, who are fine musicians and writers. I'm largely influenced by their reaction to it. If they like it, I'm knocked out. I guess I write for those people. They're really my audience." ...

Joni learned to play ukulele while attending art college, and taught herself guitar from a Pete Seeger instruction book. She left Saskatoon in 1961 to appear at the Mariposa Festival in Orillia, [Gordon] Lightfoot's birthplace. Martin Onrot, one of the organizers of the event (which was forced by injunction to change location a few hours before it began) recalls: "Joni had come in with some people from the west, and she helped us load trucks and move the entire festival. She really chipped in.

"The first time I heard her sing was in a downtown Toronto rooming house. She had a soft, beautiful voice, and an easy, melodic style. It was nice, but I had no idea that she would become a superstar."

She returned to Toronto in 1965 and stayed for a couple of summers. Finally she left when it became obvious that the world would never have the chance to appreciate her unique abilities while she remained in Toronto, unknown, undiscovered and misunderstood.

"I still feel a Canadian at heart and with the U.S. being under such peculiar circumstances I may come back, perhaps to Vancouver. Most of my friends are in the U.S. and that's why I'll stay a little longer."

There were years of dues-paying on the east coast U.S. folk circuit, but eventually, Joni's songs began to turn up on prominent folk albums. Her early compositions such as "Urge for Going," "The Circle Game," and "Chelsea Morning" are now rightly regarded as classics of the folk idiom. From there, it became easier. She gradually gained acceptance as a singer as well as writer, and began making concert tours. Her popularity grows daily, and the chances of her returning to Canada are slim despite her protestations.

Analysis

The Terror of Oxted

1. The student writer provides her reader with a candid profile of her grandmother. What is the dominating characteristic of "Nana"? Do you have a relative whose biography you would use to fulfil the requirements of this assignment?
2. The writer primarily uses several personal narratives to develop her biography. What other supporting evidence does she use?
3. What overall method of organization does she use for her biography?
4. How does the personal experience in the last paragraph tie the entire essay together?

An Interview with John Milton

1. This fascinating biography is by a high-school student. What did you learn through it about Milton's life and work?
2. Why does the writer provide footnotes and bibliography? Do you think they are necessary? Do they distract you from reading the interview?
3. Perhaps you would like to try this method for your biography.

Joni Mitchell

1. For whom and why was this biography written?
2. What is Ritchie Yorke's main technique in organizing the essay? How is it arranged?
3. Why do you think so little actual biographical information was included? Is there anything left out that you would like to know?
4. Compare the biography to the following "Who's Who" entry.

MITCHELL, Joni (Roberta Joan Anderson); singer, songwriter; b. Ft. Macleod, Alta. 7 Nov. 1943; d. William A. and Myrtle M. (McKee) A.; student Alta. Coll.; m. Chuck Mitchell, 1965, (div.); albums incl. "Song to a Seagull," "Clouds," "Ladies of the Canyon," "Blue," "For the Roses," "Court and Spark," "Miles of Aisles," "Hissing of Summer Lawns," "Hejira, Don Juan's Reckless Daughter," "Mingus" (Jazz Album of Year and Rock-Blues Album of Year, Downbeat mag. 1979); compositions incl. "Both Sides Now," "Michael from Mountains," "Urge for Going," "Circle Game"; Juno award for special achievement, 1981; Address: c/o Elliot Roberts Lookout Mgmt., 9120 Sunset Blvd., Los Angeles, CA 90212.

On your next library visit, have the librarian direct you to the biography section. You can pass many happy hours there.

Assignment **9** Review

Introduction

The review is a type of expository essay in which you give your opinion of a particular work. Unlike the writer of a literary essay, the writer of a review should assume that the reader does not know the material (book, play, film, and so on). Therefore, it is important to give the reader a general idea of what the work is about, as well as your opinion of it. A good review is generally a combination of information and opinion.

Assignment

Write a review of a book, a film, a play, a TV show, a record, or other work of art in approximately 500 words.

Prewriting Suggestions

1. The main reason for writing a review is to give your opinion about the work of art. Hence, you are expected to be critical. Criticizing a work of art, however, does not mean that you must pull it apart. You should discuss both the parts that, in your opinion, work well and the parts that do not work well.

2. You might like to look up a few back copies of your daily newspapers or national and international journals to read the reviews of books, plays, movies, and so on. But read cautiously. Professional critics often thrive on controversy, especially that which follows harsh reviews. It is suggested, though, that *you* leave statements like these out of your reviews:

This play is the worst thing that has happened to Canada since World War II.
She ran the gamut of emotions from A to B.
This is Mr. Smith's first novel. Let's hope it's his last.
The poetry in this selection seems more like autopsy than autobiography.

3. Many readers of reviews build up a short list of critics whom they trust. A trusted reviewer's opinion can serve as a guide in selecting books or movies. Over the years, you too should build your list of local, national, and international reviewers whose tastes reflect your own.

4. A review is the expression of one person's opinion. Theatre critic Wayne Edmonstone puts it clearly:

I must tell you *what* I think. I must also tell you *why* I think it. I do not tell you what *someone else* thinks I should think. I do not tell you what *you* are to think. It's as simple as that and if all you're looking for is a reflection of your own tastes, prejudices, or preferences, then – with all respect – the place to look is in the mirror.

So when you write, make sure your reader knows exactly where you stand. Be opinionated. Back up your opinions. Be emphatic. Indeed, try to include something memorable – a pun, a witty quote – something that sticks with the reader so that your opinion will be remembered.

5. To make this assignment more interesting for you, you should write a review of a show or book for your local or school paper.

Your readers will be people your own age, probably with your interests. People who read movie reviews go to the movies; those who read TV reviews watch a lot of TV.

Drafting Suggestions

1. Quickly identify the material you are reviewing: title, author, publisher, theatre, director, channel, musician, and so on.

2. Consider the purpose and emphasis of the work you are reviewing. If you are discussing a non-fiction book, for example, you may want to give the reader an idea of the information covered; for a work of fiction, you may want to discuss the plot or one or two memorable characters. Ultimately, a book should be assessed according to its purpose. Did it succeed in informing you, entertaining you, or convincing you of the author's point of view?

3. Give enough of the plot to interest your readers so that they can decide whether or not they wish to read, see, or listen to the reviewed work. Do not tell the whole story; a review is not a précis or summary. Identifying the murderer in a mystery is tantamount to committing a murder. You should merely whet the readers' appetites.

4. The inclusion of a few quotations to show the work's style enlivens a review. Attempt to fit the quotations into your own prose so that the reader can continue smoothly. (Assignment 11 gives some examples of mixing quoted material and a writer's own prose.)

5. Because a review is an expository essay, you may find it useful to read the Drafting Suggestions in Assignments 4 and 6. Most importantly, remember that you must back up your opinion with specific references to the work you are reviewing.

Revising Suggestions

After you have written your final draft, you should judge it yourself according to the set of standards in Appendix B. Then decide which method of peer feedback from Appendix B to follow. Use the list of revising suggestions from Assignments 4 and 6 as well as the following particular questions to help revise your review.

1. Does your review give enough information so that the reader knows what the work is about?

2. Is your opinion of the work clearly expressed? Have you explained *why* you feel the way you do?

3. Has the review convinced your peers? In other words, would they do as you suggest: either see or not see, buy or not buy, read or not read, the reviewed material?

4. Does the review include appropriate quotations? Do they fit in well with your own prose; that is, are they used to illustrate a particular point?

Polishing Suggestions

Use the polishing suggestions as outlined in Appendix C, making sure that your review is distinctively yours.

Models

Prehistoric Drama: an Honest Bequest

by Marke Andrews

Quest for Fire, the Canadian-French co-production which opens tonight at the Stanley Theatre, could be called a lot of other things by the people involved. "Quest for Production" by director Jean-Jacques Annaud. "Quest for Funding" by Montreal producers John Kemeny and Denis Heroux. "Quest for Comfort" by the actors and technical crew.

But the film that was a headache to inaugurate, a nightmare to shoot and a "frightening gamble" in the marketplace is on its way to becoming the most successful Canadian movie ever made....

The large-scale action in *Quest for Fire* occurs in generous doses of tribal warfare, wolf, bear and lion attacks, trumpeting mastadons and acts of cannibalism. But the *real* action is in the actors' eyes, in the way they move their heads and bare their incisors.

It's not easy showing major developments in man's evolution within a 90-minute framework, and the task is further complicated when there is no discernible dialogue.

The actors in *Quest for Fire* meet the challenge with a silent-movie flair for expression. There's a lot to watch in this film, but the main story is right there in the actors' hairy faces.

Quest for Fire is set 80,000 years in the past. The Ulam tribe loses a battle with the fierce Wagabous, who steal the sacred fire cage.

The Ulams, with no idea how to create fire, send three of their number (played by Everett McGill, Ron Perleman and Nameer El-Kadi) into the wilderness to find it.

During their journey, the three primitives encounter wild animals, cannibals and Ika (Rae Dawn Chong), a siren from the more advanced Ivaka tribe.

From the Ivaka the travelling Ulams learn how to create fire. From Ika, leader Naoh (McGill) learns ... something about his own emotional makeup.

While watching *Quest*, one is continually reminded of other films. When the trio nervously sets out on its odyssey, there's an element of *The Wizard of Oz*. The slapstick is pure "Three Stooges." ...

While parts of the film remain unconvincing – the sabre-toothed tigers are nothing more than lions with dentures and the slapstick, nudge-wink humour is terribly contrived – *Quest for Fire* upholds the integrity of its intentions.

It may teeter at times, but unlike previous prehistoric costume dramas, this one never rolls off the table into farce.

Fascinating and never dull, *Quest for Fire* represents not so much a movie, but rather a movie-going experience.

Rita: Still in Ecstasy

by Carol Vuch, student

George Ryga's *The Ecstasy of Rita Joe* is a powerful play depicting the tragic situation of a Native Indian in the city. A statement against the injustice done to the Indians, the play examines the emotions of isolation and alienation.

Rita Joe (Margo Kane), a Native Indian, comes to the city to find a place for herself, and encounters an anonymous, cement society, whose rules have no compassion. The city rejects her and her race.

The play progresses through a mingling of past and present. The present consists of the Magistrate (David Gillies) before whom Rita Joe is continually being brought on various charges, and certain city scenes with her family, her boy friend Jamie Paul (Tom Jackson), and The Society for Aid to the Indians. The past is handled through flash-backs of memory, fantasy, and lighting effects. Both blend to evolve a story of pride, deception, and rejection.

Mr. Ryga's style is very much in evidence in *Ecstasy*. The setting is unrealistic, the play without logical sequence, and the technical effects many and varied. Music, in the form of songs and a solo guitar intertwined with dialogue, is used to make comment but also serves as Rita Joe's alter ego. This is in keeping with Ryga's style; he employs these themes and techniques in many of his plays, including *Nothing But a Man* and *Grass and Wild Strawberries*.

The plays of the Sixties, when *The Ecstasy of Rita Joe* was written, were basically carefree and light. The musicals, however, adopted the message form, and statements on society's drawbacks and life's injustices were the messages of the time. Although Ryga's music is anything but escapist, it softens the harshness of his criticism of white society.

Ryga's indictment is certainly still valid today. White society has not come very far in its mastering of human prejudice. The same groups being rejected in the Sixties are still rejected today, although perhaps not as openly. Society has merely masked its prejudices, not conquered them, and the injustices still go on.

The Prairie Theatre Exchange's touring production of *The Ecstasy of Rita Joe* did justice to Ryga's play. Gordon McCall, the director, cast all the native characters with Indian actors, a first in the play's history.

In accordance with Ryga's directions, the set was a circular ramp without props or scenery. The audience surrounded the stage, some members even sitting on it. This theatre-in-the-round technique caused some problems with sight and sound, particularly in the court scenes. The set was right, though: concrete, grey, and anonymous.

Lighting was used effectively and clearly defined the transitions from past to present, reality to fantasy. The musical aspects were well done and were complemented by good performances from most of the actors. The style fit the subject and the characters: not pushy or brassy, and slightly stoic.

All in all, the production was a very good one. McCall managed to capture the playwright's style, and utilize it effectively. Set in the present, it also managed to take a fifteen-year-old play and give it a certain timelessness, considering the subject matter. The overall effect was not so much one of critical comment, but more simply a portrayal of a tragic situation.

Review of *Hold Fast*

by Irma McDonough

Hold Fast is a landmark in Canadian writing for young people. It reaches other, profounder places than most realistic writing meant for them. And it discovers Newfoundland as the source-spring of a major new talent.

In 1974 the author compiled *Dorylands*, a selection of Newfoundland writings and art, in which he shared Newfoundland's cultural past with us. Here he gives us his own work – a stunningly perceptive novel of family life in the outport and the city in his native province, and of one young person at the centre of it.

Michael at 14 loses his parents in a car accident, and suddenly his world becomes an alien place. He has to cope with a double loss: first his parents' death, then leaving his ourport home, for he goes to live in a city hundreds of miles away with his unsympathetic uncle's family.

In the space of a fortnight Michael has to begin testing the strengths of his developing maturity. What has he learned about how to conduct his life, about what to expect of life, during his short span?

His reactions to the death of his parents are typical of those bereaved of loved ones. But he begins immediately to take on the responsibility for his own life and for his young brother's. He agrees that only his brother should live with his loving aunt and favoured grandfather to relieve their economic burdens. He knows that his uncle was held aloof by his father; even so Michael goes to live with this alienated family where he finds a despot at its head. His uncle's word is law and Michael comes under it now that he had joined them.

Michael is thrust into untenable circumstances, yet his free spirit prevails because he relies on the moral touchstones of his past. His ability to think through a problem creatively helps him to logical solutions and we get to know a young man of uncommon integrity.

Major creates a sympathetic, admirable character in Michael. His empathy for young people allows for genuine appreciation of Michael's intelligence and maturity that in turn prepares him to encompass solutions that Michael can see are possible – and we get to know an author of uncommon integrity.

The first person narrative is enhanced by the delightful Newfoundland dialect that hastens a feeling of intimacy and involvement in the reader. Michael has let us into his life. Soon we accept him as he is; then we become his admirers. When he cries for his parents, when he teaches his cousin to stand up against his tyrant-father, when he reminisces with his grandfather, when he first feels the stirrings of love for a girl, he is ever a person we care about.

Hold Fast stands with other indigenous novels of stature that have pictured Newfoundland for young readers: *The Adventures of Billy Topsail* by Norman Duncan, Erle Spencer's *Yo-Ho-Ho! a story of modern piracy and smuggling*, *Dangerous Cover* by John Hayes and *The Black Joke* by Farley Mowat. And *Hold Fast* holds its own among them beautifully.

Analysis   Prehistoric Drama: an Honest Bequest

1. This review, "Prehistoric Drama," was contained within a larger article about *Quest for Fire*; the ellipses show where parts have been removed. Does what remains read smoothly?

2. Analyze the method of organization of this review. What feature tells you that it was written for a newspaper? Point out examples of parallelism in the first three paragraphs. What is the effect of repeating "Quest" in the first paragraph? Do you realize that the last three sentences of the first paragraph are sentence fragments? Do they communicate effectively?

3. Does the review tell you what you need to know about the film? Is there too much information?

4. Has Andrews made clear what he thinks?

5. What statements does he make that would cause you to see, or not see, *Quest for Fire?*

6. Though too short to qualify as a model for this assignment, the review below, from *Chatelaine*, has been included so that you can see how reviewers of the same work can strongly disagree. The work of art does not change; only the reviews differ. Both reviews of *Quest for Fire*, though, are equally valid.

Life 80,000 Years Ago — Embarrassing, Sentimental

This Franco-Canadian trip to earth 80,000 years ago has been directed by Jean-Jacques Annaud with undeterred solemnity. The film documents nothing less, nothing more than the tribes' discovery of how to make fire ... yes, by rubbing two sticks together. Between the fire and the sticks, our heroes, the Ulams, have violent encounters with various unappetizing tribes.

The trouble is that the movie is neither truly serious enough nor wildly fantastical enough to be either authoritative or fun. It is instead sentimental; the primitives are invested with feelings they surely could not have had.

The ending is embarrassing: our hero Everett McGill caressing the rounded belly of Rae Dawn Chong, striped like a zebra, under a moon. The only thing missing is a ukulele and cracked baritone to sing "By the Light of the Silvery Moon."

GINA MALLET, April, 82

Rita: Still in Ecstasy

1. This student review is written in a journalistic style. Can you find three or four examples of this style?

2. The reviewer has only hinted at the details of the plot. Can you piece it together or would you have preferred her to have told you briefly what happens to Rita Joe?

3. When do you find out what she thinks of the production? Does she make her opinions clear? Are there any parts of the production you feel should have been mentioned?

4. If you were to reorder the paragraphs of this review, which one would you begin with?

Review of *Hold Fast*

1. The reviewer of *Hold Fast* has aimed her review at a particular audience. What can you tell about the intended readers of *Hold Fast* from the review?

2. In writing a book review, the reviewer usually deals with several literary elements: character, setting, plot and theme. Which element does this reviewer stress?

3. In what ways does this book review differ from the film and play reviews?

Assignment **10** Literary Essay

Introduction

When you write a literary essay about a novel, play, short story, or poem, you should discuss your interpretation of some aspects of the work. To do this, you will need to go beyond the plot; that is, explain some deeper meaning of the work. A reader of your literary essay should acquire a better appreciation and understanding of the piece of literature by reading your explanation of one or more of its significant features. This assignment suggests a number of specific approaches to the interpretation. Retelling the story, however, is one approach for which you will receive no credit. Details of plot should only be used to support particular claims.

In your essay you should resist mentioning what you think of the work; expressing your opinion is *not* the main purpose of a literary essay. If you wish to criticize the effectiveness of a work, write a review; in a literary essay, you interpret what it, or a part of it, means.

Assignment

Write an essay explaining your interpretation of one of the short stories at the end of this assignment.

The Reading Process

Before you start to write a literary essay, you must analyze the piece of literature closely so that you can interpret it. The following suggestions may help you to develop a close-reading process.

1. Think about a few of your first meetings with friends and acquaintances. Were any of them like Howard Town's when he met Jacqueline Valentine, a famous artists' model of the forties?

> She was Venus with arms; she was Helen of the modelling stand. ... She changed me, led me to opera, candlelight, science fiction, food with garlic (which I now hate) and the boggy edges of whatever maturity I have acquired.
>
> Reading a fine piece of literature can be like meeting a new friend – it can change your life. When you read, open yourself to the possibility of experiencing something new or of being reminded of something you had forgotten.

Good writers can engage your emotions as well as your mind, so allow yourself to feel sad, happy, angry, contented, afraid, or whatever emotion the work awakens in you.

The first time you read a piece of literature, do so without stopping. Do not analyze it; just let it sweep you along. When you have finished, sit for a while and think about the piece as a whole and what it means to you. Ask yourself what you have learned, or what you have experienced in a new way. For example, you may have gained a deeper understanding of some aspect of the human condition: aging, the fickleness of fate, honesty, man's inhumanity to man, death, trust, and so on.

2. Re-read the piece, this time going beyond the plot. Good literature can often be interpreted on several different levels. For example, "The Hockey Sweater," at the end of this assignment, can be enjoyed as an amusing recollection of a childhood experience. On a deeper level, though, it can be interpreted as a parable about the emergence of French-Canadian identity.

3. We all have a tendency to put something of ourselves into what we read; a personal response makes interpretation possible. But you must be careful not to put into a work something that the author has not written or intended. Do not let your feelings get in the way of *textual evidence*. Read what the author has written and try to deduce what he or she is implying. Critically examining the following literary elements should give you an indication of what the author is trying to say.

Tone

Very early in reading a piece of literature, you should determine the author's tone. Is he or she serious or ironic? (Should you take the words at face value or should you take their opposite meaning?)

Conflict

In nearly every story, there is at least one specific conflict. What specific conflict or conflicts do the hero or heroine of the piece have with other individuals, society, the environment, or himself or herself?

Often, the experiences and conflicts of a particular character represent those of a larger group. These general conflicts are referred to as *archetypal* conflicts. Stories that have lasted through the ages often examine archetypal conflicts; hence, readers can always identify with the characters. Some examples of archetypal conflicts are the battle of the sexes, the generation gap, and the "lovers' steeplechase" (boy meets girl, boy loses girl, boy gets girl).

Character and Character Development

You can arrive at an understanding of the characters in a work through the author's description, or through analyzing their speech, actions, and the reactions of other characters to them.

Just as there may be archetypal conflicts in a story, there may be archetypal characters. To understand the concept of an archetypal character, think about yourself for a moment. Although you may think there has never been anyone quite like you, you may be similar to one or more of these archetypal characters: struggling student, whiz kid, frustrated lover, Cinderella, frustrated artist, separated lover, martyr, scapegoat, wise old man, apprentice, nature boy, the innocent, the stranger, the devil, the victim, Mother Earth, the magician, the healer, the leader, the follower, the saviour, and on and on.

Be honest. Are you an archetypal character? (You do not have to be the same age or sex as the original to be an archetypal character. Piggy in *Lord of the Flies* is an archetypal wise old man; Oliver in *Oliver Twist* is an archetypal Cinderella.)

As a result of their experiences in the story, the characters often develop or change; they become wiser, more cynical, more sensitive, or change in some other way. This change often results from a particular insight or realization. By observing and identifying with the characters in a story, you may learn something about yourself and the human condition.

Situation

The situation of a story has two elements: the external and the internal elements that affect the main character. The external factors include the other characters and the setting (time, place, and atmosphere in which the story occurs). The internal factors include the ways in which the main character deals with conflict and the archetypal experience he or she is undergoing: coming of age, losing innocence, escaping from some place or someone, being reborn, becoming disillusioned, taking a journey, losing paradise, questing, sacrificing, and so on.

Narrator and Point of View

Before you meet any of the characters in a story, you meet the narrator. The narrator may be the author, one of the characters, or an unidentified person. When interpreting a literary work, you should ask, "Who is the narrator? Is he or she to be trusted?" The narrator may be biased for or against particular characters. For example, the narrator may be in love with the heroine, or may be the hero's enemy.

The story can be told in the first person, by the author or by one of the characters, and therefore from a *limited* point of view; that is, the narrator can only tell the story as he or she sees or hears it. It can also be told in the third person, by an unidentified narrator, from an *omniscient* point of view, in which the narrator knows what *all* the characters are doing, saying, and thinking, and is also aware of external circumstances that will influence the plot. Some modern novels are told from both the first- and third-person points of view; this shifting point of view requires a careful reading to determine who the narrator is.

Symbol

A symbol is something that stands for or represents something else. A symbol often has a cluster of associations, and these associations can provide a clue to the story's more general meaning. The title of a work is often symbolic; its significance becomes clear as you read the work.

Theme

In concluding your reading process, you should be aware that the author manipulates all of the preceding elements in developing his or her *theme*, or general idea. The theme is seldom stated explicitly; you must discover it from the experiences of the characters in the story. You should express the theme of a work as a generalization about life; for example, "Our attempts to control our own lives are futile," or "Civilization corrupts."

Finally, as you prepare to write your literary essay, imagine that you are putting a jigsaw puzzle together: all the pieces are there, ready to be interlocked. Your literary essay should resemble a complete picture in which all the pieces fit together.

Prewriting Suggestions

Most of the time, when you write a literary essay, you are given a specific piece of literature and a specific topic; other times you may have a great deal of choice and are able to brainstorm topics with your peers.

1. If the choice of topic is up to you, you may want to examine the influence of one of the literary elements on the worth of the piece literature; for example, the importance of the setting, the development of the main character, the meaning of a symbol, or your interpretation of the theme.

2. If you wish, choose one of the topics following the short stories at the end of this assignment, and use it as the basis of your essay.

3. If you still feel you have nothing to say after you have read the selection, thought about it, and discussed it with others, you might like to refer to a few *secondary sources* and read what others have said about your short story. Following is a list of suggested resources; your library should have many others.

General

Atwood, M. *Survival – A Thematic Guide to Canadian Literature*
Pacey, D. *Essays in Canadian Criticism*
Siemon, F. *Science Fiction Story Index: 1950–1968*
Watters & Bell. *On Canadian Literature: 1806–1960*

Short Stories

Thurston, et al. *Short Story Criticism: 1800–1958*
Walker, W. *Twentieth Century Short Story Explication 1900–1966*

Poetry

Brown, E. K. *On Canadian Poetry*
Cline & Baker. *An Index to Criticisms of British & American Poetry*
Kuntz, J. *Poetry Explication Since 1925*
Smith, A. J. M., ed. *Masks of Poetry*

Novels

Abernethy, et al. *English Novel Explication to 1975*
Gerstenberger & Hendrick. *The American Novel, 1789–1959*
Palmer & Dyson. *English Novel Explication: Criticisms to 1972*
Smith, A. J. M., ed. *Masks of Fiction*
Woodcock, G. *The Canadian Novel in the Twentieth Century*

Plays

Coleman & Tyler. *Drama Criticism Since 1940*
New, W. H., ed. *Dramatists in Canada: Selected Essays*
Palmer & Dyson. *American Drama Criticism 1890–1965*

If you quote directly from a secondary source, use quotation marks and footnotes (Assignment 11). You may also want to include a bibliography of the secondary sources you have consulted (Activity 21).

4. Once you have chosen your short story and found a suitable topic, you should consider your audience and purpose. The audience for a literary essay is always someone who has read the piece of literature and wants to find out how someone else has interpreted it. Produce a list of your writing variables before you begin to draft your essay. (If the topic and audience for your essay have been assigned, you may not be able to follow this suggestion.)

> **Topic:** the ironic elements in *God is not a Fish Inspector*
> **Audience:** my activity partner
> **Purpose:** to point out ironic elements in the story
> **Format:** literary essay

> **Topic:** *The Old Man and the Sea*, a symbol of revolution
> **Audience:** newspaper readers
> **Purpose:** to point out the parallel between the main character and the oppressed people of Cuba
> **Format:** literary essay

Drafting Suggestions

The most difficult part of writing a literary essay is choosing a topic. For this reason, much of the work is done during prewriting. Once you have established your main claim and your writing variables, you can begin to draft your essay in the same way as you would any persuasive essay. See the suggestions as outlined in Assignment 6. However, the following are a few specific things that you should keep in mind:

1. State your claim clearly and early, as well as the title and the author of the work you are discussing.

2. Be selective in using quotations, plot summaries, and character descriptions; use only those that support your argument. Ask yourself, "Does this evidence prove what I want it to prove?" If not, you may want to look for stronger evidence, or revise your main claim.

3. Never retell the plot. If you assume that your reader knows the story and is reading your essay to reach some understanding of the selection that had not occurred to him/her, you will produce a much tighter essay. Some literature teachers, though, may ask for a brief summary of the selection.

4. Generally, your essay should be written in the third person rather than the first and usually in the present tense rather than the past. Third person sounds authoritative; present tense keeps the piece of literature alive. For example, the first person and past tense of "In my opinion, Romeo and Juliet died needlessly" are not as effective as the third person and present tense of "Romeo and Juliet die needlessly." Some people prefer to read literary essays that have been written in the past tense in order to keep the tense of the essay the same as that of the piece of literature. If your audience is your literature teacher, you should find out what he/she says about person and tense. The key is to be consistent.

Revising Suggestions

To help your own revision process when you have completed your final draft, judge your literary essay according to the standards in Appendix B. Furthermore, to help peer revision, use one of the feedback methods from Appendix B. Make sure that the students who are going to edit your literary essay have read the piece of literature. Consider the following specific items to help revise your literary essay:

1. Are the main claim, title, and author of the piece clearly stated?

2. Is the main claim backed up by textual evidence? Will it thoroughly convince the intended reader?

3. Are the quotations introduced smoothly into the prose of the essay? Are the techniques of blending prose and quoted material varied? (See Assignment 11 for examples.)

4. Is any of the textual evidence unnecessary or irrelevant?

5. Will the reader have a new or deeper understanding of the story after reading the essay?

Polishing Suggestions

Just before you give your literary essay to your intended reader, polish it according to the suggestions in Appendix C.

Selection

The Hockey Sweater

by Roch Carrier

The winters of my childhood were long, long seasons. We lived in three places –
the school, the church and the skating-rink – but our real life was on the
skating-rink. Real battles were won on the skating-rink. Real strength appeared
on the skating-rink. The real leaders showed themselves on the skating-rink.
School was a sort of punishment. Parents always want to punish children and
school is their most natural way of punishing us. However, school was also a
quiet place where we could prepare for the next hockey game, lay out our
next strategies. As for church, we found there the tranquillity of God: there
we forgot school and dreamed about the next hockey game. Through our
daydreams it might happen that we would recite a prayer: we would ask God
to help us play as well as Maurice Richard.

We all wore the same uniform as he, the red, white and blue uniform of
the Montreal Canadiens, the best hockey team in the world; we all combed
our hair in the same style as Maurice Richard, and to keep it in place we used
a sort of glue – a great deal of glue. We laced our skates like Maurice Richard;
we taped our sticks like Maurice Richard. We cut all his pictures out of the
papers. Truly, we knew everything about him.

On the ice, when the referee blew his whistle, the two teams would rush
at the puck; we were five Maurice Richards taking it away from five other
Maurice Richards; we were ten players, all of us wearing with the same blazing
enthusiasm the uniform of the Montreal Canadiens. On our backs, we all
wore the famous number 9.

One day, my Montreal Canadiens' sweater had become too small; then it
got torn and had holes in it. My mother said, "If you wear that old sweater
people are going to think we're poor!" Then she did what she did whenever
we needed new clothes. She started to leaf through the catalogue the Eaton
company sent us in the mail every year. My mother was proud. She didn't
want to buy our clothes at the general store; the only things that were good
enough for us were the latest styles from Eaton's catalogue. My mother didn't
like the order forms included with the catalogue; they were written in English
and she didn't understand a word of it. To order my hockey sweater, she did
as she usually did; she took out her writing paper and wrote in her gentle
schoolteacher's hand; "Cher Monsieur Eaton. Would you be kind enough to
send me a Canadiens' sweater for my son who is ten years old and a little too
tall for his age and Docteur Robitaille thinks he's a little too thin? I'm sending
you three dollars and please send me what's left if there's anything left. I
hope your wrapping will be better than last time!"

Monsieur Eaton was quick to answer my mother's letter. Two weeks later
we received the sweater. That day I had one of the greatest disappointments
of my life! I would even say that on that day I experienced a very great

sorrow. Instead of the red, white and blue Montreal Canadiens' sweater, Monsieur Eaton had sent us a blue and white sweater with a maple leaf on the front – the sweater of the Toronto Maple Leafs. I'd always worn the red, white and blue Montreal Canadiens' sweater; all my friends wore the red, white and blue sweater; never had anyone in my village ever worn the Toronto sweater, never had we even seen a Toronto Maple Leafs' sweater. Besides, the Toronto team was regularly trounced by the triumphant Canadiens. With tears in my eyes, I found the strength to say, "I'll never wear that uniform."

"My boy, first you're going to try it on! If you make up your mind about things before you try, my boy, you won't go very far in this life."

My mother had pulled the blue and white Toronto Maple Leafs' sweater over my shoulders and already my arms were inside the sleeves. She pulled the sweater down and carefully smoothed all the creases in the abominable maple leaf on which, right in the middle of my chest, were written the words "Toronto Maple Leafs." I wept.

"I'll never wear it."

"Why not? This sweater fits you ... like a glove."

"Maurice Richard would never put it on his back."

"You aren't Maurice Richard. Anyway, it isn't what's on your back that counts, it's what you've got inside your head."

"You'll never put it in my head to wear a Toronto Maple Leafs' sweater."

My mother sighed in despair and explained to me, "If you don't keep this sweater which fits you perfectly I'll have to write to Monsieur Eaton and explain that you don't want to wear the Toronto sweater. Monsieur Eaton's an *Anglais;* he'll be insulted because he likes the Maple Leafs. And if he's insulted do you think he'll be in a hurry to answer us? Spring will be here and you won't have played a single game, just because you didn't want to wear that perfectly nice blue sweater."

So I was obliged to wear the Maple Leafs' sweater. When I arrived on the rink, all the Maurice Richards in red, white and blue came up, one by one, to take a look. When the referee blew his whistle I went to take my usual position. The captain came and warned me I'd be better to stay on the forward line. A few minutes later the second line was called; I jumped onto the ice. The Maple Leafs' sweater weighed on my shoulders like a mountain. The captain came and told me to wait; he'd need me later, on defense. By the third period I still hadn't played; one of the defensemen was hit in the nose with a stick and it was bleeding. I jumped on the ice; my moment had come! The referee blew his whistle; he gave me a penalty. He claimed I'd jumped on the ice when there were already five players. That was too much! It was unfair! It was persecution! It was because of my blue sweater! I struck my stick against the ice so hard it broke. Relieved, I bent down to pick up the debris. As I straightened up I saw the young vicar, on skates, before me.

"My child," he said, "just because you're wearing a new Toronto Maple

Leafs' sweater unlike the others, it doesn't mean you're going to make the laws around here. A proper young man doesn't lose his temper. Now take off your skates and go to the church and ask God to forgive you."

Wearing my Maple Leafs' sweater I went to the church, where I prayed to God; I asked him to send, as quickly as possible, moths that would eat up my Toronto Maple Leafs' sweater.

Suggested Topics

1. The conflict between the narrator and his mother may represent the opposing attitudes of the older and younger generations in Quebec. Discuss the differences in the attitudes towards English Canada of these two characters. Support your ideas by presenting direct quotations.

2. Roch Carrier makes use of symbol in developing his theme in "The Hockey Sweater." What is your interpretation of the following symbols: the skating rink, Monsieur Eaton, the hockey sweater? Your opinions must be supported by direct textual proof.

3. The National Film Board has made a film of "The Hockey Sweater." Discuss the interpretation of the film by comparing it to your interpretation of the story. Are there any important elements in the story that are not in the film? Refer to specific incidents in the story.

Models   Inferiority

Topic: The letter the boy's mother writes to the Eaton Company shows that she feels inferior. Discuss in a single paragraph of about 200 words.

(The italics in this mini-literary essay show how the main claim is reinforced by using key words.)

The letter written by the boy's mother in Roch Carrier's "The Hockey Sweater" reveals her feelings of *inferiority*. The fact that she must write a letter "in her gentle schoolteacher's hand," rather than being able to use the English order forms provided with the Eaton's catalogue, shows her *inability* to communicate. The words she uses ("would you be kind enough," and "please send me what's left if there is anything left") and even the way she criticizes the wrapping of a previous package demonstrate *her desire to avoid* angering the superior "Monsieur Eaton." When the wrong sweater arrives, she *is too timid* to return it, saying "Monsieur Eaton ... [will] be insulted because he likes the Maple Leafs. And if he's insulted do you think he'll be in a hurry to answer us?" She even *lacks the self-confidence* to attempt to correct the mistake Eaton's made; rather than insulting a member of the English-Canadian Establishment, she *will allow her son to be persecuted.*

Vive Les Canadiens!

Topic: On one level, "The Hockey Sweater" is an amusing story about a childhood experience, but on another level it is a parable about the emergence of French-Canadian separatism. Discuss.

Roch Carrier's "The Hockey Sweater" can be read not only as a quaint story about a childhood experience, but also as a parable about the emergence of French-Canadian separatism.

In the 1950s the Montreal Canadiens, "the best hockey team in the world," perennial Stanley Cup champions and masters of hockey skills, were the idols of French Canadians of all ages. At that time the Québécois had little economic or political power; English Canadians ran the businesses and controlled the flow of jobs and money, and Maurice Duplessis' dictatorship allowed the people no say in their government. The only arena where French Canadians could demonstrate their superiority and live their "real life" was the hockey rink.

The young boy and his friends, "all of us wearing with the same blazing enthusiasm the uniform of the Montreal Canadiens," identify with the only heroes their society has. The Canadiens' hockey sweater with "the famous number 9" represents their search for a way to separate their cultural identity from that of "Monsieur Eaton" and the Toronto Maple Leafs.

This same desire to save the culture of Quebec from assimilation in the North American melting pot motivated both the Quiet Revolution of the early 1960s and the separatist movement of today. Charles de Gaulle's cry of "Vive le Québec libre!" stirred the generation that had grown up cheering Maurice Richard. Their struggle culminated in the election of René Lévesque and the Parti Québécois in 1976.

Pride in one's identity is the central theme of "The Hockey Sweater." Maurice Richard and René Lévesque, each struggling in his own way against the Toronto Maple Leafs and "Monsieur Eaton," symbolize the triumph of that pride.

1. How do you know that the writer has a great deal of knowledge about the Quebec situation?
2. Does she back up the points she makes with textual evidence? Do you think she has read anything into the story that is not there?
3. Are there any points you think she has overlooked?

Araby

by James Joyce

North Richmond Street, being blind, was a quiet street except at the hour when the Christian Brothers School set the boys free. An uninhabited house of two storeys stood at the blind end, detached from its neighbours in a square ground. The other houses of the street, conscious of decent lives within them, gazed at one another with brown imperturbable faces.

The former tenant of our house, a priest, had died in the back drawing-room. Air, musty from having been long enclosed, hung in all the rooms, and the waste room behind the kitchen was littered with old useless papers. Among these I found a few paper-covered books, the pages of which were curled and damp: *The Abbott*, by Walter Scott, *The Devout Communicant* and *The Memoirs of Vidocq*. I liked the last best because its leaves were yellow. The wild garden behind the house contained a central apple-tree and a few straggling bushes under one of which I found the late tenant's rusty bicycle-pump. He had been a very charitable priest; in his will he had left all his money to institutions and the furniture of his house to his sister.

When the short days of winter came dusk fell before we had well eaten our dinners. When we met in the street the houses had grown sombre. The space of sky above us was the colour of ever-changing violet and towards it the lamps of the street lifted their feeble lanterns. The cold air stung us and we played till our bodies glowed. Our shouts echoed in the silent street. The career of our play brought us through the dark muddy lanes behind the houses where we ran the gauntlet of the rough tribes from the cottages, to the back doors of the dark dripping gardens where odours arose from the ashpits, to the dark odorous stables where a coachman smoothed and combed the horse or shook music from the buckled harness. When we returned to the street light from the kitchen windows had filled the areas. If my uncle was seen turning the corner we hid in the shadow until we had seen him safely housed. Or if Mangan's sister came out on the doorstep to call her brother in to his tea we watched her from our shadow peer up and down the street. We waited to see whether she would remain or go in and, if she remained, we left our shadow and walked up to Mangan's steps resignedly. She was waiting for us, her figure defined by the light from the half-opened door. Her brother always teased her before he obeyed and I stood by the railings looking at her. Her dress swung as she moved her body and the soft rope of her hair tossed from side to side.

Every morning I lay on the floor in the front parlour watching her door. The blind was pulled down to within an inch of the sash so that I could not be seen. When she came out on the doorstep my heart leaped. I ran to the hall, seized my books and followed her. I kept her brown figure always in my eye and, when we came near the point at which our ways diverged, I quickened my pace and passed her. This happened morning after morning. I had never spoken to her, except for a few casual words, and yet her name was like a summons to all my foolish blood.

Her image accompanied me even in places the most hostile to romance. On Saturday evenings when my aunt went marketing I had to go to carry some of the parcels. We walked through the flaring streets, jostled by drunken men and bargaining women, amid the curses of labourers, the shrill litanies of shop-boys who stood on guard by the barrels of pigs' cheeks, the nasal chanting of street-singers, who sang a *come-all-you* about O'Donovan Ross, or a ballad about the troubles in our native land. These noises converged in a single sensation of life for me: I imagined that I bore my chalice safely through a throng of foes. Her name sprang to my lips at moments in strange prayers and praises which I myself did not understand. My eyes were often full of tears (I could not tell why) and at times a flood from my heart seemed to pour itself out into my bosom. I thought little of the future.I did not know whether I would ever speak to her or not or, if I spoke to her, how I could tell her of my confused adoration. But my body was like a harp and her words and gestures were like fingers running upon the wires.

One evening I went into the back drawing-room in which the priest had died. It was a dark rainy evening and there was no sound in the house. Through one of the broken panes I heard the rain impinge upon the earth, the fine incessant needles of water playing in the sodden beds. Some distant lamp or lighted window gleamed below me. I was thankful that I could see so little. All my senses seemed to desire to veil themselves and, feeling that I was about to slip from them, I pressed the palms of my hands together until they trembled, murmuring: "*O love! O love!*" many times.

At last she spoke to me. When she addressed the first words to me I was so confused that I did not know what to answer. She asked me was I going to *Araby*. I forgot whether I answered yes or no. It would be a splendid bazaar, she said she would love to go.

"And why can't you?" I asked.

While she spoke she turned a silver bracelet round and round her wrist. She could not go, she said, because there would be a retreat that week in her convent. Her brother and two other boys were fighting for their caps and I was alone at the railings. She held one of the spikes, bowing her head towards me. The light from the lamp opposite our door caught the white curve of her neck, lit up her hair that rested there and, falling, lit up the hand upon the railing. It fell over one side of her dress and caught the white border of a petticoat, just visible as she stood at ease.

"It's well for you," she said.

"If I go," I said, "I will bring you something."

What innumerable follies laid waste my waking and sleeping thoughts after that evening! I wished to annihilate the tedious intervening days. I chafed against the work of school. At night in my bedroom and by day in the classroom her image came between me and the page I strove to read. The syllables of the word *Araby* were called to me through the silence in which my soul luxuriated and cast an Eastern enchantment over me. I asked for leave to go to the bazaar on Saturday night. My aunt was surprised and hoped it was not some Freemason affair. I answered few questions in class. I watched my master's face pass from amiability to sternness; he hoped I was not beginning to idle. I could not call my wandering thoughts together. I had hardly any patience with the serious work of life which, now that it stood between me and my desire, seemed to me child's play, ugly monotonous child's play.

On Saturday morning I reminded my uncle that I wished to go to the bazaar in the evening. He was fussing at the hallstand, looking for the hatbrush, and answered me curtly:

"Yes, boy, I know."

As he was in the hall I could not go into the front parlour and lie at the window. I left the house in bad humour and walked slowly towards the school. The air was pitilessly raw and already my heart misgave me.

When I came home to dinner my uncle had not yet been home. Still it was early. I sat staring at the clock for some time and, when its ticking began to irritate me, I left the room. I mounted the staircase and gained the upper part of the house. The high cold empty gloomy rooms liberated me and I went from room to room singing. From the front window I saw my companions playing below in the street. Their cries reached me weakened and indistinct and, leaning my forehead against the cool glass, I looked over at the dark house where she lived. I may have stood there for an hour, seeing nothing but the brown-clad figure cast by my imagination, touched discreetly by the lamplight at the curved neck, at the hand upon the railings and at the border below the dress.

When I came downstairs again I found Mrs. Mercer sitting at the fire. She was an old garrulous woman, a pawnbroker's widow, who collected used stamps for some pious purpose. I had to endure the gossip of the tea-table. The meal was prolonged beyond an hour and still my uncle did not come. Mrs. Mercer stood up to go: she was sorry she couldn't wait any longer, but it was after eight o'clock and she did not like to be out late, as the night air was bad for her. When she had gone I began to walk up and down the room, clenching my fists. My aunt said:

"I'm afraid you may put off your bazaar for this night of Our Lord."

At nine o'clock I heard my uncle's latchkey in the halldoor. I heard him talking to himself and heard the hallstand rocking when it had received the weight of his overcoat. I could interpret these signs. When he was midway through his dinner I asked him to give me the money to go to the bazaar. He had forgotten.

"The people are in bed and after their first sleep now," he said.

I did not smile. My aunt said to him energetically:

"Can't you give him the money and let him go? You've kept him late enough as it is."

My uncle said he was very sorry he had forgotten. He said he believed in the old saying: "All work and no play makes Jack a dull boy." He asked me where I was going and, when I had told him a second time he asked me did I know *The Arab's Farewell to his Steed*. When I left the kitchen he was about to recite the opening lines of the piece to my aunt.

I held a coin tightly in my hand as I strode down Buckingham Street towards the station. The sight of the streets thronged with buyers and glaring with gas recalled to me the purpose of my journey. I took my seat in a third-class carriage of a deserted train. After an intolerable delay the train moved out of the station slowly. It crept onward among ruinous houses and over the twinkling river. At Westland Row Station a crowd of people pressed to the carriage doors; but the porters moved them back, saying that it was a special train for the bazaar. I remained alone in the bare carriage. In a few minutes the train drew up beside an improvised wooden platform. I passed out on the road and saw by the lighted dial of a clock that it was ten minutes to ten. In front of me was a large building which displayed the magical name.

I could not find any sixpenny entrance and, fearing that the bazaar would be closed, I passed in quickly through a turnstile, handing a shilling to a weary-looking man. I found myself in a big hall girdled at half its height by a gallery. Nearly all the stalls were closed and the greater part of the hall was in darkness. I recognised a silence like that which pervades a church after a service. I walked into the centre of the bazaar timidly. A few people were gathered about the stalls which were still open. Before a curtain, over which the words *Café Chantant* were written in coloured lamps, two men were counting money on a salver. I listened to the fall of the coins.

Remembering with difficulty why I had come I went over to one of the stalls and examined porcelain vases and flowered tea-sets. At the door of the stall a young lady was talking and laughing with two young gentlemen. I remarked their English accents and listened vaguely to their conversation.

"O, I never said such a thing!"

"O, but you did!"

"O, but I didn't!"

"Didn't she say that?"

"Yes. I heard her."

"O, there's a ... fib!"

Observing me the young lady came over and asked me did I wish to buy anything. The tone of her voice was not encouraging; she seemed to have spoken to me out of a sense of duty. I looked humbly at the great jars that stood like eastern guards at either side of the dark entrance to the stall and murmured:

"No, thank you."

The young lady changed the position of one of the vases and went back to the two young men. They began to talk of the same subject. Once or twice the young lady glanced at me over her shoulder.

I lingered before her stall, though I knew my stay was useless, to make my interest in her wares seem the more real. Then I turned away slowly and walked down the middle of the bazaar. I allowed the two pennies to fall against the sixpence in my pocket. I heard a voice call from one end of the gallery that the light was out. The upper part of the hall was now completely dark.

Gazing up into the darkness I saw myself as a creature driven and derided by vanity; and my eyes burned with anguish and anger.

Suggested Topics

1. "Joyce places the boy in a situation that limits his choices." Discuss this statement, emphasizing the significance of the boy's age, the other characters, and the setting (time and place). They all seem to be against him. Support your claims with direct textual evidence.

2. The boy imagines himself a kind of Sir Galahad, searching for the Holy Grail. Joyce sustains the knight-errant imagery by presenting him in a number of situations reminiscent of the days of King Arthur and the Round Table. Discuss by presenting background information on Sir Galahad and the Holy Grail and quotations from "Araby" to explain the imagery Joyce has used.

3. Discuss the ways in which each of the characters (even the dead priest) shows the conflict between reality and illusion. Present direct textual proof in your essay.

Elements of Realization in "Araby"

Model   *Topic: In "Araby," James Joyce is essentially concerned with the world of illusion and reality, and with a young boy's journey from innocence to maturity. Discuss.*

James Joyce's story "Araby" was published in a collection of short stories, *Dubliners*, on June 15, 1914. In "Araby," the author is essentially concerned with the world of illusion and reality, and with a young boy's voyage from innocence to the brink of maturity. In the final scene, we see that the references to money, the boy's failure to be reassured by darkness, the subtle reminder of the real world of politics, and what he discovers from the girl at the bazaar are all vital elements in the boy's final realization that he has been deluding himself.

Upon his arrival at the bazaar, the boy is immediately confronted with one aspect of reality by the fact that he must pay an admission. Normally, a person of his age would be let in at half-price, but he says, "I could not find any sixpenny entrance, and ... I passed in quickly through a turnstile handing a shilling to a weary-looking man." To the boy, money has no place in his world of illusion, but he pays twice as much as he should have, not caring to think about the economics of his actions. Later, when he encounters "two men counting coins on a salver," he is made aware that to nourish his imaginary needs, he must depend on money, a very real commodity. This brings him a step closer to maturity.

After gaining entry, the boy finds another disturbing element to deal with in his losing battle between fact and fantasy. He sees that "the greater part of the hall was in darkness," and he begins to question his preference of dark to light. Previously, he had depended on the dark to reinforce his world of illusion: now he finds himself looking into the dark, but it is impossible for him not to accept the real world around him, in all its decay and drabness. He admits to walking "into the centre of the bazaar timidly," as if he realizes that he is on the verge of a self-realization that has been eluding him.

Beyond this sense of discovery, the boy must also contend with the harsh, concrete reality of politics.

He notices two men talking to a young lady, overhears "their English accents," and is reminded that the country of his birth, the very soil from which his illusions spring, is beset by England. This theme, although only mentioned in the story once, is important because, although the boy is young and not politically inclined, he is sensitive enough to realize the implications. To find this element at "Araby" adds another weight to the balance of his realization.

Most importantly, however, the girl at the bazaar is crucial to his final realization. He encounters her flirting with "two young gentlemen," and the boy, at this point desperately attempting to find things to fuel his imagination, transfers to this girl the qualities that he sees in Mangan's sister. From the vapid interchange between the "young lady" and the two men, he realizes that Mangan's sister is capable of flirting too, and that if so, his chances of winning her love with a cheap trinket from a depressing bazaar are minimal. Perhaps, with a wisdom beyond his years, he is granted some insight into the real world of love and sees that to fall in love with a flirt can be very disconcerting to the novice. Especially when he hears her say, "O, there's a ... fib," he realizes that even though she is addressing a different issue, the remark can be interpreted as Mangan's sister's making a comment on his hopeless illusions. Again, when she asks him if he wants to buy anything, he faces the disheartening reality that her voice was not encouraging" and that she seemed to speak to him "out of a sense of duty." If, as I believe, he was seeing the girl at the bazaar as Mangan's sister in a last-ditch attempt at holding on to his fantasy, her attitude towards him must certainly demoralize him into accepting what can and cannot be.

Through these elements, it is clearly seen how the boy comes to his final realization. Having what is real thrust at him from so many directions undermines his illusions, and now he understands that in a world of such contradictory realities, to place fantasy over fact is indeed foolish. It is this admission to himself at the end of the story which leaves him despairing and alone.

Analysis

1. The writer uses the technique of rephrasing the question as his main claim; this is a widely used and acceptable technique when writing a literary essay.

2. He chooses four incidents from the story and elaborates on each of them in a separate paragraph. What incidents does he use? Why did he choose these? Are there others he could have used?

3. He comments on Mangan's sister indirectly, through his comparison of her with the girl at the bazaar. How does he prove that Joyce introduced the girl for this purpose? Are there other points about Joyce's attitude to women that he could have mentioned?

4. As the writer says, there is only one reference to politics. Was he wise to make a point of it?

Selection

God Is Not a Fish Inspector

by W. D. Valgardson

Although Emma made no noise as she descended, Fusi Bergman knew his daughter was watching him from the bottom of the stairs.

"God will punish you," she promised in a low, intense voice.

"Render unto Caesar what is Caesar's," he snapped. "God's not a fish inspector. He doesn't work for the government."

By the light of the front ring of the kitchen stove, he had been drinking a cup of coffee mixed half and half with whisky. Now, he shifted in his captain's chair so as to partly face the stairs. Though he was unable to make out more than the white blur of Emma's nightgown, after living with her for 48 years he knew exactly how she would look if he turned on the light.

She was tall and big boned with the square, pugnacious face of a bulldog. Every inch of her head would be crammed with metal curlers and her angular body hidden by a plain white cotton shift that hung from her broad shoulders like a tent. Whenever she was angry with him, she always stood rigid and white lipped, her hands clenched at her sides.

"You prevaricate," she warned. "You will not be able to prevaricate at the gates of Heaven."

He drained his cup, sighed, and pulled on his jacket. As he opened the door, Fusi said. "He made fish to catch. There is no place in the Bible where it says you can't catch fish when you are three score and ten."

"You'll be the ruin of us," she hissed as he closed the door on her.

This morning, as every morning, he had wakened at three. Years before, he had trained himself to get up at that time and now, in spite of his age, he never woke more than five minutes after the hour. He was proud of his early rising for he felt it showed he was not, like many of his contemporaries, relentlessly sliding into the endless blur of senility. Each morning, because he had become reconciled to the idea of dying, he felt, on the instant of his awakening, a spontaneous sense of amazement at being alive. The thought never lasted longer than the brief time between sleep and consciousness, but the good feeling lingered throughout the day.

When Fusi stepped outside, the air was cold and damp. The moon that hung low in the west was pale and fragile and very small. 50 feet from the house, the breakwater that ran along the rear of his property loomed like the purple spine of some great beast guarding the land from a lake which seemed, in the darkness, to go on forever.

Holding his breath to still the noise of his own breathing, Fusi listened for a cough or the scuff of gravel that would mean someone was close by, watching and waiting, but the only sound was the muted rubbing of his skiff against the piling to which it was moored. Half a mile away where the land was lower, rows of gas boats roped five abreast lined the docks. The short, stubby boats with their high cabins, the grey surface of the docks and the dark water were all tinged purple from the mercury lamps. At the harbour mouth, high on a thin spire, a red light burned like a distant star.

Behind him, he heard the door open and, for a moment, he was afraid Emma might begin to shout, or worse still, turn on the back-door light and alert his enemies, but she did neither. Above all things, Emma was afraid of scandal, and would do anything to avoid causing an unsavoury rumour to be attached to her own or her husband's name.

Her husband, John Smith, was as bland and inconsequential as his name. Moon faced with wide blue eyes and a small mouth above which sat a carefully trimmed moustache, he was a head shorter than Emma and a good 50 pounds lighter. Six years before, he had been transferred to the Eddyville branch of the Bank of Montreal. His transfer from Calgary to a small town in Manitoba was the bank's way of letting him know that there would be no more promotions. He would stay in Eddyville until he retired.

A year after he arrived, Emma had married him and instead of her moving out, he had moved in. For the last two years, under Emma's prodding, John had been taking a correspondence course in theology so that when he no longer worked at the bank he could be a full-time preacher.

On the evenings when he wasn't balancing the bank's books, he laboured over the multiple-choice questions in the Famous Preacher's course that he received each month from the One True and Only Word of God Church in Mobile, Alabama. Because of a freak in the atmosphere one night while she had been fiddling with the radio, Emma had heard a gospel hour advertising the course and, although neither she nor John had ever been south of Minneapolis and had never heard of the One True and Only Word of God Church before, she took it as a sign and immediately enrolled her husband in it. It cost $500.

John's notes urged him not to wait to answer His Call but to begin ministering to the needy at once for the Judgment Day was always imminent. In anticipation of the end of the world and his need for a congregation once he retired, he and Emma had become zealous missionaries, cramming their Volkswagen with a movie projector, a record-player, films, trays of slides, religious records for every occasion, posters and pamphlets, all bought or rented from the One True and Only Word of God Church. Since the townspeople were obstinately Lutheran, and since John did not want to give offence to any of his bank's customers, he and Emma hunted converts along the grey dirt roads that led past tumble-down farmhouses, the inhabitants of which were never likely to enter a bank.

Fusi did not turn to face his daughter but hurried away because he knew he had no more than an hour and a half until dawn. His legs were fine as he crossed the yard, but by the time he had mounted the steps that led over the breakwater, then climbed down fifteen feet to the shore, his left knee had begun to throb.

Holding his leg rigid to ease the pain, he waded out, loosened the ropes and heaved himself away from the shore. As soon as the boat was in deep water, he took his seat, and set both oars in the oar-locks he had carefully muffled with strips from an old shirt.

For a moment, he rested his hands on his knees, the oars rising like too-small wings from a cumbersome body, then he straightened his arms, dipped the oars cleanly into the water and in one smooth motion pulled his hands toward his chest. The first few strokes were even and graceful but then as a speck of pain like a grain of sand formed in his shoulder, the sweep of his left oar became shorter than his right. Each time he leaned against the oars, the pain grew until it was, in his mind, a bent shingle-nail twisted and turned in his shoulder socket.

With the exertion, a ball of gas formed in his stomach, making him uncomfortable. As quickly as a balloon being blown up, it expanded until his lungs and heart were cramped and he couldn't draw in a full breath. Although the air over the lake was cool, sweat ran from his hairline.

At his two-hundredth stroke, he shipped his left oar and pulled a coil of rope with a large hook from under the seat. After checking to see that it was securely tied through the gunwale, he dropped the rope overboard and once more began to row. Normally, he would have had a buoy made from a slender tamarack pole, a block of wood and some lead weights to mark his net, but he no longer had a fishing licence so his net had to be sunk below the surface where it could not be seen by the fish inspectors.

Five more strokes of the oars and the rope went taut. He lifted both oars into the skiff, then, standing in the bow, began to pull. The boat responded sluggishly but gradually it turned and the cork line that lay hidden under two feet of water broke the surface. He grasped the net, freed the hook and began to collect the mesh until the lead line appeared. For one he had been lucky and the hook had caught the net close to one end so there was no need to backtrack.

Hand over hand he pulled, being careful not to let the corks and leads bang against the bow, for on the open water sound carried clearly for miles. In the first two fathoms there was a freshly caught pickerel. As he pulled it toward him, it beat the water with its tail, making light, slapping sounds. His fingers were cramped, but Fusi managed to catch the fish around its soft middle and, with his other hand, work the mesh free of the gills.

It was then that the pain in his knee forced him to sit. Working from the seat was awkward and cost him precious time, but he had no choice, for the pain had begun to inch up the bone toward his crotch.

He wiped his forehead with his hand and cursed his infirmity. When he was twenty, he had thought nothing of rowing five miles from shore to lift five and six gangs of nets and then, nearly knee deep in fish, row home again. Now, he reflected bitterly, a quarter of a mile and one net were nearly beyond him. Externally, he had changed very little over the years. He was still tall and thin, his arms and legs corded with muscle. His belly was hard. His long face, with its pointed jaw, showed his age the most. That and his hands. His face was lined until it seemed there was nowhere the skin was smooth. His hands were scarred and heavily veined. His hair was grey but it was still thick.

While others were amazed at his condition, he was afraid of the changes that had taken place inside him. It was this invisible deterioration that was gradually shrinking the limits of his endurance.

Even in the darkness, he could see the distant steeple of the Lutheran church and the square bulk of the old folk's home that was directly across from his house. Emma, he thought, grimly, would not be satisfied until he was safely trapped in one or carried out of the other.

He hated the old folk's home. He hated the three stories of pale yellow brick with their small, close-set windows. He hated the concrete porch with its five round pillars and the large white buckets of red geraniums. When he saw the men poking at the flowers like a bunch of old women, he pulled his blinds.

The local people who worked in the home were good to the inmates, tenants they called them, but there was no way a man could be a man in there. No whisky. Going to bed at ten. Getting up at eight. Bells for breakfast, coffee and dinner. Bells for everything. He was surprised that they didn't have bells for going to the toilet. Someone watching over you every minute of every day. It was as if, having earned the right to be an adult, you had suddenly, in some inexplicable way, lost it again.

The porch was the worst part of the building. Long and narrow and lined with yellow and red rocking chairs, it sat ten feet above the ground and the steps were so steep that even those who could get around all right were afraid to try them. Fusi had lived across from the old folk's home for 40 years and he had seen old people, all interchangeable as time erased their identities, shuffling and bickering their way to their deaths. Now, most of those who came out to sleep in the sun and to watch the world with glittering, jealous eyes, were people he had known.

He would have none of it. He was not afraid of dying, but he was determined that it would be in his own home. His licence had been taken from him because of his age, but he did not stop. One net was not thirty, but it was one, and a quarter-mile from shore was not five miles, but it was a quarter-mile.

He didn't shuffle and he didn't have to be fed or have a rubber diaper pinned around him each day. If anything, he had become more cunning for, time and again, the inspector had come and destroyed the illegal nets of other fishermen, even catching and sending them to court to be fined, but they hadn't caught him for four years. Every day of the fishing season, he pitted his wits against theirs and won. At times, they had come close, but their searches had never turned up anything and, once, to his delight, when he was on the verge of being found with freshly caught fish on him, he hid them under a hole in the breakwater and then sat on the edge of the boat, talked about old times, and shared the inspectors' coffee. The memory still brought back a feeling of pleasure and excitement.

As his mind strayed over past events, he drew the boat along the net in fits and starts for his shoulder would not take the strain of steady pulling. Another good-sized fish hung limp as he pulled it to him, but then as he slipped the mesh from its head, it gave a violent shake and flew from his hands. Too stiff and slow to lunge for it, he could do nothing but watch the white flash of its belly before it struck the water and disappeared.

He paused to knead the backs of his hands, then began again. Before he was finished, his breath roared in his ears like the lake in a storm, but there were four more pickerel. With a sigh that was nearly a cry of pain, he let the net drop. Immediately, pulled down by the heavy, rusted anchors at each end, it disappeared. People were like that, he thought. One moment they were here, then they were gone and it was as if they had never been.

Behind the town, the horizon was a pale, hard grey. The silhouette of rooftops and trees might have been cut from a child's purple construction paper.

The urgent need to reach the shore before the sky became any lighter drove Fusi, for he knew that if the inspectors saw him on the water they would catch him as easily as a child. They would take his fish and net, which he did not really mind, for there were more fish in the lake and more nets in his shed, but he couldn't afford to lose his boat. His savings were not enough to buy another.

He put out the oars, only to be unable to close the fingers of his left hand. When he tried to bend his fingers around the handle, his whole arm began to tremble. Unable to do anything else, he leaned forward and pressing his fingers flat to the seat, he began to relentlessly knead them. Alternately, he prayed and cursed, trying with words to delay the sun.

"A few minutes," he whispered through clenched teeth. "Just a few minutes more." But even as he watched, the horizon turned red, then yellow and a sliver of the sun's rim rose above the houses.

Unable to wait any longer, he grabbed his left hand in his right and forced his fingers around the oar, then braced himself and began to row. Instead of cutting the water cleanly, the left oar skimmed over the surface, twisting the handle in his grip. He tried again, not letting either oar go deep. The skiff moved sluggishly ahead.

Once again, the balloon in his chest swelled and threatened to gag him, making his gorge rise, but he did not dare stop. Again and again, the left oar skipped across the surface so that the bow swung back and forth like a wounded and dying animal trying to shake away its pain. Behind him, the orange sun inched above the sharp angles of the roofs.

When the bow slid across the sand, he dropped the oars, letting them trail in the water. He grasped the gunwale, but as he climbed out, his left leg collapsed and he slid to his knees. Cold water filled his boots and soaked the legs of his trousers. Resting his head against the boat, he breathed noisily through his mouth. He remained there until gradually his breathing eased and the pain in his chest closed like a night flower touched by daylight. When he could stand, he tied the boat to one of the black pilings that was left from a breakwater that had long since been smashed and carried away.

As he collected his catch, he noticed the green fisheries department truck on the dock. He had been right. They were there. Crouching behind his boat, he waited to see if anyone was watching him. It seemed like a miracle that they had not already seen him, but he knew that they had not for if they had, their launch would have raced out of the harbour and swept down upon him.

Bending close to the sand, he limped into the deep shadow at the foot of the breakwater. They might, he knew, be waiting for him at the top of the ladder, but if they were, there was nothing he could do about it. He climbed the ladder and, hearing and seeing nothing, he rested near the top so that when he climbed into sight, he wouldn't need to sit down.

No-one was in the yard. The block was empty. With a sigh of relief, he crossed to the small shed where he kept his equipment and hefted the fish onto the shelf that was nailed to one wall. He filleted his catch with care, leaving none of the translucent flesh on the back-bone or skin. Then, because they were pickerel, he scooped out the cheeks, which he set aside with the roe for his breakfast.

As he carried the offal across the backyard in a bucket, the line of gulls that gathered every morning on the breakwater broke into flight and began to circle overhead. Swinging back the bucket, he flung the guts and heads and skin into the air and the gulls darted down to snatch the red entrails and iridescent heads. In a thrumming of white and grey wings, those who hadn't caught anything descended to the sand to fight for what remained.

Relieved at being rid of the evidence of his fishing – if anyone asked where he got the fillets he would say he had bought them and the other fishermen would lie for him – Fusi squatted and wiped his hands clean on the wet grass.

There was no sign of movement in the house. The blinds were still drawn and the high, narrow house with its steep roof and faded red-brick siding looked deserted. The yard was flat and bare except for the dead trunk of an elm, which was stripped bare of its bark and wind polished to the colour of bone.

He returned to the shed and wrapped the fillets in a sheet of brown waxed paper, then put the roe and the cheeks into the bucket. Neither Emma nor John were up when he came in and washed the bucket and his food, but as he started cooking, Emma appeared in a quilted housecoat covered with large, purple tulips. Her head was a tangle of metal. "Are you satisfied?" she asked, her voice trembling. "I've had no sleep since you left."

Without turning from the stove, he said, "Leave. Nobody's making you stay."

Indignantly, she answered. "And who would look after you?"

He grimaced and turned over the roe so they would be golden brown on all sides. For two weeks around Christmas he had been sick with the flu and she never let him forget it.

"Honour thy father and mother that thy days may be long upon this earth."

He snorted out loud. What she really wanted to be sure of was that she got the house.

"You don't have to be like this," she said, starting to talk to him as if he was a child. "I only want you to stop because I care about you. All those people who live across the street, they don't... ."

"I'm not one of them," he barked.

"You're 70 years old... ."

"And I still fish," he replied angrily, cutting her off. "And I still row a boat and lift my nets. That's more than your husband can do and he's just 50." He jerked his breakfast off the stove. Because he knew it would annoy her, he began to eat out of the pan.

"I'm 70," he continued between bites, "and I beat the entire fisheries department. They catch men half my age but they haven't caught me. Not for four years. And I fish right under their noses." He laughed with glee and laced his coffee with a finger of whisky.

Emma, her lips clamped shut and her hands clenched in fury, marched back up the stairs. In half an hour both she and John came down for their breakfast. Under Emma's glare, John cleared his throat and said, "Emma, that is we, think – " He stopped and fiddled with the knot of his tie. He always wore light grey ties and a light grey suit. "If you don't quit breaking the law, something will have to be done." He stopped and looked beseechingly at his wife, but she narrowed her eyes until little folds of flesh formed beneath them. "Perhaps something like putting you in custody so you'll be saved from yourself."

Fusi was so shocked that for once he could think of nothing to say. Encouraged by his silence, John said, "It will be for your own good."

Before either of them realized what he was up to, Fusi leaned sideways and emptied his cup into his son-in-law's lap.

The coffee was hot. John flung himself backward with a screech, but the back legs of his chair caught on a crack in the linoleum and he tipped over with a crash. In the confusion Fusi stalked upstairs.

In a moment he flung an armload of clothes down. When his daughter rushed to the bottom of the stairs, Fusi flung another armload of clothes at her.

"This is my house," he bellowed. "You're not running it yet."

Emma began grabbing clothes and laying them flat so they wouldn't wrinkle. John, both hands clenched between his legs, hobbled over to stare.

Fusi descended the stairs and they parted to let him by. At the counter, he picked up the package of fish and turning toward them, said, "I want you out of here when I get back or I'll go out on the lake and get caught and tell everyone that you put me up to it."

His fury was so great that once he was outside he had to lean against the house while a spasm of trembling swept over him. When he was composed, he rounded the corner. At one side of the old folk's home there was an enclosed fire escape that curled to the ground like a piece of intestine. He headed for the kitchen door under it.

Fusi had kept on his rubber boots, dark slacks and red turtle-neck sweater, and because he knew that behind the curtains, eyes were watching his every move, he tried to hide the stiffness in his left leg.

Although it was early, Rosie Melysyn was already at work. She always came first, never missing a day. She was a large, good natured widow with grey hair.

"How are you today, Mr. Bergman?" she asked.

"Fine," he replied. "I'm feeling great." He held out the brown paper package. "I thought some of the old people might like some fish." Although he had brought fish for the last four years, he always said the same thing.

Rosie dusted off her hands, took the package and placed it on the counter.

"I'll see someone gets it," she assured him. "Help yourself to some coffee."

As he took the pot from the stove, she asked, "No trouble with the inspectors?"

He always waited for her to ask that. He grinned delightedly, the pain of the morning already becoming a memory. "No trouble. They'll never catch me. I'm up too early. I saw them hanging about, but it didn't do them any good."

"Jimmy Henderson died last night," Rosie offered.

"Jimmy Henderson," Fusi repeated. They had been friends, but he felt no particular sense of loss. Jimmy had been in the home for three years. "I'm not surprised. He wasn't more than 68 but he had given up. You give up, you're going to die. You believe in yourself and you can keep right on going."

Rosie started mixing oatmeal and water.

"You know," he said to her broad back, "I was with Jimmy the first time he got paid. He cut four cords of wood for 60¢ and spent it all on hootch. He kept running up and down the street and flapping his arms, trying to fly. When he passed out, we hid him in the hayloft of the stable so his old man couldn't find him."

Rosie tried to imagine Jimmy Henderson attempting to fly and failed. To her, he was a bent man with a sad face who had to use a walker to get to the dining-room. What she remembered about him best was coming on him unexpectedly and finding him silently crying. He had not seen her and she had quietly backed away.

Fusi was lingering because after he left, there was a long day ahead of him. He would have the house to himself and after checking the vacated room to see that nothing of his had been taken, he would tie his boat properly, sleep for three hours, then eat lunch. In the afternoon he would make a trip to the docks to see what the inspectors were up to and collect information about their movements.

The back door opened with a swish and he felt a cool draft. Both he and Rosie turned to look. He was shocked to see that instead of it being one of the kitchen help, it was Emma. She shut the door and glanced at them both, then at the package of fish.

"What do you want?" he demanded.

"I called the inspectors," she replied, "to tell them you're not responsible for yourself. I told them about the net."

He gave a start, but then was relieved when he remembered they had to actually catch him fishing before they could take the skiff. "So what?" he asked, confident once more.

Quietly, she replied, "You don't have to worry about being caught. They've known about your fishing all along."

Suddenly frightened by her calm certainty, his voice rose as he said, "That's not true."

"They don't care," she repeated. "Inspector McKenzie was the name of the one I talked to. He said you couldn't do any harm with one net. They've been watching you every morning just in case you should get into trouble and need help."

Emma stood there, not moving, her head tipped back, her eyes benevolent.

He turned to Rosie. "She's lying, isn't she? That's not true. They wouldn't do that?"

"Of course, she's lying," Rosie assured him.

He would have rushed outside but Emma was standing in his way. Since he could not get past her, he fled through the swinging doors that led to the dining-room.

As the doors shut, Rosie turned on Emma and said, "You shouldn't have done that." She picked up the package of fish with its carefully folded wrapping. In the artificial light, the package glowed like a piece of amber. She held it cupped in the hollows of her hands. "You had no right."

Emma seemed to grow larger and her eyes shone.

"The Lord's work be done," she said, her right hand partly raised as if she were preparing to give a benediction.

Suggested Topics

1. What impression do you get of Fusi and Emma and their conflict? Concentrate on the opening paragraphs of the story. What does Emma want for her father?

2. What is the significance of Fusi's statement, "Render unto Caesar what is Caesar's"? He is quoting from the Bible. Can you complete the quote? What is the significance of *not* completing the rest of the quotation?

3. Why is Fusi so afraid of the fish inspector?

4. Though John Smith and Rosie Melysyn are minor characters in the story, Valgardson nevertheless paints a clear picture of them. What does he tell you about each? What else do you learn about them? How do you learn it?

5. Which character in the story is the true Christian? Why?

6. How is the title significant?

7. If you have seen the film of the same name, what insights into the characters are brought out by the director that you do not find in the story?

Assignment **11** Short Research Report

Introduction

Reporting information is one of the most common tasks you will have in school or in business. While the research report requires a careful and diligent search for facts, the facts should be presented in your own style. The report should include a blend of your own prose and quotations from authorities.

This short research essay is intended as a first step toward writing the longer research paper (Assignment 12). The suggested topics are limited in scope, and you are not required to include a bibliography.

Assignment

In about 250 words, write a report on a nursery rhyme, a Canadian holiday, the use of a word, the name of one of your schools, or an invention or discovery. You must include a minimum of one direct quotation in your essay.

Prewriting Suggestions

1.   The first step in writing a report is *selecting a topic*. Several are suggested for this assignment. Ask yourself what you, or your readers, want to know about that topic. You may wish to draft a list of questions. For example:

a) **nursery rhymes**
Why and how did the nursery rhyme begin? (Choose one whose origin you have always wondered about.) If you cannot think of a nursery rhyme, start by trying to answer one of these: Who was "Little Jack Horner"? Why was "Mary, Mary, Quite Contrary"? Why was it that "Jack Spratt Could Eat No Fat"? Why was "Old King Cole" so merry?

b) **holidays**
When and why did it come into existence? Who was responsible for its creation? For whom or what is it named? Has its name ever been changed? What are people expected to do on this holiday? What do most actually do? Here are a few holidays to consider: *Remembrance Day*, *Victoria Day*, *Boxing Day*, *Labour Day*.

c) **words**
What is the derivation of the word? When did it come into use? (The *Oxford English Dictionary* gives this information.) Has the meaning changed through

the ages? Include the actual word in one of your sentences. Here are some words to research if you cannot think of one yourself: *bluestocking, pemmican, grog, laconic, Bluenose, toboggan.*

d) **the name of a past school**

When and why did it come into being? Was it always in its present location? For whom or what is it named? Has its name ever been changed? Has its size changed?

e) **inventions or discoveries**

When, by whom, why, and how was it invented or discovered? (In other words, give all the details.) Has its use changed through the ages? Here are some things to research if you cannot think of one yourself: *a thumb-tack, an umbrella, the man whose picture is on the $100 bill, Magnetic Hill, Standard Time.*

2. The next step in writing a research report is *gathering information.* Before you start the actual research, take a look at your resources. Encyclopedias, newspapers, and reference books are common sources of information. Visit your library and do not hesitate to consult the library's most important and often most helpful resource – its staff. Before proceeding, do Activity 21, which deals with research techniques.

3. Once you have located your sources of information, *read the material carefully and take notes.* Use index cards – they are easy to carry, use, and organize. Your general topic can likely be divided into several sub-topics. On each card, list the topic, sub-topic, and the facts that are relevant to that sub-topic. Record direct quotations under the sub-topic that they refer to. If you are only using one quotation from a book, record your source – author, title, publisher, and page number – at the bottom of the card.

> *Eavesdropping*
> *First use:*
> *- 1580 (Old English)*
> *- "eaves" - overhanging edge of roof*
> *- "eavesdrop" - the place where*
> *water dropped from the*
> *eaves*
>
> The Shorter Oxford English Dictionary,
> 3rd ed., C.T. Onions (ed.), (London:
> Oxford University Press), p. 580.

4. Your completed cards will help you *organize your report*. By arranging them in front of you, you may discover not only an ideal organization for your essay, but also a possible need for further research.

Once you have organized your cards, make a working outline. The outline should consist of your topic, several sub-topics, and supporting facts. The following is a possible outline for the research report in the model section.

Origin of the Word "Eavesdropping"

I. First use
   A. 1580 – Old English
   B. "Eaves" – overhanging edge of a roof
   C. "Eavesdrop" – the place where water dropped from the eaves
II. Origin of verb
   A. 1606
   B. Verb "to eavesdrop" – "to stand within the 'eavesdrop' of a house in order to overhear secrets"
   C. Eaves were an excellent place for snoopers to listen to private conversation
   D. Snoopers were called "eavesdroppers"
III. Today's meaning
   A. Dictionary meaning similar to original
   B. Everyday use expanded to include "eavesdropping" on telephone, etc.

5. *Consider your writing variables* so that you can fulfil your reader's needs. Remember that your purpose is to *inform* your reader. As a result, you should be thorough, honest, and objective in the presentation of your facts.

6. Before you write, determine whether your treatment of your subject will be *serious or comic*. (Yes, a research paper can be humorous.) Once you have decided on a definite style, follow that style consistently.

Drafting Suggestions

1. With diligent research, and thorough note taking and outlining, your research report should almost write itself. In a short report, indicate your subject in your first sentence. Rather than beginning with

   "This research paper is about ... "
   or   "In this paper I will show that ..."
tell something interesting or important about your topic.

2. Acknowledge material from your references with the use of footnotes. You may use information that is common knowledge without footnoting. However, if you present other people's specific words or even other people's ideas without acknowledging the source, you are plagiarizing. See Activity 21 for information on setting up a footnote.

3. A quotation adds authority to your work. If you re-phrase material from another source, do not put quotation marks around it, but do give it a footnote number and record the source in the usual way. However, if you use a direct quote (a specific word or phrase from another source), you should credit it with quotation marks and a footnote.

4. For this assignment, include a minimum of one direct quotation from your research material. *Shorter quotations* should be integrated as smoothly as possible into your own writing. Notice the different ways of integrating the following short quotations into a research report.

> I know of no bird or animal that can equal the Canada Goose for getting well after being wounded. It is said that a cat has nine lives; if that is true, the Canada Goose has at least eighteen, nine on each side of the border.
>
> *Jack Miner*

> Nobody has asked me but if I were to choose a national bird for Canada, it would be the starling. He struts self-reliantly, asks no favours of anybody, and never puts out his claw for relief.
>
> *Gordon Sinclair*

Both quotations are taken from *Colombo's Concise Canadian Quotations*, ed. John Robert Colombo (Edmonton: Hurtig Publishers Ltd., 1976.)

a) Jack Miner, operator of the famous bird sanctuary at Kingsville, Ontario, complimented the Canada goose on its phenomenal capacity "for getting well after being wounded."[1]

b) Which bird did famed naturalist Jack Miner admire most? The Canada goose. "I know of no bird or animal," he said, "that can equal the Canada Goose for getting well after being wounded."[2] Columnist and broadcaster Gordon Sinclair cast his vote for the starling. "He struts self-reliantly, asks no favours of anybody, and never puts out his claw for relief."[3]

c) Discussing the question of a national bird for Canada, Gordon Sinclair says that his choice "would be the starling," because, among other reasons, it "never puts out his claw for relief." (Colombo, p. 21b)

d) According to naturalist Jack Miner, "it is said that a cat has nine lives; ... a Canada Goose has at least eighteen ... ." (Colombo, p. 21b)

Ellipses indicate that something from the original quotation has not been included. Ellipses have only three dots. If you ever see four, it means that the ellipses end a sentence; the fourth dot is the period.

e) Jack Miner says "the Canada Goose has at least eighteen [lives], nine on each side of the border." (Colombo, p. 21b)

Brackets are needed around "lives" because it does not appear in the original quotation, but has been added for clarification. Notice that these brackets are squared; do not confuse them with the standard parentheses.

The rules for including *longer quotations* of three lines or more are a little different: you indent the entire quotation for both left and right margins, single space, and omit the quotation marks.

f) Jack Miner gave the majestic Canada goose this remarkable tribute:

> I know of no bird or animal that can equal the Canada Goose for getting well after being wounded. It is said that a cat has nine lives; if that is so, a Canada Goose has at least eighteen, nine on each side of the border. (Colombo, p. 21b)

Each quotation must then have an appropriate footnote number or the last name of the author and page number in parentheses. If you use the latter method, you must provide a bibliography.

5. To assist you with the final draft of your short research paper, read over the models at the end of this assignment. Notice particularly their use of quoted material and footnotes.

Revising Suggestions

When you or your peers edit your short research report, apply the check list from Appendix B as well as the following specific questions:

1. Has your report achieved its purpose? That is, have you informed your reader of the important facts about your topic? If there are questions that have not been answered, perhaps your research was insufficient.

2. Is the topic of your report clear? Have you introduced your topic in an interesting manner?

3. Do all your facts relate to the topic? Are they organized in a logical manner?

4. Are the quoted material and your prose blended smoothly?

5. Is the scholarship correct? Are the quotations punctuated correctly? Are the footnotes set up and punctuated correctly?

Polishing Suggestions

Besides using Appendix C, make a last-minute effort to see that all the commas, quotation marks, and so forth are correct. Also, make sure your reader will accept your method of crediting your quotation(s): footnoting or including the information within the body of the essay.

Models

Under the Eaves

by Judy Chapelsky, student

In researching the origins of unusual words, I came upon a particularly interesting account of the verb "eavesdropping."

An Old English word first used in 1580, "eaves" referred to the overhanging edge of a roof.[1] Also originating at the same time, the noun "eavesdrop" referred to the place where the water dropped from the eaves of a house.[2]

But it wasn't until 1606 that the verb "to eavesdrop" originated and was defined as "To stand within the 'eavesdrop' of a house in order to overhear secrets; hence, to listen secretly to private conversation."[3] This meaning was based on the fact that there was about two feet of space between the edge of the eaves and the wall of the house, which turned out to be an excellent place for snoopers to crouch and listen to private conversations. These snoopers were defined by the law as "Such that listen under windows or the eaves of a house to hearken after discourse, and thereon to frame slanderous and mischievous tales."[4] The snoopers were called "eavesdroppers" and were said to be "eavesdropping."

Today's dictionary meaning of "eavesdropping" is strikingly similar to the original meaning of the word, but its everyday use has expanded to include more than just snooping from standing under the eaves of a house. We now refer to eavesdropping on the telephone and through closed doors, and use it casually to refer to the many other ways we listen to private conversations.

---

[1]The Shorter Oxford English Dictionary, 3d ed., s.v. "eaves."
[2]SOED, p. 580.
[3]SOED, p. 580.
[4]Bergen Evans, Comfortable Words (Toronto: Random House of Canada, 1959), p. 137.

The Dynamic Duo

by Steven Greenaway, student

Most of us use them, one on top of the other, at least twice a day. Some spend hours polishing with them while others just retain the pair for a quick rinse. Yet, have any of us ever bothered to look into the history of our beloved bathroom buddies – the faithful toothbrush and its underrated partner, toothpaste?

Toothbrushes are of uncertain origin. While the Romans are said to have used them in hopes of preserving their teeth, judging from their skeletal remains, the practice seems to have had little success.

Laurence Wright, a noted authority on the subject of toothbrushes, believes the first recorded toothbrush in England was one commissioned by Queen Elizabeth I in 1561, "whose teeth, once yellow, were in her old age, jet black." (Wright, p. 421)

Along with the toothbrush, the aristocracy of England often used tepid water to clean their pearly whites every morning. For a majority of the working class, however, soot was a popular dentifrice. Other recipes for homemade "tooth soap" included ashes mixed with honey, charcoal, areca nuts, and cuttlefish bone. (Wright, p. 409)

Perhaps the next time we squeeze a cylinder of breath-freshening *Aim* or *Colgate* (with *MFP*) onto our specially tapered *Squibb* or *Reach*, we should pay tribute to the wonders of modern technology!

Bibliography

Wright, Laurence. Clean and Decent. Toronto: University of Toronto Press, 1967.

Analysis

Under the Eaves

1. This is a student's short but thorough explanation of the origin of "eaves-dropping." Do you think anything is missing? Is there anything else you would want to know about her information or its sources?

2. What does *SOED*, in the footnotes, stand for?

The Dynamic Duo

1. This is a student's well-written research paper about two parts of our daily hygiene most of us take for granted. Are there some aspects of toothpaste he does not discuss? For example, we do not find out how toothpaste gets into the tube. (You might research how this feat is accomplished.)

2. The writer has included some humour in his essay, by using words such as "The Dynamic Duo" and "beloved bathroom buddies." Can you find other examples? Is his use of humour effective? Why does he use it? (You might like to try humour in your short research paper.)

3. Notice that the writer does not use footnotes. He, therefore, provides a bibliography. If you are permitted to write your essay without footnotes, turn to Assignment 12 for instructions on how to write a bibliography.

4. Notice that the writer first uses a direct quotation, then a paraphrase. This explains why he needs quotation marks the first time, but not the second.

Assignment **12** Long Research Report

Introduction

Before you begin this assignment, make sure that you carefully read through Assignment 11. Much of what is said there also applies to the long research essay.

Assignment

Write a research essay of at least 1000 words on a topic of your choice.

Prewriting Suggestions

1. *Selecting a Topic*

When choosing a topic, select one that is limited enough for you to handle. For example, "The Canadian Government" is too broad a topic for a 1000-word report. It would be more effective to report on some aspect of that topic: Canadian prime ministers, the organization of the government, the election process, and so on.

In choosing a topic for this assignment, you may wish to select a topic on which you have to write for another course, such as social studies. This will allow you to benefit from the revision suggestions of your peer/editors and English teacher/editor before you submit your final paper to your subject teacher. (Make sure you have your subject teacher's approval *before* you begin such an assignment.)

2. *Locating Sources of Information*

If you have not already done so, become familiar with Activity 21.

3. *Note taking*

If you are quoting extensively, you may wish to record each quotation on a separate index card, making sure to include the page number and the author's name. (Researchers sometimes use different coloured cards in order to distinguish quotations from information.)

Before you put your books away, make sure that you record the bibliographic information on another card or sheet of paper. (Nothing is more frustrating than sitting down to complete your bibliography, only to find that you do not have all the details about your sources.)

4. *Organization*

There are a number of ways of organizing the facts in a research report: chronological order, sequential order, order of importance, cause and effect, comparison and contrast, and so on. Whatever method of organization you choose, prepare an outline of your sub-topics and supporting facts.

5. State your writing variables, for example:

Topic: the types of hamburgers sold around town
Audience: my boss
Purpose: to help him select a new type of hamburger for our menu
Format: a proposal report (which contains a research essay)

or

Topic: Brutus as a tragic hero
Audience: my literature teacher
Purpose: to show the qualities of a Shakespearean tragic hero
Format: a research report

Drafting Suggestions

1. Follow the drafting suggestions outlined in Assignment 11.

2. Longer research papers are made up of several parts; however, depending on the complexity of your paper and the requirements of your teacher, you may or may not need all of the following:

Title Page

Includes the title of your essay, your name, the name and section (if there is one) of the course for which the paper is written, your instructor's name, the name of your school, and the date. (Your instructor may wish you to use a particular layout for the title page, so check before you begin.)

Table of Contents

Depending on how long or complex your paper is, you may or may not need a table of contents. If you do use one, it should contain the headings of each section and the page on which each section begins.

Appendices, Charts

If you use material which is essential but, because it's too long or too complex, cannot be included within the text, you must put it as an appendix in a separate section between the body of the text and the page of footnotes. Charts, graphs, and other illustrations should, if possible, be included near the part of the text to which they relate.

Footnotes

The modern trend is to avoid footnotes and include the name of the author and page number in parentheses within the body of the essay. If you are required to use notes, you may group them on a separate page at the end of your paper. It is wise to include an unattached photocopy of these endnotes so that your reader is not constantly flipping to the back of the essay.

Bibliography

All the books and other materials you used in compiling your paper, whether or not you quote from them in the text, should be mentioned in a bibliography after the appendices or footnotes. For information on setting up a bibliography, see Activity 21.

3. Before you draft your paper, read the model research essay at the end of this assignment. Notice particularly the organization and structure of the essay, the style, the use of quotations, and the organization of the footnotes and bibliography.

Revising Suggestions

Use the revising suggestions outlined in Assignment 11.

Polishing Suggestions

Besides using the polishing suggestions outlined in Appendix C, concentrate on the *appearance* of your presentation. Research papers should be written and spaced neatly – in fact, to add an authoritative touch to your paper, you should *type* it (or have it typed) double-spaced on one side of the paper only.

Model

Acupuncture

by Lynn Stefonovich, student

Tai chen tseng – to "insert a golden needle"[1]

Acupuncture, the ancient Chinese art of healing, is the practice by which a needle is inserted a few millimetres into the skin, left for a predetermined amount of time, and then withdrawn. Fine, flexible, and sharp, the needles may be made of any substance, but silver and stainless steel needles seem to be the most popular. Insertion of the needles should not cause pain or draw blood.[2] Though the Western scientific theory about acupuncture differs considerably from the Chinese theory, the art of healing is undeniably effective.

According to traditional Chinese theory, the human body is divided into twelve passages (meridians):

> The means whereby man is created, the means whereby disease occurs,
> the means whereby man is cured, the means whereby disease arises:
> the twelve meridians are the basis of all theory and treatment.
>
> (Ling Shu, jingbie pian)[3]

Through these passages flow the vital forces of life. There are two life forces, *Yin* (the feminine force) and *Yang* (the masculine force). If a person is healthy, the life forces are said to be in proper proportion. An acupuncturist will manipulate the forces by inserting the needles at critical points until a proper balance is achieved.[4] The doctor is concerned with the energy behind the invisible forces of Yin and Yang.

Western theory differs considerably from the Yin/Yang theory. Scientific research performed on rats proves that acupuncture relieves pain but does not cure disease. When the needles are inserted, impulses are sent to the brain by way of the central nervous system, which acts as a conductor. The brain causes the body to secrete natural chemicals that resemble pain-killing drugs such as morphine and heroin.[5] Scientists believe that "acupuncture produces analgesia rather than anesthesia; that is, the reduction of pain rather than the loss of sensation."[6]

Before a diagnosis is made, the patient must have a complete examination from head to toe. Acupuncture points and the organs they are associated

---

[1] Mark Duke, Acupuncture (New York: Pyramid Books, 1973), p. 31.
[2] Austin Kipling, "A Curious Cure That Works," Changing Times, November 1980, p. 38.
[3] Felix Mann, Acupuncture (New York: Random House, 1973), p. 35.
[4] James Hassett, "Acupuncture Is Proving Its Point," Psychology Today 14 (December 1980): 86.
[5] Hassett, p. 82.
[6] Hassett, p. 89.

with are usually not close together. For example, the acupuncture points on the leg are associated with the liver, gall bladder, kidney, bladder, spleen, and stomach. Any points that are painful, even if no pressure is applied to them, are connected with a diseased organ. When the disease is cured, whether by acupuncture, Western medical methods, or the passage of time, there will be no pain at the acupuncture point.[7]

Another way to reach a diagnosis requiring the application of acupuncture is by taking the patient's pulses. There are twelve different pulses, six on each wrist within a given area. Six are taken by the doctor applying a light pressure on the area, and the other six by a heavier pressure on the same area. Each pulse is associated with a certain organ. The acupuncturist compares the characteristics of each pulse with those of a healthy pulse to form his decision. He believes that by feeling the pulse he "can detect illness long before it appears as a noticeable symptom."[8] The pulses and the tender acupuncture points are the two most important factors in a diagnosis, but many minor observations also affect the doctor's decision.

Since all the organs have counterparts on the body's surface, the well-trained acupuncturist observes changes in his patient's skin and body openings. He studies the patient's eyes, tongue, and colouring because different colours relate to different organs. His senses of hearing and smell also assist the doctor. Body odours and changes in a patient's voice can mean a Yin/Yang disturbance.[9] Combining all the necessary information from observing and touching, the acupuncturist reaches a diagnosis. Before treatment begins, he knows precisely where the needles will go, how deep they will be placed, how long they will be left in, and how many times they will be used. The aim of the acupuncturist is to "stimulate the affected organ through its meridian and restore the harmonious flow."[10] He will balance the Yin and Yang energy among the various organs, the nervous system, and the blood.

To stimulate the Yang, the acupuncturist inserts the needle slowly, withdraws it rapidly, and massages the spot after the needle is taken out. He stimulates the Yin in the same way. He uses hot needles for Yang treatment, cold ones for Yin. If, as he inserts the needle, the acupuncturist twists it clockwise, Yang will be influenced; a counter-clockwise motion will produce a change in Yin.[11] Response to the treatment differs from patient to patient: some respond within a few seconds of the first needle, some require as many as forty-two needles and several visits. A very small proportion of the patients who do not improve while being treated may notice a cure some months later.

---

[7]Mann, p. 27.
[8]Duke, p. 150.
[9]Duke, p. 140.
[10]Louis Moss, M.D., Acupuncture and You (Secaucus: Citadel Press, 1964), p. 40.
[11]Duke, p. 162.

Following each treatment, a patient may feel an increase in energy, due to the stimulating effect of the needles, and a pleasant drowsiness due to the sudden release in tension.[12]

Although acupuncture will continue to be a topic of controversy, physiologist David Mayer summed up the general feelings of researchers when he said, "I don't think any researcher in this field now doubts that acupuncture can reduce experimental pain in the laboratory."[13]

More people are turning towards the "golden needles" as a last resort to alleviate pain and disease. Some are finding that it should perhaps have been their first resort. In the future, Western medical technology may be combined with acupuncture, to give the patient the best of both medical worlds.

---

[12]Mann, p. 200.
[13]Hassett, p. 85.

Bibliography

Duke, Mark. Acupuncture. New York: Pyramid Books, 1973.

Hassett, James. "Acupuncture Is Proving Its Point." Psychology Today 14 (December 1980): 81–89.

Kipling, Austin. "A Curious Cure That Works." Changing Times, November 1980, pp. 36–41.

Mann, Felix. Acupuncture. New York: Random House, 1973.

Moss, Louis, M.D. Acupuncture and You. Secaucus: Citadel Press, 1964.

Analysis

1. Why do you think the student writer chose to write on acupuncture? Who is her audience?

2. Can you tell that she has used basic essay structure (Assignment 6)? What is her main claim? What supporting evidence does she use? What method of organization does she use?

3. Comment on her use of quoted material. Does she blend quotations and her own prose smoothly?

4. How acupuncture works is something few non-Chinese people understand. Has she explained the procedures of acupuncture thoroughly? Was her explanation easy to understand? Did she leave out any important information?

5. After she wrote this research essay, she wondered if she should have written it as a saturation report (Assignment 13). Because she knows a number of people who have had acupuncture as well as a few doctors who administer it, she could have interviewed them and used the techniques of journalism to write her essay. Do you think the essay would have been better had she produced a saturation report? Why?

Assignment 13 Saturation Report

Introduction

A saturation report, sometimes called a feature article, is another example of informative writing. The term refers to a type of "soft" journalism that usually deals with some up-to-date topic and relies on material gathered from every possible source. Typical examples appear in newspapers and magazines with titles such as "The Immortality Pill," "Video discs," "The SPCA," and "New Wave." Unlike a traditional research essay, the saturation report usually deals with less academic topics, relies on a combination of sources, includes "first-hand" sources, and presents the information in a lively and informal manner.

Assignment

Write a saturation report of no fewer than 1000 words.

Prewriting Suggestions

1. Choose as your topic some newsworthy aspect of our society: a controversial group, a famous or interesting individual, or a recent development in education, fashion, medicine, and so on. Here are a few suggestions: the latest fashion trend, dances of the 80s, a local monument or historic site, a controversial cancer treatment. The purpose of your saturation report will be to inform your reader as fully as possible about your topic.

2. In selecting a topic, consider the audience for your report. Since saturation reports normally appear in newspapers and magazines, they are written specifically to appeal to the interests of the readers of that particular magazine or paper. You may wish to imagine that you are writing an article for a particular publication. Get to know its readership by examining the articles and advertisements that appear, and comparing them to those in other publications. What are the readers' interests?

Then draft your writing variables; for example,

Topic and Purpose: to expose the manner in which discos entice young people into their clubs with gimmicks, fads, and crazes

Audience: the readers of the "Young People" section of our local newspaper

Format: saturation report

3. Because the success of a saturation report usually relies on research, you should allow plenty of time for thorough reporting. Choose your topic at least six weeks before you plan to submit your paper to your final audience.

In order to write a good saturation report, you must become a sponge, soaking up details as you perform various kinds of research. *First-hand* knowledge is an important source of information for the saturation report. You will want to arrange personal interviews with your subject, or with people who are knowledgeable about your topic. Prepare the questions for your interview in advance, and determine how you will record your subject's responses. (A tape recorder is ideal for this purpose.)

Your research will take you into the library, primarily into the periodical section, but you will have to watch TV and listen to the radio, read newspapers and magazines, and collect pertinent articles. You may even want to take photographs or collect illustrations. All this is enjoyable, but it does take time.

Drafting Suggestions

1. In all probability you will collect your information in bits and pieces – conversations you have had or overheard, descriptions, interviews, researched facts, articles you have read, and so on. Once you have collected all your material, you must spend time piecing it together into a unified whole.

As in any type of exposition, your report will have unity only if your material supports your main claim or thesis. Quotations, observations, descriptions, and anecdotes will lend interest to your report, but make sure that each technique illustrates a point about your topic that you want to emphasize.

2. One of the main differences between the saturation report and the longer research paper is the way in which each presents its research. The research paper is organized and presented formally, displaying its data in a traditional manner, whereas in the saturation report the research material is blended so subtly and effectively into the writer's prose that the reader scarcely notices its presence.

Unlike the research essay, the saturation report requires no footnoting or bibliography. When you quote, you should include your source in the body of your report.

3. You can have a great deal of fun with your point of view because it can be as flexible as you want. As long as you prepare the reader for shifts, you can be a participant in the action, then remove yourself, and come in again. You can switch from first- to third-person point of view. This technique will become clear when you read one of the model saturation reports.

4. Illustrative material is often provided in saturation reports. Graphs, charts, illustrations, photographs, cartoons – all or any can add to your article.

Revising Suggestions

Use ideas in Appendix B and the check list from Assignment 6 to help in revising your saturation report.

Polishing Suggestions

Use Appendix C to help polish your saturation report. Remember that presentation is important. Make sure you label all your diagrams and pictures clearly. Type your saturation report if you can (especially if you are going to send it to a newspaper or magazine).

Models

The Fascinating World of Dreams

by Mike Chan, student

In recent years the study of dreams has become increasingly popular. Theories and conjectures about dreams abound, as they have throughout history, yet only recently has dreaming been investigated seriously on a large scale. The modern scientific techniques of dream research now provide very reliable data. However, much of the mystery of dreaming still remains; many questions on the topic are still unanswered.

According to *Psychology*, the earliest Greeks believed dreams came from the Gods – several passages in *The Iliad* refer to dreams sent by Zeus. During the middle ages, religious authorities held demons responsible for bad dreams. According to *Psychology Today*, not until Sigmund Freud's work in the nineteenth century were psychological facts recognized as the cause of dreams.

Although my aunt insists she never dreams, psychologists have confirmed that everybody dreams every night. The reason for forgetting dreams, however, is still not clear.

Many people have wondered whether or not animals dream. Studies performed at the University of Southern California were designed to answer their question. Dr. C.Y. Vaughn conducted various experiments with monkeys, concluding that "Animals also perceive visual images during sleep." Unable to communicate verbally with his subjects, Dr. Vaughn was uncertain what his monkeys dreamt about. Nevertheless, the doctor reports, "Judging from their facial expressions, the dreams were most likely hostile in nature."

Eye movement is the predominant physical activity during the dreaming process; authorities report rapid eye movements nearly always accompany dreams.

Contrary to popular belief, dreaming of an activity takes approximately as long as carrying out the activity in waking life. According to *Psychology*,

"Dreams do not occur in a split second, as many of us believe." A conversation I had with Dr. I. Olsen confirmed this hypothesis. Dr. Olsen states, "People think dreams occur in a split second, but actually it takes equally as long to dream of an activity as it does to carry out the activity in the waking state. When we are asleep, our perception of time is lost."

Many people argue that dreams completely lack colour. An avid dreamer myself, I tended to support this claim. Much to my surprise, an investigation done by doctors Allen Kahn and Stuart Fisher at Texas State University provides evidence to prove all dreams are in colour, but the colour may be forgotten when the subject recalls the dream.

Interestingly enough, studies have shown that we dream an average of four times per night, each dream separated by a ninety-minute interval. The first dream usually occurs one hour after the onset of sleep; the last dream is nearly always the only one people remember.

A film entitled "Sleep," shown to our class, claims that a major shift in body position indicates a dream has just ended. Dr. Joseph Collins, featured in the film, stresses the relationship between rapid eye movement and shifts in body position. According to Dr. Collins, "Rapid eye movement ceases after a major shift in body position, thus indicating the termination of a dream."

As outlined in *Psychology*, dreams develop from four primary sources: day residue, past experience, external stimuli, and physiological states. Day residue and past experience are the dominant factors in determining our dreams, but the other two are equally as important.

External stimuli incorporated into our dreams fascinate me the most. Upon hearing my alarm clock some mornings, I have incorporated the sound into my dream. Before awakening, I have dreamt the phone was ringing; subsequently in my dream, I have gone to answer it.

Dreams are infinitely diverse, their contents inexhaustibly varied. Scientists have divided the contents of dreams into three main categories: aggression and friendliness, misfortune, and sex. Studies conducted on 250 college students at Texas State University show eighty per cent of the subjects dreamt of misfortune most of the time. As Dr. John Roscoe states, "Misfortune is constantly in our subconscious thought, and, therefore, predominant in our dreams."

Dreaming has always been associated with the mysterious, supernatural world of precognition and mental telepathy. History is filled with tales of prophetic dreams, and yields many eerie, unexplained accounts of the supernatural. Abraham Lincoln, for example, dreamt he entered the East Room of the White House and saw a coffin. When he asked who had died, the reply was, "The President." Lincoln died three days later, the victim of an assassin's bullet. Lincoln's dream and its subsequent realization have been considered coincidental. According to Dr. William Levy, a prominent psychologist in Boston, "Lincoln was preoccupied with death. He often dreamt of being assassinated, and I see no correlation between his last dream and the fate that befell him."

Dr. Levy does point out, on the other hand, that telepathic messages can be transmitted through dreams. A team of scientists at Maimonides Hospital in New York conducted systematic studies of thought transmission to sleeping subjects. Their findings were incredible. Dr. Peter Krippner, head of the investigation, states, "Certain people are able to perceive thoughts while dreaming. Further studies will hopefully teach us how these messages are sent and received."

Although the study of dreams has become much more widespread over the years and although greater knowledge of the subject has been gained, dreaming is still one activity that continues to amaze us. Fascinating, mysterious, elusive – the profound world of dreams will undoubtedly continue to enlighten man for many years to come.

The Frisbee

by Murray Suid and Ron Harris

The Frisbee, the plastic flying disc that has become one of [North] America's favourite toys, owes its life to pies and men from Mars.

People have been throwing things since the dawn of time, beginning with rocks being thrown at enemies. Somewhere along the way the ball was invented and games like catch followed. Even the throwing of discs goes back quite a ways. The ancient discus of the Greeks is still used today in Olympic competition.

But the flying disc which gave the Frisbee its name was nothing more than a pie tin from the Frisbie Pie Company of Bridgeport, Connecticut. The firm was going strong in the 1920s, when a great many Frisbie pies were eaten by students at nearby Yale University. Whether the pies were any good, nobody seems to know. But the empty tins were great! Students quickly discovered that Frisbie tins, when flipped through the air, would soar like birds. Skilled tin-flippers could even get the pie trays to do tricks, like hovering or returning to the thrower. The new sport was named "Frisbie-ing," in honor of the pie manufacturer.

Years passed. Walter "Fred" Morrison had never heard of Frisbie-ing. Walt Morrison was a California-based carpenter and part-time inventor. Invention ran in the family. Morrison's father had invented the sealed-beam headlight for automobiles. As a boy, Morrison, like most kids, had tried his own hand at pie-tin-tossing, paint-can-lid-hurling and plate-skimming. All this experience might have remained little more than a childhood memory had it not been for the flying-saucer craze.

In 1947 Kenneth Arnold, a Washington State businessman, was flying his private plane past Mount Rainier. Suddenly he spotted a formation of nine strange aircraft. They weren't ordinary aircraft. They were discs that flew without wings or engines and disappeared at impossible speed as Arnold drew nearer. When the pilot told reporters about his encounter, he said the mysterious objects looked like "upside down saucers." The newspapers coined the term "flying saucers" and the name stuck. In less than a year, the whole country was flying-saucer crazy. People began seeing flying saucers everywhere, wondering if they came from outer space. The government studied flying saucers. Authors wrote millions of words on the subject.

As the saucer craze grew, Walt Morrison's inventive mind saw a fantastic opportunity. Why not cash in on the mania by making his own flying saucers? Why not turn those tossed pie tins into a full-scale fad? Morrison began experimenting with commercial pie tins in an effort to make them more stable. He failed. A metal saucer, Morrison decided, would never work.

Luckily, Morrison lived in the early days of the Plastic Age. Crude plastics had been around for several decades, but it wasn't until World War II that really modern plastics were developed. In those days plastic was looked upon as a miracle substance, the wave of the future. Only after plastic began replacing other materials did people begin thinking of it as "cheap." Walt Morrison took a block of tenite, one of the early plastics, and carved out a cupped disc with sloping, rounded edges – the great-grandaddy of all modern Frisbees. The inventor scrounged up the money to buy a plastic molding machine and went into the flying saucer business.

Morrison sold his first Flyin' Saucers at a Los Angeles county fair. Actually, he didn't sell the discs themselves. He sold pieces of "invisible wire." Morrison and a helper would walk through the fair crowds, holding their hands in the air as if they were carrying a wire between them. "Make way for the invisible wire!" they would shout. Curious fairgoers followed the strange procession. When they reached the booth, Morrison and the assistant pretended to attach the "wire" to two posts. Then the inventor pulled out a Morrison Flyin' Saucer. He had practised so well that he could send the saucer straight from one post to the other. The disc seemed to be guided by an invisible string. Onlookers crowded around asking how the gadget worked and how they could buy one.

"Oh, I don't sell the saucers," Morrison explained. "I only sell the wire. It comes in hundred-foot lengths for a penny a foot. If you buy the wire, I'll toss in the saucer for free."

The biggest problem with the Morrison Flyin' Saucer was the tendency of its plastic to become brittle when cold. If a saucer hit something hard, like an asphalt street after the sun went down, it would burst into a million pieces. Morrison offered a free replacement Flyin' Saucer to players whose saucers had broken if the owner brought in every single piece. The company had to replace only four saucers.

Despite the shattered saucers, Morrison's toy began to catch on. He refined his invention in 1951, using a tougher plastic. He still drew heavily on the flying-saucer idea. (This disc had a raised "cabin" with portholes in it.) He named his new model the Pluto Platter. At about that time, Rich Knerr and A.K. Melin were nursing along their small California toy company. Wham-O, as the company was called, specialized in slingshots. In their travels the two men saw many Pluto Platters flying through the California skies. The saucer caught their interest, and they tracked down Walt Morrison. History was made when Morrison, Knerr and Melin signed on the dotted line. Wham-O bought the Pluto Platter design and began to produce the first of over one hundred million flying discs that have filled the heavens during the last twenty years.

The Pluto Platter's popularity grew slowly. The saucer was pushed aside in 1958 when Wham-O's miracle product, the Hula Hoop, caught on. The new fad nearly killed the Platter. But the Wham-O people were sure they had a hit on their hands. They went on sales trips throughout the country. One of them took Rich Knerr close to Yale University, where he heard of the legendary Frisbie tins and the sport of Frisbie-ing. Knerr liked the name and decided to use it for the Wham-O saucer. However, as he had only heard but had never seen the name, he misspelled it "Frisbee." The new name was first used in 1959.

In the early 1960s, Ed Headrick, the vice-president of Wham-O, came up with the refinement that saved the Frisbee's life. He found that by putting raised "flight rings" on the saucers, the Frisbee would be more stable and accurate. Headrick pushed the plastic disc as a sport, not just a toy, and his strategy worked. The Frisbee shot to fame in the middle and late 1960s and has been going strong ever since.

Analysis

The Fascinating World of Dreams

1. Obviously the student writer of this very good saturation report has done a great deal of research on his topic. How many different sources has he used? What are they? Who do you think his intended audience is?

2. Has he told you more or less about dreaming than you wanted to know?

3. He breaks down his paper into discussions of many different aspects of dreams, such as whether or not we dream in colour. Which did you find most interesting? Which was the best handled? Did you find any that should have been handled more fully?

4. Did you find the writer's references to his own or his family's dreaming habits interesting or distracting?

5. In what ways would this paper be different had it been written as a research essay (Assignment 12)?

The Frisbee

1. This saturation report discusses in detail the history of the Frisbee. Can you tell where the reporters found their information?

2. This article was designed to convey information about Frisbees. To what audience?

3. What types of supporting evidence (Activity 2) were used?

4. Is there anything you would like to know about Frisbees that the article does not mention? (If you would like to learn how to throw a Frisbee, see Assignment 14.)

5. Perhaps you would like to write a saturation report about the history of a past or current fad, such as video games, pet rocks, or hula hoops.

Assignment 14 Instructions

Introduction

We spend much of our lives in giving or receiving instructions: recipes, grocery lists, directions to an out-of-the-way spot, assembly or operating instructions, explanations of how to do any number of projects, and so on. In all cases, the key to writing effective instructions is making sure they can be followed.

Assignment

In 200 to 400 words, write a set of instructions or directions.

Prewriting Suggestions

1. For this assignment, choose a topic for yourself or modify one of these: how to scuba dive, slalom, macramé, raise guppies, change a typewriter ribbon, or any other activity that you know how to do.

2. Your format for this assignment can be a letter, report, memo, expository paragraph, or whatever you wish. Furthermore, you can use lists and diagrams. State your writing variables; for example:

> **Topic:** how I do my math homework
> **Audience:** my math teacher
> **Purpose:** so I can explain what my procedure is – if I am doing anything incorrectly, my math teacher will tell me
> **Format:** letter (which includes directions)
>
> or
>
> **Topic:** how to change the typewriter ribbon
> **Audience:** my sister
> **Purpose:** so she will change the ribbon correctly
> **Format:** memo (which includes a set of instructions)
> **Persona:** I am going to write as though I were the typewriter (see Activities 1 and 19)

Drafting Suggestions

1. List all the information that your reader will need. Do not be concerned about the order, simply list information as it occurs to you. What materials will be required? What terms will you have to define? What steps will your reader have to take to perform the activity?

2. Number the steps in your list in the order you expect your reader to follow them.

3. Write your first draft following the order you have set up.

4. If you need to define a term, try to work the definition into your prose smoothly and unobtrusively. Your reader does not want to learn terminology, but to be able to follow the instructions or directions as easily as possible.

5. Use simple, direct sentences.

6. Usually instructions are written in the second person: "After you do that, do this."

7. Keep an appropriate list of transitional devices from Activity 3 near you as you write to help you make your instructions coherent.

8. Listing may be used; in fact, it may be advisable. (You may want to list items needed to assemble something, for instance.)

9. Diagrams may sometimes explain a process better than words, so, if you begin to bog down in wordiness, try a graph, map, or diagram.

10. Often one- or two-sentence paragraphs are clearer than long, complicated ones. Shorter paragraphs also produce more clean space on the paper and make instructions look less complicated for your reader.

11. Check your draft to ensure that your reader will understand how the activity is performed. Are the directions complete and in the right order? There is nothing more frustrating than discovering, after you have completed one step, that something else should have preceded it.

12. Numbering each step may be appropriate.

13. You have just read a set of instructions.

Revising Suggestions

The true test of whether your instructions or directions work is, of course, in the hands of your reader. If he or she successfully completes your instructions, your writing works. However, you should test your instructions *before* you present them to your reader by following them yourself. As you go through them, ask yourself, "Have I left anything out? Is what I have said in logical sequence?"

When you or your peers edit your set of instructions, apply the check list from Appendix B as well as the following specific items:

1. Are further details, more precise wording, or illustrations needed to clarify your directions?

2. Have you explained each step in the order in which it is performed?

3. Would the use of transitional words such as "first," "next," "then," and "finally" lead the reader more easily from one step to the next?

4. Are the directions divided logically into paragraphs or some kind of listing?

Polishing Suggestions

Besides using Appendix C to help you polish your instructions, make sure that your entire presentation is set up in a clear way. A cluttered page is hard to read.

Models

How to Throw a Frisbee
by Murray Suid and Ron Harris

Frisbee tossers use dozens of different throws and catches. These range from the simplest techniques to elaborate trick shots only an expert can do. Here are the basics of throwing a Frisbee. Once you have them down pat, you can work on fancier throws.

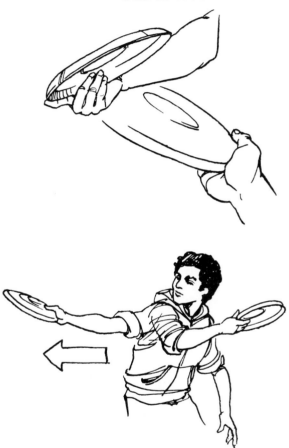

The *basic Frisbee grip*. Hold the Frisbee comfortably in the palm of your throwing hand. Your first finger should rest along the rim of the Frisbee. The other three fingers curl underneath. Your thumb is on top of the Frisbee.

The *backhand toss* is one of the most common Frisbee throws. Turn your shoulder toward the target. Extend your arm so that your index finger points where you want the Frisbee to go. Bring your throwing arm back, bending your elbow and cocking wrist around. Then straighten your arm. At the moment your arm is fully extended, let the Frisbee go with a snap of the wrist. At the same time take a step forward with your right foot (if you're right-handed). At the end of the throw your finger should be pointing at the target.

The key to accurate throws is to keep the Frisbee as flat as possible when you let it go. The flatter your throw, the straighter the Frisbee's path will be. When you start out, throw at a target that isn't too far away; 25 or 30 feet will do. Once you've perfected your short-range aim, begin moving the target back.

Another popular throw is the *underhand toss*. Face the target squarely, your arm pointing where you want the Frisbee to go. Use the same basic grip. But this time bring your arm behind you until it's nearly parallel to the ground. To toss the Frisbee, bring your arm forward, bending the elbow slightly as your hand comes under. Extend your arm, launching the Frisbee with a flip of the wrist. As you throw, take a step forward with the foot opposite your throwing arm (the left foot if you are right-handed). Once again, try to keep the Frisbee on a level, flat flight path.

Even if you are a beginning Frisbee thrower, you have probably learned how to throw *curves*. You simply tip the disc as it is released. To make the Frisbee's flight path curve to the right, toss the disc with the left side up and the right down. For a left-hand curve, keep the left side of the Frisbee lower than the right.

Know How to Complain

Most of us have probably experienced problems with products or services and wondered about the best way to remedy the situation. Yet when we make a complaint, we often seem to be sent running in circles, directed from one salesperson to another, receiving little, if any satisfaction.

Knowing how to complain effectively is an important consumer skill. It can make the difference between a satisfactory settlement and a complete rejection of your request, says Consumer and Corporate Affairs Canada.

The first step towards resolving a justified consumer problem is to make your complaint to someone in authority in the company with which the problem arose.

Identify yourself and explain your problem clearly and concisely.

If possible, provide the bill of sale, the name and model number of the product, and the date of purchase. State what action you want the store to take on your complaint, such as replacing the item or refunding your money.

If you are making the complaint by letter, be specific. Include photocopies of receipts, guarantees, cancelled cheques, copies of previous correspondence, and any other relevant material.

If your local merchant cannot, or will not, help you to resolve your problem, complain to the manufacturer. If he ignores you or refuses to remedy your complaint, it's time to seek help elsewhere.

If the problem involves a specific law, a government agency may be able to help.

If your complaint falls within an unlegislated area, try sending a letter to your local newspaper if it has a consumer-action-line column, or to a trade association to which the company in question belongs.

A copy of your correspondence could also be sent to any local consumer association.

It's best to avoid problems, of course, so before you buy from any store, check its reputation with the Better Business Bureau.

Preparation is the Key to Success

To succeed at a job interview, career advisers and interviewers suggest that you:

1. Research the firm you are interested in joining. If possible, talk to people who already work there. Be prepared to show interest in and ask questions about the company. Include such things as company policies and future plans.

2. Find out as much as you can about the interviewer. Ask friends who work in the firm about interests, temperament, idiosyncracies.

3. Know specifically what you want to do. Be prepared to explain how your skills relate to a specific opening.

4. Make a list of positive points about yourself. If asked about your strengths, don't be afraid to say, "I'm good with numbers" or "My human-relations skills are good."

5. Practise your responses. Ask a friend to join you in role-playing and to possibly alert you to annoying characteristics, such as distracting slang or speech patterns.

6. Be on time, or phone ahead if you are delayed.

7. Watch your appearance. You don't have to appear in "your best bib and tucker," but you should appear to be neat and professional. Some companies are more formal than others; if possible, note how people doing similar jobs to the one for which you are applying dress.

8. Give the interviewer your full attention. Employers love to hear someone wants to work for them.

9. Don't *initiate* salary discussions in the first interview, but be prepared to discuss salary so that you don't sell yourself too cheaply.

10. Be prepared to answer questions such as the following in an interview:
a) Why should I hire you?
b) Why do you want to work here?
c) What interests you about this position?
d) How long will you stay with the company?
e) What are your ambitions?
f) What are your greatest accomplishments?
g) Why do you want to change jobs?

11. Relax. Consider the interview as a conversation.

12. Be tenacious. Don't be afraid to ask when a decision will be made. If your interviewer says he or she will call you in four days, but fails to do so, call back and ask politely if a decision has been reached yet.

Excerpt from *Doing It with Style*

by Quentin Crisp and Donald Carroll

Style in speech is simply the ability to say exactly what you mean in a way that is distinctive. It is a skill that few possess.

The most crucial element in speaking with style is your voice, the perfect instrument for conveying your distinctiveness. The challenge is to make your voice even more distinctive than it is already, so that one word from you over the telephone identifies you as unmistakably as would a glimpse of you in person.

... we would now like to enumerate seven subsidiary ways to refine your speaking style.

1. Be consistent: Just as you shouldn't have a different type of dress for different people or occasions, you shouldn't have a different manner of speaking.

2. Learn to listen: In our eagerness to get our own message across, we often fail to hear what is actually being said to us. And thus we miss the opportunity to make a comment that is both pertinent and arresting. So remember that a good conversationalist is, first and foremost, a good listener. In fact, among people who are widely regarded as great conversationalists, there are some who hardly ever open their mouths at all.

3. Pause before speaking: This is not merely a rephrasing of the standard advice to think before you speak (although that is certainly sound advice). The point here is that you should be seen to be thinking before you speak, and therefore to be taking seriously what has been said to you.

4. Speak softly: Actually, there is nothing wrong with speaking loudly. It's just that you should always speak with more or less the same voice level, and as there are times when a loud voice is inappropriate, it is easier to keep your speaking voice style intact if you keep your voice down. This is something that Mafia dons have long known, and that Muhammad Ali has recently learned.

5. Don't try to be funny: Real humour has nothing to do with jokes, or with any other prefabricated narrative form. Somerset Maugham once observed that if you make people laugh, they will think you trivial. While that isn't strictly true, he had a point: the effort to make people laugh is certainly trivializing.

6. Avoid jargon and slang: Both have two major drawbacks, either of which would be sufficient to disqualify them from having any place in the vocabulary of a stylist. They are both fashions [fads], and someone with style doesn't follow fashions in speaking any more than in dressing. And both are forms of group-speak, and someone with style shuns identification with a group.

To see just how bad it can get, consider this gaseous emission from a Boston television reporter who was sent to do a story on how the airlines would fare with large numbers of people staying home over Christmas.

His report consisted of a solemn discourse on "how the no-show factor will impact on the airlines in a holiday situation." Sad to say, the man's tongue was not cut out on the spot.

7. Avoid certain subjects, such as personal disasters, your [personal relationships], your past, the flaws of others, and any subject on which your opinion is too eagerly solicited. The best way for a stylist is to single out something, anything, about the subject for which you can profess admiration. And, where possible, that something should be thoroughly inconsequential.

Ronald Firbank, the English author, demonstrated his mastery of this technique on one notable occasion when a fellow author doggedly tried to get a literary opinion out of him. Firbank at last responded, sweetly: "I adore italics, don't you?" Firbank had style.

Analysis

How to Throw a Frisbee

1. For whom do you think the Frisbee instructions were written?

2. Are they easy to follow?

3. Why were the drawings included? Are they helpful?

4. After you perfect these basic Frisbee-throwing techniques, what do you think the next step would be?

5. For some information about the history of the Frisbee, see "The Frisbee" in Assignment 13.

Know How to Complain

1. In what order have the steps been arranged? Do any seem out of place?
2. Are the instructions clear and easy to understand?
3. Is there any other advice that you think should have been included?

Preparation Is the Key to Success

1. Do you think all the necessary instructions are included?
2. Which instruction do you think is the most important?

Excerpt from *Doing It with Style*

1. What do you think is the style of this set of instructions? Do you think the style is appropriate for the subject?
2. Are the ideas clearly expressed? Are there any words you do not understand? Should they be defined?
3. Find the sentence in point two beginning, "In fact, among people ...." Of what kind of humour is it an example? Can you find at least one other example of the same kind of humour?
4. Most instructions are arranged in the order in which the author thinks they should be followed. Are these instructions arranged in that way? Why or why not? Can you suggest another method of organization?
5. Are there any instructions you would add or delete?

Assignment **15** Memo

Introduction

A memo (or memorandum) enables easy, fast communication between people in the same club, school, company, or business. Basically, a memo is a concise, informal message from one person to another. The purpose can be to make a request, to give instructions, to make an announcement, to answer a question, to confirm the main points of a conversation, and so on. Whatever its purpose, the memo saves time and provides a written record of the date of the communication, the message, the name of the sender, and the name of the recipient.

Assignment

Write two memos to someone in your school or club, to a member of your family, or, if you work, to a fellow employee. Your memos should illustrate different purposes; choose from a request, an announcement, or a summary of a meeting or conversation.

Prewriting Suggestions

1. Determine the topic and purpose of your memo: to make a request or announcement, to confirm arrangements, to summarize a conversation, and so on. If you are having difficulty choosing a topic, modify these lists of writing variables:

> **Topic and Purpose:** to request that students deposit lunch leftovers in the wastebasket
> **Audience:** my fellow students
> **Format:** memo
>
> or
>
> **Topic and Purpose:** to announce that we will be having a farewell party for Dick Jones on Saturday night
> **Audience:** my fellow employees
> **Format:** memo
>
> or
>
> **Topic and Purpose:** to summarize the arrangements for our field trip on June 8
> **Audience:** members of the camera club
> **Format:** memo

2. It is important that you have a complete knowledge of the situation about which you are writing. You may need to research or ask questions before continuing.

3. Consider the needs and interests of your reader. If you are making a request, what reasons will convince your reader to grant it? If you are supplying information, which information is essential?

Memos are often used in a business environment, where the reader needs to be informed quickly but thoroughly, so be concise.

Drafting Suggestions

1. Write a summary sentence for the memo, clearly stating the main idea of the message.

2. Jot down all of the supporting facts and ideas that you wish to include.

3. Set up your memo in the same way as one of the models. Make sure you have included at the top left corner these captions:

> **Date:**
> **To:**
> **From:**
> **Subject:**

You do not sign a memo; however, you may initial it at the bottom. There is also no need to close formally, as you would in a letter.

4. Now re-read your entire memo. Add, omit, or change anything that does not fulfil your purpose. Make sure you have caught your reader's attention and interest. You can do this by keeping the message brief and to the point, and by beginning and ending on a positive note.

5. Repeat the above suggestions for the second memo.

Revising Suggestions

When you or your peers edit your memos, apply the check list from Appendix B as well as the following specific questions:

1. Does the opening sentence summarize the content and purpose of the memo?

2. Has any vital information been omitted?

3. Can the memo be abbreviated without eliminating important information?

4. Is the *you* point of view consistent?

5. Is the end of the memo too abrupt? (Since there is no formal ending for memos, the message must end smoothly.)

6. Will your memo fill your reader's needs or produce the results that you need?

Polishing Suggestions

Besides following the suggestions in Appendix C to help you polish your memos, make sure you consider the reaction of your readers to what you have said. Perhaps your word choice may need to be slightly altered.

Models

DATE: Sept. 17, 1982
TO: Members of the Basketball Team
FROM: Coach Reed
SUBJECT: Coach Reed's Tension Release Program

I would like to draw your attention to the truly successful mess you made in the locker room the other day. I think the wet towels and unrolled bandages scattered all over the floor have never been arranged more interestingly. And I'm sure the overturned benches piled on top of each other will actually improve the psychological well-being of the team.

Since you guys seem to have an overabundance of energy, I will personally try to relieve you of some of it by having early morning practices.

"Coach Reed's Tension Release Program" will begin *tomorrow* at 7:30 A.M., under the authority of captain Bob Horton, and will continue for two weeks.

So don't forget to tell your mommies to wake you up a little bit earlier tomorrow, or you might find yourself warming the bench for the rest of the season.

DATE: March 5, 1982
TO: Members of the Pioneers' Club
FROM: Joanne Day, Acting President
SUBJECT: Next meeting

The next meeting of the Pioneers' Club will be held on Tuesday after school in the meeting room beside the library.

Items on the agenda will be:
1. election of a new President (as you know, Tony Carver had to resign for personal reasons);
2. discussion of ideas for putting together a pamphlet on the school's history;
3. discussion of the results of interviews with three elderly local residents;
4. anything else the members want to talk about.

I hope to see you there.

```
DATE:  March 11, 1982
TO:  Members of the Pioneers' Club
FROM:  Joanne Day, President
SUBJECT:  Summary of the last meeting


At the meeting of the Pioneers' Club held last Tuesday afternoon, the following
events took place:
1.  Joanne Day, Acting President, was elected President by acclamation;
2.  Mike Wong proposed, and those present agreed, that the Club advertise
in the school newspaper for old photographs of the school;
3.  Mike also suggested that students ask any parents who were also students
here for a short note about their experiences;
4.  Susan Delorme said that Mrs. Cranes, the wife of the school's first
principal, would be happy to come and talk with us about the school's
beginnings, and it was agreed that Joanne should ask her to attend our next
meeting on Tuesday.
5.  There was no other business; the meeting adjourned at 4:05 P.M.

                                   JD
```

Analysis

From Coach Reed

1. This is an example of a request memo. What is being requested? Does the memo fulfil its purpose?

2. It contains several examples of sarcasm, such as "the truly successful mess." Can you find others? Why are they included?

3. What do you think the members of the team would think of this memo?

From Joanne Day, Acting President

1. This is an example of an announcement memo. What is being announced? Does the memo fulfil its purpose?

2. The writer uses the technique of listing. Do you think this is a good idea? What is the effect of making a list?

From Joanne Day, President

1. This is an example of a summary memo. What is being summarized? Does the memo fulfil its purpose?

2. If you were a member of the Pioneers' Club and could not attend the meeting, would this memo provide enough information for you?

Assignment 16   The Proposal and Report

Introduction

In many situations a proposal must be presented in order to obtain approval for a project. Often, once the project has been completed, a report must be submitted outlining the success or failure of the project.

Therefore, this assignment has two parts. First, you are to write a proposal where you present either a problem, with your suggestions for solving it, or an idea with your methods for making it feasible. Second, you are to write a report based on the success or failure of your proposal.

Part One

Write a proposal for a solution to a problem or an idea that you would like to see become a reality. The subject of your proposal may concern your school, club or organization, job, or family.

Prewriting Suggestions

1. Decide on a real problem or idea about which to write your proposal. Here are a few topics to get you thinking:
   a) Propose that a rock band come to your school for a lunch hour or a school dance.
   b) Propose to your parents that your curfew be extended to midnight.
   c) Propose that you and a friend set up a business to cut your neighbours' lawns.
   d) Propose that you enlarge your office at work.

2. If your proposal presents a solution to a problem, summarize the problem before attempting to arrive at a solution. There may be several possible solutions; consider the advantages and disadvantages of each before settling on the best solution.

3. State your proposal in a concise statement. Be specific. Now, outline the reasons that support your proposal. This may involve research or interviews. (Knowing how to obtain the correct information will save you a lot of time and effort, as well as making it more likely that your proposal will be accepted.)

4. Investigate all the factors involved in your proposal: costs, materials, time, labour, and so on.

5. Once you have all your data, jot down your intentions, for example:

Topic and Purpose: to increase my allowance
Audience: my father
Format: letter (which includes a proposal)

or

Topic and Purpose: to invite a rock band to give a concert
Audience: the principal
Format: memo (which includes a proposal)

Drafting Suggestions

1. Your main purpose in writing the proposal should be to gain the interest and support of your audience. Consider what your reader's interests will be. Money? Time? Potential profits? Do the advantages of your proposal outweigh the disadvantages?

2. Prepare an outline of your proposal. A suggested outline presenting a proposal to invite a rock band to give a concert, follows.

Outline

Proposal to Mrs. Hayes, Principal, Macdonald Secondary School

I. Nature of proposal
   To invite "High Strung" to give a concert at noon in the cafeteria

II. Reasons for the invitation
   A. Desire expressed for lunch-time entertainment
   B. The popularity of "High Strung" among the students
   C. Success of previous concerts
   D. Possible source of funds for student council

III. Arrangements to be made
   A. Rate
   B. Publicity
   C. Sale of tickets
      1. Pre-concert
      2. At the door
   D. Preparation of the cafeteria
      1. Setting up band equipment and chairs
      2. Pre- and post-concert clean-up
      3. Supervision
   E. Responsibility for damage

IV. Conclusion
   Highly beneficial for everyone

3. In order for your proposal to be taken seriously, it should be well constructed and written in a businesslike manner. Therefore, make sure your word choice, sentence structure, transitions, and paragraphs follow the principles of quality writing.

4. Read the proposal (in the Model section) that uses the preceding outline.

Revising Suggestions

You may want to ask your peers to assume they are the final reader of your proposal: your principal, vice-principal, employer, boss, and so forth. They should mention any problems that might cause them to turn your proposal down. Ponder their reasons, then revise your report.

When you or your peers edit your proposal, apply the check list from Appendix B as well as the following specific points:

1. Is your proposal clearly and concisely stated?

2. Have you supplied all the information that a reader would require to assess your proposal?

3. Is the information in your proposal organized into general categories? Have you followed an outline?

4. Is your tone straightforward and businesslike?

Once you have heard your teacher/editor's comments on your proposal, you may either go to Part Two of this assignment, or you may submit your proposal in earnest to its intended reader. This is by far the best test for your proposal. If you make the proposal a real one and obtain acceptance, you will feel more successful than if you receive an "A" for a classroom assignment.

Polishing Suggestions

Apply the suggestions from Appendix C before you submit your proposal to its final reader.

Part Two

Write a report on the successful or unsuccessful execution of your proposal.

There are so many different kinds of reports that in order to gain experience in writing all of them, you would have to take a special course in report writing. In such a course you would learn the characteristics of progress reports, analytic reports, feasibility reports, history reports, procedural reports, informative reports, interpretive reports, status reports, and narrative reports. For this assignment, you can become familiar with the general characteristics of report writing by writing one to follow your proposal assignment.

Prewriting Suggestions

1. If you indeed wrote a real-life proposal for the first part of this assignment, and had that proposal accepted, you may be in an ideal situation to write the second part of the assignment. You should now prepare an analytical report for the same audience who accepted your original proposal.

If you composed a fictitious proposal, you should now assume that your proposal was accepted, and the event has occurred, so that you can prepare an analytical report.

2. The purpose of this assignment is to report on the success or failure of the execution of your proposal to the person who accepted it originally.

3. Begin to gather information on your project: the time it took, the costs, and most importantly, the results. Compare this information with the estimates you presented in your proposal.

4. Once you have all your necessary information, you should jot down your writing variables, for example:

> **Topic and Purpose:** to report the results of my increased allowance
> **Audience:** my father
> **Format:** letter (which includes a report)
>
> or
>
> **Topic and Purpose:** to report the results of the concert and to thank those responsible for making it a success
> **Audience:** the principal
> **Format:** report

Drafting Suggestions

1. Formal reports have many parts: title page, letter of transmittal, preface or foreword, table of contents, list of illustrations, abstract or summary, body, and appendices. When you write your report for this assignment, however, you need include only a letter of transmittal and the body.

a) Letter of Transmittal
This letter follows the conventional letter format and states its message simply. What you basically need to say is, "Here is the report." However, you may include your main conclusion and acknowledgements for any help you received in preparing the report.

b) Body
This is the main part of your report. It should be written as an expository essay with an introductory paragraph, developmental paragraphs, and a concluding paragraph.

2. In the body of the report, present the details of the event in some logical order. You may want to begin with an overall assessment of the project, then go on to discuss specific aspects: costs, results, and so on. A common method of concluding a report is to give a recommendation for future action.

3. In many cases, the project will have been a "mixed success" – partially successful, partially unsuccessful. Consider both the positive and negative aspects; then decide if, on balance, the advantages outweighed the disadvantages. Your decision will form the summary or conclusion of your report.

4. Prepare an outline for your report. A suggested outline, presenting a report on the noon-hour concert, follows.

Outline

Report to Mrs. Hayes, principal of Macdonald Secondary School

   I. Very successful concert

  II. Evaluation of success
     A. Over $300 raised for student council
     B. Students' comments
     C. Teachers' reactions
     D. Band's reaction

 III. State of cafeteria
     A. Relatively clean
     B. One broken chair

 IV. Recommendation
     "High Strung" be invited back

5. After you have written your first draft, rewrite it, including any pertinent information that you have left out, omitting any unnecessary repetitions, and changing anything that does not present the facts accurately. Although you no doubt wish to present a favourable report, you must be truthful about your findings. You do not want to be caught in an embarrassing position when your final reader says, "But what about the riot? You didn't mention the broken vending machines."

6. Read the report (in the Model section) that uses the preceding outline.

Revising Suggestions

Ask your peers to read the report as though they were the intended reader. Is your report well-organized (have you followed an outline) and complete (are all facts included and are they accurate)? Does your writing pass the check lists outlined in Appendix B?

Polishing Suggestions

After you have made your report uniquely yours, cover your report to protect the inner pages. On the cover place your name and the title of your report, then present it to your final reader.

Models   Proposal

DATE: January 30, 1982
TO: Mrs. Hayes
FROM: Henry Ballard
SUBJECT: "High Strung" concert

Statement of intent:

As a member of the student council of Macdonald Secondary School, I would like to propose that the council be allowed to invite the popular local group "High Strung" to perform at a.lunch-time concert.

Proposal:

Several students have requested that a band visit our school during a noon hour to give a concert. "High Strung" has played in several local clubs, as well as at a dance at Whitton Secondary School. The band, one of whose members was a student here, is very popular among the students, so sales of tickets for a lunch-time concert by them would probably raise several hundred dollars for the student council.

If we receive your permission to invite "High Strung," we will arrange with the group's manager a date when the band would be free and the cafeteria could be prepared.

Members of the student council would put advertising posters supplied by the group on all school bulletin boards and would also place an advertisement about the concert in the school newspaper.

Pre-concert ticket sales would take place in the main lobby during the three lunch hours before the concert. Student council members would sell the tickets then, as well as selling tickets at the door on the day of the concert.

Volunteers chosen by the council would be responsible for arranging and cleaning up the cafeteria before and after the concert. If anything should be damaged during the concert, the student council will repair or replace it.

We would appreciate your choosing several faculty members to stay in the cafeteria during the concert, to ensure that everything goes smoothly. Mr. Smithers has already agreed to attend.

I believe that everyone in the school would benefit if a concert by "High Strung" took place here.

I feel strongly that further funding for this project is absolutely necessary and

Letter of Transmittal

Student Council Office
Macdonald Secondary School

February 24, 1982

Mrs. H.G. Hayes
Principal
Macdonald Secondary School

Dear Mrs. Hayes,

    Here is my report on the concert by "High Strung" that took place last Tuesday. Please feel free to share it with the faculty.

    Thank you very much for your interest and co-operation in making the concert such a success.

Sincerely,

Henry Ballard

Henry Ballard

Report

REPORT ON THE CONCERT BY "HIGH STRUNG" AT MACDONALD SECONDARY SCHOOL

The lunch-time concert by "High Strung," which took place last Tuesday, February 17, was, in the opinion of the members of the student council, very successful.

The council's net profit on ticket sales was $315.00. $285.00 was taken at the door. Although we are very pleased with this amount, we regret that the concert did not start on time because not everyone was inside the cafeteria by 12:30. It was also difficult to get rid of those students still eating their lunches. Some stayed for the concert without paying.

Students commented that the band performed very well. They especially enjoyed their renditions of "Rock and Roll" by Led Zeppelin, "Wanna Rock" by April Wine, "The Mob Rules" by Black Sabbath, and "21/12" by Rush. The lighting effects and the use of the fog machine were also well received. Not everyone enjoyed their use of explosions, however; some of the students were afraid that real gunpowder had been used. Pete Willows, from Division 12, was pleased to have been asked to assist their lighting man in changing the gels on the follow spot. He told us later that he may help "High Strung" with a few of their evening shows.

Mr. Swalloas and Miss Williams - who supervised the concert - had said before the concert that they did not want the band to come, but told members of the student council afterwards that they were surprised at how well-behaved the students were and how well "High Strung" played. "In fact," Mr. Swalloas said, "we enjoyed ourselves a great deal." "I never knew a rock concert could be so enjoyable," said Miss Williams.

The band's manager wrote us to say that the band had enjoyed playing here and that it would be happy to play here again.

The clean-up crew had to spend only half an hour tidying and rearranging the cafeteria, even though not all the people who volunteered actually stayed behind. The student council will replace one chair, broken by a student, with the council and the student sharing the cost.

The council's overall recommendation is to invite "High Strung" to perform here again in about one month's time; however, we feel that tickets should only be sold before the day of the concert. Also, we recommend that future noon-hour concerts be held in the auditorium or gymnasium.

The student council wishes to thank our sponsor, Mr. Smithers, and you, Mrs. Hayes, for allowing the concert to be held.

Proposal

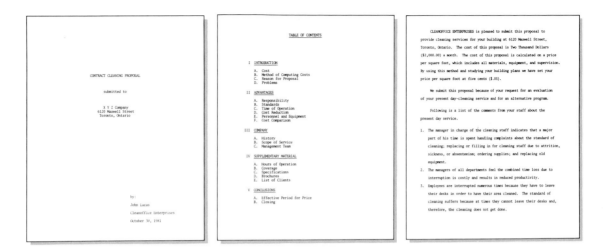

CLEANOFFICE ENTERPRISES is pleased to submit this proposal to provide cleaning services for your building at 6120 Maxwell Street, Toronto, Ontario. The cost of this proposal is Two Thousand Dollars ($2,000.00) a month. The cost of this proposal is calculated on a price per square foot, which includes all materials, equipment, and supervision. By using this method and studying your building plans we have set your price per square foot at five cents ($.05).

We submit this proposal because of your request for an evaluation of your present day-cleaning service and for an alternative program.

Following is a list of the comments from your staff about the present day service.

1. The manager in charge of the cleaning staff indicates that a major part of his time is spent handling complaints about the standard of cleaning; replacing or filling in for cleaning staff due to attrition, sickness, or absenteeism; ordering supplies, and replacing old equipment.

2. The managers of all departments feel the combined time loss due to interruption is costly and results in reduced productivity.

3. Employees are interrupted numerous times because they have to leave their desks in order to have their area cleaned. The standard of cleaning suffers because at times they cannot leave their desks and therefore, the cleaning does not get done.

4. Employees find the noise of the vacuum cleaners is, at times, disturbing.

5. Employees' work quality suffers because they become annoyed with too many disturbances.

After a careful analysis of these comments, we feel our proposal gives the following advantages over your present day service:

1. We assume all responsibility for cleaning staff, equipment, supplies, and supervision. This will free the manager presently in charge of service for more important matters.

2. Our supervision will maintain acceptable standards of cleaning and help reduce employee complaints.

3. Cleaning will not be performed during your work day, eliminating any disturbances. This will also reduce time loss and costs, as well as improve quality and productivity.

4. Our cleaning staff are professional people who use the most up-to-date equipment. This eliminates the need for replacing equipment and ensures work will be completed.

5. We invite you to compare present costs for wages, fringe benefits, supplies, equipment, and supervision with the cost of this proposal. We feel confident that our price will result in a saving or at least be comparable.

CLEANOFFICE ENTERPRISES has been in the contract cleaning business since 1925 and is the largest company in this field in North America. We presently have a cleaning staff of more than nine thousand (9,000) employees who are responsible for the maintenance of forty million (40,000,000) square feet of floor space a night. Our programs have been implemented in hospitals, sports complexes, office buildings, colleges, universities, elementary and high schools, and industrial plants.

Our management team has specially trained professionals in methodology, operations, sales, and supervision that are available to you.

The time which our cleaning staff will be on your premises is between 6:00 P.M. and midnight Monday to Friday. The complete service provided will include window washing, waxing and polishing floors, wall washing, cleaning of all furniture and fixtures, washroom cleaning, and all other nightly housekeeping tasks.

This work will be performed with the latest equipment, which will be stored on your premises. A list of our staff, brochures of equipment and supplies to be used, and a detailed copy of specifications outlining the above accompany this proposal. Also included is a list of clients for your reference.

The price quoted in this proposal is in effect for sixty (60) days, commencing November 1, 1981.

We thank you for the opportunity of submitting this proposal and look forward to hearing from you. We welcome any comments concerning this proposal and can be contacted at 489-0314.

Analysis

"High Strung" Concert Proposal

1. How closely did the writer follow his outline? Was anything left out?

2. Are his reasons for wanting to invite the group clear? Do the reasons convince you?

3. Do you think he has considered all the objections the principal might raise?

Report on the Concert

1. Does the letter of transmittal for this report seem necessary?

2. How closely does this report follow its outline?

3. Does the report make clear to you why the writer thought the concert was successful?

4. Are the recommendations Henry makes consistent with his report of how the concert went?

Contract Cleaning Proposal

1. This student model is written as a professional proposal from a cleaning firm to a prospective client. Have the details of the proposal been made clear?

2. The writer indicates that the proposed contract is based on the recommendation of employees. How do you think this fact will affect the client's decision whether or not to accept it?

3. Within the introduction, the writer indicates that he has been asked by XYZ Company to prepare a report on the present cleaning service. The report is included in the introduction. If Cleanoffice Enterprises do not satisfy XYZ Company, who would write a report to follow up this proposal? What would it deal with? To whom would it be written?

4. Examine the outline. Can you find all the parts of the outline in the body of the proposal? Would it have been better to introduce each part of the proposal with the headings from the outline? If you think so, where would you place "Introduction," "Advantages," "Company," "Supplementary Material," and "Conclusions"?

5. Legitimate business jargon ("time loss") is used throughout. Find other examples.

Assignment **17** The Personal Letter

Introduction

In these days of instant communication by telephone and satellite, you may not think it is necessary to develop the ability to write a clear and sincere personal letter. But receiving a letter, simply because the writer had to make an effort to compose it and put it on paper, has an impact that a phone call cannot duplicate.

More than 200 years ago, the Earl of Chesterfield, one of the most famous letter writers, recommended to his son that the writer of a personal letter should use the "charm and wit of extemporaneous conversation." If you follow the Earl's advice, your readers will look forward to your next personal letter.

There are two parts to this assignment. The first deals with the conversational or friendly letter, the kind you are most likely to write to a friend or relative; the second deals with personal letters written for specific purposes. Your teacher may ask you to do one or both parts.

Part One

Write a friendly letter of about 250 words.

Prewriting Suggestions

1. Before you begin this assignment, do a bit of personal stocktaking. Do you owe letters to anyone? Would you like to begin corresponding with someone? If possible, make this assignment a real-life one.
2. When you write a conversational or friendly letter, follow these suggestions:
   a) Keep in mind the personality of the person to whom you write.
   b) Re-read the last letter you received from this person and discuss the things that he or she has shown an interest in.
   c) Write about people and events you are both familiar with and curious about.
   d) Avoid a patronizing tone or an artificially literary style.
3. The very fact that you take time to write denotes thoughtfulness; recall your reaction when you last received a personal letter. Because receiving personal mail should always be a pleasant experience, remember that your letter should be easy to read. And it should be characterized by naturalness, sincerity, and originality.

4. List your writing variables; for example:
   Topic: my first month of school
   Audience: Herbie
   Purpose: to tell him how much I miss him and my old school
   Format: friendly letter

Part Two

Write one of the following: a "bread and butter" letter, a "thank-you" letter, a congratulatory letter, a letter of condolence, or an invitation.

Prewriting Suggestions

1. To help you determine what kinds of letters to write, read these definitions:

   a) **The "Bread and Butter" Letter:** When you have been a guest for a meal, holiday, trip, or the like, write a brief letter of appreciation within a day after your visit. Even though you have already thanked your host or hostess in person, a personal letter is still appropriate.

   b) **The "Thank-you" Letter:** When you have received a present or any kind of favour, write an acknowledgement letter as soon as possible. Do not become too sentimental, but do reveal your sincere appreciation for the thoughtfulness that was shown to you.

   c) **The Congratulatory Letter:** When a friend has achieved some kind of honour or won an award, a congratulatory letter from you ensures the continuation of a solid friendship.

   d) **The Letter of Condolence:** All friends really look forward to "get well" letters; friends who have had a death in their family appreciate knowing that someone else is sharing their sadness. Be brief but be sincere in your statements of sympathy.

   e) **The Invitation:** Everyone likes to be invited to a special function. Make sure you send your invitation at least two weeks in advance of the event, and include all the details of the function.

2. If you have not done part one of this assignment, you should read the prewriting suggestions there.

3. Do you know someone who would like one of these letters? If so, write up your intention, including the variables, in a form similar to this:

   Topic and Purpose: to congratulate him on getting a job
   Audience: Joe
   Format: congratulatory letter
   or
   Topic and Purpose: to invite them to a Valentine's Day party
   Audience: twelve friends
   Format: invitation (which I'll photocopy)

Drafting Suggestions

1. In writing a personal letter you have much more leeway than in writing a business letter (Assignment 18): in your choice of stationery, in whether you type or write in longhand, and in your organization. Your personal letter, though, should be legible and neat. Avoid crowding margins: left, right, top, and bottom. You want your letter to be enjoyed and appreciated.

2. Most personal letters should have the following sections:

a) Sender's address
b) Date line
c) Salutation (Dear ...)
d) Body of the letter
e) Complimentary close (Yours sincerely)
f) Signature

See if you can find the six parts of a personal letter in the model letters at the end of this assignment. Also note the form and punctuation of each. (If you are confused, see the details of form and punctuation in the drafting suggestions in Assignment 18.)

Revising Suggestions

When you or your peers edit your letter, apply the check lists from Appendix B as well as the following specific items.

1. Is your letter interesting? If not, perhaps you have not considered your reader's interests, or have not written about topics that matter to you.

2. Is the tone of your letter appropriate for your intended purpose and audience? If you are writing a conversational letter to a close friend, the tone of your letter should be warm, informal, and reflect your personality.

3. Is your letter honest? If your "thank-yous," congratulations or condolences are stilted, perhaps it's because you have not written about how you truly feel.

Polishing Suggestions

Use the polishing suggestions in Appendix C as well as these specific items.

1. Write or type your final copy.

2. Fold the letter, and place it in an envelope which has the receiver's address in the centre and your address in the upper left corner.

3. Send it off to your intended reader and await a reply.

Models

13 Smuffow Avenue
Toronto, Ontario
M1C 4T5
March 12, 1982

Dear Angelina,

So much has happened to me since I've come to Canada that I haven't had time to sit down and tell you about everything. Today, I have time.

The plane was three hours late arriving in Toronto because of bad weather; in fact, we almost turned around and went back to London but the pilot decided to go on instead. The Customs inspector opened all my suitcases and checked everything. When I finally arrived in the area where people were waiting for arriving passengers, I could not find Uncle Giuseppe. I didn't want to start looking for him in case I got lost in that big airport. Finally I went to one of the Alitalia counters and the lady phoned Uncle Giuseppe for me and found out he was on his way. He arrived about half an hour later and took me home, where Aunt Rita had supper ready. I was so tired I fell asleep right after supper.

Toronto is a very big city. It has an underground like London's (they call it the subway) but not so old and dirty. There are many big buildings downtown with shops underground that connect right to the subway. Toronto is filled with many wonderful sights, but the most beautiful place I've visited is a house called Casa Loma that was built by a millionaire; it even has a cannon in the bedroom!

I must go to my next class now, so I can't write any more. I miss you and Carlo and Mama very much.

Would you believe that I wrote this letter in my writing class and I am going to get a mark for it?

Write soon.

Love,

Lucia

5633 12th Ave.,
Langley, B.C.,
V4C 1X6.
December 12, 1981.

Dear Heather,

I was thrilled to hear about the new addition to your trophy collection.
The regional award for Best Pianist is really hard to win, but I was not
surprised to find out that you left the other contestants behind in a
cloud of music notes.

Where do you play next? Are you going to the "All Ontario Music
Festival"? Wherever you go, I am sure that you will play your best,
more than likely winning whatever prize is being offered.

I feel congratulations are in order at present and am sending them along
with my love and heartfelt wishes. May you succeed at whatever you try.

Take care of yourself; watch those fingers!

Best wishes always,

Ida

1916 Granville St.,
Swift Current, Sask.,
S5T 4L2.
30 March 1980

Dear Mike,

On behalf of myself and my family I want to express our deepest and
most sincere sympathy to you on the death of your sister.

Lorraine was a truly loving person, and I know that to lose her so
suddenly and so young must have been a great shock.

I know there is little I can say or do that can comfort you at a
time like this, but if there is something I can do to make your burden
easier, I hope you will let me know.

Sincerely,

Marianne

July first,

Dear Betty,

Please come to a pool party on Friday, July 19, 1982 at 4:30 P.M.

PLACE: my home, 9821 Rustic Drive,
REASON: to help celebrate my birthday

Bring your bathing suit, a towel, and a hearty appetite. Mom is making an Italian dinner with a huge five-layer cake.

I'm inviting fourteen friends in all and thought it might be fun if we all did something together after the party. So, everybody is going to get a chance to write down one suggestion on a piece of paper and put it in a hat. At 7:30, I will draw one out. We all have to agree to follow the suggestion. Great idea?

I sure hope you can come, but in case you can't please phone me at 224-5302.

Barny

February, 5th

Dear Frank,

I am writing to thank you and your brother for having me as a guest at your cabin in Ste. Agathe last weekend. What a feast you provided on Sunday morning! I can still see the view of the Laurentians glistening in the sunlight from my bedroom window. And I can still smell the Eggs Benedict we had for breakfast. I didn't know you were such a good cook!

I look forward to entertaining both of you in the next few months at my family's cabin on Lake Memphremagog. I just hope the fish will be biting. I'll be in touch with you as soon as I can make the arrangements.

Once again, thanks for an unforgettable weekend.

Hank

#306 3165 W. 39th Ave.
St. John's, Nfld.
02C 5M4
10, 31, 1980

Dear Bill,

On behalf of the Fall Weekend Committee, I would like to express our thanks for your assistance in making our Smallwood-Lake-Weekend such a success.

In the past, the Saturday evening entertainment has been a bit difficult because people were very reluctant to accept responsibility for it. Therefore, you have no idea what relief and gratitude I felt when you so readily agreed to organize it. You were certainly responsible for the most enjoyable moments of the weekend; both audience and performers enjoyed themselves.

I deeply appreciate your assistance. When people like you take on these responsibilities, my job becomes much easier.

Sincerely,

Billie-Lee Binkley

Billie-Lee Binkley
(Chairperson of the Fall Weekend
Committee)

Analysis

Lucia's Friendly Letter

Such a letter between friends who have moved from one country to another can be a joy to receive and, if you think about it, quite easy to write. The reader will be eager to hear any news about the new country. What does Lucia say in her letter that will be of interest to her friend?

Ida's Letter of Congratulations

1. Why was this letter written? Does Ida give Heather her message in a clear and friendly way?
2. Is the letter long enough for its message? Can it be shortened?

Marianne's Letter of Condolence

1. If you were Mike, would you feel that you could call upon Marianne?
2. How has she shown her support?

Barny's Invitation

1. Does the party sound like fun? Would you go?
2. Do you think this invitation should be typed and duplicated, or written by hand fourteen times?
3. Why is the sender's address not needed?

Hank's *Bread and Butter* Letter

This kind of a thank-you letter is appreciated by the receiver. What features of the letter would Frank and his brother particularly enjoy?

Billie-Lee's *Thank-you* Letter

1. In what ways has she complimented Bill?
2. Do you think he will say yes to her next request for assistance?

Assignment **18** The Business Letter

Introduction

Almost everyone needs to know the principles of writing an effective business letter.

The advice of the Earl of Chesterfield is still relevant today. "Every paragraph should be so clear and unambiguous that the dullest fellow in the world may not be able to mistake it, nor obliged to read it twice in order to understand it."

If you follow the Earl's advice, you should be able to produce an acceptable business letter.

Assignment

Write two of the following: a letter of inquiry, reply, request, acknowledgement, complaint, or a letter in which you place an order or enclose a remittance. Make sure you use a different style and form for each letter.

Prewriting Suggestions

1. Before you begin this assignment, think. Can you make this assignment a real-life one? Maybe you would like to do one of the following:
   a) Ask someone to be your reference for a job application.
   b) Ask your local newspaper to cover your school's soccer games.
   c) Complain to a mail order company that has not filled your order but has cashed your cheque.
   d) Request a particular speaker to come to your club's next meeting.

Or perhaps you can think of other reasons for doing this assignment.

2. Once you have decided to whom you are writing, keep this person's personality in mind. It will determine the style and tone of your letter.

If you are writing to a company, try to find out – by telephoning – the name of the person to whom you should write. If this is not feasible, use a formal tone and style in the salutation and body of the letter.

3. Write out your intentions, using the writing variables. These examples may be useful:

> **Topic and Purpose:** to get a refund for a racquetball racquet that cracked after six months
> **Audience:** president of the racquet company
> **Format:** letter of complaint
>
> or
>
> **Topic and Purpose:** to obtain a character reference for a job
> **Audience:** my English teacher
> **Format:** letter of request

Drafting Suggestions

1. Business letters generally have more features than personal letters. The sections peculiar to business letters are underlined:

Sender's address	street address city, province postal code
Date line	day, month, year
Receiver's address	name and title (if known) street address city, province postal code
Attention line	title of a person or department (not always used)
Salutation	greeting (followed by a colon; a comma is used for a personal letter)
Subject line	subject of the letter (not always used)
Body of the letter	
Complimentary close	a polite ending
Pen signature	writer's signature
Typewritten signature	typed name of writer
Title or position of person who signs the letter	title (not always used)
Identification initials	initials of typist (if typist is not writer)
Special notations	enclosure notations, carbon copy note (not always used)

In order to see clearly all of the parts of a business letter, read the models and analyses.

2. There are many different ways to punctuate a business letter. The most important rule is to be consistent. The models in the polishing suggestions include examples of block, modified, and indented forms with open, mixed, and closed punctuation. Here are examples of how to present the sender's address, the receiver's address, the salutation, the subject line, the body, the complimentary close, and the signature, for each combination:

Block style, open punctuation

```
123 Fourth Street
New City, Saskatchewan
C2N 4H5
June 1, 1982

Reader's Ltd.
567 Eighth Avenue
Old City, Ontario
M3V 6H7

Dear Mr. Jones

SUBJECT:  Magazines

_____
_____
_____

Yours very truly
Bill Smith
Bill Smith
```

Block style, closed punctuation

```
123 Fourth Street,
New City, Saskatchewan,
C2N 4H5.
June 1, 1982.

Reader's Ltd.,
567 Eighth Avenue,
Old City, Ontario,
M3V 6H7.

Dear Mr. Jones:

SUBJECT:  Magazines

_____
_____
_____

Yours very truly,
Bill Smith
Bill Smith
```

Modified block style, mixed punctuation

```
                    123 Fourth Street
                    New City, Saskatchewan
                    C2N 4H5
                    June 1, 1982

Reader's Ltd.
567 Eighth Avenue
Old City, Ontario
M3V 6H7

Dear Mr. Jones:

          SUBJECT:  Magazines

_____
_____
_____

                    Yours very truly,
                    Bill Smith
                    Bill Smith
```

Indented style, closed punctuation

```
                    123 Fourth Street,
                      New City, Saskatchewan,
                        C2N 4H5.
                          June 1, 1982.

Reader's Ltd.,
  567 Eighth Avenue,
    Old City, Ontario,
      M3V 6H7.

Dear Mr. Jones:

          SUBJECT:  Magazines

_____
_____
_____

                    Yours very truly,
                    Bill Smith
                    Bill Smith
```

3. Good business letters, like memos, proposals, and reports, should be planned before they are drafted, and revised during and after the composing process. As you write, keep asking yourself:

a) Am I clear, correct, and natural?
b) What facts are involved?
c) What message do I want to convey?

4. You should not write business letters in a stilted, overly formal style. There is no reason to feel nervous when you must write to a lawyer, doctor, bank manager, or other professional person. Lengthy phrases like "I hereby acknowledge your letter of the 16th and in reply wish to advise" and "I trust the above action meets with your entire approval" are better left out.

Notice the difference between these two complaints:

I received my parcel from you today. In regards to the aforementioned parcel, there is an error in filling catalogue item No. 332 534 567 B at $16.99 on invoice No. 636.

On the enclosed order No. 636 you will see that I ordered a size forty-two. I received a size two.

Good business letters go directly to the point and explain the facts in a natural way.

5. Your writing should also be direct, clear, and grammatically correct. Notice the difference between these two requests:

Have you anything that would be good for a project on Spain and how to start a project on that country? Like travel brochures, maps, posters, etc. Hopefully free.

I am planning a social studies project on Spain, because I have always wanted to visit there. I have heard that your travel agency is very helpful to students; therefore, I would like to ask your assistance. Could you recommend any reading references, film strips, or other audio-visual aids? If you have any free brochures or posters, I would appreciate receiving them.

After he/she has untangled the bad prose in the first example, the reader will probably be able to figure out what the writer wants. Such a letter, though, is more likely to be discarded than answered.

6. To help keep your business letters less formal and more direct, consider some of these alternatives:

Formal	Friendly
communication	letter
the writer	I or me
discrepancy	difference
assistance	help
we regret most sincerely	I am very sorry

Use active voice rather than passive:

Passive	Active
no billing has been received	I did not get a bill
an immediate reply will be appreciated	I would appreciate a prompt reply
the question was raised by you	you asked
your letter of July 5th has been received and the content of same has been carefully noted	(Leave it all out.)

Roundabout	Straightforward
I am in receipt of	I received
please arrange to return	please return
I am not in a position to	I cannot
I will take steps to	I will

A Phrase	A Word
in order to	to
along the lines of	like
in the event that	if
in regard to	about
for the reason that	because
in the amount of	for

Archaic	Modern
attached please find	here is (or) I am attaching
I wish to advise that	(omit)
for your information	(omit)
under separate cover	(say how sent – by mail, express)
at this writing	now
forward	send
I trust	I hope, believe, think
at your earliest convenience	please answer promptly (or say when you need a reply)

7. Be courteous in all your business letters. Even if you have been unjustly treated, you are more likely to solve the problem if you write pleasantly but firmly.

Revising Suggestions

Before you let your peers read your business letters, tell them about your intended readers and the circumstances that caused you to write each of the letters. If you are writing these letters only as an assignment, make up a fictitious audience and purpose for each so that your peers can assume the reader's position.

When you and your peers edit your business letters, apply the check lists from Appendix B as well as the following specific items:

1. Can you answer these questions regarding each of your letters:
  a) *Why* was the letter written? Would a telephone call have made your letter unnecessary?
  b) *When* should your letter have been written? Will your letter reach its destination in time for the reader to act upon its contents?
  c) *What* does your letter contain? Are important things included and unimportant things left out?
  d) *How* will your letter accomplish its purpose? Is your message clear, businesslike, and friendly? Is your letter interesting? Will your letter bring the result you want?

2. Is your letter organized and punctuated according to the formats discussed in this assignment?

Polishing Suggestions

Use Appendix C to help prepare your letters for your final readers. Also, note the following specific items:

1. Business letters are generally typed on one side only, on 210 × 297 mm or 8^1/$_2$ × 11 inch white paper. The letter should be positioned on the paper so that it becomes a picture, with white space framing it.

2. When you send it to your final reader, have it folded properly (in three) and in a standard, long commercial envelope, approximately 100 × 250 mm (4 × 9 inches). Make sure the address of the receiver and sender are set up on the envelope similarly to the form and punctuation you used in the main letter.

Models

11045 Swann Street
Richmond, B.C.
V3R 5B6
November 5, 1981

Fine Fashions Ltd.
1222 Waterloo Street
Toronto, Ontario
N1J 1S3

Attention The President

Dear Sir or Madam:

    Yesterday I bought a blouse in the Fine Fashions store at Wildford Shopping Centre. It was not inexpensive. When I brought it home I noticed that it was very poorly made and in many places the seams were not caught under, leaving raw edges.

    I have returned the blouse and received a refund, but as I am sure you are concerned with the quality of your merchandise, I felt that you should be aware of this matter.

Yours truly,

Kimi Kap

cc. Manager, Fine Fashions, Wildford Shopping Centre

1338 Whitebird Avenue
St. Joseph's, N.B.
N9B 7M4
October 16, 1981

Canadian Appliance Ltd.
333 Flourier Avenue
St. Joseph's, N.B.
N3V 2L9

Attention The President

Dear Sir:

My CGIT group is in the process of arranging a drive for funds. The
last time our group solicited for our cause was five years ago.

I would very much like to see you sometime next week - at your
convenience - to discuss our fund drive and how you and your employees
might help the CGIT.

Would you please consider meeting me for a half hour? I shall call you
in a few days to arrange an appointment.

Sincerely,

Marie Mitchell

Marie Mitchell

34 Whistler Place,
Myplace, B.C.,
M5C 4R5.
August 1, 1978.

Jimmy Hamilton,
    Captain of the Green Bay Leafs,
        112 Yourplace Ave.,
            Myplace, B.C.,
                M3B 5S6.

Dear Jimmy,

    I was happy to receive your letter requesting a leave of absence
for you and your Little League team members. It pleases me to see how
enthusiastic you all are about baseball.

    I understand how important it is to you and the team to play an
exhibition game in the U.S., and I would very much like to be able to
give my consent. However, at this time, I cannot give permission for
you to go unless you can raise at least $100.00 to help finance the
trip.

    I am sorry not to be able to give you a happier answer, but I wish
you luck in your fund raising.

                                Yours sincerely,

                                J.B. Nicholls

                                J.B. Nicholls, President,
                                Gordon Little League Baseball
                                Association.

658 Griffins Avenue,
Mytown, B.C.,
V8E 2X1.
February 4, 1981.

Ms. L. Gerard, President,
Vanner School for Disabled Children,
1010 Charles Drive,
Kidtown, B.C.,
V2V 3H1.

Dear Ms. Gerard:

   I am writing to inform you of my desire to perform volunteer work for your organization.

   Having received the list of services you need, I am requesting that I be assigned the following duties:

   1. Children's tutor
   2. Delivery of library books
   3. Organizing accommodation for out-of-town parents

   I feel that I could be of help in these areas, having worked in my high school library for two years while holding a part-time job as a tutor in mathematics. I also have strong organizational abilities and would like to use them in a constructive manner.

   I will be available for work Monday through Thursday from 6:00-9:00 P.M., and Fridays, 1:30-3:00 P.M.

   I hope that my services will be of some benefit to your organization. Please contact me at 555-5555 if an interview is granted.

                                        Sincerely,

                                        Julia Leung

                                        Julia Leung

Analysis

Letter to Fine Fashions

1. Does the writer make the nature of her complaint clear?

2. Is her manner courteous?

3. What sort of response do you think her letter would bring from the company president? (What effect do you think her carbon copy would have on Fine Fashions?)

4. Perhaps, in fulfilling the requirements of this assignment, you could respond to the letter using the persona of either the president of Fine Fashions Ltd. or the manager of the Wildford store.

Marie Mitchell's Letter

1. Has the writer made clear what she wants?

2. If you were the president, would you see her? Why?

J. B. Nicholls' Letter

1. Does Mr. Nicholls make his position clear? To say no in a letter is often very difficult. Does the writer succeed?

2. Is his style appropriate to the subject and to Jimmy?

Julia Leung's Letter

1. Notice the difference between this letter of application and those in the next assignment. What is the main difference?

2. If you were Ms. Gerard, would you want to see the writer?

Assignment 19 Application and Résumé

Introduction

Sometimes you will be able to find a job through personal contact, but more often you will be required to write a letter of application and include a résumé. Your chances of even obtaining an interview will often depend on how well you have presented yourself on paper.

Assignment

Write a letter of application and a résumé.

Prewriting Suggestions

1. You can write this assignment either for an imaginary situation or for a real one. Writing for the former could be fun and creative; writing for the latter could get you a job.

2. Find ads to which you want to reply. You can find them in newspapers, Canada Employment Centre offices, local bulletin boards, or school notices.

Here is a sampling of advertisements that you may respond to if you are not actually applying for a job:

Babysitter

Reliable girl is needed for Friday nights. 7 to midnight. For two children. Box 78

Mackenzie's

3400 E. Hamburger St.
Part-time counter help applications are now being accepted. Apply in writing please.

Accompanist

Needed to assist in auditions for musical. Must be able to sight read. Box 77

Rock Band

Am forming a rock band. Looking for instrumentalists and singer. Apply in writing. Box 80

3. Study the job descriptions of the ads you have selected. Narrow them down to the one that you would like to answer and to the job that you feel most qualified for.

4. Work on your résumé before you write your letter of application. Respond to these items before you begin to draft your résumé.

a) What are the objectives of the job?

b) In what ways do you qualify for the job?

c) What direct experience do you have? (In answering this, point out the previous jobs you have had that are similar to your intended new job.)

d) What indirect experience do you have? (In answering this, consider other jobs you have had that have something in common with your intended new job.)

5. List the information you will want to include in your résumé and letter:

a) Educational background – especially pertinent courses

b) Previous jobs – include outstanding accomplishments

c) Other courses – especially pertinent ones

d) Personal information – age, height, weight, health

e) Activities and interests – especially pertinent ones

f) Availability – specify a date

g) References – have them ready if requested

HERMAN

"Strange how all six of your previous employers left the 'C' out of the word 'excellent'."

6. Once you have all your details jotted down, you should list your writing variables. Then you will be able to draft your résumé and letter of application. Something like this will suffice:

Topic: the position of assistant chef
Audience: Mr. Douglas
Purpose: to obtain an interview with Mr. Douglas of Douglas Catering Ltd.
Format: résumé and letter of application

Drafting Suggestions for Your Résumé

1. Generally, your résumé should be no more than one page long. Busy employers do not have time to read four- and five-page résumés.

2. The most widely used method of organization for a résumé format is chronological order. This is the method you will probably use for this assignment. It is particularly suitable for a person who has a consistent work and education history. The employer can easily check on the progress of the applicant.

There are other methods of organizing résumés that better suit the applicant whose history contains intermittent periods of work and education or a varied career or outstanding accomplishments.

3. The following résumé shows a forthright attitude. Yours should too.

a) List your name, address, and phone number at the top of the page, so that your prospective employer can contact you easily.

b) Next comes a list of your education, job experience, interests and hobbies, and personal information. Describe these topics under separate headings, clearly set off with capital letters, underlining and spacing.

c) In describing your educational history, list the school, college, or university that you attended, and the level of education that you achieved. You may also want to list specific courses you have taken that relate to the job. Do not forget to also list night courses or other types of specialized training that you have received.

In listing your employment history, begin with your most recent job and work backwards. Specify the dates, the *full* name of the company (the employer may want to contact them), and your position. Then give a brief, but specific, description of what your job entailed. A phrase such as "helped in the lunch-room" is too vague; it does not tell your prospective employer *how* you helped.

d) Paragraphs or even whole sentences are not necessary. Phrases in the third person seem to work effectively in a résumé.

e) If you provide names of people as references, make sure you ask them first. Why is this a good policy?

Try to get your references from a variety of sources: your work, your school, your church, your club, your team, or any other organization you belong to.

4. Set up your information in a format such as the following (this résumé is based on one written by a student, but the names and addresses are fictional):

```
                                    RESUME

                                    Kim James Marks
                                    1515 Awards Avenue
                                    Saskatoon, Saskatchewan
                                    S6Y 3Y4
                                    Phone: 333-6767

EDUCATIONAL DATA

Sept. 77-present            McNair Secondary School, Saskatoon, Sask.

                            Areas of Concentration:  three years
                            specializing in foods and catering with grades
                            of A in all related courses.

Sept. 70-June 77            Nugget Elementary School, Toronto, Ontario

EMPLOYMENT DATA

Jan. 1981-present           Cafeteria helper, McNair Senior Secondary
                            School, Saskatoon, Sask.
                                    served lunches to students, prepared
                                    salads and garnishes

Sept. 1979-present          Bus boy, Dino's Place, 3, Main Street,
                            Saskatoon, Sask.
                                    picked up dishes, swept and cleaned
                                    restaurant

July 78-Sept. 79            Counter person, McCleod's, 1414 #4 Road,
                            Saskatoon, Sask.
                                    served public, prepared hamburgers

June 77-Aug. 78             Newspaper Sub-manager, Saskatoon, Sask.

May 75-June 77              Carrier, Saskatoon Star-Phoenix, 4310 Staves
                            St., Saskatoon, Sask.

PERSONAL DATA

Age                         18
Health                      Excellent
Weight                      160
Height                      6'0"
Relocation                  Yes, anywhere in Canada

Activities and Interests:
Reading, filmmaking, basketball

Awards:
Most Promising Cook Award, McNair School, June, 1980
Best Cook Award, 1978, Elphin's Summer Camp

REFERENCES (By permission)

Mr. J. J. James, Principal of McNair School, 330 Allen Ave.,
    Saskatoon, Sask.
Mr. Nathan John, McCleod's, 1414 #4 Road, Saskatoon, Sask.
Mrs. Jane Taylor, Dino's Place, 3 Main Street, Saskatoon, Sask.
Mrs. T. Chef, McNair Home Economics Department.
```

Drafting Suggestions for Your Letter of Application

1. As the letter of application is a business letter, you should look over all the suggestions in Assignment 18. Like all your business letters, your application letter should be clear and correct, direct and natural, as well as courteous and personalized.

2. Specifically, the letter of application has to perform four tasks:

a) Establish a point of contact with the employer by mentioning what job you are applying for and how you know about the vacancy (advertisement, employment agency, third person, or whether you are simply writing an unsolicited letter of application).

b) Arouse the interest of the employer by stating why you are interested in the position.

c) Convince the employer by briefly mentioning your qualifications. Make him or her want to read your résumé.

d) Gain an interview with the employer by politely asking for one and by showing that you would come at any time that would be suitable to his or her schedule.

Do you think the letter of application on page 180 performs the four tasks?

3. If you do not have any work experience, or if your experience is not related to the job you are applying for, emphasize in your letter of application the personal qualities that you feel might make you a suitable candidate for the position. For example:

Although I do not have any direct sales experience, I have discovered through my participation in various clubs that I do have an ability to get along well with others. This, coupled with a competitive spirit, would, I believe, enable me to make a contribution to your organization.

You should carefully consider the requirements of the job. A sales position, for example, might require someone who is personable, well-spoken, and aggressive, while a clerical position might require good organizational ability and attention to detail.

4. Here is a sample letter of application to accompany the previous résumé:

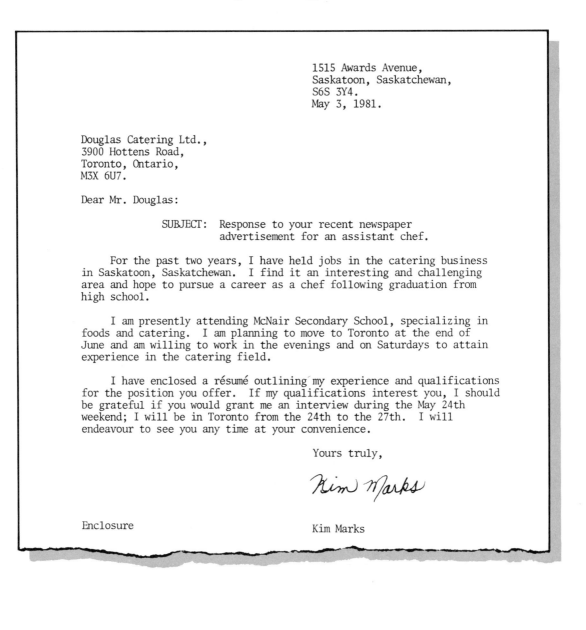

1515 Awards Avenue,
Saskatoon, Saskatchewan,
S6S 3Y4.
May 3, 1981.

Douglas Catering Ltd.,
3900 Hottens Road,
Toronto, Ontario,
M3X 6U7.

Dear Mr. Douglas:

SUBJECT: Response to your recent newspaper
advertisement for an assistant chef.

For the past two years, I have held jobs in the catering business
in Saskatoon, Saskatchewan. I find it an interesting and challenging
area and hope to pursue a career as a chef following graduation from
high school.

I am presently attending McNair Secondary School, specializing in
foods and catering. I am planning to move to Toronto at the end of
June and am willing to work in the evenings and on Saturdays to attain
experience in the catering field.

I have enclosed a résumé outlining my experience and qualifications
for the position you offer. If my qualifications interest you, I should
be grateful if you would grant me an interview during the May 24th
weekend; I will be in Toronto from the 24th to the 27th. I will
endeavour to see you any time at your convenience.

Yours truly,

Kim Marks

Enclosure   Kim Marks

Revising Suggestions

You may want to ask your peers to read the advertisements you are answering before reading your résumé and letter.

When you or your peers edit your résumé and letter of application, apply the check lists from Appendix B as well as the following specific points:

1. Does the interviewer know

a) *Who* you are?

b) *What* experience you have?

c) *Where* you have gained your experience?

d) *When* you gained your experience?

e) *Why* you want the job, or *why* you wish to change jobs?

2. You may want to have your peers pretend that they are the employer and conduct an interview with you. During an interview, an employer may discuss some aspect of your résumé that you have only mentioned briefly, or aspects of the job, such as salary, hours, travel, or career opportunities.

Polishing Suggestions

1. Make a clear copy of your résumé, especially if you plan to use it to answer several similar ads. You can easily photocopy your original, but be sure to seek out a photocopy machine or an instant print outlet that can produce clean copies from your original. Make sure you type your résumé (or have it typed) in order to add a professional touch.

2. Your résumé should, of course, be accompanied by your letter of application. (This may be handwritten. In fact some employers may insist that letters of application be handwritten. Why?)

Whenever possible, direct your letter to a particular person. With a little searching, you can usually find out who that person is.

Make sure your application letter is short, saying very quickly why you are applying, asking for an interview, and promising a follow-up phone call in the near future.

3. Now send your letter of application and résumé in a suitably addressed envelope to your future employer.

4. Before you go for your interview, read the model "Preparation Is the Key to Success" in Assignment 14. Good luck!

Models

26 Horseshoe Drive
Willowdale, Ontario
M7P 4X1
March 18, 1982

Addison-Wesley (Canada) Ltd.
26 .Prince Andrew Place
Don Mills, Ontario
M3C 2T8

Dear Sirs:

I am writing to you because I am fascinated by the publishing
industry and want to learn more. A résumé, listing my past experience
and qualifications, is enclosed.

Although my exposure to the industry is limited, I am enthusiastic
and eager to learn. I am also adaptable, and believe that I could
become an effective employee in a number of areas.

Should you find me a potential candidate for employment after
reviewing my enclosed résumé, I would be most happy to meet with you at
your convenience.

I remain,

Yours very truly,

Janet Dexter

Ms. Janet Dexter

RESUME

JANET DEXTER
26 Horseshoe Drive
Willowdale, Ontario
M7P 4X1

S.I.N.   110 002 812
Home Phone: (416) 988-8938

OBJECTIVE: To work as an employee of a publishing company. To
utilize organizational skills, experience in education,
and interest in literature.

EDUCATION: 1979-80 - Dalhousie University
                       B.A. degree (English)
             1975-76 - Dalhousie University
                       T.C. 5.
             1969-71 - N.S. Teachers' College
                       T.C. 3.
             1969   - New Glasgow High School
                       Grade 12 diploma

WORK
EXPERIENCE:

1980-
present   Municipality of Halifax County - Public Library Assistant
             P.O. Box 890, Armdale Post Office
             Halifax, N.S.
             Phone: (902) 488-6353

             Branch Supervisor - Mr. Frank Boplaw
             I worked as a library assistant, performing regular clerical
             duties, as well as assisting the Children's Librarian (Mrs.
             Debbie Day) with the children's programming. I resigned
             after my husband was transferred to Toronto.

1979   Halifax City School Board - Library Assistant
Jan-June   1849 Bruns Street, Halifax, N.S.
             Phone: (902) 487-2389 (Mr. O'Hale)

             Library Services Supervisor - Mrs. Maggie Cross.
             The job consisted of occasional substituting in elementary
             and junior high-school libraries, and two weeks at the
             Teachers' Resource Center.
             I discontinued in order to complete my B.A. degree.

1971-78   Queens County Amalgamated School Board - Teacher
             P.O. Box 820, Kentville, N.S.
             Phone: (902) 827-1232

Elementary Supervisor - Mr. George Carver
I taught at the Port Smithers Consolidated Elementary
School under Mr. Douglas M. Shand (44 Palls Dr.,
Kentville, N.S.) for six years and under Mr. N.D. Henry,
present principal, for one year.
I left because I moved to Halifax and hoped to change the
direction of my professional career.

PROFESSIONAL
INTERESTS: While employed by Queens County Amalgamated School Board:

- Involved in public communications
  * Edited Primary and Elementary Teachers' Association
    Provincial Newsletter for two years.
  * Edited N.S. Teachers' Union Queens County Regional
    Newsletter for one year.
  * Edited Queens County Teachers' Center Newsletter
    for one year.

- Chairperson of Queens County Regional Teachers' Office
  Clearing House.

- Assisted in setting up Queens County Teachers' Resource
  Centre and member of the Board of Directors.

REFERENCES: Professional-
               Mr. N.D. Henry
               Principal
               Port Smithers Cons. Elementary School
               Port Williams, N.S.
               BOP 1T3   Phone: (902) 544-8765

               Academic-
               Dr. Bruce Stinger
               Dalhousie English Department
               1313 Henny Street
               Halifax, N.S.
               B9H 3G3   Phone: (902) 484-3397

               Personal-
               Mr. Ralph Candy
               1546 Hazzle Street
               Halifax, N.S.
               B3H 3S3   Phone: (902) 484-3829

Qualifications Brief
Sherri L. McLennan
Richmond, B.C. V7A 4A6
277-4011

Objective
Photography Studio assistant where a desire for job variety, a friendly and courteous manner, and a sharp mind are desirable assets. Salary expected – $4.50 to $5.00 per hour.

Related Achievements
Worked with an author of "Richmond and You" printing photographs to accompany the article for publication. Participated in Drama course. Printed school letterheads and professional business cards. Limited publication of anthology of personal writings.

Education
High School graduate of Matthew McNair Senior Secondary (June, 82.) Emphases on Advanced Photography and Graphic Arts. Studied the use of process camera, plate maker, and printing press. Skills learned were layout, plate burning, business card designing, and production, as well as studio portrait and darkroom techniques.

Other Training
Wrote and broadcast regular "CISL" Radio school programs. Helped backstage and in performance for Christmas plays at elementary schools.

Personal
Born December 23, 1964... single... excellent health... considered fast learner... enjoy dealing with people... like to use imagination and creative ability to solve problems... energetic

PERSONAL RESUME

PERSONAL

Sherri McLennan
9871 Seacote Rd.
Richmond, B.C.
V7A 4A6   277-4011

Date of Birth: December 23, 1964
Place of Birth: Queen Charlotte City, B.C.
Health: Excellent.   S.I.N. 721 568 616

EDUCATION

1980-82   McNair Senior Secondary School, Richmond
1977-80   McRobert's Junior Secondary School, Richmond

Will graduate in June, 1982.

Specialty courses: Graphics, Creative Writing, Ceramics, Typing,
                    Drama.

Skills: Ability to use 35 mm camera, darkroom equipment, printing
         press, process camera, and plate maker typewriter.

ACTIVITIES

Richmond and You, free-lance photographer, 1982
Softball scorekeeper, 1979-82
Christmas Plays, performing and backstage work, 1980
Girls' Cosom Hockey Team, Player, 1977-80

EXPERIENCE

Municipal Election work (ballot counting) 1981
Babysitting 1978-81

REFERENCES

Mr. D. Nakamura   Mrs. N. Jamieson   Mrs. B. Morrison
Cosom Hockey Coach   Teacher   9851 Seacote Rd.
4821 Park Rd.   McNair Sr. Sec.   Richmond, B.C.
Richmond, B.C.   9500 #4 Rd.   V7A 9B3
V6B 8L9   Richmond, B.C.   271-1195
274-8257   V7A 2Y9
                       274-7258

Analysis

Janet Dexter Letter and Résumé

1. Even though the details are fictitious, this application letter and résumé present a serious, real-life situation. Would you grant Ms. Dexter an interview?

2. What kind of a job does she seem qualified to perform?

3. Is there anything missing in her résumé?

Sherri McLennan Qualifications Brief and Résumé

1. The advertisement and response is from a real-life situation. Instead of writing a letter of application, Ms. McLennan sent in a qualifications brief. (Note: her qualifications brief is in her own handwriting.) What is the difference between a qualifications brief and a letter of application? Which do you think is more effective? Why?

2. Ms. McLennan was granted an interview from her qualifications brief. To her interview she took her personal résumé as well as three letters of reference. What differences are there between her qualifications brief and her personal résumé?

3. Do you think Ms. McLennan got the job?

Assignment 20 Letter to the Editor

Introduction

When you read a newspaper or magazine, certain articles often capture your attention. Sometimes you support what a reporter or columnist has written; sometimes you violently disagree. In other words, you react to what you read. But have you ever sat down and put your feelings into a letter? Here is your opportunity.

Assignment

Choose an article from a recent newspaper or magazine and write a letter to the editor, agreeing or disagreeing with what the article says.

Prewriting Suggestions

1. Go through recent newspapers and clip out articles that catch your eye. Arrange them in the order of their importance to you. Decide which contains a statement you agree or disagree with strongly. Jot down your thoughts about the article.

2. Read the editorial pages and the letters to the editor in newspapers and magazines to study the format. What do the letters have in common? Try to analyze the readers of letters to the editor. What do you think the readers have in common? Your answers to these questions will help you to determine your audience, as well as the purpose and approach of your letter.

3. Before you begin to draft your letter to the editor, you should state your writing variables. Something like this would be useful:

> **Topic:** reaction to Denny Boyd's columns
> **Audience:** readers of *The Sun*
> **Purpose:** to disagree with his opinions
> **Format:** letter to the editor

4. If you have any strong opinions after reading an article in a newspaper or magazine, you might become involved in a debate with someone who disagrees with you. The discussion that follows will give you practice in argument techniques that you need when you compose a letter to the editor. Like a good persuasive essay (Assignment 6), an effective letter to the editor should clearly state and support your opinion.

Drafting Suggestions

1. Follow the guidelines for persuasion outlined in Assignment 6. As with the persuasive essay, your purpose is to convince someone of your point of view; however, you will have to do so in very little space.

2. Address yourself to the arguments outlined in the article or editorial. You may want to summarize the argument briefly before refuting it. For example:

Mr. Boyd states that it is not "pixie dust," but a thorough grounding in grammar, that is responsible for his professional writing skills. But why did "Pop Garner's" system of parsing, prevalent in the schools for so many years, work for Mr. Boyd and fail for so many other students?

3. Have a strong opening. You must catch the editor's attention in order for your letter to be published.

4. Make your points clearly and concisely. There is little space in most newspapers for letters; the briefer you are, the more likely your letter is to be published intact.

5. Use positive or negative slant wisely. (Activity 18)

6. The use of rhetorical devices will make your viewpoint worth remembering. (Activity 9.)

7. Have a strong ending. Leave your readers with your most important thought.

Revising Suggestions

When you submit your letter for peer and teacher/editor feedback, be sure to clip the original newspaper article to it. This saves the reader a great deal of time. If you are not responding to a particular article, include a short summary about what you are reacting to.

If you are using peer feedback, you may want to set up a newspaper office situation. The readers of the letter should assume they are editors. As they read the letter to the editor they should be concerned with fitting it into the smallest possible space. They should always think about what could be removed without changing the original sense.

When you or your peers read the final draft of your letter to the editor, apply the check lists from Appendix B as well as the following specific items:

1. Does your opening capture your reader's interest?

2. Does your letter follow the guidelines for persuasion as outlined in Assignment 6?

3. Can you delete anything, or state it in a more concise manner?

Polishing Suggestions

Use Appendix C to help you polish your letter to the editor.

Why not send your letter to the newspaper or magazine? You may see your ideas in print.

Models

Sir:

Over the last decade, and particularly over the last couple of years, an organization has been going from strength to strength, gaining power and control in British Columbia. It is widespread throughout Canada, but in British Columbia it was allowed to escalate faster and gain control of all the Province's workers in every form of industry. This organization, fast becoming the dictator, lurks under the guise of the friend of the worker: the Unions.

The province has been beset by strikes that have crippled the economy and put many people out of work who could ill afford it. The people and the government of B.C. are now completely disenchanted with the Unions: they have been held to ransom long enough.

At the peak of labour unrest, strikes, and ludicrous pay demands, the provincial government in a surprise move, introduced legislation to end the strike and ordered the industries back to work. Although labelled interference by the Unions, the legislation included reasonable bargaining power: it was a welcome and necessary act by the government.

Unions have abused their bargaining privileges, shut down major industries in the province, and lost the province great sources of revenue because of their outrageous demands.

Society is changing, and sadly for the worse. What incentives will there be left for future generations to improve their minds or enter a profession? Why waste five or six years paying for further education to reap (if you're lucky!) no more financial reward than a garbage collector?

There is something drastically wrong with society when a bus driver is earning $25,000 plus a year, and a Crown Counsel with 7 year's education, who cannot strike under pain of being disbarred, is earning $20,000 a year. Perhaps our Attorney General thinks prosecuting criminals is a menial task and it is far more important that we keep the bus drivers happy.

Now the country has been hit by a nationwide postal strike, the duration of which may extend until after Christmas. In this instance the Unions are trying to defy federal government legislation. This strike could prove a disaster for the millions of people in Canada reliant on the mail for their livelihood.

How can anybody remain a Socialist?

Miss Frankie Kirby

[The second model is the published version of the above. Notice carefully what the editor cut out of the original. Much of this cutting should have been done during the revision process.]

All Credulity Strained

Sir:

The people and the government of B.C. are now completely disenchanted with unions: they have been held to ransom long enough. Unions have abused their bargaining privileges, shut down major industries in the province, and lost the province great sources of revenue because of their outrageous demands.

There is something drastically wrong with society when a bus driver is earning $25,000 plus a year, and a Crown counsel with seven years' education, who cannot strike under pain of being disbarred, is earning $20,000 a year.

Now we have a nation-wide postal strike. In this instance the unions are trying to defy government legislation. This strike could prove a real disaster for the millions of people in Canada relying on the mail for their livelihood.

How can anybody remain a socialist?

(Miss) Frankie Kirby

With Apologies to Virginia

Dear Editor:

I'm 7 years old so I don't read your paper much. But I like to look at the pictures and I saw something that confuses me.

It was a front page picture of eight Santas on a street corner waving at cars passing by. They were selling Christmas trees. I wondered if the picture was true so I asked my older brother and he seemed hurt. You see, my brother is 21 years old.

It makes me scratch my head and think. I wonder who is the real Santa Claus anyway? I guess you couldn't tell me, but if you see the guy who took the picture, please ask.

Reggie

Analysis

Frankie Kirby's Letters

1. Does the published version still have the style and genuineness that the original had? Do you notice that the editor included a title? Do you think it is appropriate?
2. When you edit your letter to send it in, try to make sure that nothing will need to be cut so that your authentic voice rings loudly and clearly.

Reggie's Letter

1. The student writer announces at the beginning of the letter that he is using a persona. What effect does this have on how you read the letter? Does he use the persona consistently?
2. Would this letter have been as effective without the persona? Why?
3. Can you write a reply, answering his question about who the real Santa Claus is?
4. What does the reference to "Virginia" in the title mean?

Assignment **21** Exam Essays

Introduction

Writing under pressure is a harrowing experience for many people. This assignment is designed to give you strategies for writing a "demand" paper so that you will be able to hand it to your reader with confidence. A "demand" paper is any piece of writing which must be written during a specific time limit. Generally, it involves expository writing, but with two major differences: the topic is specified and the time is limited. Exam essays and classroom projects are the most common types of "demand" papers.

Assignment

Write a "demand" paper as an in-class assignment.

Your writing teacher may provide you with a series of "demand" essay topics, expecting you to hand in a completed paragraph or essay within a specific time period.

You might like to ask one of your course teachers to provide an exam question in a sealed envelope. At the beginning of the writing class, break the seal to find out what the question is and write the "demand" paper. This kind of real assignment can be very useful.

If the preceding suggestions are not feasible, use one of the back-up topics for "demand" papers below.

Back-up Topics

1. In a single paragraph discuss how racial attitudes in Lower Canada contributed to the Rebellion of 1837.

2. What is the difference between irony and sarcasm? In an essay of approximately 500 words compare and contrast irony and sarcasm. Also, illustrate your claims with specific reference to something you have read, said, or heard.

3. In a detailed essay, trace the life cycle of a mosquito.

4. In an essay, criticize *The Writer's Workshop* from your personal point of view.

5. In a literary essay, compare the narrators (the person who is telling the story) of "The Hockey Sweater" and "Araby." (The stories are in Assignment 10.)

6. In a literary essay, compare and contrast Fusi ("God is Not a Fish Inspector," Assignment 10) with Nana ("The Terror of Oxted," Assignment 8).

Prewriting Suggestions

As a student, you will perhaps have little experience with "demand" papers other than those you write in school. Exams and tests do, however, prepare you for the many instances where you will be obliged to write under pressure because of your job or circumstances.

What follows are suggestions which apply to exam writing; however, many of the suggestions can be applied to all kinds of "demand" writing.

1. Being well prepared for an exam is the best prewriting strategy. There is nothing quite like the feeling of confidence that comes from knowing the material well.

2. Predict a few exam questions and do some "dry runs" at home. Think of how happy you will feel if you have predicted the exact question on an exam! Even if you are only partly right, that is better than being completely surprised by the exam question.

3. When you receive your exam, read over the entire paper. Underline all the significant words in the directions. (Missing the "or" in a question that tells you to do "1, 2, or 3," could be disastrous.) If the exam presents a choice, identify the questions you feel most competent to answer. So that you will not run out of time, estimate the time that you will spend on each question. It's a good idea to answer first the questions that you know; this gives you a sense of accomplishment.

Also observe the value of each question and write accordingly. To spend the majority of your time on the first half of the exam, which is worth only 20 marks, to find that the second half is worth 80 marks, shows poor organization and results in panic.

4. When you have decided on the order in which you will answer the questions, and the time you will allot to each, re-read your first question carefully. Do not begin to write until you have a clear idea of what the question asks you to do. A summary of the facts will not do if you are asked to "compare" or "criticize." Key words, discussed in the Drafting suggestions below, will guide you.

5. Plan your general answer before you begin to write. Since there is little time available for revision in an essay examination, time spent on planning is a good investment. Needless to say, wear a watch. Know generally what you want to say before you start; in other words, make sure you understand the question.

State your purpose for writing; list your supporting evidence; finally, decide on your method of organization. Re-phrasing an exam question often guides you in the right direction. Read the following examples:

Essay Question: In a 500-word essay explain what you would do to stop a particular company from dumping wastes into the sea.

Main Claim: There are five things that I would do to stop XXX Company from dumping wastes into the sea. (Note: do not use weak openings like "In this essay I am going to ..." or "My purpose in writing is to ....")

Essay Question: Point out how you would put a zipper in a skirt.
Main Claim: There are three main steps in putting a zipper into a skirt. (When you write, plan to describe each step in about fifty words.)

6. Finally, come into the exam room with proper tools: pens, pencils, erasers, rulers, a dictionary (if permitted), and any other required material.

Drafting Suggestions

1. The wording of the exam questions will not only assist you in drafting your main claim, but will guide you in choosing a method of development.

Key Words

illustrate

Questions and Strategies

In "God is Not a Fish Inspector" how is it made obvious that Fusi is going to lose? Use specific evidence to illustrate your proof.

A question on an English or history exam, which asks you to illustrate with specific, concrete examples, usually requires that you explain or clarify your answer by presenting textual evidence. Your opinion by itself is not what is required. If you are not able to bring a primary source (that is, a copy of the material) into the exam room, you will have to paraphrase rather than give direct quotations to support your claims.

Note: begin your essay by re-phrasing the question and then follow basic essay structure (Assignment 6). If you cannot think of a good introduction, the re-phrased question will have to do. For example, "In *God is Not a Fish Inspector*, Valgardson makes it obvious that Fusi is going to lose from the moment he wakes up." By re-phrasing the question in this way, you will find that all you have to do is provide illustrations to prove your claim.

2. All essay exam questions can be started in this way. For the questions which follow, jot down suitable opening sentences for an essay. Even if you have no idea what the answers are, you should still write some opening sentences. This will prove to you that it is possible to master exam techniques. If you have your technique under control right from the beginning, you will have much more confidence as you proceed through the exam essay.

compare

Compare Darwin's theory of evolution with the Biblical theory of creation.

When you compare, you should look for qualities and characteristics that resemble each other. The term "compare" is usually accompanied by *with*, implying that you are to emphasize similarities.

contrast   *Contrast the laws pertaining to women and property in Quebec fifty years ago with those in effect today.*

When you are asked to contrast, you should emphasize differences. Focus on the things, qualities, events, or problems that you can contrast.

discuss   *Discuss Sir John A. Macdonald's role in the "Pacific Scandal."*

The term "discuss" appears often in exam questions. You should analyze, examine, and present the pros and cons regarding the problems involved in the question. You will receive a good mark if your answer is complete and thorough.

explain   *Explain the Pythagorean theorem in no more than 100 words.*

If you know Assignment 4 well, you will know that you are expected to write an expository paragraph when asked to explain. It is important that you explain clearly and concisely from a strong personal point of view. You should appear to your marker as an authority on the subject; therefore, write with conviction.

list   *List five symptoms of coronary artery disease.*

The term "list" can confuse. Are you to write an essay, or are you to present a list? If you are asked to write an essay, obviously you must enumerate in paragraph form; but if you are not, you should present a brief itemized series. Indicate that you are presenting a list because that is what is asked for in the question.

summarize   *Summarize the causes of Alberta's dispute with Ottawa over energy pricing.*

To summarize means you are to condense. You may, at times, be given a longer passage to summarize; however, if you are given a question as above, you should present only the main facts. Details, illustrations, and elaborations should be left out. But indicate to your reader that you are summarizing, and that you *know* the details.

trace   *Trace the route of Simon Fraser across Canada.*

Obviously a map or diagram would help to answer this question; but if you are asked to write an essay, you should give a description of his progress, the historical significance of his journey, and a general development from the point of origin to his final destination. Use chronological order.

criticize   *Criticize the federal government's policy on the constitution.*

When you are asked to criticize, you should not merely find fault, but give *your* opinions about both the merits and demerits of something. Take a strong stand, but do present all the facts; in other words, you should discuss the reasons the government did what it did.

justify   *Justify the execution of Louis Riel.*

You must prove that an event is socially beneficial when you are asked to justify. Show evidence for your decisions. You must convince your reader that you are right.

review   *Review Zeffirelli's film **Romeo and Juliet**.*

A review demands critical examination. Do not mention only the bad points, but what you liked as well. Jot down what you wish to discuss *while you are watching* the film: the acting, the scenery, the costumes, the sound, and so forth. Afterwards, organize your points in a satisfying order, and briefly analyze or comment on each.

relate   *Relate the construction of the transcontinental railway to the settlement of Saskatchewan.*

When you are asked to relate, you should link the two things by what relates them to each other. Emphasize the relationships, connections, or associations of your subjects.

3.   Do not be afraid to tell your reader how you are interpreting the question. Terms are always open to interpretation. If you misinterpret the term, but you explain what you are doing and answer with conviction, you will receive more credit than if your reader has to figure out what you were trying to do.

4.   If you are having trouble defining a term, you might be able to ask your teacher, "What exactly does this term mean?" Then, you should be able to answer with confidence.

5.   As you continue to study and write exams, add to the list of key words.

Revising Suggestions

During an exam, you will, of course, not be able to receive any feedback from your peers. Instead, you will have to check your paper yourself, using check lists similar to those in the first half of Appendix B. When you have finished writing, re-read the questions, then re-read your answers.
1.   Make sure you have answered all the required questions.
2.   Check to see that you have not forgotten any important points.
3.   Correct any careless errors.
4.   If your answers are illegible, recopy them, *if time permits.*

Polishing Suggestions

After your exam is returned, look it over and learn from it. Find your strengths and weaknesses; build for your next exam by eliminating your weaknesses.

Models

Read the three student responses to this question: "In a single paragraph, discuss how racial attitudes in Lower Canada contributed to the Rebellion of 1837."

1. Racial Attitudes

In the 1830s the English controlled government and commerce in Lower Canada. This, the French Canadians resented. The English made money off the French by building roads, bridges, and canals. They did this to create more trade and more settlement. The French didn't like these improvements because they found out they had to pay for them. How? Through their taxes, that's how. They showed the English, by rebelling, that they wanted what was French to always be French. Just like today. The English thought that the French were just being stubborn. Just like today.

2. Rebellion of the 1830s

The rebellion in Lower Canada, like that in Upper Canada, was mainly due to political and economic causes, but in Lower Canada the racial issue made things worse. The group which controlled the government and commercial life of Lower Canada was almost all English, and it was this fact that French Canadians resented most. The English minority wanted to make money by developing the province's resources by building roads, bridges, and canals to promote trade and settlement. Since the English controlled the government, it would usually help them in promoting such projects. However, French Canadians didn't want any "improvements," especially when they had to pay for them. They believed that the resources of Lower Canada, which had been discovered by French Canadians, should be developed by French Canadians for their benefit. To the English, this attitude seemed to be against progress.

3. English and French

Really it was the "Chateau Clique" that made the rebellion of 1837. But the French don't like the English because they want to build roads and other things on their land and make them pay for it. The English don't like the French. Because they thought they're backward and a conquered people. They thought the land belonged to them. The Act of Union in 1822 said the French are a minority in the legislature. The French want to keep their language and religion. Louis-Joseph Papineau was a lawyer. He told Canadiens to fight for their rights. So there was the rebellion.

What makes the paragraphs different? (To help you answer, look at the introductions, main claims, development, and conclusions. Examine the sentence variety, transitions, and style. Is there anything irrelevant in any of the paragraphs?) If you had to assign a "C," "B," and "A," how would you distribute them to the three papers? Use the check list of standards in Appendix B. See below for a history teacher's comments and grades.

Analysis   History Teacher's Comments

Racial Attitudes

Your paragraph is correctly focussed on racial attitudes. Your interpretation is slightly superficial – try analyzing the reasons behind the attitudes you describe. You develop your ideas logically but could further improve your paragraph by using a variety of subjects (you use "they," "the English," and "the French" too frequently) and sentence types. Finally, avoid sentence fragments. They are unacceptable in formal writing – too casual.
Grade: C

Rebellion of the 1830s

Your paragraph is well developed and thorough, considering that this was an in-class assignment. Facts are well set out, in logical order, and are adequately supported. Vocabulary includes key words that demonstrate your understanding of the topic. Paragraph also has structural strengths – proper form, effective use of transitional words to link sentences. A most satisfactory example of expository writing.
Grade: B/A

English and French

Facts are not enough! You have crammed in many, many facts but haven't put them together to form a coherent paragraph. First, state your topic, then stick to it. Order your supporting statements so that they seem to flow naturally, from one to the other, in supporting your topic. Also, watch verb tense and avoid sentence fragments. You are so close – you talk all around the topic, but without focus and order you aren't communicating. Thoughts need structure.
Grade: Withheld. Rewrite using a written outline as a guide. No mark until rewritten.

Author's Observations

The above comments are presented just as the history teacher wrote them. It is interesting to note that her comments emphasize the need for good writing. The writer of the third paragraph obviously knows more about the Rebellion of 1837 than the other two, yet his inability to express his ideas resulted in a failing paper.

Activity
Section

About the Activities

Introduction

In this section you will find exercises, games, and special writing activities to help you refine and improve particular aspects of your writing. At times you may need to refer to a dictionary, thesaurus, or handbook. Perhaps your teacher will recommend specific ones so that you and your classmates will be using the same authorities.

You can apply each activity to any writing you are doing. If you are writing a narration, for example, and are worrying about your word choice, look at Activity 15; if you are writing a letter and want to make your feelings more apparent, look at Activity 18.

If you take a few moments to discover what the Activity Section contains, you can use it to fulfil your needs. If you cannot decide which activity to begin with, do the first few. Later, your teacher/editor or your peers may suggest that you should work on a particular activity to sharpen an aspect of your writing.

How To Do an Activity

The Activity Section is designed so that you work with one other person: a fellow student at school as well as a friend or relative at home. (Although you can get some benefit from working alone, you really need someone to talk to, to check with, to ask and answer questions.)

Throughout each activity you will need to talk to your partner. You will soon get used to working in an active writing lab.

Each activity begins with background information, then offers specific projects to help you refine an aspect of writing or correct an error.

1. Exercises

Whenever possible, talk through the exercises with your partner rather than write them out; you will be able to do many more exercises this way.

2. Games

The games will work better if you and your partner prepare for them. By coming to each game with word lists and example sentences as well as a dictionary, thesaurus, and handbook, you will be able to have a great deal of fun while you learn.

Establish the rules of each game before you play; each one is introduced in the textbook, along with a few suggestions. You and your partner should decide on how you will score points, when you will stop playing, what may constitute an invalid response, and so on.

3. Special Writing Activities

Most of the activities culminate in a writing project for you to do *for* your partner. It is possible to do it for your teacher/editor as well.

Sometimes it may be necessary to do an entire activity; sometimes not. Sometimes you may start at the beginning of an activity; sometimes in the middle. If only one partner needs to do an activity, the other should act as an adviser and help his/her partner. (By teaching your partner, you will learn new things yourself.) The important thing to remember, when you work in the Activity Section, is that it should fulfil *your* writing needs.

Activity **1** Getting to Know the Writing Variables

Background

In order to understand and appreciate the writing variables, take a moment to think about how you speak. You communicate effectively by adjusting, even changing, your speech. You can talk loudly, softly, slowly, or quickly. Your tone of voice can be happy, sad, or angry. You can sound sincere or insincere. You can use simple or complex words, jargon or slang. You can be still when you speak, or you can use gestures to emphasize certain points. You can use your normal voice or try to imitate someone else. There are an endless number of things you can do with your voice. The same variety is possible when you write.

When you are writing, there are several factors or variables that will affect your writing: *topic*, *audience*, *purpose*, *format*, *persona*, and *situation*.

Exercise One

Topic

Most of *The Writer's Workshop* emphasizes the fact that you go through various steps as you write. Because *content* is the most important aspect of your writing, the first step of your writing process should deal with generating an idea or topic. With your partner, examine each of the following prewriting methods.

Think/Write
Take a few minutes for you both to list some of the things that have been concerning you. They may be about society, the environment, politics, or very personal problems.

Share with your partner a topic from your list that you would like most to write about. Explain why you want to write about it. For whom would you like to write?

Many writers keep a daily journal. By doing this, they constantly practise the Think/Write Method. Turn to Appendix A of *The Writer's Workshop* for ideas on how to keep a journal.

Talk/Write
Sometimes you can brainstorm a topic by talking with one or more people. By listening to other people voice their opinions, you are often able to clarify your own opinions.

Where do you do your best brainstorming: at school, around your dinner table, at a party?

Choose a topic and brainstorm it with your partner. If you cannot think of a topic, look over the following list. Find one on which the two of you have differing opinions and brainstorm it to the point where you could use it for a piece of writing.

Men are stronger than women.
Teenagers should have a curfew.
Animals should not live in the same houses as humans.
English Canadians should learn French.
Sex education should not be taught in schools.

Read/Write

Tell your partner about your reading habits. Which newspaper do you read? What parts of the paper do you read regularly? Do you have favourite columnists? Which magazines do you read? Other than required school books, name the last three books you have read. Who are your favourite authors? Why are they your favourites?

Share with your partner something you have read recently that you would like to write about. To whom do you want to write? Why?

Write/Write

This method is linked closely to that of the daily journal. If you force yourself to fill a blank page every day, you will often unearth worth-while topics for future assignments.

So that you and your partner can practise this method, give each other a key word (such as *money*, *sports*, or *clothes*). Write it down and start writing about the first thing that comes to mind. If nothing comes to mind, just keep writing the key word. Return to the key word if you feel yourself getting sidetracked or if you cannot think of anything more to write. When you have filled a page, see if you have written anything that might become a suitable topic for a piece of writing.

Assign/Write

As a student, you will use this method in most of your classes. Assignment 21, Exam Essays, offers several useful suggestions on how to write on an *assigned* topic.

If you have such an assignment coming up for one of your courses, ask your partner to predict an essay question. Explain how you would attempt to answer it.

Exercise Two   Audience

There is no special order in which you should think about the writing variables; they should be considered collectively. This exercise, however, deals only with *audience*.

Most people know what will please or displease their relatives, friends, and acquaintances, so they speak and act accordingly. You may say something to one friend or relative and receive a laugh; you may say the same thing in the same way to someone else and receive a rebuke. Why is this so?

Decide on a problem or issue that has been bothering you, one that deals with society, parents, morals, school, religion, or the environment. Share it with your partner.

1. Explain the problem as clearly as you can so that your partner understands it.
2. Ask your partner to assume the role of your best friend of the same sex. Explain the problem as though you are speaking to this friend.
3. Repeat the explanation to your partner, who now assumes the role of your best friend of the opposite sex. (Notice that by changing your audience, you will have to change your words, expressions, and so on.)
4. Next, your partner should assume the role of one of your parents.
5. Next, a complete stranger. (Your partner should tell you the stranger's age, sex, and so on, before you begin your explanation.)
6. Next, a child of six.
7. Finally, someone you do not like.

When you have completed this oral exercise, discuss with your partner the differences among your various explanations.

Reverse the exercise to give your partner an opportunity to speak.

Exercise Three   Purpose

Sometimes we write simply for the pleasure of playing with language or expressing ourselves; for example, when we write in a diary or journal. But generally when we write for someone else, we write for a specific *purpose*.
1. There are two basic reasons for writing: first, because you want to communicate your ideas to someone; second, because someone else wants you to communicate with him or her. The former is usually done sporadically by student writers at home; the latter, because of teachers' assignments, is usually done more systematically at school. Nonetheless, purpose plays an important part in both the writing you *want* to do and the writing you *have* to do.

With your partner discuss some piece of writing that you would like to do. Then, talk about an assignment that you have to do. Discuss thoroughly your reasons for writing both.

2. There are also several specific reasons why you write; for example, to convey information, to persuade, to describe, to tell a story, or to entertain.

Think about a particular part of your environment that you consider interesting or beautiful. Independent of your partner, write about the area for two of the following specific reasons. Take only five minutes for each reason.

To inform
Provide facts about the area, similar to an encyclopedia entry, that will *inform* your partner.

To persuade
Argue that the area should, or should not, be developed for commercial purposes.

To describe
Create a "word picture" of the area in free verse, rhymed verse, or a paragraph format.

To tell a story
Tell one of many adventures you have had in the area.

Personal expression
Write a journal entry in which you express your feelings or thoughts about the area.

With your partner, compare the differences in the content and organization of your two pieces of writing.

Exercise Four   Format

Words can be arranged so that they are in the *format* of sentences, paragraphs, essays, letters, memos, reports, proposals, poems, short stories, novels, plays, and so on.

Paragraphs and essays can be further categorized into exposition, narration, and description. Exposition explains ideas, narration tells a story, and description describes someone or something. Notice the difference in the following opening sentences for each category:

Exposition
Young and old alike should know how to swim.

Narration
Last night I went for a swim before I went to bed.

Description
The swimmers splashed in the refreshing water eddying around them: above, the heavens twinkled; below, fishes hid.

1. With your partner determine whether each sentence below is expository, narrative, or descriptive. (The answers are at the end of the Activity Section.)

a) There are two main species of elephants: Indian and African.

b) My first glimpse out the window at the Chateau Lake Louise revealed a spectacular view.

c) Charles Joseph Clark first saw the light of day in High River, Alberta, in 1939.

d) One night I took off my shoes and socks and walked barefoot through the park.

e) Anyone who has seen a duck-billed platypus will agree that it is a most unusual-looking animal.

f) Criminal penalties for the personal use of marijuana should not be removed.

g) My brother gave me a huge surprise on Christmas morning.

h) Marty Hogan is one of the world's finest racquetball players.

i) Drive, lob, Z, and cross-court are the four basic racquetball serves.

j) Yesterday, I played my first game of racquetball against my much more experienced cousin.

2. Independently, you and your partner write a narrative, descriptive, and expository sentence for each of these topics: love, a textbook, one of your parents, the sun, school. (Exchange your sentences and see if you can each determine the most appropriate category for each sentence.)

3. Writers decide which of the many formats to use in order to best illustrate their topic, satisfy their audience, and fulfil their purpose.

With your partner discuss the formats that you most often use. Why do you use these formats so often? Which formats have you never used? Why?

Exercise Five

In review, the four main writing variables are *topic, audience, purpose,* and *format.* Once you have established your topic, the combinations and permutations of the other three writing variables make one piece of writing different from another.

1. With your partner, examine how the following specific idea would be affected every time a writing variable changed:

Topic: the use of insecticides near heavily populated areas

If you were to write on this topic, what characteristics would your piece of writing have if you used the writing variables below? In discussing "characteristics," refer to word choice, sentence structure, types of paragraphs, style, content, and so on.

Audience: the editor of your local newspaper

Purpose: to explain why you are nervous about a recent spraying of insecticides

Format: a letter

2. How would the characteristics of the letter be affected if you changed only *purpose?*

Purpose: to suggest that even more insecticides be used

or

Purpose: to link infant deaths to the recent spraying of insecticides

or

Purpose: to point out that there are even more mosquitoes in your back yard than there were before the spraying began

or

Purpose: to provide information on exactly what the insecticides contain and what the dangers are

With your partner, suggest two or three other purposes for writing the same piece. What new characteristics would the letter have?

3. How would the characteristics of the letter be affected if you changed only *audience?*

Audience: close neighbours whose baby is ill for no apparent reason

or

Audience: Member of Parliament

or

Audience: science teacher

or

Audience: your journal

With your partner, suggest two or three new readers for the same piece. What new characteristics would the letter then have?

4. Assume that you are no longer going to write a letter. How would the piece be affected if you changed only *format?*

Format: research essay

or

Format: expository paragraph

or

Format: narrative essay

or

Format: proposal and report

With your partner, suggest two or three new formats for the same piece. What new characteristics would each new format have?

5. Independently, each of you write several new combinations of the preceding variables. Discuss the characteristics of each new set. For example, what would be the characteristics of a piece with this particular combination?

Topic: the use of insecticides near heavily populated areas
Audience: science teacher
Purpose: to link infant deaths to recent spraying of insecticides
Format: research essay

Exercise Six   Persona

A fifth writing variable is *persona* (discussed in detail in Activity 19). Most of the time you will write from your own point of view, voicing your opinions openly in a straightforward style. There may be times, however, when you pretend someone else wrote your piece. If you do this, you are assuming a *persona*. By using a persona, you can often make the expression of your point of view more effective than if you spoke in your own voice.

You can, for example, pretend that you are a visitor from outer space because you want to criticize a particular injustice in society. By looking at the injustice from a non-human point of view, you may make your readers see the problem more clearly. You might use the persona of a young child (even yourself at the age of six) to tell what a child's Christmas is really like. You could write from the persona of an animal on the endangered species list. What could be the effect?

With your partner, take turns pointing out three things you would want to criticize about the eating habits of Canadians. First, explain from your own point of view; then alternate with the following personae: a Masai, a sixteenth-century Elizabethan, a Martian, a French chef.

Where, in your writing, do you think you will be able to use persona effectively?

Exercise Seven   Situation

Situation is perhaps the most complex of all the writing variables. It involves all the external circumstances (where you live, who your friends and acquaintances are, what you are doing) and internal circumstances (how you are feeling) that influence you, as a writer.

1. Assume that you have been assigned to do a research report on the Unification Church (the so-called "Moonies"). Your treatment of the topic will vary if one of the following is true:

a) You know very little about this group, and are simply curious.
b) You are presently a member of the Unification Church and feel that it has given new meaning to your life.

c) Your sister, to whom you were once very close, has joined the "Moonies" and lost contact with her family.

Discuss other situations with your partner which could affect your treatment of this topic.

2. Your situation is what will help give each piece of writing your own particular stamp. Occasionally, you might like to write from a different persona, or point of view. Then you might also want to invent a situation for the imaginary author of your material.

Independent of your partner, invent a persona and situation for an essay about the "Moonies." For example, you might assume a persona of someone who has been a "Moonie" and a situation where your parents forcibly took you from the group.

Afterwards, discuss how different the piece of writing would be from one that was written using your own voice as a student in a classroom.

3. The writing variable of *situation* is further enriched by your audience's situation. Your treatment of the topic of the Unification Church will vary if either of the following is true:

a) Your audience knows very little or a great deal about this group.

b) Your audience is a happy (or unhappy) member (or ex-member) of the "Moonies."

When you consider *your* situation as well as *your audience's* situation, your piece of writing takes on a uniqueness which makes it unlike any other piece of writing.

Special Writing Activity

So that you can take all six writing variables into consideration, write a short piece for your partner. Use this specific set of writing variables or make up one of your own:

Topic: sport of your choice
Audience: friend in Africa
Purpose: to show how silly the sport really is
Format: letter
Your situation: you are very poor at playing the sport
Your audience's situation: your audience has never heard of the sport

Ask your partner to comment on the appropriateness of *each* use of the writing variables.

Last Words

For everything you write in the future, consider the writing variables of *topic*, *audience*, *purpose*, and *format*. Also if you think your piece of writing needs enriching, consider *persona* and *situation*.

Activity 2 Organizing for Unity

Background

When a piece of writing (expository, descriptive, or narrative) is unified, everything within it deals with the same topic and contributes to supporting the main claim. Every word and sentence becomes an inseparable part of the whole.

In this activity you will learn how to collect the evidence you need to support the main claim, list it, organize it in the most effective way for your purposes, and make sure it is unified. All the relevant points will be contained in your work; all the irrelevant ones will have been discarded.

This activity is divided into four major parts:
 I. Collecting Supporting Evidence
 II. Listing Supporting Evidence
III. Organizing Supporting Evidence
IV. Unifying Supporting Evidence

I. Collecting Supporting Evidence

There is an old recipe for rabbit stew that begins, "First, shoot your rabbit." Similarly, before you begin to collect evidence to support your main claim, you must have a claim you want to support. Each of the assignments contains suggestions on choosing and formulating your main claim.

You will find anything that you decide to collect – stamps, matchbooks, pictures of Wayne Gretzky – in both likely and unlikely places. The most likely place to start collecting is right around your own home and neighbourhood. Similarly, when you collect supporting evidence for a piece of writing, start with what you already know.

... the storage capacity of your grapefruit-sized brain is staggering – conservatively estimated at ten billion units of information. If you want to find out what you *do* know, Michael Phillips suggests this little exercise. 'Suppose that you sat down with paper and pencil to write out everything you remembered, including names of people you know or have heard about, experiences from childhood on, plots of books and films, descriptions of jobs you've held, your hobbies, and so on.' But you'd better have a lot of time for proving this point to yourself because, as Phillips goes on to say, 'If you wrote 24 hours a day, you'd be at it for an estimated two thousand years.'

Dr. Wayne Dyer, Pulling Your Own Strings

Say, for example, that you want to write a descriptive paragraph and have settled on your brother's messy room as your topic. Collecting evidence for your paragraph is easy: go to your brother's room, open the door (if you can), and take a good look.

Collecting evidence to support other main claims may not be this simple, but you should be able to find more evidence by consulting people you know, books and other library materials, or the broadcasting media.

What types of supporting evidence do you need? To answer, you will have to decide which types serve your purpose best. To describe your brother's messy room, you will want to use *examples* to convey the disorder in the room (an unmade bed, clothes all over the floor, books piled high on his desk, a row of dessert bowls under his bed). If, on the other hand, you were writing a persuasive essay on the dangers of smoking, you would collect *reasons* why people should not smoke (increased chance of lung cancer and heart disease, air pollution, the risk to unborn children). Other types of supporting evidence are *facts*, *results*, *incidents*, *details*, *illustrations*, *questions*, *lists*, and *quoted material*. You will find examples of all of these types in this activity.

Exercise One

Independent of your partner, choose one of the following main claims. List at least three places you would go to start collecting evidence, in the order in which you would consult them. Then, discuss your choices with your partner.

a) Salmon no longer spawn in a river near you.

b) What is on the moon?

c) The most important year of schooling is grade one.

d) Travelling should be fun.

e) There is something I never leave home without.

II. Listing Supporting Evidence

Once you have established where to collect your evidence, you must record it in some way. You will probably start by simply jotting down items at random as they occur to you or as you find them. There are ways, however, in which you can list your evidence that will help to organize it at the same time.

Exercise Two

The simplest type of an organized list is shaped like a ladder. Each rung contains one piece of information: the bottom rung represents the least important piece of evidence; the top rung represents the most important. For instance, the following ladder contains the main claim and provides supporting evidence for an essay, "Reasons to Quit Smoking."

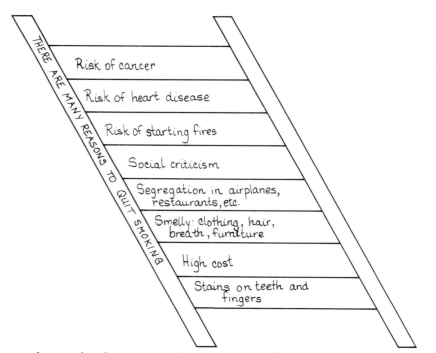

As you place items on your ladder, you may find that some pieces of your evidence contrast with others. You then may decide to start two ladders: one containing evidence confirming your main claim, the other containing items opposing it; for example, you may come up with reasons to continue smoking. If you have enough facts on both ladders, you may want to write a contrast paper, "The Pros and Cons of Smoking."

1. Here is a list of steps you might follow when you clean your room. Independent of your partner, organize these steps on a ladder. If you do not think that you would use some of the items, do not include them; if you can think of others, include them on your ladder.

a) Open a can of Coke.

b) Bring in the vacuum cleaner.

c) Put all my junk on my bed.

d) Remove everything from the floor.

e) Fill a bucket with warm water.

f) Ask my mother to help.

g) Open the window.

h) Take the sheets and pillowcases off the bed.

i) Sweep under the bed.

j) Turn on the stereo.

k) Take everything off the dresser.

l) Put dirty clothes into the laundry hamper.

m) Make myself a peanut butter sandwich.
n) Sort through the junk on my bed.
o) Plug in the vacuum cleaner.
p) Clean my windows.
q) Phone a friend for company.
r) Put soap into the pail of water.
s) Get some ice.
t) Plan which movie to see after I clean my room.

2. Compare your ladder with your partner's. Are they very different? Is the difference in the items themselves, or the order in which they are arranged on the ladder?

Exercise Three

The more you write, the more ways of listing evidence you will discover and want to try. Another method uses an ancient design called a *mandala*. A mandala is a circular drawing representing wholeness and harmony.

1. You can use a mandala to list evidence by putting your main claim in the centre and the supporting facts, reasons, details, and so on around it. For instance, the following mandala states the main claim and provides supporting evidence for it:

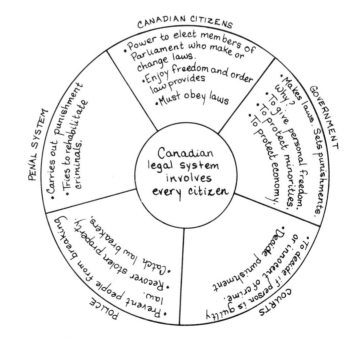

Notice how the supporting evidence is listed: on the outside of the circle are listed the names of groups involved in the Canadian legal system, while within the divisions of the mandala are listed the specific tasks of each group.

2. Use one of the following main claims (or one of your own choice) and, independent of your partner, construct a mandala with the main claim in the middle. You should both use the *same* main claim so that you can compare mandalas; so, take time to find a claim that you both agree upon.
a) Everyone should learn to ski.
b) Whistler Mountain offers magnificent facilities for skiers.
c) Skiing is a great sport for young and old alike.
d) You may think you cannot afford to ski, but skiing can be quite inexpensive.
e) My ski trip to Banff was filled with exciting moments.

3. Compare your word mandala with your partner's. Should anything be added or deleted? If you were to turn your mandala into an essay, would it be narrative, descriptive, or expository?

Exercise Four

There are many other ways of listing supporting evidence besides *ladders* and *mandalas*. You can use *flow charts*, which play such an important part in computer science. You can put items into *boxes* ("pigeonhole" them), use a *family tree*, draw *pictures* or *cartoons*, make a word or picture *collage* – in fact, you can use any *graphic* or visual method that you can think of to list and arrange your evidence.

Assume that you must write an essay on the topics mentioned below. Independent of your partner, decide in what way you would list supporting evidence: flow chart, pigeonhole boxes, family tree, cartoons or pictures, a collage, or line or bar graph. Use each only *once*.
a) History of the fork as an eating utensil.
b) Ways to eat with a fork.
c) Duties of the executive of a club you belong to.
d) Contrast of a typical North American meal and a Masai meal.
e) Ways to study.
f) What great world thinkers said about reincarnation.
When you finish, compare and talk about the suitability of your choices.

III. Organizing Supporting Evidence

While you are listing your evidence, as you have just seen, you are probably also organizing it in a way that best suits your writing variables. Now is the time to decide what formal method of organization your piece needs.

Exercise Five   Comparison/Contrast

One method of organization is pointing out similarities (comparisons) and differences (contrasts) between two subjects. You might first talk about Subject A and then talk about Subject B. That would produce a paper using the AAA/BBB method. If you were to mention items from A, at the same time pointing out similarities or differences to B, you would be using the ABABAB method. You can use the AAA/BBB or ABABAB method for either comparison or contrast. Furthermore, it is possible to write a *comparison/contrast* paper in which you use either method to point out similarities *and* differences.

What are the benefits of the AAA/BBB and ABABAB methods both for the writer and reader?

1. Choose two things to compare or contrast.
 a) Life in a small town and life in a city.
 b) Life when your parents were sixteen and life now.
 c) Your elementary school and your high school.
   (Or choose your own comparison or contrast topic.)

2. Draw up two columns, labelling each with the appropriate topic. List similarities or differences between the two topics. Whenever you put something in one column, add a similar item to the other one.

Life in a Small Town	Life in a City
a) slower	faster
b) clean, fresh air	smog in the air
c) clean streets	debris in streets
d) safe to walk streets	crime-infested streets
e) everyone knows each other	people are lonely

3. Exchange your lists. Discuss their completeness and decide on the best method for organization of your paper, the AAA/BBB or the ABABAB method.

4. If you like, you can make a collage of pictures contrasting or comparing two things or places. Then point out the differences or similarities to your partner. You will find that a good collage will provide an excellent beginning for an essay.

The following are possibilities for collages contrasting sleeping patterns:
 a) pictures of people sleeping in beautiful beds contrasted to people sleeping on the streets.
 b) different styles of beds.
 c) different customs of sleeping.
 d) the history of beds.
 e) different sleep positions.

Exercise Six   Cause and Effect

A piece of writing can be solidly unified by presenting either the causes of a problem followed by the effects, or the effects of a problem followed by the causes.

1. Find two pictures: one a cause of a problem; the other an effect. Give them to your partner. (If you cannot find pictures, provide a word picture.) For example, you could provide a picture of an oil tanker and another of a dead bird.

2. Your partner must find pictures, draw other pictures, or provide word pictures that bridge the cause and effect relationship. For example, pictures of a storm, a grounded tanker, an oil spill, and a bird caught in oil provide a cause/effect relationship.

3. Your partner should then give you an oral explanation of the cause/effect relationship. Use of a sequential order should make the explanation clear. For example, your partner should explain how each picture logically leads from the cause (oil tanker) to the effect (dead bird).

4. Repeat the exercise by reversing the instructions. Explain the effect and cause relationship orally. For example, point out the effect (dead bird) first, and the cause (oil tanker) last.

5. Decide which order was better, cause/effect or effect/cause.

6. Repeat the exercise with a different topic.

Exercise Seven   Sequential Order

In arranging supporting evidence in sequential order, you place items in a list of instructions in the order in which they should be carried out.

Choose one of the following *general* topics. Make up a list of instructions, writing each instruction on a separate piece of paper. Then have your partner organize the list in sequential order. Repeat the exercise, reversing roles.

a) How to pass history.

b) How to prepare spaghetti and meat balls.

c) How to serve a tennis ball.

d) How to hold a racquetball racquet. (Or make up another "How to ...")

Exercise Eight   Spatial Order

In arranging supporting evidence in spatial order, you place descriptive details in terms of how you want your reader to see them: near to far, far to near, right to left, up to down, and so on.

1. Describe orally the room in which you sleep so that your partner can draw a map of it. (You are not allowed to look at your partner's map during your description.)

2. Begin with the dimensions of the room, giving the location, number, and size of the doors and windows.

3. In your description you must mention at least twenty things to be included in the map. To help your partner draw the room accurately, begin with the exact position of the bed so that your partner can position everything else in relation to it. To achieve coherence through spatial organization, you can use transitional words like *underneath, above, opposite to*, and *behind*.

4. When your partner finishes the map, see how accurate the picture of your room it is. If there are glaring mistakes, discuss why they occurred.

5. Repeat the exercise, reversing the roles.

Exercise Nine Chronological Order

In arranging supporting evidence in chronological order, you arrange events in the order in which they occur. If you introduce events out of order (flashbacks or flash forwards), you should prepare your reader for the shift in time.

1. Tell your partner a story from the first person viewpoint (I) or the third person viewpoint (he/she). Use a chronological order. All your partner has to do is number each new event that happens in your story.

To keep your narrative coherent, you might like to repeat key words like the names of your characters and *I, my, him, she*, and *they*. Also use transitional devices like *although, as, in order that, then*, and *since*.

2. Discuss with your partner the order of each of your events. Did your story have a beginning, middle, and end? Was there an apparent order? Were the events in the best order? In what other order could the story have been told?

3. Now your partner should do the exercise.

Exercise Ten Climactic Order

In arranging supporting evidence in climactic order, you should arrange the events in terms of their importance.

1. Ask your partner to provide six or seven reasons, facts, and examples to prove a statement. Because this is an oral exercise, allow a few minutes for preparation.

Examples
a) Some of the rules at our school could be eliminated.
b) There are many kitchen gadgets that are useless.
c) Teenage clothing is conformist.
   (Or choose your own statement.)
Make sure your partner takes a strong stand, either for or against something. The argument should open with a *general* main claim and then have *particular*

examples to prove the statement. Transition words like *furthermore*, *similarly*, *moreover*, *in additon*, and *finally* will help organize each idea coherently according to its importance.

2. When your partner finishes his/her proof, challenge any piece of information that was either incorrect or inappropriate. If a fact is not absolutely accurate, it should be researched and corrected or omitted.

3. Discuss the order of each item of proof. If you start with the least important and end with the most important, you are building to a climactic ending for your audience. If you organize from the most to the least important, you are giving the beginning the greater impact. Which method did your partner use? Was it effective? Should any item be moved?

4. Now reverse the exercise so that you prove a statement.

Exercise Eleven   Unfamiliar to Familiar

In arranging supporting evidence in unfamiliar-to-familiar order, you should introduce the unfamiliar item, explain it in terms of something familiar, and conclude with the unfamiliar item.

1. Orally, explain one of the following technically difficult subjects or abstractions to your partner. Take a few minutes to decide on something familiar that you can compare your subject to; for example, a *byte* is similar to a letter or punctuation mark.

  a) logarithms
  b) bytes on a computer disk
  c) body language
  d) theory of relativity
  e) IQ testing
  f) hypnosis
  g) kilopascals
  h) transistors
  i) Rubik's cube
  j) satellite TV transmission
  k) communication

To help your explanation, use transitional expressions like *similarly*, *on the other hand*, or *somewhat like*.

2. Do not stop your explanation until your partner says, "I understand." Then, your partner should explain one of the other items to you, following the same instructions.

3. You and your partner may like to make up your own variations of this method of organization. For example, you might want to organize a piece of writing from *general to particular* or from *particular to general*. You might want to use an *analogy* or sustained figurative comparison. You might want to use *restatement* of the main claim in different words. Which of the above methods would you use to organize an essay about

a) Mother Teresa,
b) Love makes the world go 'round,
c) The method of delivering babies under water,
d) Your heritage?

Exercise Twelve

Each of the following pieces of writing has been developed mainly with one type of supporting evidence and organized in one specific manner. The heading on the left of each paragraph indicates the type of supporting evidence; that on the right, the method of organization.

With your partner, find examples within each piece of both the type of supporting evidence and the organization.

Type of Supporting Evidence   Method of Organization

Details   *Spatial Order*

A giraffe is the tallest animal in the world. He has long legs in order to outrun most of his enemies. His body is protectively coloured with large sandy–to–chestnut angular spots, closely spaced. A giraffe's most distinctive feature is his long neck, which he uses to reach for his favourite foods, acacia and mimosa leaves. As he quickly strips a tree with his extensible tongue and mobile lips, a giraffe looks positively indifferent, especially if he lowers his long eyelashes. But, if he lifts his head to look at you, his two short hairy horns seem to crown one of the haughtiest faces in the world.

Incidents   *Cause/Effect*

Last night I borrowed my dad's car without asking. It was just my luck that I hit the only patch of ice on an otherwise clear road and skidded into a telephone pole. To make matters worse, I discovered that I was a little short of money, so I had to call dad to pay the tow-truck driver for towing the car to the garage. Now I'm grounded for a month. Talk about bad luck!

Incidents   *Effect/Cause*

My dad won't let me out of the house after school for a month, just because of some bad luck. Last night I borrowed his car without asking and had the misfortune to skid on a piece of ice and hit a telephone pole. Then I found out that I didn't have enough money to pay to have the car towed to the garage, so I had to borrow fifty dollars from dad. That's bad luck for you!

Facts   *Comparison*

Julie and Julian are the two best-looking students in the room. Although of opposite sexes, they are similar in every other aspect. Their hair is blond and curly; their eyes are pools of liquid blue; their complexion smooth and healthy.

They sound the same; even their laughs are indistinguishable. With their slim, athletic bodies, they wear their clothes like professional models. To be with them for an hour or so is to be blessed with intelligent, stimulating conversation; when one stops speaking, the other one picks up mid-sentence. And no wonder. Julie and Julian are fraternal twins.

Examples   *Contrast*
Glenda Jackson is a buzz saw of an actress and *Rose* is a toothpick of a play. This sense of imbalance sets the tone of the evening. Jackson possesses a feral magnetism; the play is nerveless, somnolent, inert. She is direct; the play is diffuse. In vocal inflection and delivery, she is a wicked font of wit and irony; the play is parched for either.

Details   *Climactic Order*
When I entered her bedroom, I could not help thinking that it was the untidiest place I had ever seen. On first glance, the unmade bed dominated the room, with discarded clothes and books strewn among the sheets and blankets. But the mahogany dresser with half-empty cosmetic bottles, jars with lids off, and upturned boxes covering its top was even more disorganized. The once orange shag carpet, however, was the most revolting sight of all. The patches of shag that were not hidden under a blanket of old newspapers, smelly running shoes, and bags of leftover lunches, were distinctly green.

Examples   *Order of Importance*
Have you ever listened to our political leaders' voices as they debate? Not what they say; just their vocal range. The Liberals use their middle registers, indicating confidence. The Conservatives use their lower registers, indicating that they really know the truth. The NDP use their upper registers, indicating the hysteria that they believe is about to take over the country.

Illustration Through Description   *Climactic Order*
To appreciate a zoo, you should spend time in front of each cage. If you just walk by a tarsier's cage, for example, you might miss this monkeylike little beast altogether. Because the tarsier chooses darkness as protection from his enemies, you will have to be patient to get a glimpse of him. When you do, though, you will see his round head, closely set in his shoulders, his froglike face, his naked ears, and his enormous eyes. Without moving his tiny body, the tarsier can turn that head of his so that he can look directly to the rear – almost instantly. And if what he sees alarms him, he can jump six or seven times his length.

Details   *Unfamiliar to Familiar*
Few people have seen the rare and endangered sandhill crane. Unlike the great blue heron, with which it is often confused, the sandhill crane is unable to escape human disturbance by perching and nesting in tall trees. A bird of

the open plains, marshes, and bogs, the sandhill crane spends its entire life on the ground. Because it is very sensitive to disturbance, its only defence is to put distance between itself and its enemy.

Illustration Through Narration   *Climactic Order*

Some people would not have a cat in their house, and now I know why. Before our cat died, I never left the house without having to get my mom to defur me. Bossy shed all year long; her long, white hairs clung to my clothes like miniature magnets. Bossy also liked to scratch everything in the house except her scratching post. Our furniture was always in tatters. Whenever we had company, Mother would cover the arms of the sofa and chairs to hide Bossy's latest tears. I always thought cats were supposed to be clean. Bossy wasn't told this. Before she consumed it, she would drag her food onto something soft: the carpet, my bed, clothes that were lying around. And the only place where she would noisily court the neighbour cat was on the front porch. Goodbye, Bossy, and good riddance!

Facts   *Chronological Order*

The Beatles were the most remarkable musical team of all time. After getting together in Liverpool, they struggled for recognition for several years. Becoming a hit in England, the Beatles soon became a world phenomenon. Wherever they played, crowds screamed hysterically for more. Besides giving concerts on stage and television, they became film stars in the film, "A Hard Day's Night." At the height of their fame, they broke up, married, and went their own ways. Their fans hoped and speculated that they would eventually get together. These hopes were shattered in December, 1980 with the murder of John Lennon.

Questions   *Particular to General*

Do you remember the Sixties? Do "flower power," Haight-Ashbury, Woodstock, the Maharishi, anti-war demonstrations, and the Kennedys mean anything to you? Do Kent State and the computer centre at Sir George Williams University ring a bell? Have you had a nostalgic urge lately to flash a peace sign at someone? Well, you're not alone – some of us remember the Sixties as the most exciting years of our lives.

Quoted Material   *Restatement*

There are as many ways of describing love as there are lovers. It is "like a red, red rose," and "like sunshine after rain." It "makes the world go 'round." It is "a flame," or "a sickness"; it is "nature's second sun" or "the coldest of critics." It is "that orbit of the restless soul" and "the sweetest thing on earth." My favourite definition of love, though, is "that state in which the happiness of another person is essential to your own."

Reasons   *Cause/Effect*

Do lake monsters exist? Many people believe they have actually seen them.
However, I cannot believe that they exist in our lakes. The evidence is not
convincing. Most reported sightings come after there has been newspaper
publicity, suggesting that people are responding to mob psychology. There is
no physical evidence for lake monsters other than photographs, and photographs can be faked. Most reported sightings turn out to be hoaxes. Many
towns around lakes that supposedly are the homes of monsters rely on tourists;
talking about lake monsters is good for business.

Results   *Sequential Order*

After you fill a separator with a pail of fresh cow's milk, and operate it for a
while, you will have one container of milk and one of cream. Placing the
cream into a churn, you can – after half an hour's pumping – have a couple of
kilograms of butter and a jug of buttermilk. Then, you're all set for a hearty
breakfast: buttermilk pancakes smothered in butter and syrup with a glass of
wholesome milk.

Details   *Analogy*

A campfire is a thing of sensual delight, as entertaining and appealing as any
ballet. Consider the flaming whirling dervishes, roaring and sighing as they
perform their suicidal fandango. This antediluvian performance (bequeathed
by Prometheus), divinely choreographed, duplicates no movements. The sparks
of lust and desire ignite in a frantic conflagration, kindled by the caressing
fingers of heat massaging away the nocturnal fears and bugaboos.

IV. Unifying Supporting Evidence

Once you have learned to organize your writing, unifying it should pose no
difficulty. You should be able to see which pieces of evidence support your
main claim and which are irrelevant or illogical.

Constructing an outline is a natural, easy, logical outcome of all the work
you have done in collecting, listing, organizing, and unifying your supporting
evidence. Read over the following outline, based on the mandala in Exercise
Three. Notice how parallelism is used.

Canadian Legal System Involves Every Citizen
  I. Introduction
  II. Government
    A. Makes laws
    B. Sets punishments
    C. Gives personal freedom
    D. Protects minorities
    E. Protects economy

III. Courts
    A. Decide if person is guilty or innocent of crime
    B. Decide punishment
IV. Police
    A. Prevent people from breaking the law
    B. Recover stolen property
    C. Catch lawbreakers
 V. Penal System
    A. Carries out punishment
    B. Tries to rehabilitate criminals
VI. Canadian Citizens
    A. Have power to elect members of parliament who
       1. make laws
       2. change laws
    B. Enjoy freedom and order the law provides
    C. Must obey laws
VII. Conclusion

The final step would be to draft an essay from your outline. Do you see how easy it would be to write an essay from the above outline?

Exercise Thirteen

From your mandala of Exercise Three provide an outline. Work independently. When you and your partner have both completed your outlines, compare them. They should be similar. Check to see that all the items are parallel.

If you have been using this exercise in connection with a real assignment, you should now be ready to write your essay.

Special Writing Activity

On a topic of your choice, compose a short paragraph for your partner (similar to one of those in Exercise Twelve). Use the ideas discussed above to collect, list, and organize your supporting evidence. Be sure you know how every item relates to the main claim.

When you present it to your partner he or she should be able to indicate the type of supporting evidence you used (facts, details, reasons, and so on) and your method of organization (contrast, sequential order, general to particular, and so on).

Last Words

Whenever you write, make sure that you take time to organize all your supporting evidence so that your paper is unified.

Activity 3 Coherence

Background

When your writing is coherent, your reader cannot help but understand what you are saying: everything is tied together in a clear and logical manner.

There are several techniques that you can use to help your readers follow your ideas. First, you should use some logical method of organization (discussed fully in Activity 2). Second, you may want to repeat a key word or phrase to remind your reader of the important points of your essay. Third, you should connect sentences and paragraphs by introducing particular transitional devices.

Exercise One   Key Words

One method of achieving coherence is to repeat your subject's name throughout your writing. Your reader will thus be kept constantly aware of your subject.

But repetition of a word for its own sake, without a specific purpose, can be boring. You might find it a good idea to use replacement nouns or pronouns instead. You might, for example, in a paragraph discussing John Diefenbaker, refer to him as "the late John Diefenbaker," "the former prime minister," "the member from Prince Albert," "the Chief," as well as using pronouns such as "he," "his," "himself."

Prepare a one-minute talk for your partner on one of the following topics. As you talk, your partner should record your use of key words.
 a) The Queen of England
 b) Burt Reynolds
 c) Margaret Atwood
 d) Your father
 e) Your grandmother.

Special Writing Activity

Beginning a paper with three key words can also give it coherence. Read this paragraph, paying attention to the linking lines:

The Squirrel

Wary, delicate, beautiful – the squirrel reluctantly approaches my food-laden hand. Its quivering nose accentuated by a fluttering tail, the tiny creature lingers in the near distance. Startled by the faint scratch of a single falling leaf, it freezes momentarily. Darting closer, it exemplifies nature's perfection, as filtered sunlight reflects prisms of radiance from the squirrel's silvery tail. Determination outweighing fear, the little fellow momentarily abandons its post to accept my friendship; it retreats to safety just as rapidly as it appeared. On this late autumn day, the squirrel has given me a charming glimpse of life in the forest.

Study the lines that tie particular words to the first three words. Do you see how the words that have been connected give the paragraph coherence? Can you draw further lines?

Besides key words, what type of supporting evidence (facts, details, reasons, and so on) and which method of organization (comparison, cause/effect, analogy, and so on) have been used?

For your partner, write a paragraph beginning with three key words; for example: "Slippery, juicy, and tasty"; "Self-confident, stubborn, but good-natured"; "Tall, dark, and ugly." When you finish, see if your partner can draw lines similar to those in the above paragraph.

Exercise Two   Transitional Devices

Transitional expressions show relationships between thoughts and give a sense of direction and continuity. They assist the reader to move not only from detail to detail within a single sentence, but also from sentence to sentence and paragraph to paragraph. They are a vital factor in coherence.

1. With your partner, examine the following sentences

Weak Transition
Imported oil is now over $30.00 per barrel, and it has become a very expensive fuel.

Stronger Transition
Imported oil is now over $30.00 per barrel; *hence*, it has become a very expensive fuel. (*Note the punctuation.*)

No Transition
Canada's energy policy calls for Canadianization. The government believes that Canada's resources should be owned by Canadians.

Transition Added
The government believes that Canada's resources should be owned by Canadians; *moreover*, Canada's energy policy calls for Canadianization.

No Transition
The United States advocates a continental energy policy for North America. Canada and Mexico disagree with this approach.

Transition Added
The United States advocates a continental energy policy for North America. *On the other hand*, Canada and Mexico disagree with this approach.

No Transition
CANDU reactors use natural uranium and heavy water. They are considered safer to operate than other types of reactors. The uranium contained in them has been used by some countries to make atomic bombs.

Transition Added
CANDU reactors use natural uranium and heavy water. They are, *consequently*, considered safer to operate than other types of reactors. *Nevertheless*, the uranium contained in them has been used by some countries to make atomic bombs.

(Notice the position of the two transitional expressions. Could they be placed in other positions?)

2. Here is a list of some useful transitional expressions. As you and your partner read the list, notice the specific reasons for the use of certain transitional devices. Then, reread the four examples above. Which *new* transitional expressions could you substitute for the ones that have been used? As long as the meaning does not change, you could easily change the transitional expression.

Addition
in addition, again, moreover, further, furthermore, finally, lastly, at last, in conclusion, first, second, in the third place, (not *firstly*, *secondly*, and so on) once again

Comparison
similarly, likewise, in like manner, whereas, but, on the other hand, except, by comparison, where, compared to, up against, balanced against, vis-à-vis

Contrast
but, however, yet, still, nevertheless, on the other hand, after all, for all of that, on the contrary, notwithstanding, in contrast

Emphasis
in fact, indeed, in any event, certainly, definitely, never, extremely, absolutely, always, forever, perennially, eternally, emphatically, unquestionably, without a doubt, certainly, undeniably, without reservation

Example
for example, for instance, in this case, in another case, on this occasion, in this situation, take the case of ..., proof of this, evidence of this, thus, in this manner

Exception
yet, still, however, nevertheless, in spite of, despite, of course, once in a while, sometime

Place
near, beyond, opposite to, adjacent to, at the same place, here, there

Proof
for the same reason, obviously, evidently, furthermore, moreover, besides, indeed, in fact, in addition

Purpose
to this end, with this object, for this purpose

Result
accordingly, thus, consequently, hence, therefore, wherefore, thereupon

3. Notice how the following conjunctions function in the same way as transitional devices.

No Transition
The Alberta tar sands are considered an almost unlimited source of oil. Exploration in the Beaufort Sea has revealed large supplies.

Correlative Conjunctions Added for Transition
Not only are the Alberta tar sands considered an almost unlimited source of oil, *but* exploration in the Beaufort Sea has *also* revealed large supplies.

No Transition
In Canada, garbage is considered a nuisance and a health hazard. In some parts of the world it is burned to generate electricity.

Co-ordinate Conjunction Added for Transition
In Canada garbage is considered a nuisance and a health hazard, *yet* in some parts of the world it is burned to generate electricity.

Subordinate Conjunction Added for Transition
Although in some parts of the world garbage is burned to generate electricity, it is considered a nuisance and a health hazard in Canada.

Exercise Three

1. Independent of your partner, choose a reason for joining each of the following sentences. Then use an appropriate transitional device or conjunction.
   a) Negotiations were successfully completed with Native Peoples. Quebec began the vast James Bay hydro-electric project.
   b) Churchill Falls in Labrador furnishes power to nearby Quebec. It exports excess capacity to New York State.
   c) The Ark was built in Prince Edward Island. It has become world-famous. It uses energy efficiently.

d) Canada's energy policy stresses the ownership of Canadian resources by Canadians. Petro-Canada purchased Philips Petroleum. It purchased Petrofina. It may purchase other foreign-owned oil companies.

e) Nova Scotia has no hydro-electric generating capacity. It must purchase expensive foreign oil to provide electricity. Its citizens pay the highest electricity rates in Canada.

(Compare your use of transition with your partner's; then, both of you compare yours with the Suggested Answers at the end of the Activity Section.)

2. The following sentences support the main claim "Nuclear power can be dangerous." Rearrange the supporting evidence in a logical order, making sure *every* sentence is relevant to the claim. Change some key words to pronouns, and use a few transitional devices. Compare your paragraph with your partner's. Have you both produced coherent paragraphs? See the Suggested Answers for another treatment.

Nuclear power can be dangerous.
There was an accident at Three Mile Island in Pennsylvania.
You never know when there might be an accident at a power plant.
The movie *The China Syndrome* dramatized a disastrous accident at a plant like Three Mile Island.
People should be more concerned about problems like the disposal of radio-active waste.
Many people from nearby Middletown were evacuated by the U.S. National guard and the Pennsylvania state authorities.
A near disaster occurred in Mississauga, Ontario.
Authorities were afraid the radioactive core of the reactor would melt.
Thousands of people must protest.
There were no casulties at Three Mile Island.
Authorities may listen.

Last Words   Besides using a solid method of organization, you can enhance your coherence by repeating key words and using specific transitional devices.

Activity **4** Beginnings and Endings

Background

Most writers find that beginning and ending their pieces are their most difficult tasks. The King of Hearts' advice in *Alice in Wonderland*, "Begin at the beginning, go on until you come to the end, and then stop," is much harder to follow than would appear at first glance.

What do you want to accomplish at the beginning and end of your piece of writing? At the beginning you hope to capture your reader's attention, introduce your main claim and indicate your purpose for writing. At the end, you should sum up your piece in a new and interesting way so that your reader will think about what you have written.

This activity deals with ways to compose beginnings and endings for expository pieces, although much of the information in the following exercises may also be useful for narrative and descriptive writing. Specialized formats such as letters, proposals, memos, and résumés, are not specifically dealt with in this activity.

Exercise One   Beginnings

©1969 United Feature Syndicate, Inc.

First impressions are important. And in writing, composing a catchy sentence or two that grabs the reader's attention is what every writer dreams of doing. Many writers, unable to think of a way of starting, will compose an entire essay before they work on the opening. They may not even think of a title for their work until they have completed it.

With your partner, choose a topic that you both know something about. Examine the following methods of beginning a paragraph on the topic of "Racquetball." Try to write *seven* similar beginnings for your main claims.

1. The *statement*, the most commonly used opening, does not exactly serve as an attention-getter, but it does state what you are going to write about:

Racquetball has become very popular throughout North America.

Then you are ready to write your main claim:

It is one of the easiest games to learn.

This sentence implies that the body of the paragraph will explain how to play racquetball. If the reader is interested in the game, he or she is hooked.

2. The *generalization*, another common introduction, simply introduces your paragraph with a broad statement.

Everyone should have some way to stay physically fit.

Then state your particular main claim:

Racquetball is both good exercise and fun.

What do you think will follow?

3. The *attention-getting tactic* is to be used judiciously:

Racquetball can help save your life.

This beginning contains the "hook." What will the body of the paragraph be about?

4. The *question*, another frequently used method of introduction, asks one or two questions:

Who says exercise can't be fun?

The main claim can provide a logical answer:

Racquetball provides more exercise and more fun than any other court game.

What do you think will be included in the paragraph?

5. The *summary*, a useful introduction, tells your reader of several possible approaches, and then, in the main claim, states the one to be dealt with in the paragraph:

Every racquetball player has his or her reasons for taking up the game. My reason is a desire to find a sport in which both sexes can compete on equal terms.

The word "reason" gives you a clue to what will follow.

6. The *quotation*, if it is apt, can give authority to your paragraph:

A leading physical fitness expert says, "Racquetball provides one of the best ways to achieve all-round fitness."

This sentence hooks the reader and indicates what will follow. How?

7. The *analogy*, a comparison which will be sustained figuratively throughout the paragraph, can result in an accomplished piece of writing:

For many people today, the war against flab is waged on a square, whitewashed
battlefield – the racquetball court.

What does the "battle" imagery in this sentence suggest about the rest of the paragraph?

When you both complete your seven beginnings for your own topic, discuss their effectiveness, trying to decide which one would produce the best paragraph.

©1969 United Feature Syndicate, Inc.

Exercise Two Endings

Ending a piece of writing can be a difficult task for writers. From the time you first started to write paragraphs, you were probably told that your conclusion should summarize your writing in a new and interesting way. Frankly, this suggestion can be frustrating. What kind of ending qualifies as "new and interesting"? Is novelty for its own sake always a good idea? A better conclusion to strive for would be one which fulfils the expectations of the topic.

1. As you move toward your conclusion, keep an eye on your topic in general and on your main claim in particular. In that way your conclusion should satisfy you, your purpose, and your reader. Assuming that the paragraph has been developed along the lines of the beginnings in Exercise One, can you and your partner match these endings with their beginnings?
a) Tennis is out; I have become a racquetball maniac.
b) That a sport can be so much fun and at the same time so healthful makes it a natural choice for almost anyone.

c) Why not try it?

d) Fight flab; take up racquetball.

e) If fitness is important to you, consider starting a racquetball program.

f) Any time my court and my opponent are ready, so am I.

g) These are just a few of the reasons I enjoy racquetball.

2. For one of the beginnings that you and your partner were working on in Exercise One, compose three different endings. Discuss the appropriateness of each, and then decide on the best one.

©1969 United Feature Syndicate, Inc.

Exercise Three   Titles

Many writers think of a title before they begin to write; others use a "working title" which they may or may not use for their finished work; still others do not even think of a title until they have completed their work. No matter what method you use, consider the importance of a good title.

In composing a title, do not merely put down the name of your topic or repeat your main claim. A title should catch the reader's attention and let him or her know what to expect from the work.

From your experience, discuss the importance of titles with your partner. Use the following questions or make up others:

a) Which musical group do you think has the most suitable name? Which one do you think does not suit its name? Why?

b) What are the different names that people call you? Which one(s) do you like? Do you not like? Why? Which name is the real you?

c) What kind of title would make you pick up a book? Why?

If you want to see a paragraph which uses one of the beginnings and endings in the above exercises, turn to "Racquetball Mania" in the Models at the end of Assignment 4. What do you think of the title?

Exercise Four   Narration

1. Assume that you and your partner are going to write a narrative about a haunted house. Independent of each other, compose two different beginnings.

2. Compare them, and determine which one would make the best opening for the narrative.
3. Then, for that beginning, independently compose two different endings.
4. Compare them, and determine which one would be the best conclusion for the narrative.
5. Then, for the beginning and ending, independently compose two different titles.
6. Compare them, and determine which one would be the best title for the narrative.

Exercise Five

Description

1. Assume that you and your partner are going to write a description of each other's face. Independent of each other, compose two different beginnings.
2. Compare them and determine which one would make the best opening for the description.
3. Then, for that beginning, independently compose two different endings.
4. Compare them and determine which one would be the best conclusion for the description.
5. Then, for the beginning and ending, independently compose two different titles.
6. Compare them, and determine which one would be the best title for the description.

Last Words

Before you give a piece of writing to your intended reader, check three things: the title, the beginning, and the ending.

Activity 5 Consistency

Background

Your writing can be unified and coherent, as described in the preceding activities, but it can still confuse your audience if it is not consistent. You should not shift from one verb tense to another, from active to passive voice, from a singular subject to a plural verb, from a third person point of view to a second, and so on.

The following exercises and games, which are varied and detailed, will involve you and your partner in oral rather than written activities so that you can quickly correct any inconsistencies that occur. Because this activity deals with many types of consistency, you should do only the exercises you really need.

Exercise One

Verb Tenses

1. Tell your partner, in two or three sentences, about the last time you bought something. Use the simple past tense.

Examples

I *went* to the box office because I *wanted* to buy tickets for a "Loverboy" concert.

I *was able* to get good seats, so I *paid* for them and *started* to leave.

Fortunately, I *remembered* to check my tickets because I *had received* the wrong ones.

If you do not have a good memory, write these sentences down because you are going to use them many times in this exercise. You only need to write the group *once*, for reference; the rest of this exercise is oral.

2. So that you can experiment with other forms of the past tense, retell the story in various ways. If your partner hears any inconsistencies, he or she should interrupt you. Make sure you keep your entire story in the past.

Examples

I *had gone* to the box office because I *wanted* to buy ... .

I *went* to the box office because I *had been wanting* to buy ... .

3. Retell the story using verbs in one of the present tenses:

Examples
I *go* to the box office because I *want* to buy ... .
I *am going* to the box office because I *want* to buy ... .

4. Retell the story using verbs of the future tense:

Examples
I *shall be going* to the box office because I *want* to buy ... .
I'll go to the box office because I *want* to buy ... .

From now on, when you write, consider the advantages of rewriting your work in various tenses. Rewriting a piece in the present tense may result in a piece more vital and immediate than one written in the past tense.

5. To be able to change from one tense to another, you should have a knowledge of the three main forms of a verb: present, past, and past participle. With your partner, look over this list, which contains some irregular verbs in common use.

Present Tense	Past Tense	Past Participle (always used with auxiliary verbs *to be* or *to have*
arise	arose	(has) arisen
begin	began	begun
bring	brought	brought
catch	caught	caught
choose	chose	chosen
come	came	come
dive	dived, dove	dived
do	did	done
draw	drew	drawn
drink	drank	drunk
drive	drove	driven
eat	ate	eaten
fall	fell	fallen
fly	flew	flown
get	got	got
go	went	gone
hang	hung	hung
hang (execute)	hanged	hanged
know	knew	known
lay	laid	laid
lend	lent	lent
lie (recline)	lay	lain
lie (tell a falsehood)	lied	lied
ride	rode	ridden
raise	raised	raised
rise	rose	risen
set	set	set
speak	spoke	spoken
swim	swam	swum
teach	taught	taught
write	wrote	written

Game One

Tense Tenses

In preparation for the game, you and your partner will each need to draw up a list of verbs. Taking turns, give each other the present tense of the verb. The object of the game is for your opponent to provide the past tense and the past participle. For example:

"A" gives "B" "run."
"B" responds with "ran" and "ran" for two points. Then gives "A" "grow."
"A" responds with "grew" and "grew." "B" says, "The past participle is 'grown'; you only get one point." Then "A" gives "B" "do."
The game continues.

6. Using the sentences you worked with in steps 1 to 4, tell the story using the auxiliary verbs below. (You will not be able to use each auxiliary with every verb, but every verb will be affected.)

Examples
  a) *will* (showing determination)
     I *will go* to the box office because I *want* to buy ... .
  b) *should, would, could* (use various tenses)
     I *should go* to the box office because I *want* to buy ... .
     I *would have gone* to the box office because I *wanted* to buy ... .
     I *could go* to the box office because I *want* to buy ... .
  c) *may, can, might, must* (use various tenses)
     I *may go* to the box office because I *want* to buy ... . (permission)
     I *can go* to the box office because I *want* to buy ... .(ability)
     I *might have gone* to the box office because I *wanted* to buy ... .
     I *must go* to the box office because I *want* to buy ... .
  d) *ought*
     I *ought to go* to the box office because I *want* to buy ... .

Exercise Two   **Active and Passive Voice**

Beginning writers often shift between active and passive voice because they want to bring variety to their writing, but this shift often leads to confusion on the part of the reader. Remember that in *active voice* the subject is the doer of the action, while in *passive voice* the subject is the receiver of an action. Generally, active voice is stronger because it is direct; passive voice is weaker and indirect. Passive voice, however, is appropriate and effective in some circumstances. To ensure that your reader will stay on track, keep the verbs in a single sentence (and perhaps in your entire piece of writing) in the *same* voice.

1. For practice, ask your partner to provide a sentence in the passive voice which you can convert to the active. Decide which sentence is better for your purpose.

Examples
  a) *Passive:* My neighbour *was bitten* by my dog.
    (The subject "neighbour" receives the bite.)
    Active: My dog *bit* my neighbour.
    (The subject "dog" is doing the biting.)
  b) *Passive:* The bell *could be heard* for miles.
    (The subject "bell" is not doing the hearing.)
    Active: Everyone for miles *could hear* the bell.
    (The subject "everyone" is doing the hearing.)

2. After working from passive to active, reverse the procedure.
  a) *Active:* I *hit* the ball.
    Passive: The ball *was hit* by me.
  b) *Active:* The tree *cast* a shadow.
    Passive: A shadow *was cast* by the tree.

3. When you are certain of the difference between active and passive voice, examine a recent piece of your writing. Underline all the verb forms, including auxiliaries. Do you shift from active to passive within your sentences?

Before you rewrite your piece, look at these two excerpts, taken from student writing.

  a) ...After two years in Brisbane, Australia *was abandoned* for the second time. After *enjoying* six months on a temporary nursing assignment in Dallas, Texas, I *travelled* to Europe to *spend* a year *touring* the many splendid places which *were* previously *missed*. ... The next three years *were spent working* in Canada, the United States, and Britain. Each new experience *was relished*.

"Was abandoned," "were missed," "were spent," and "was relished" are passive. The inconsistencies in voice are confusing. In the first sentence, it appears that Australia was "two years in Brisbane." The following version is clear and consistent:

...After two years in Brisbane, I abandoned Australia for the second time. After enjoying six months on a temporary nursing assignment in Dallas, Texas, I travelled to Europe to spend a year touring the many splendid places which I had previously missed. ... (Continue revising so that the last two sentences use active verbs.)

  b) ...First of all dives *should be done* in deep water *to avoid* injuries. *Stand* on the edge of the pool deck. Feet *should be* shoulder-width apart with toes *curled* over the edge. Arms *are placed* directly above the head, *interlocking* thumbs *to ensure* this position *is maintained* throughout the dive. Second, knees and upper body *are bent* forward. After *adopting* this position, *fall* forward, *kicking* the feet out behind. If these directions *are followed*, mastery of this dive *will result* after only a few tries.

With your partner, try to rewrite this excerpt, ensuring that you use only active voice. (When you finish, turn to the Suggested Answers to compare the student's rewrite with yours.)

Exercise Three   Subject/Verb Agreement

Subjects and verbs must agree in number with each other. Unknowingly, beginning writers often provide a plural verb for a singular subject, or vice versa. Look over these examples.

Inconsistent
Multiple births for a couple is seldom anticipated.
Consistent
Multiple births for a couple are seldom anticipated. ("Births" and "are" are plural.)

1. Before dealing specifically with consistency in number, look at the following sentences. Taking turns with your partner, change everything that is in italic to the plural.

a) *An* Ontario *citizen* in the thirties could never have anticipated the impact of the *birth* of *each* of the quintuplets on May 28, 1934 to Elzire and Oliva Dionne.

b) *A person* from *one walk of life* came to *her* hometown to see *her*, including *a star, a member of royalty, an ordinary commoner.*

c) The quintuplets were seen in *a newspaper, a movie,* and during *a personal appearance.*

2. It seems obvious that a singular subject requires a singular verb, and a plural subject requires a plural verb; however, difficulties often arise in determining whether a subject is singular or plural. Review with your partner the following points:

a) Nouns that act as collective units take singular verbs:

The Dionne *family was* constantly on display in its special home, Quintland. The *press was* always ready to publicize their smallest action.

If the parts of the collective unit are considered more important than the collective whole, however, the verb must be plural:

The *family were* never really close, despite Mr. Dionne's efforts to unite them.

The *press were* never told that Emilie had epileptic seizures.

b) Plural nouns that are singular in meaning take singular verbs; (for example, *measles, mumps, billiards, news, economics, mathematics, logistics, linguistics*).

Economics was an important factor in the quints' early lives.

These, however, are always considered plural: *trousers, tongs, wages, tactics, pliers, scissors, odds, glasses, barracks, insignia.*

Glasses were worn by at least one of the quints.

And these nouns can be either singular or plural, depending on their meaning: *acoustitcs, gymnastics, ethics, politics, statistics, acrobatics.*

Politics was indirectly responsible for the quints' estrangement from their family.

("Were" would also be correct since *politics* can be used to refer to a single entity or several political groups.)

Quoted literary titles and names of organizations are always singular.

We Were Five, by James Brough, *was* based on the quints' remembrance of their childhood.

The Board of Guardians *was* set up by the Ontario government to oversee the quints' professional and financial activities.

c) Co-ordinate nouns (joined by *and*) that refer to the same person or thing take singular verbs:

A TV special and documentary *was* made from Pierre Berton's book, *The Dionne Years.*

A country doctor and instant celebrity *was* Dr. Allan Dafoe, who delivered the quints.

Use a singular verb when *every* or *each* precedes co-ordinate nouns.

Every man and woman who saw the quints *was* captivated by them.

d) Singular subjects followed by parenthetical expressions introduced by *with, along with, together with, as well as, like, including, in addition to,* and *no less than,* take singular verbs:

Mrs. Elzire Dionne, together with her seven other children and her husband, *was* living in a house nearby.

To avoid this rather formal construction you might use *and*. Note, the verb changes because the number changes:

Mrs. Elzire Dionne, her husband, and her seven other children *were* living in a house nearby.

e) Compound singular objects joined by *and* take plural verbs:

Cecile, Yvonne, Emilie, Annette, and Marie *were* raised in isolation.
Raised in isolation *were* Cecile, Yvonne, Emilie, Annette, and Marie.

f) The constructions *one of those ... who, one of those ... which,* and *that* take plural verbs:

Dionne was one of those *people* who *have* trouble handling sudden fame.

Locate the antecedent of the pronoun *who, which,* or *that.* In the above sentence, the antecedent of "who" is "people." Hence, the plural verb "have" is needed, not the singular "has." (*Note:* an *antecedent* is the word a pronoun replaces.)

g) When a compound subject is joined by *or, either ... or, neither ... nor, not only ... but also,* the verb agrees with the nearest subject:

Neither their *father* nor their *mother was* allowed to live in the same house they did.
(Two singular subjects; verb is singular.)
Either the resident *nurses* or *Dr. Dafoe was* in charge at all times.
(Plural subject plus a singular subject; verb is singular.)
Either *Dr. Dafoe* or the resident *nurses were* in charge at all times.
(Singular subject plus a plural subject; verb is plural.)

h) When the subject of the verb differs in number from the complement, the verb always agrees with the subject rather than the complement:

The quints' *births were* a phenomenon.
The only *company* for the first few years of their lives *was* nurses.

A *complement* follows a verb that has no action, and therefore needs to be completed. The above sentences make no sense without the complements, "phenomenon" and "nurses."

i) The number of the noun in a prepositional phrase does not affect the number of the verb:

The father of the quintuplets *was* Oliva Dionne, a farmer.

If you read the sentence *without* the prepositional phrase, you will then have no problem with agreement:

The father *was* Oliva Dionne, a farmer.

j) *There* and *here* are adverbs, not subjects, and do not affect the number of the verb:

There *were* five little girls whom all wanted to claim as their own.
("Girls" is the subject, therefore, you would not use "was.")

k) Indefinite pronouns often cause problems with agreement. Take a few minutes to study these lists.

Indefinite pronouns that take a singular verb			Indefinite pronouns that take a plural verb	
anyone	everybody	nothing	both	many
everyone	somebody	anything	several	few
no one	someone	everything	a number	
each	either	neither	a variety	

Everything about the quints *was* news.
A number of films *were* made about them.

A third list of indefinite pronouns needs more attention: *none, some, any, most, all, more.* When you use one of these, remember this: use a singular verb when the pronoun refers to nouns of quantity or bulk; use a plural verb when it refers to units or numbers.

Most of the *money* the quints made *was* kept in trust for them.
None of their *brothers and sisters were* close to them.

Game Two | Agreement

Rules: In preparation for the game, collect a number of sentences where there could be some confusion over the agreement between the subject and the verb. Remove the verb and supply a choice for your opponent, who gets one point for choosing the correct verb and one point for naming its subject.

Example:
"A" *gives* "B": "*Country Doctor*, as well as several other films, (is, are) about Dr. Dafoe."
"B" answers, *is* and *Country Doctor* for two points. Then "B" gives "A": "The odds of the birth of identical quintuplets (is, are) one in 57,000,000.
"A" answers, *are* and *odds* for two points, then gives "B": "There (was, were) a countryman and his wife, faced with this extraordinary occurrence." The game continues.

Exercise Four | Agreement of Pronouns and Their Antecedents

Both pronouns and possessive adjectives should agree in gender, person, and number with their antecedents (the words they refer to).

Consistency in gender
Mr. Dionne fought to regain the custody of *his* daughters.
(You would never write "her daughters.")

Consistency in person

Dr. Dafoe, on the other hand, wanted the quints under *his* control.
(You would never consider "their control.")

Consistency in number

Each of the quints noticed that *she* was different from other people.
(The pronoun "she" has "each" as its antecedent. Both are singular in number.)

1. Pronouns must agree in *number* with their antecedents. Read and discuss the following suggestions with your partner.

a) A plural pronoun is used to refer to two or more singular antecedents joined by *and*:

As nurses, Yvonne Leroux and Mollie O'Shaughnessy devoted *themselves* to the quints for several years.

b) But a singular pronoun is used to refer to two or more singular antecedents joined by *or* or *nor:*

Neither the doctor nor Fred Davis, the publicity photographer, allowed the parents to interfere with *his* time with the quints.

c) If, however, the first antecedent is singular and the second is plural, the pronoun reference should be plural. (It should agree with the nearest antecedent.)

Neither Dr. Dafoe nor the nurses would allow *their* charges to have pets or associate with other children.

d) If the nearest antecedent is singular, the pronoun reference is singular.

Neither the nurses nor Dr. Dafoe would allow *his* charges to have pets or associate with other children.

e) When a pronoun refers to a collective antecedent, you must determine its meaning in the sentence.

Singular in meaning

The public had *its* appetite for news of the quints whetted on every special occasion by pictures and newsreel appearances.

Plural in meaning

The public, writing from all over North America, thought of the quints as *theirs*.

f) Notice the use of the indefinite pronoun in the following sentences.

Singular

Everyone sent a post card home to *his* wife, saying "I was here."

Plural

A variety of companies used the quints in *their* advertising.
(If in doubt, refer to the list of indefinite pronouns in the previous exercise.)

2. Pronouns must agree in *gender* with their antecedents. This seems an obvious thing to do, but it does pose a few problems. For instance, what pronoun should a writer use when the antecedent is obviously both male and female?

No one left Callander without *his* souvenir.
No one left Callander without *her* souvenir.
No one left Callander without *his* or *her* souvenir.
No one left Callander without *her* or *his* souvenir.
No one left Callander without *his/her* souvenir.

All of the above would be correct; the choice is yours.
You may not write:
No one left Callander without *their* souvenir.

Even though it gets around the gender problem nicely, *their* does not agree in number with *no one*. However, through usage, *their*, or some other word meaning *his or her* may one day become standard.

3. Finally, pronouns must agree in *person* with their antecedents.

Inconsistent
Even today *we* enjoy talking about the quints, and *you* can still visit the house where they were born.

Consistent
Even today *we* enjoy talking about the quints, and *we* can still visit the house where they were born.

Game Three

Antecedent Difficulties

Rules: Use the same rules as Game Two, except that you get one point for naming the correct pronoun or possessive adjective and one point for naming its antecedent.

Example:
"A" gives "B": "Both Yvonne and Marie announced (her, their) intention to become nuns."
"B" answers, "*their* because its antecedent is *Yvonne and Marie*" for two points. Then "B" gives "A": "A convention would be held in Toronto to allow (its, it's, their) delegates to visit the quints."
"A" answers, "*its* because its antecedent is *convention*." "A" gives "B": "An American, with his fiancee, travelled to Callander for (his, their) wedding." Continue the game.

Exercise Five   Point of View

It is possible to write from several points of view: first person (I), second person (you), or third person (he/she; one). Normally, once you have established your point of view, you should maintain it throughout the selection.

1. Explain something to your partner from your point of view. You must use *I*, *me*, *my*, *myself*, and *mine*.

If *I* want to spend the summer with *my* relatives in Manitoba, *I* will have to go by *myself* as *my* parents are working. *My* sister will have to lend *me* her suitcase as *my* brother has borrowed *mine*.

2. Orally, re-explain to your partner from the second person point of view. Use *you, your, yours, yourself*.

If *you* want to spend the summer with *your* relatives in Manitoba ...

(Notice that other words may need to be changed.)

3. Now, use the third person male or female point of view: *he, her, him, herself*.

If *she* wants to spend the summer with *her* relatives in Manitoba ... .

4. Now, use the impersonal third person: *one, one's, oneself*.

If *one* wants to spend the summer with *one's* relatives in Manitoba ... .

5. Reverse the exercise with your partner.

6. Which point of view did you find the most comfortable to use? The most awkward?

7. There may be times when you want to change your point of view within a piece of writing. If this is so, you should always inform your readers. Notice how this writer shifts from second person to first:

You want to spend the summer with your relatives in Manitoba? Well, let me tell you about my experiences there.

(What follows will obviously be in the first person.)

8. If you wish, you could repeat the point of view exercise using plural forms: First person (we, our, ours, ourselves) and third person (they, them, their, theirs, themselves). The second person is the same for singular and plural except for "yourselves" in the plural point of view.

Sentence Work

Do you and your partner see inconsistencies in person in these sentences? If not, see the Suggested Answers.

a) If you want to go to Yellowknife, North West Territories, the most convenient way one can travel is by plane.

b) When I moved to Vancouver, I discovered that you are able to live quite contentedly without snow.

c) The government of Alberta has made a historic site of their first oil well, Imperial Leduc Number One; it's not far from the Trans-Canada Highway.

d) If one wants to give credit for the discovery of Saskatchewan, he should go to Henry Kelsey.

Exercise Six

Tone

Although handled in Activity 15, consistency in levels of word choice will be mentioned briefly here. If you start informally, for example, do not shift to formal word choice; if you establish formality, do not introduce colloquialisms.

Sentence Work

Decide whether to change or omit the italicized words in these sentences so that the tone is consistent. If you cannot think of a way to solve the problem, look in a thesaurus *before* turning to the Suggested Answers.

a) Indubitably, the province of Manitoba, being in the geographical centre of the country, is *pretty well fixed* to obtain goods and services from the East and West.

b) If you have to do *hard time* in a federal prison in Ontario, chances are you'll find yourself in the *metropolis* of Kingston, where several penitentiaries are situated.

c) A stone wall surrounds the older section of Quebec City, and some of the streets are *stoned* too.

d) Legally, Moncton should be spelled with a "k," since it was given its *nomenclature* in honour of General Monck.

e) Halifax has been and continues to be one of the *premier* seaports in North America.

Last Words

During your polishing process make sure you have cleared up any inconsistencies; for example, see that your subjects agree with their verbs, that you do not start with one point of view and shift to another, and that you do not begin a sentence in the past tense and end it in the present tense.

Activity 6 "Unwriting" – Paraphrase, Précis, Summary, Outline

Background

As a student, you have probably had to take notes during lectures, condense essays, boil down chapters of textbooks, or rewrite complicated passages. In doing these tasks, you reversed the writing process. Rather than building a piece of writing from main claim to finished product, you reduced a finished product to its main ideas. This process can be called "unwriting." In this activity you will examine several forms of unwriting: the *paraphrase*, *précis*, *summary*, and *outline*. As well, you will learn how to pick out the *main claim*.

Exercise One

1. Tell your partner a story, anecdote, joke, personal experience, or anything else that you can think of. Your partner should listen and enjoy, without interrupting. (This is difficult for most listeners, but your story will be easier to paraphrase if its continuity is not broken.)

2. When you have finished, your partner should retell in his/her own words what you have said. This repeated story in your partner's words is a *paraphrase* of your original words.

3. Now, ask your partner to retell the story, condensing it to half its original length. He or she must decide what to include and what to omit. Only the main claim and the most important parts of the development should remain. This condensation is a *précis* of the original. (By the way, the précis can use your original words or the words of your partner's paraphrase.)

4. Then, ask your partner to tell you about the story in even fewer words. He or she must mention the main point of the story and, very briefly, what happened. This is a *summary*. (It, too, can be in your own or your partner's words.)

5. Next, ask your partner to tell you the story in point form, using numbers: first, second, third, and so on. This is an *outline*.

6. Finally, your partner should state the main point of your story. This is the *main claim* or *thesis statement*.

7. Then repeat the activity. This time your partner tells a story, and you do the unwriting.

Exercise Two

1. Your partner and you should read one of the short stories from Assignment 10. After reading the selection, discuss with your partner anything that you don't understand.

2. Look up unfamiliar words or metaphors and allusions. Study the structure of the story, the length and types of sentences that the author has used, what sort of transitions are made, and how the story as a whole fits together. (This advice applies to anything you want to unwrite.)

3. Jot down all the ideas that you think are important. Include each idea only once, though the author may mention it several times.

4. In your own words restate each point, changing its order if you feel it necessary. Remember you are the audience, and the purpose for your unwriting is to make the original clearer and more concise.

5. Work with your partner to collectively write a paraphrase, précis (in the author's or your own words), summary (in the words of either), outline, and main claim.

Exercise Three

You may often find that you are obliged to read something that contains difficult or archaic words, phrases, and allusions. If you "unwrite" it, suddenly it makes much more sense.

Take turns with your partner in paraphrasing the following speech from *Romeo and Juliet.*

ROMEO:	If I profane with my unworthiest hand This holy shrine, the gentle sin is this, My lips, two blushing pilgrims, ready stand To smooth that rough touch with a tender kiss.
JULIET:	Good pilgrim, you do wrong your hand too much, Which mannerly devotion shows in this, For saints have hands that pilgrims' hands do touch, And palm to palm is holy palmers' kiss.
ROMEO:	Have not saints lips and holy palmers too?
JULIET:	Ay, pilgrim, lips that they must use in prayer.
ROMEO:	O then dear saint, let lips do what hands do – They pray. Grant thou, lest faith turn to despair.
JULIET:	Saints do not move, though grant for prayers' sake.
ROMEO:	Then move not while my prayer's effect I take. Thus from my lips, by thine, my sin is purg'd.
JULIET:	Then have my lips the sin that they have took.
ROMEO:	Sin from my lips? O trespass sweetly urg'd! Give me my sin again.
JULIET:	You kiss by th' book.

(If you have paraphrased correctly, Romeo will have kissed Juliet twice.)

The importance of paraphrasing pieces of literature will become evident when you write literary essays. If you come across a difficult patch of writing in any short story, novel, poem, or play that you are studying, talk through a paraphrase with someone until you completely understand what you are reading.

Exercise Four

(For this exercise, choose a partner who is unfamiliar with your writing.)

1. Read an essay that you have written to your partner.

2. When you finish, ask your partner to paraphrase, in his/her own words, what the essay is about.

3. Your partner should repeat steps 1 and 2 so that you can hear and paraphrase his/her essay.

4. You can both carry this exercise further by presenting a précis and summary of each other's essay. Then present an outline and the main claim.

... THE GREAT ONE, WAYNE GRETZKY, HAVING AN UNBELIEVABLE NIGHT, DASHED THROUGH THE MAPLELEAF DEFENDERS, PROJECTING A BLISTERING DRIVE PAST HELPLESS NETMINDER BUNNY LAROCQUE BUT THE SHOT RICOCHETED UP OVER THE CROSSBAR INTO THE THUNDERING CROWD!

GRETZKY HIT THE POST!

Exercise Five

1. Find a somewhat difficult piece of writing of no more than 300 words from the editorial pages of a newspaper or a magazine.
2. Read the article aloud to your partner. Your partner may make notes but may not interrupt you or look at what you are reading.
3. When you finish, ask your partner to tell you what the article is about. Remember, whether the paraphrase is shorter or longer than the original, it should be easier to understand.
4. When your partner finishes the paraphrase, discuss whether any important points were either left out or not clarified.
5. Repeat the exercise, with your partner reading his/her article to you.

Exercise Six

In many universities and colleges, students are expected to write a test to determine whether they will be admitted into the regular first-year English course. Often, as part of the test, they are required to write a précis. The original material is usually about 600 words long; the students are required to write a précis of approximately 300 words.

Using the short piece of writing in this exercise, imagine that you are writing a university entrance test. Keep in mind the university wants to see how well you can read and write.

A Political Manager Is Born

by Michael Nolan

The household in which Joe [Clark] grew up was politically ambidextrous. Charles, his father, was a Conservative and his mother a Liberal. "I voted for Mackenzie King when I was twenty-one," says Grace, "because at that time it was sacrilege not to." Yet the political life of High River was predominantly Social Credit. Followers of the old-line parties were clearly in the minority and, in light of this fact, Grace and her husband's sister, an active Conservative like Charles, used to joke that they were the only two of their breed in town.

Looking back on his High River days, the Conservative leader considers the perception of him as a serious youngster determined at an early age to become prime minister as overblown.

"There is a feeling that I started at age two," he says. "That, in my judgment, is just not true." He admits that he was clearly not cut out to be a rancher or a rodeo rider during high school days. "I think there were some people in town who were certain that I was going to go on and do something. But I think that has to be put into the context of the certainty that a number of other teachers in a number of other towns have about the future progress of somebody else who turns out to sell insurance."

At times, the memories of parents and friends seem to conflict. Yet there emerges the general picture of a serious youngster, mature for his years and fond of talking to older people; a determined, individualistic youth given more to reading, debating and essay-writing than to athletics. His friend Jim Howie, now a fertilizer dealer in the town, describes him as "not that well co-ordinated physically" and a student "who was always trying to tie the teachers in knots with his big words." His parents maintain that, at one time, he had an ambition to be a sportswriter and sports broadcaster; he played a lot of baseball, because he was too small for hockey. They recall him memorizing the *Encyclopedia of Sports*.

1. Before you write a précis of this excerpt from *Joe Clark*, you and your partner should each write a separate paraphrase, following the instructions outlined in Exercise Two.

2. Now write your précis in paragraph form. There are two kinds of précis: the kind in which you use the author's language to condense the original to one-third or one-half of its length, or the kind in which you use your own words (that is, you condense a paraphrase). Both kinds of précis should include the main claim and some of the original development.

3. When both you and your partner complete your paraphrase and précis (with suitable titles), compare them to see how similar they are. If you are having difficulty, turn to the Suggested Answers to see a sample paraphrase and précis of this article.

Exercise Seven

1. Working with your partner, write a précis of Robert Hunter's account of one of his first voyages with the Greenpeace Foundation. Before you start, decide between yourselves who will do the first kind of précis (a condensed version using the author's language) and who will do the second kind (a condensed version of a paraphrase).

from *The War Within Greenpeace*
by Robert Hunter

In June, 1975, after a year of organizing and three months at sea in an old fishing boat, we finally came upon a fleet of Russian whalers less than fifty miles off the coast of California. We tossed highspeed rubber boats into the water, leapt aboard, and roared into the line of fire between a harpooner and his prey. One boat stayed off to the side, its crew's cameras focused on the action. The ordeal was nerve-wracking, but we got what we wanted; spectacular footage of a harpoon rocketing over our heads, exploding in the body of a whale. We turned and chugged directly to the nearest port – San Francisco, as luck would have it – and released our footage to the TV networks. It was Walter Cronkite who got on the air first, and from that moment we had a reputation as the most macho environmentalists in the world.

Our footage also showed undersized (less than thirty-foot) sperm whales being hauled up the slipway of a gargantuan Russian factory ship, like sardines being gulped by a bear. For the first time, the TV-watching masses saw that the whale was no longer Leviathan and that Man was no longer a puny, fearless Captain Ahab. We had rewritten *Moby Dick* in living colour on the seven o'clock news. From that moment, humanity's image of whales was altered. From that moment, too, although none of us saw it at the time, our essential job was done. Our original aim had been to act as a catalyst in a process of consciousness transformation. Beyond that, we had no plan at all.

2. When you have each completed your précis, compare them. Which is easier to understand: the précis of the original or the précis of the paraphrase? If you would like to compare either of yours with another, turn to the sample précis in the Suggested Answers.

Exercise Eight

1. For this final unwriting activity, write a paraphrase, précis, summary, outline, and the main claim for this excerpt from Owen Phillips's *The Last Chance Energy Book*:

from *The Last Chance Energy Book*
by Owen Phillips

In the search for new energy sources, the sun is an obvious candidate. It is generally believed that solar energy is surely the long-term answer, and this belief is almost certainly justified. In the United States, we have been somewhat behind other countries in developing solar power. Even a casual visitor to Western Australia would notice that many of the new houses there have solar panels built into their roofs. It is quite routine, not at all exceptional. That part of the world has always been energy poor – there is no oil, not much coal (the deposits that do exist being of indifferent quality), and little hydroelectric power. On the other hand, the climate is generally sunny with a month of cloudy weather per year so that solar panels, together with a small back-up system, provide plenty of hot water for heating and for household use. Why cannot we do the same thing in this country on a larger scale?

No doubt we shall; this is one of the personal options open to us. It takes no great foresight to anticipate that domestic solar panels will become increasingly more economical over the long run as the technology for their manufacture improves and as the prices of alternative fuels rise. They will make a great difference to our personal budgets and will help to reduce the national demand for oil and natural gas. But solar panels are not for everyone. What about all the people who live in apartment houses, hotels, and condominiums? Or in areas of the country where the sun shines only intermittently in winter, precisely the time when the heat is needed most? It is probably an over-statement of the case, but not an outrageous one, to assert that domestic solar collectors will provide for the energy problem the same kind of contribution that backyard vegetable plots provide for our food supply – sufficient for a relatively few fortunate people and a valuable supplement for others, but that's all.

Solar energy may indeed be the long-term answer, but the use of domestic collectors is not the only way to capture it. Another option could be to cover the deserts with solar collectors, using the heat to generate electric power. But there are problems. Do we really want to cover the deserts with solar collectors? New Englanders may not mind, but the people who live in Arizona may be less than enthusiastic. The ecology of the desert is a fragile thing and the impact of large farms of solar collectors may be difficult to assess. Are we prepared for the enormous capital costs? Solar collectors work very well when the sun is shining, but they are not very useful at night. Energy would need to be stored in very large amounts to carry us through for nighttime use or during extended cloudy periods; either this or a back-up system of large capacity that is used only intermittently and is consequently expensive. Solar power from the deserts may well be part of the solution, but we should not assume that it is the whole solution.

2. Compare your pieces of unwriting with those of your partner.

If you do not agree on the essentials, go back to some of the directions in the various exercises. If you remain confused, look at the paraphrase, précis, summary, outline, and main claim of this excerpt in the Suggested Answers.

Special Writing Activity

Ask your partner to find you a fairly difficult piece of prose of approximately 600 words, for which you are to write a paraphrase, précis, summary, and outline. When you have completed them, give them to your partner, who will use the principles of unwriting to evaluate your work.

Last Words

If you ever feel that an essay you have written is incomplete, you should make an outline in short sentences of *exactly* what your essay contains. In this way, you can often see what your essay is lacking.

Making an outline may also be the very thing you should do *during* the drafting process if you are stuck on part of the development.

Activity 7 Figurative Language and Allusions

Background

We learn early the value of using comparisons: "My dad's bigger 'n your dad!" A comparison can relate something that is unfamiliar with something that is familiar, and thereby make a description more effective.

Figurative language relies on comparison, either stated (she runs *like the wind*) or implied (she *breezed* through the exam). By using a figurative comparison, a writer can help his or her readers see something or someone in a new way.

Exercise One

A comparison can be either literal or figurative. *She looks like her mother* is a literal, or factual, comparison. *She looks like a million dollars* is a figurative comparison. If taken literally, the latter expression does not make much sense!

1. Provide three literal (factual) comparisons on the appearance of a friend. You should use someone or something who actually looks like your friend. For example,
   a) Bob looks like _____ (Henry).
   b) Bob looks like _____ (his father looked at the same age).
   c) Bob looks a little like _____ (Marty Feldman).

2. Now provide three figurative (imaginary) comparisons. (In choosing your comparisons, you should think of at least one aspect of your friend's appearance, so that you can compare it with a similar aspect of something or someone else.)
   a) Bob looks like _____ (a young prince.)
   b) Bob looks like _____ (a Greek god.)
   c) Bob looks like _____ (death warmed over.)

3. Check your responses with your partner to see that you have made literal and figurative comparisons.

Exercise Two

Working with your partner, try to complete some of these sentences with an original figurative comparison. Discuss the effectiveness of each comparison.

Examples

Getting married is like *travelling to a strange country.*

Going to sleep is like *blowing out a candle.*

Going to school is like …

Falling in love is like …

Driving a car is like …

Playing football (or another sport) is like …

Watching TV is like …

Going on a date is like …

Getting up in the morning is like …

Going on stage is like …

Exercise Three

There are several different kinds of figurative comparisons. Read each term and example below. Then, make up a sentence about your friend, using that type of figurative comparison.

1. A *simile* is a figurative comparison that uses "like" or "as."

Valerie runs like a gazelle.

Valerie's temper is as hot as boiling tar.

2. A *metaphor* is a figurative comparison that states or implies one thing is something else.

Valerie is a gazelle.

Valerie burns everyone with her temper. (Implies she has a hot temper)

3. *Personification* gives inanimate objects life.

The branches wrapped themselves around Valerie's arms.

4. An *allegory* gives life to an abstract quality or condition; for example, *death*, *love*, *hunger*, or *friendship*. When a word is used allegorically, it is usually capitalized.

Valerie saw the movie *Bedazzled*, in which Dudley Moore played Everyman.

5. An *allusion* makes a comparison by reference to a character from literature, mythology, history or legend.

Valerie thinks she is Princess Leia, but she is actually more like Olive Oyl.

6. An *analogy* keeps up a figurative comparison for a certain length of time: sometimes a paragraph, sometimes an entire essay, or even an entire book.

Auntie Muriel is both the spider and the fly, the sucker-out of life juice and the empty husk. Once she was just the spider and Uncle Teddy was the fly, but ever since Uncle Teddy's death Auntie Muriel has taken over both roles. Elizabeth isn't even all that sure Uncle Teddy is really dead. Auntie Muriel probably has him in a trunk somewhere in the attic, webbed in old ecru lace tablecloths, paralyzed but still alive. She goes up there for a little nip now and then. Auntie Muriel, so palpably not an auntie. Nothing diminutive about Auntie Muriel.

from *Life Before Man*

After you have written your simile, metaphor, personification, allegory, allusion, and analogy, discuss your sentences with your partner.

Exercise Four

Once you begin to think figuratively, your writing can improve tremendously. But there are a few pitfalls to avoid when writing figurative comparisons.

Read these rules and study the examples. Then, with your partner, follow the suggestions to write a sentence with a figurative comparison.

1. *Rule One:* In a figurative comparison the two things compared are usually not alike in every respect. In order for the comparison to work, however, they must have at least one thing in common.

My aunt's sapphire eyes frightened me more than all her harsh words.

(The aunt's eyes are being compared to sapphires. Both eyes and sapphires are blue and hard.)

Subject
A relative's eating habits.
Comparison
the way a bird eats.

2. *Rule Two:* In a figurative comparison, the object you compare your subject to should be able to do in reality what you want it to do figuratively. If your comparison does not make complete sense, your metaphor will be strained. Why does this metaphor not work?

Jim's fists stabbed his opponent like rocks.

(Generally, rocks *smash*; they do not *stab*. If the writer wanted to keep *stabbed*, what could *rocks* be changed to?)

Subject
Your report card.
Comparison
a battlefield (Make sure that whatever happens in, on, or to your report card also happens on a battlefield.)

3. *Rule Three:* In a figurative comparison you should not begin with one comparison and end with another. Why would a mixed metaphor such as this be confusing?

After Susan's campaign caught fire, she snowballed her way into the presidency of the students' council.

(A snowball cannot catch fire any more than a fire can snowball. If you changed *snowballed* to *flamed*, the metaphor would not be mixed. What would you change *caught fire* to, if you wanted to keep *snowballed*?)

Subject
Some time of the day.
Comparison
an animal. (Do not mention anything that either the animal or the time of day cannot do.)

Exercise Five

1. When using figurative comparisons you must avoid dead metaphors, that is, metaphors that have been used too often and are now clichés. You and your partner should each study these three examples:

When she got the job at the supermarket, Nancy was *as happy as a lark*.
The principal *hit the nail on the head* when he declared that students from other schools were responsible for spray-painting our school walls.
When our houseboat sank, all our possessions went to *Davy Jones' locker*.

2. Now, you and your partner work separately, each trying to substitute new figurative comparisons for the italicized clichés. As you both do so, test each one according to the three rules in Exercise Four.

You would not use *happy as a swan*, *hit the log on the head*, or *Davy Browns' locker* because they have nothing in common with anything in the comparison (rule one).

You would not change *happy as a lark* to *happy as a frog* because in reality a frog is not known for its cheerful noise (rule two).

If you changed *hit the nail on the head* to *hit the bucket*, you would be mixing metaphors (rule three). The metaphor is *kicked the bucket*.

3. After you have compared your answers with your partner's, discuss both sets of answers in relation to the following. Are yours more original?

When she got the job at the supermarket, Nancy was *as happy as a newlywed*.
The principal was *right on the mark* when he declared that students from other schools were responsible for spray-painting our school walls.
When our houseboat sank, all our possessions went *the way of the Titanic*.

4. Now, you and your partner write three sentences with dead metaphors. Give them to each other. Each must substitute three original figurative comparisons for the clichés. Evaluate your responses by applying the three rules.

Exercise Six

1. Choose one of these epigrams and write about it, continuing the analogy until you can no longer sustain the figurative comparison; for example, with Oscar Wilde's epigram "Illusions are like umbrellas; you no sooner get them than you lose them," you should write about illusions in terms of umbrellas. Here are other epigrams to choose from:

All the world's a stage.   (Shakespeare)
Memory is the diary that we all carry about with us.   (Wilde)
Our little life is rounded with a sleep.   (Shakespeare)
It is with rivers as it is with people: the greatest are not always the most agreeable nor the best to live with.   (Henry Van Dyke)

2.   Have your partner check your analogy according to the rules in Exercise Four.

Exercise Seven

1.   Find five cartoons with figurative comparisons in your local newspaper or in magazines you have around the house. (Many cartoonists use figurative comparisons, especially allusion.)
2.   Bring them to school to share with your partner and see if he/she recognizes the two things that are being compared.
3.   What two things are being compared in this cartoon?

HERMAN

"Listen...if we get this right, we'll be famous."

Exercise Eight

Writers who use allusions can save themselves dozens of words. When they see a similarity between their subject and something else that they know well and expect their readers to understand, they will unhesitatingly link them together.

Readers will not fully appreciate a particular allusion unless they are familiar with the specific reference. Let us hope that as you work through this exercise, you will not find yourself like Paul on the road to Damascus, blind and uncomprehending.

1. Find five *written* allusions in your local newspaper or in any magazines. (Reporters often use them in their daily columns.)

2. Bring them to school to share with your partner and see if he/she recognizes the two things that are being compared.

3. As you read these excerpts from a recent edition of *Maclean's*, record which of the allusions you know for sure, which ones you could make a reasonable guess at, and which ones pass you by.

Discuss the full significance of each allusion that you recognize with your partner. As these were written by magazine correspondents who wanted the general public to understand what they had written, you can certainly see that they expected their readers to have had many varied experiences.

- a) "*If the 20th century did, in fact, ever belong to Canada,* James Alan Roberts, the author of this compelling memoir, must be ranked as one of its curators."
- b) "What has happened to turn poverty from the rallying cry of the *Just Society* and *Great Society* [programs which were conceived in the] '60s into the non-issue of the '80s?"
- c) The headline of an article about Marshall McLuhan: "*Medium for the Message.*"
- d) "Although ardent McLuhanites may feel that the university has not sufficiently atoned for short-shrifting their *guru,* his spirit lives on in these inspired proceedings."
- e) A headline reads: "*Landlords in sheep's clothing.*"
- f) "But *the unkindest cut of all* came last week from a significant change in the political pitch of [Quebec] provincial Liberal Claude Ryan ...."
- g) Headline reads: "*Encounter of a Chilly Kind.*"
- h) "Like *Sisyphus,* the president [Ronald Reagan] is pushing uphill against powerful gravitational forces.
- i) Says Imperial Oil President Jim Livingstone of the recent [Ottawa-Alberta oil pricing] deal: "*The large print giveth and the small print taketh away.*"

j) [Author Jack] Hodgins' folksy golly gee Vancouver Islanders ... venture out in thought or deed to *strut and fret upon a larger stage* – Ottawa, Toronto, Ireland, Japan."

4. If you cannot solve all of these, turn to the Suggested Answers.

Exercise Nine

Did you find Exercise Eight difficult? If you did, it may indicate that you do not read enough. The main reason that allusions escape readers is that the readers are not informed.

Most professional writers know something of the classics, the Bible, other religions, world history, the arts, sports, and so on. When they write, it is perfectly natural for them to dip into their knowledge in order to sharpen a particular comparison. They do so with no apology. Instead of spelling out their comparison literally, they delight in comparing literarily.

If you want to understand and appreciate a particular reference, you can ask a friend who is better read for an explanation, or you can refer to a dictionary, encyclopedia, or other reference work in hopes that the allusion will have received a mention.

The best solution, though, is to fill in the gaps in your own knowledge by reading the classics, listening to news programs and documentaries, reading newspapers and periodicals, as well as listening to well-informed people. In other words, absorb as much as you can from your surroundings.

Following are questions that will help you determine your knowledge in several fields. If you are unable to supply one or two correct answers to each set of questions, you should start to fill your spare time with some necessary reading.

1. What was each character's tragic flaw (the quality in their natures that destroyed them)? Othello, Romeo, Hamlet, Macbeth, Oedipus, Brutus.

2. What adjective best describes each character? Falstaff, Puck, Bottom, Uncle Tom, Stanley Kowalski, Peter Pan.

3. For what quality is each political figure known? Hitler, Alexander the Great, Richard Nixon, John A. Macdonald, Elizabeth I, Napoleon, Idi Amin.

4. What sort of philosophy would you associate with each figure? Sartre, Freud, Plato, Karl Marx, Mahatma Gandhi, Socrates.

5. What do you think of in connection with each Biblical character? Eve, David, Ruth, Joshua, Salome.

6. What is the essence of each place? Paradise, Shangri-la, Valhalla, Elysian Fields, River Styx, the end of the rainbow.

7. What is each god and goddess famous for? Zeus, Woden, Neptune, Bacchus, Athena, Yama, Glooscap, Aphrodite. (And in what religion would you find these messengers of the gods: Cupid, Mercury, Gabriel, Yamapurusha?)

8. What is the allusion in each title? *Apocalypse Now, 10, Nine to Five, China Syndrome, The Pale Horseman, The Grapes of Wrath.*

9. Which movie stars are known by these nicknames? The Duke, Ski Nose, The Great Profile, America's Sweetheart (she was a Canadian), The King, The Little Tramp.

10. You could probably make up similar lists of people or things that a great many people know about. Make up your own list of famous people or things and test them on your partner. Here are two to get you thinking:

What do these symbols stand for? Stars and stripes ...

What is the significance of these TV titles? M★A★S★H ...

Special Writing Activity

The true test of mastering figurative comparisons is recognizing them in your reading and using them in your writing.

1. For your partner, write a short paragraph in which you create an analogy by sustaining a figurative comparison. You can use similes, metaphors, personifications, allegories, and allusions.

2. Ask your partner to evaluate the paragraph according to the rules in Exercise Four.

3. Read these student models. Test the figurative comparisons and discuss their effectiveness with your partner. Study how the student writers created successful analogies by sustaining certain images: waves on a beach compared to a sea battle, a talker's words compared to waves drowning the listener, a girl's death compared to the plucking of a rose, and trees on a cliff compared to tired soldiers.

Sea Battle

The waves attack the shore like soldiers in battle – charging the beach in frenzy, dying in foamy agony. And as each wave slowly falls, then retreats into the sea, the next one comes in its place. It, too, seems eager to make its hopeless assault; it, too, is doomed, as sure of defeat as its predecessor. On and on the battle goes, an incessant and futile struggle against the impregnable defenses of the shore.

Drowning

by Gordon Bookey, student

Whenever he talked to me I felt as if I were drowning. His words poured out in torrents, hitting me like sweeping waves determined to pull me under. I would struggle onward, and with my head bobbing to and fro try to concentrate on his speech. At times, he would grow calm, and I'd feel my ordeal was at an end. But then, with all the hidden energies of the deep, the onslaught would continue until, drained and overcome, I'd helplessly go under.

Why?
by M. A. Clarkson, student

My neighbour, Mrs. Frances, has a lovely family that she has nurtured and cared for like a garden. Her four children, like beautiful flowers, blossomed around her. But she had one special rose, Zoe, her first-born, who came into this world a very frail child. No one expected her to live. For 17 years, Mrs. Frances, like a devoted gardener, nursed and watched over Zoe in a special way. She admired her daily as she matured into a strong, beautiful rose, bringing joy to everyone. Suddenly, on a Sunday morning, Mrs. Frances' rose was plucked from her garden, and her every heartbeat asks why ...

The March
by Mike Hawkins, student

Marching up the jagged cliff like tired soldiers, the young pines drop their heavy arms toward the ground. At first, they march in rigid formation, only occasionally interrupted by one (perhaps gunned down by a shot of lightning) lying at the feet of his fellows, or another leaning on his neighbours for strength. Closer to the top, all semblance of order disappears; the trees, virtually unprotected, tremble and shiver in the biting wind. Some sway with fright, others surge forward, determined to overcome the merciless enemy. At the top stands their leader, a tall pine, strong and immortal. He surveys his disorderly troops as they struggle up the jagged steps to join him in their eternal battle.

Last Words

A Canadian Joke

A little boy was using bad language in his backyard. His uncle, overhearing him, said, "I'll not have that kind of language around here."

The little boy looked up at him and said in a firm voice, "But Margaret Atwood uses those words. And so does Margaret Laurence. And so does Mordecai Richler."

His uncle gave him a steely-eyed look and retorted, "Then you'll just have to stop playing with those kids."

Activity 8 Sentence Variety

Background

In the labs of *The Writer's Workshop* you work alone on sentence combining techniques. In this activity you have the opportunity to study the infinite variety of sentence structure with someone else, asking questions, testing emphasis, clearing up problems.

Exercise One

Every sentence contains one basic idea, but some sentences decorate their basic idea with additional words, making the sentence more complex.

Simple Idea
Guy Lafleur scored a goal.

Complex
The fair-haired boy, Guy Lafleur, scored a fourth straight goal when he dashed through the Maple Leaf defence with the puck.

1. Do you see the simple idea, "Guy Lafleur scored a goal," within the complex idea?

2. You and your partner work separately to convert these simple ideas into complex ones:
a) The Montreal Canadiens won the Stanley Cup.
b) Canadian children play hockey.
c) The team won a medal.
d) The goalie stopped Smyl's shot.
e) The players took off their gloves.

3. Compare your sentences. Chances are that no sentence is identical to another. Already you are noticing the possibilities of sentence variety.

Exercise Two

The reverse process is just as easy to apply. To be able to isolate the kernel parts of a complex idea is useful when you practise sentence combining.

Complex Idea
The stalking boxer chased his running opponent into the corner.

By taking every important word, you can put the kernel parts into simple sentences.

Kernel Parts
There is a boxer.
The boxer is stalking.
The boxer chased.
There is an opponent.
The opponent is running.
There is a corner.
The opponent is in the corner.

1. Working separately from your partner, break these sentences into their kernel parts.

a) Muhammad Ali has won the world heavyweight boxing championship three times.
b) Mack Truck lost an important fight to champion Larry Holmes in 1981.
c) Dedicated boxers train for hours every day on the light and heavy punching bags.
d) *Rocky*, starring Sylvester Stallone, is an Academy Award-winning movie about boxing.
e) "Little Chocolate," from Nova Scotia, was the world featherweight and bantamweight champion in the early 1900s.

2. Compare your kernel parts with your partner's. They should be nearly the same. Sentence variety does not occur in the kernel, but only in the ways in which several kernels can be combined.

Exercise Three

Notice how the following sentence can be broken into seven kernel parts.
The silly skier flew down the hill and hit a solitary tree.

Kernel Sentences
There is a skier.
The skier is silly.
The skier flew.
There is a hill.
There is a tree.
The tree is solitary.
The skier hit a tree.

Read the different ways of combining these seven kernels:

a) The silly skier flew down the hill and hit a solitary tree.
b) Flying down the hill, the silly skier hit a solitary tree.
c) The silly skier who flew down the hill hit a solitary tree.
d) After flying down the hill, the silly skier hit a solitary tree.

e) Hitting a solitary tree was the silly skier who had flown down the hill.
f) The silly skier who hit a solitary tree had flown down the hill.
g) The silly skier, flying down the hill, hit a solitary tree.
h) Flying down the hill and hitting a solitary tree was the silly skier.
i) Hitting a solitary tree after flying down the hill was the silly skier.
j) A solitary tree was hit by the silly skier who had flown down the hill.
k) The silly skier, the one who flew down the hill, hit the solitary tree.

See how many ways you and your partner can combine the following kernel sentences:

1. *Two kernel sentences*

Nancy Greene won two Olympic skiing medals in 1968.
She did this at the Winter Olympics in Grenoble, France.

2. *Three kernel sentences*

Steve Podborski is a downhill skier.
He is a Canadian.
He won the World Cup in 1982.

3. *Four kernel sentences*

Gerry Sorenson is from Kimberley, B.C.
She is a downhill skier.
She won two World Cup Races.
She did this in 1981.

Exercise Four

Because there are so many ways of combining sentences, you will need to determine which combination serves your purpose, or which is the most emphatic.

If you are dissatisfied with the way you have written one of your sentences, rearrange the most important words to achieve the greatest impact for a specific purpose and audience. The places for key words are at the beginning and end of sentences. Why?

Example
a) In the 1981 Wimbledon tennis finals, five-time champion Bjorn Borg lost to American John McEnroe on a hot July day before a packed Centre Court.
b) Five-time champion Bjorn Borg lost to John McEnroe in the 1981 Wimbledon tennis finals on a hot July day before a packed Centre Court.
c) In the 1981 Wimbledon tennis finals on a hot July day before a packed Centre Court, five-time champion Bjorn Borg lost to American John McEnroe.

Which of the above sentences creates the most impact? Why? The least impact? Why?

2. You and your partner separately rearrange the kernels in the following sentences to create the greatest impact for an imagined audience and purpose. First pick out the idea you want to stress and place it in a position of importance.

    a) Over the last ten years, because of extensive television coverage, tennis has become a very popular sport in North America and around the world.

    b) Teenagers such as Andrea Jaeger, as well as Canada's Carling Bassett, are playing as professionals because of large cash prizes.

    c) Tennis courts have not been common in Canada, except on the West Coast, where the climate allows people to play almost all year.

    d) The Davis Cup, open to both amateur and professional players, is a world championship frequently won by American players.

    e) Coveted by every player is the "Grand Slam" of tennis, for which in one year a player must win the Australian Open, Wimbledon, the French Open, and the United States Open.

3. Compare and discuss each sentence by deciding which one creates the greater impact: yours or your partner's.

Exercise Five

1. Working separately, you and your partner combine each group of kernel ideas into a single sentence in what you consider the best way. Concentrate on making your sentence emphatic.

    a) Many Canadian boys become good skaters.
        They want to be hockey players.
        Toller Cranston became a superb figure skater.
        He is not interested in playing hockey.

    b) Barbara Ann Scott is Canada's most famous skater.
        She was Canada's darling in the late 1940s.
        She won World and Olympic gold medals.
        She was born in Ottawa.

    c) Petra Burka won the Canadian figure skating championship.
        She also won the North American and world championships.
        She won all three within a month.
        Her mother, Ellen, coached her.

    d) Sheila Burka is not related to Petra Burka.
        She is a skater too.
        Her sport is speed skating.
        She has won the Canadian championship.

    e) She was a petite blonde skater from North Vancouver, B.C.
        Her name was Karen Magnusson.
        She won the Canadian Senior Women's Championship in 1968.
        She was only sixteen.

2. Compare and discuss each sentence with your partner to determine which is more emphatic.

Exercise Six

So far you have had practice in combining and rearranging in order to create emphatic sentences. By subtracting certain unnecessary words, you can give even more emphasis and variety to your sentences.

From
The team, consisting of Jim Elder, Tom Gayford, and Jim Day, who were equestrians, won a gold medal at the Olympics in Mexico City in 1968.
To
The equestrian team of Jim Elder, Tom Gayford, and Jim Day won a gold medal at the 1968 Olympics in Mexico City.

Working with your partner, subtract the unnecessary words from these sentences.

a) Tom Magee is from Vancouver and he has become the first Canadian who has lifted more than 2,000 pounds (this is the equivalent of over 900 kg) in a powerlifting competition.

b) Her ability in the five events which make up the pentathlon has won Diane Jones-Konihowski, who is from Saskatchewan, much acclaim.

c) Ned Hanlan, who was nicknamed "The Boy in Blue" because of the costume he usually wore, won three hundred consecutive sculling races one after the other and has been honoured with a statue on the grounds of the Canadian National Exhibition in Toronto.

d) The Silver Broom, a trophy which was donated by Air Canada, is the prize that is competed for by curlers who come from Scotland, Sweden, Switzerland, Canada and other countries.

e) A young man from Vancouver whose name is Greg Joy gave the Canadian audience a thrill they did not expect when he won a silver medal in the high jump event at the 1976 Olympics, which were held in Montreal.

Exercise Seven

Because you should always be aware of your audience when you write, you should strive to create the greatest impact by combining, rearranging, and subtracting ideas. If there is the possibility that your reader may be confused, you should also be prepared to expand your ideas. By posing the questions *who*, *what*, *where*, *when*, *why*, and *how*, you may discover the effectiveness of adding something extra to a sentence.

Key Idea: kicking a field goal
Who: Lui Passaglia
When: with only three seconds left on the clock
Where: from the fifty-yard line
Why: winning the game

How: accuracy and strength
What: (already indicated)

Notice the processes of *combining, rearranging, subtracting,* and *expanding*:

a) Lui Passaglia, showing his strength and accuracy, kicked a field goal from the fifty-yard line, and won the game with only three seconds left on the clock.
b) Showing his strength and accuracy by winning the game in the last three seconds, Lui Passaglia kicked a field goal from the fifty-yard line.
c) During the last three seconds of the game, the strong and accurate Lui Passaglia kicked a game-winning, fifty-yard field goal.

1. Which sentence shows the most emphasis through combining, rearranging, subtracting, and expanding?

2. You and your partner work *separately* to expand each of the following key ideas into full sentences. Then, by combining, rearranging, subtracting, and expanding, present to each other the one sentence which you consider the most emphatic. Discuss the effectiveness of each choice.

a) playing high-school football
b) playing on artificial turf
c) seeing a Grey Cup game
d) becoming a cheerleader

Exercise Eight

1. Using *rearrangement* and *subtraction*, combine the following sentences into one well-formed paragraph. You and your partner work separately, making sure your sentences are varied. Use some short sentences, some long. Put key words first in some, last in others. Make sure, though, that your whole paragraph flows logically.

Lacrosse is Canada's national game. Not many people watch lacrosse. Even fewer play it. Hockey is much more popular. At first lacrosse was an Indian game. The Indians called it baggataway. More than 200 men played on each team. Now both Indians and non-Indians play the game. There are two kinds of lacrosse. Field lacrosse is played outdoors, with ten men on each team. Box lacrosse is played indoors. Each team has five men and a goal tender. The rules of lacrosse are simple. They are similar to the rules of hockey. Lacrosse is a fast-moving game. There is a great deal of action. More people should be interested in lacrosse.

2. When you both finish, compare the variety of your sentences and the emphasis of your paragraphs.

Exercise Nine

There are three kinds of common sentence errors to avoid when you combine, rearrange, subtract, and expand kernel sentences.

1. It is an error to run one sentence into another without indicating where one sentence stops and the next one starts.

Sentence runs on
Thousands of people have taken up running in recent years joggers have become a common sight on streets and parks.
Repaired
Thousands of people have taken up running in recent years. Joggers have become a common sight on streets and parks.

2. It is an error to express one of your kernel ideas in a word group that does not provide a complete thought.

Incomplete thought
Their foreheads dripping with perspiration.
Complete thought
Their foreheads drip with perspiration.
or
Their foreheads are dripping with perspiration.

3. It is an error to have one kernel near another kernel if they do not have any logical connection with each other.

a) Sometimes all you have to do is move a word or two:

Illogical
Anyone who runs around a track knows frequently the joys of jogging.
Logical
Anyone who frequently runs around a track knows the joys of jogging.

b) Sometimes you may need to rearrange a number of words:

Illogical
Held in early April, some runners dream of entering the Boston Marathon.
Logical
Some runners dream of entering the Boston Marathon, held in early April.

c) Sometimes you have to introduce new words into the sentence because there is no word in the sentence to which a particular group can relate:

Illogical
By jogging every day, muscles and joints can break down.
Logical
By jogging every day, people may break down muscles and joints.

Logical
If you jog every day, you may break down muscles and joints.

If a word group does not make sense within itself, it must have a word near it to which it can relate. "Muscles and joints" cannot jog, but "people" or "you" can.

If you read your sentences aloud, you can usually discover whether you have made any of these three common sentence errors. Then all you have to do is rearrange, subtract, or expand your kernel ideas into a new combination.

Sentence Work

Something is wrong with each of these sentences. Work separately from your partner on rearranging, subtracting, or expanding each one.

a) Spreading its message through radio and TV, Canadians hear "Participaction" encouraging them to exercise.
b) Jacqueline Gareau won the women's division of the Boston Marathon in 1980. After Rosie Ruiz was disqualified.
c) James F. Fixx, author of the best-selling book *The Complete Book of Running*.
d) Magazines such as *Runner's World* contain articles of interest to runners, published in Mountain View, California.
e) Terry Fox became Canada's best-known runner, he ran halfway across Canada on one leg.
f) Recent research indicates women may not become pregnant who run long distances.
g) People who find running too strenuous often turn to walking senior citizens are especially fond of it.
h) Everyone should benefit from physical fitness who wants to lead a healthy life.

Check your responses with your partner's to see if you have both corrected the sentence faults. If your responses are different, go through the sentences together until you are both in agreement. For other ideas turn to the Suggested Answers.

Exercise Ten

All the sentences used in Exercises One to Nine have made statements (declarations). *Declarative sentences* are the most common in English. There are three other types of sentences, however, that can add variety to your writing: *questions*, *exclamations* and *commands*.

Notice what can be achieved without using a declaration:

Who is the best hockey player of all time? Stop and think a minute. Is it the explosive "Rocket" Richard, who scored fifty goals in fifty games? The elegant Bobby Orr, unquestionably the greatest of modern defencemen? The lightning-quick Guy Lafleur, always there where he's needed? The ageless Gordie Howe, with more than thirty years' service as a professional? Or today's superstar, the great Wayne Gretzky? Decide for yourself!

1. Notice the puctuation of each of the sentences. Which are questions? Exclamations? Commands?

2. Although you should not overuse these three kinds of sentences in your writing, try to write a paragraph without using a single declaration.

3. Ask your partner to check that you have not used any declarative sentences and that your paragraph holds together.

Exercise Eleven

In your early writing days, you learned that a sentence is a group of words with a subject and a verb. If you forgot the subject or the verb, you were told your sentence was incomplete. You had written a sentence fragment, and that was taboo. You were told, "A sentence must contain at least one complete thought." So through your schooling you avoided anything resembling a fragment, and spent those years perfecting whole sentences. Complete thoughts.

But writers do use non-sentence fragments in order to communicate. Which sentence in the preceding paragraph is a fragment? Did you understand it? Also, did you spot the interrogative fragments in the paragraph about the "best hockey player of all time"? The missing parts of these *minor sentences* can easily be supplied from the context, so the statements will not be misunderstood.

Before you use the non-sentence fragment with confidence, you must know the difference between this useful word group and an accidental fragment fault. Here are a few examples:

Fragment Fault
Pele, the greatest soccer player of all time.
(Expand this sentence by supplying the missing verb.)

Fragment Fault
Vancouver, Toronto, and Calgary being three of the Canadian cities with professional soccer teams.
(Expand by supplying a more complete verb.)

Fragment Fault
North American soccer teams have imported many European players. Because of their greater experience.
(Combine these.)

1. See if your partner has repaired the above sentences in the same way you have.

2. Perhaps the following paragraph uses the non-sentence fragment excessively. But how does the style of the writing relate to its topic? Do the fragments communicate complete thoughts?

Feet flying. Ball sailing. Crowd roaring. Goal! Free kicks, penalty kicks, goal kicks. Whistles. Cheers. The Black Pearl. The Kaiser. Chinaglia. Professional soccer, the most popular game in the world, has reached North America, and fans are crowding into stadiums all over the continent to watch their heroes.

For another look at non-sentence fragments, read "The Locker Room," in Assignment 3.

3. Write a short piece with at least one legitimate non-sentence fragment.

4. Exchange it with your partner and discuss whether you have written a fragment that works or a fragment fault that should be revised.

Special Writing Activity

On a topic that you think will please your partner, write a paragraph in which you include various kinds of sentences, including non-sentence fragments. Ask your partner to discuss the effectiveness of your sentence variety.

Last Words

If this activity has whetted your appetite, you should plan to spend time learning the finer details of sentence variety in the various labs in *The Writer's Workshop*. There, you can work alone. At your own pace. In school. At home. Anywhere. Any time. By the time you have mastered the entire laboratory section, you will have acquired the habit of good writing.

Activity 9 Rhetorical Devices

Background

Rhetorical devices are techniques that are used to create a certain effect on an audience. When used with discretion, rhetorical devices can help achieve your purpose; that is, to emphasize, to shock, to add humour, to draw attention to word choice, to create suspense, and so on.

Some rhetorical devices mentioned in this activity have been included in other parts of *The Writer's Workshop*; therefore, only the ones not found elsewhere will be discussed in detail.

Exercise One

Read through each rhetorical device with your partner and discuss what purpose it serves. Take turns thinking of a new example of each rhetorical device before you go on to the next one.

1. Use a *rhetorical question* when you want to ask a question to which the answer is already known or implied.

Do Canadian actors have to leave home to make their fortunes?
Can we as Canadians not afford to give actors the chance to succeed here?

2. Use *abnormal word order* – a variation on the usual subject-verb-object sentence pattern – to give variety and emphasis to your writing.

Normal Word Order
Bob and *Doug*, the outrageous McKenzie brothers, *came* from the Great White North to American television screens.
Attractive, talented, statuesque actress Alexis Smith has starred in films, on Broadway, and at the Stratford Festival.

Abnormal Word Order
From the Great White North to American television screens *came Bob and Doug*, the outrageous McKenzie brothers. (The verb comes *before* the subject.)
Actress Alexis Smith, *attractive, talented, statuesque*, has starred in films, on Broadway, and at the Stratford Festival. (Adjectives come *after* the noun.)

3. Use a *non-sentence fragment* when a full sentence is not necessary for sense (Activity 8).

Who co-starred in *Superman?* Canada's Margot Kidder.
Lights! Camera! Action!

4. Use *repetition* for emphasis and rhythm.

When I was a child, I understood as a child, I thought as a child; but when I became a man, I put away childish things. *The Bible*

5. Use a *pun* when you want to play with words.

Michael Sarrazin was murdered twice in *The Reincarnation of Peter Proud.* Now that is overkill!

A recent article about Newfoundland actor Robert Joy was called – you guessed it – "The Joy of Acting."

In *Eye of the Needle*, in which Donald Sutherland plays an assassin nicknamed "the Needle," some people had trouble following the thread of the plot. (Or, if you wish to be more obvious, "...some people didn't get the point.")

6. Use *exaggeration (hyperbole)* when you want to emphasize a fact.

Boris Karloff was so scary in the movies that no one would dare speak to him in real life for fear of having his or her blood congeal.

Bela Lugosi became so famous as Dracula that blood banks locked their doors when they saw him coming.

7. Use an *understatement* when you want to create the reverse effect (and add a touch of irony) by making the fact seem less significant.

Norman Jewison has had some success as a movie director; he made *Fiddler on the Roof* and *Jesus Christ Superstar.*

Since he left Canada, he has earned a few dollars for his work.

8. Use *climactic parallelism* when you wish to present several facts in order of importance. (Lab 14).

Margaret Trudeau has been many things to many people over the past years: Vancouver flower child, photographer, author, movie star, and child-bride to our prime minister.

9. Use a *balanced sentence* when you wish to parallel two or more equal ideas. (Labs 4 and 14 have many examples.)

Raymond Burr left British Columbia to become a star in Hollywood; he returned to British Columbia to become a real estate agent in TV commercials.

10. Use *opposites* when you want to contrast two opposing ideas.

Arthur Hill, who left law school to become an actor, has earned more by playing a lawyer than he could have by working as one.

11. Use *reversals (chiasmus)* when you want to make a balanced sentence even more memorable.

Remember Mae West's famous saying: "It's not the men in my life that counts – it's the life in my men."

12. Use a *periodic sentence* when you wish to withhold an important part of the sentence until the end. The sentence should not make complete sense until you have read the last word (Lab 15).

One of the highlights of *Little Big Man*, a successful film that dealt with the story of Custer's Last Stand as told by a 122-year-old survivor, was the portrayal of Old Lodge Skins by North Vancouver actor Chief Dan George.
Not only was Chief Dan a longshoreman, a logger, a fisherman, honorary chief of the Squamish Indians, but, in his sixties, he received an Academy Award nomination as a movie star.

13. Use a *figurative comparison* when you wish to present your audience with a strong image (Activity 7).

The career of character actor John Vernon took a 180-degree turn from serious actor to comedian when he starred in the outrageously funny film *Animal House*.
He portrayed the dean of a college where John Belushi behaved like a rampaging animal.

14. Use an *allusion* when you want to save yourself a great number of words and you think your audience will appreciate the reference (Activity 7).

Glenn Ford's success as a Western hero has made him the John Wayne of Canadian actors.

15. Use an *aphorism* or short, memorable statement.

Anyone who wants to become famous in Canada must first become famous somewhere else.

16. Use *alliteration* to draw attention to a string of words.

Lorne Greene's pellucid, precise, and portentous delivery earned him the
nickname of "The Voice of Doom" on CBC radio.
Even when he sells dog food, Greene appears aristocratic, authoritative, and
awe inspiring.

17. Use *rhyme* to make two or more words memorable.

Yvonne de Carlo's career has been described as going from vamp (in *Salome*)
to camp (in the TV series *The Munsters*).

18. Use *onomatopoeia* when you want to draw attention to the sound of a
word.

In films about Canada, rippling streams and cascading falls have played
prominent parts.
The thundering rumble of avalanches and the howling whine of blizzards
have convinced audiences throughout the world that Canada is a land of
eternal snow.

19. Use *underlining (or italics)* and *quotation marks* to emphasize certain words.
(Activity 14)

Many Americans would be amazed to know that Mary Pickford, known throughout the world as "America's Sweetheart," was Gladys Smith, a <u>Canadian.</u>

Exercise Two

Can you and your partner find these rhetorical devices in "The Shape of
Things to Come": alliteration, climactic parallelism, exaggeration, non-sentence
fragment, pun, rhyming words, rhetorical question, opposites, allusion, analogy, and word punctuation?

If you cannot find all of the rhetorical devices, turn to the Suggested
Answers.

The Shape of Things to Come
by Patricia Davies, student

Hey, guys and gals! If you've been dreaming about a slim, strong, sleek phy-
sique, now is the time to <u>do</u> something about it!

If you're pining for a willowy figure, and want to whittle the excess "waste"
off your trunk, there's no need to be stumped for a solution. We have
numerous branches in the city ready to help you.

In our centres, there are as many different kinds of equipment as there are clients. Everyone can find facilities to suit his or her taste: an indoor track, dance studio, exercise room, swimming pool, sauna, whirlpool, and even a licensed restaurant.

Some people visit "The Shape of Things to Come" to enlarge their bodies; others go there to shrink them. We design programs to suit each person's individual needs.

Come and have a personal talk with one of our thousands of helpful representatives. They will be pleased to provide you with full details on all our equipment and programs.

Who doesn't want to look great? A dynamic physical appearance can be a great confidence builder when looking for employment and when meeting new people.

Use your head! Think ahead! The time to start doing something is <u>now</u>. Satisfaction guaranteed or money refunded.

Special Writing Activity

Write a publicity piece, in which you include at least five rhetorical devices. Your task in this activity is to attract your partner's attention so that he/she will come, go, buy, sell, or do whatever you want her/him to do. When you finish, list the rhetorical devices that you used so your partner knows which ones to evaluate.

Last Words

In the future, consider using a few of these tricks of a writer's trade. An effective rhetorical device can often enliven a dull patch of prose. Use these devices with discretion, however; overuse of rhetorical devices can result in an unnatural, or even unintentionally humorous, effect.

Activity **10** Sentence and Word Errors

Background

Looking at a list of things that can go wrong with your writing is a little like looking at a list of all the diseases that can kill you. You can die of anorexia, pernicious anemia, leukemia, infectious hepatitis, coronary thrombosis, Hodgkin's disease, tuberculosis, and a host of other unpleasant diseases. Your writing can also "die" from one of a long list of diseases.

Editors have been known to put the fear of death in a beginning writer. They may say gravely, "Your writing is suffering from ambiguity," or they may nod in agreement and in unison whisper, "Redundancy!" You take your dying paper home and try to save it from a disease you have never heard of. After hours of rewriting, you think that you have revived it, so you submit your paper for a second opinion. When you see it a week later, you barely recognize it. Red blotches cover its poor body. There is a huge "V" in its midsection; "ROS" on every long sentence; and "AWK" scattered over its margins. You limp home, wondering if you can ever revive your bloodied piece of writing.

But do not despair when you see writing terms or symbols on your work. They are part of your editors' efforts to help you become a better writer. You and your editors need a common terminology to save time when talking about your writing.

Exercise One

As you read the following long list, do not panic – look up the definitions of these terms only if someone who edits your writing uses them.

Word Errors	Sentence Errors
faulty agreement	awkward construction
ambiguous	balance needed
capitalization needed	comma fault (splice)
confusing word	confusing construction
reword	coherence needed
transitional word needed	co-ordination faulty
concreteness needed	subordination faulty
colloquial	dangling modifier
slang	misplaced modifier

Word Errors	Sentence Errors
too formal	unemphatic
euphony	fragment inappropriate
redundant	run-on sentence
be exact	fused sentence
tone shift	illogical
unidiomatic	punctuation wrong
italics needed	faulty parallelism
lower case needed	parallelism needed
shift of person	passive ineffective
shift of number	periodic sentence better
shift of tense	precision needed
misspelling	subordination needed
trite	support needed
hackneyed	sentence variety needed
verbose	ineffective
verb form questioned	faulty comparison
wordy	incomplete
wrong word	word order confusing
confusing antecedent	revise sentence
double negative	inconsistent
split infinitive	false analogy
hyphen needed	logical fallacy
apostrophe needed	sentence out of place
wrong *it's*	vague
undesirable repetition	sentence too long
do not abbreviate	sentence too short
faulty pronoun reference	jerky sentences
write number in full	start new paragraph
faulty complement	use climactic parallelism
be specific	faulty logic
jargon	shift in style
inappropriate slant	undesirable separation
used adverb instead of adjective	remold
used adjective instead of adverb	something omitted
figurative language inconsistent	does not make sense
verb and subject disagree	careless error
pronoun in wrong case	vary punctuation
verisimilitude shattered	illegible

1.   Spend a few minutes with your partner looking over the list. Both of you answer these questions:

   a) Which terms are you familiar with?

b) Which ones are you totally unfamiliar with?

c) Which ones seem to be duplicates?

2. If, during a feedback session on one of your papers, a peer/editor or a teacher/editor uses a term you do not understand, ask your partner to explain it so that you understand it completely. Your partner should use everything at his/her disposal to clear up your confusion: other textbooks, handouts, diagrams, drawings, drills, filmstrips, encouragement.

You can test each other on the meaning of any of the terms in Exercise One by playing a game. You can, however, win the game without knowing any of the terms, because being able to name an error will always be less important than being able to correct it.

Many professional writers avoid mistakes because they know instinctively how to use the various word groups, but they could not tell you what a dangling gerundial phrase is if their lives depended on it.

Game One

What's Wrong With the Word?

Rules

1. Each of you make up a predetermined number of sentences in which you deliberately create a "word" error. (*Hint*: Save yourself time by finding sentences that have already been made up for this purpose – in textbooks, workbooks, handbooks, or handouts. Often you will find the answers as well. Just make sure you do not show them to your partner.)

2. Take turns presenting the sentences one at a time to each other.

3. Use this scoring procedure: one point for naming the error, three points for correcting it. Remember, being able to correct an error is more important than being able to identify it.

Example

"A" presents this sentence: "Between you and I, we will learn how not to make mistakes."

"B" says, "It should be 'Between you and me, we will learn how not to make mistakes' because *me* should be in the objective case." ("B" earns four points.)

"B" presents this sentence: "Her dress is very unique."

"A" says, "It should be 'Her dress is unique.' I don't know why though." ("A" earns three points.) If "B" says something like "*Very* is superfluous because *unique* is already the ultimate," then he/she earns one point. "A" then presents the next sentence for "B" to answer: "Neither of the boys are coming to my party."

Continue the game.

Game Two

What's wrong with the sentence?

Rules
The rules are exactly as in Game One, except that you must deal with sentence errors rather than word errors.

Example
"A" presents this sentence: "Coming down the street, my house was on fire." "B" says, "It should be 'Coming down the street, I saw my house on fire.' It sounds better that way." ("B" earns only three points because the reason for the correction is not exact.) "A" says, "It's a dangling modifier" to earn an extra point. Then "B" presents these sentences: "We left early. We had work to do."
"A" says, "It should be something like this: 'We left early because we had work to do' or 'Because we had work to do, we left early.' The reason is that subordination is needed." ("A" earns four points for that answer.) "A" then presents: "At the rummage sale a shovel could be bought for a dollar. A tea pot cost a dollar. A dollar would buy a pocket knife."
Continue the game.

Exercise Two

Following is a list of "fumblerules" of grammar; sentences that illustrate the errors they describe. Using the list of errors in Exercise One, try to create your own "fumblerules."

1. Avoid run-on sentences they are hard to read.
2. Don't use no double negatives.
3. Use the semicolon properly, always use it where it is appropriate; and never where it isn't.
4. Reserve the apostrophe for it's proper use and omit it when its not needed.
5. Do not put statements in the negative form.
6. Verbs has to agree with their subjects.
7. No sentence fragments.
8. Proofread carefully to see if you any words out.
9. If any word is improper at the end of a sentence, a linking verb is.
10. Steer clear of incorrect forms of verbs that have snuck in the language.
11. Take the bull by the hand and avoid mixed metaphors.
12. Avoid trendy locutions that sound flaky.
13. Never, ever use repetitive redundancies.
14. Everyone should be careful to use a singular pronoun with singular nouns in their writing.
15. If I've told you once, I've told you a thousand times, resist hyperbole.
16. Also, avoid awkward or affected alliteration.
17. Don't string too many prepositional phrases together unless you are walking through the valley of the shadow of death.

18. Always pick on the correct idiom.
19. "Avoid overuse of 'quotation "marks."'"
20. The adverb always follows the verb.
21. Avoid commas, that are not necessary.
22. If you reread your work, you will find on rereading that a great deal of repetition can be avoided by rereading and editing.
23. A writer must not shift your point of view.
24. Eschew dialect, irregardless.
25. And don't start a sentence with a conjunction.
26. Don't overuse exclamation marks!!!
27. Place pronouns as close as possible, especially in long sentences, as of ten or more words, to their antecedents.
28. Hyphenate between syllables and avoid un-necessary hyphens.
29. Write all adverbial forms correct.
30. Don't use contractions in formal writing.
31. Writing carefully, dangling participles must be avoided.
32. It is incumbent on us to avoid archaisms.
33. Last but not least, avoid clichés like the plague; seek viable alternatives.

Last Words

Over the years educators have argued about when to correct a student's sentence errors. The philosophy of the writing process, to which this text is dedicated, supports the notion that early editing damages the process. At the same time, you should be aware that the end product must be correct. You must not give your audience the impression that you do not know right from wrong. If your readers see grammar and spelling mistakes, they will then begin to doubt the accuracy of what you are saying.

Activity **11** For the "Be-Whiched" Writer

Background

Many writers are "be-whiched" and never know it. Indeed, they live happy, normal lives – that is, until they realize that their audience is always bored with their writing. Their constant use of *to be* and similar verbs, and *which*, *it*, and similar pronouns, makes their writing tedious.

These exercises have the purpose of improving your writing style by getting rid of any be-whichment.

Exercise One

Before you and your partner work on this exercise, you should both find out if you are be-whiched.

1. Test your latest piece of writing by bracketing all parts of the verb *to be* – *is, am, are, was, were, being, been*;
every *which, who, whom, that*;
and *it, this,* and *there*.

2. Notice how the following piece of writing has been tested for be-whichment.

The Twenties vs. the Thirties

The stock market crash of 1929 [was] one of the worst days for the citizens of Canada. [This was] the day [which] began the Depression, soon [to be] worldwide. The value of Ford stock, [which was] one of the richest companies in Canada, went down fifty per cent. They lost over sixty-two million dollars in less than two months, and [this was] only the beginning. The drought on the Prairies [was] soon to follow. What [was] once fertile land, with valuable fields of wheat, [was] now barren desert. Its precious topsoil [was being] swept away with every gust of wind. The Maritimes [were] also in bad shape as they had no natural resources to support them. The inhabitants of the Prairies and the Maritimes [were] forced to go on relief, [which was] a program set up to help desperate people during the Depression. [This was] a large blow to the pride-filled Canadian citizens.

(This paragraph was taken from a student's five-page essay.)

3. Look back at your marked pieces of writing. Do they look like this one?

4. Now, answer honestly: are you suffering from be-whichment? If so, you should do the following exercises.

5. Leave Exercise One for the moment. You will continue with it at the end of this activity.

Exercise Two

1. The various parts of the verb *to be* are essential to many sentences. You do not have to banish them from your writing. Sentences like these are effective:

W.D. Valgardson *is* a poet, short-story writer, and novelist.

The harsh but haunting wilderness of northern Manitoba *has been* the background for many of his stories.

You and your partner write a similar sentence making sure that the form of *to be* is essential to your sentence.

2. Only when you excessively use the parts of *to be* does your writing suffer. In most cases your sentences will be healthier with other, stronger verbs. Note the difference between these two pairs of sentences:

W.O. Mitchell and Jack Hodgins *are* two authors who *are* from Western Canada.
(Excessive use of *to be*.)
W.O. Mitchell and Jack Hodgins *are* two Western Canadian authors.

Hodgins has *been* living on and writing about Vancouver Island.
(*To be* as an auxiliary verb.)
Hodgins lives on, and writes about, Vancouver Island.

Find a sentence from your work with a similar overuse of *to be*. You and your partner rewrite it in the same way as one of the above sentences.

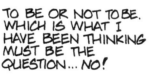

Exercise Three

Sometimes the intentional use of *which*, *who*, or other similar relative pronouns can create a strong sentence.

> Women *who* are stronger than the men around them and *who* triumph by making the best of their circumstances are the main characters of Margaret Laurence's novels.

Many beginning writers, though, use this type of dependent clause because it's easy to use. Consequently, their writing becomes tedious.

1. Overuse of the *which* clause is easy to cure; change the clause to a verbal phrase, or appositive. Study these sentences:

> Robertson Davies, *who* was formerly the Master of Massey College and *who* is now retired, has recently published a provocative novel, which is called *The Rebel Angels*.

> Robertson Davies, *retired former Master of Massey College*, has recently published a provocative novel, *The Rebel Angels*. (The appositives are more concise.)

> Dennis Lee, *who* has written several books of poetry for adults, is now much more famous as a writer of children's poetry.

> Dennis Lee, *having written several books of poetry for adults*, is now much more famous as a writer of children's poetry. (The verbal phrase is more emphatic.)

2. Find a similar sentence that you or your partner has written and rewrite it in the same way as the above samples.

Exercise Four

Many writers are fond of using *it* and *there*. Their sentences contain these patterns:

There is ... which ...

or

It is ... that ...

These patterns produce verbs in the passive rather than the active voice and wordy dependent clauses rather than effective phrases and appositives.

Passive

> There is one of Canada's finest female novelists who is scarcely known of by most Canadians, and her name is Constance Beresford-Howe.

Active

> Most Canadians scarcely know of one of Canada's finest female novelists – Constance Beresford-Howe.

Passive

> It is Mavis Gallant who has been termed by critics one of Canada's finest short-story writers and who was living for many years in self-imposed exile in Paris.

Active

Critics have termed Mavis Gallant, who lived for many years in self-exposed exile in Paris, one of Canada's finest short-story writers.

(Notice that the active voice is stronger than the passive in both these sentences.)

If you or your partner has used an *it* or *there* with part of *to be* in one of your sentences, rewrite it in the same way as the above.

Exercise Five

The verbs *to do* and *to have* often cause the same problems as *to be*.

Many students do prefer non-fiction to fiction.
Many students prefer non-fiction to fiction. (The *do* is unnecessary).

Stanley Burke and Roy Peterson's books have frequent criticism of politicians.
Stanley Burke and Roy Peterson's books frequently criticize politicians.

It is often easy to eliminate a general verb like *have* for a specific one like *criticize*, because all you have to do is change a word that is already in the sentence (*criticism*) to a verb.

If you or your partner have used any parts of *to do* (*do*, *did*, *done*, *does*) or *to have* (*have*, *has*, *had*) in your writing, try to substitute specific verbs for them.

Exercise Six

1. For more practice, you and your partner tighten the following be-whiched sentences. Check to see that you have deleted unnecessary words such as the following:

it	be	is	am	was	were	being
there	been	are	which	that	who	whom
this	do	done	have	has		

a) It is Timothy Findley's fascinating book, which is called *The Wars*, that has become a film which was directed by Robin Phillips and stars Brent Carver.

b) There is a book by Farley Mowat which is called *A Whale for the Killing*, in which a beached animal was killed by the inhabitants of a village that is located in Newfoundland.

c) Bruce Hutchison is best known as a political commentator, but it is his most recent book, *Uncle Percy's Wonderful Town*, which is his first work of fiction.

d) Peter Newman wrote *Renegade In Power*, which described John Diefenbaker in terms which were not flattering to him.

e) Richard Rohmer's military career has made him aware of international intrigue, and he has used his knowledge in such novels as *Exxoneration* and *Patton's Gap*.

f) There is a Vancouver author whose name is Keith Maillard and whose third novel has recently been published; it is called *The Knife In My Hands*.

g) The works of such Québécois authors as Roch Carrier have been translated by Sheila Fischman.

h) In latter years Margaret Atwood has done more to bring Canadian literature to world prominence than has Margaret Laurence.

2. Do not look at the Suggested Answers until you have both worked on each sentence.

Exercise Seven

1. Now you and your partner go back to Exercise One and rewrite "The Twenties vs. the Thirties." Try to get rid of every unnecessary form of *to be*, *to do*, *to have*, as well as every *which*, *who*, *that*, *this*, *it*, and *there*.

2. After you have rewritten the paragraph, turn to the Suggested Answers to compare your version to the one provided.

3. Now, by yourself, rewrite your own piece, using the ideas in this activity to rid your writing of unnecessary be-whichment.

4. Ask your partner to read your piece to see if you have succeeded. Has your style changed significantly?

Special Writing Activity

Write a piece of approximately 200 words for your partner, on a topic you think he/she will enjoy. In this activity, however, you are not permitted to use any of these words:

it	be	is	am	was	were	being
there	been	are	which	that	who	whom
do	does	done	have	has	had	having

Last Words

In future, strive to keep your writing free of "be-whichment."

Activity 12 For the Wordy Writer

Background

A wordy sentence or selection is one that contains unnecessary words or details. A long selection is not necessarily wordy. If the extra details add meaning, they will help you communicate what you want to say; if they do not, they will merely confuse your reader.

Following three simple rules will help keep you from being snared in words.

Rule One
Use only words necessary to fulfil your purpose; avoid superfluous descriptive words and roundabout phrases.

Rule Two
Use words which your audience is likely to know.

Rule Three
Use precise and concrete words for your topic, rather than vague and abstract ones.

Exercise One

1. Explain your feelings about one of these topics to your partner:
   a) the school newspaper
   b) jogging
   c) corporal punishment
   d) democracy
2. Your partner should interrupt you to ask for further explanation if he/she is confused. When this happens, clarify your statement, then pass on to the next part of your explanation.
3. Record how many times you were interrupted.
4. Now let your partner do the exercise.
5. Who had more legitimate interruptions: you or your partner? Why?

Exercise Two

Beginning writers, in their enthusiasm to express their ideas, often inject too many words into their sentences. Words such as *very*, *actually*, and *really*, are often used unnecessarily to add emphasis. In the following sentence, which words could you leave out?

It is *so* easy to use words like these *very* ones, that *actually* most people are *quite* unaware that they *usually* do so.

1. The following words are often misused to add emphasis, but they also have legitimate meanings. Try to use one of these words in a sentence so that it is necessary to the meaning.

actually, very, really, tremendously, too, quite, totally, especially, even, important, deeply, completely, positively

Necessary
The lunch-room is usually untidy, but is *especially* untidy after a food fight.
Unnecessary
There are *actually* whole lunches lying uneaten in wastebaskets.

2. Try the same thing with these words:

rather, a little, slightly, somewhat, sort of, something like, kind of

Necessary
I would *rather* go today than tomorrow.
Unnecessary
The classrooms are *rather* unattractive under their layer of garbage.

3. Now try the same with these words:

simply, generally, basically, always, obviously, particularly, effectively, as far as … concerned, incidentally, usually

Necessary
She dressed *simply* for her interview.
Unnecessary
There *simply* seems to be no respect for property.

Exercise Three

1. Work with your partner to remove any wordiness from these sentences:

a) Margaret Atwood is a well-known novelist in Canada who has also gained fame as a poet and critic.
b) Her initial taste of fame occurred after the publication of a number of books of her poetry; two examples of these are *The Circle Game* and *The Animals in That Country.*
c) She has also written several novels, all of which have appeared in listings of books which have sold well.
d) *Survival – A Thematic Guide to Canadian Literature* is the book in which Atwood spills the beans about the really important aspects related to what has been called her "victim theory."
e) *Life Before Man*, a recently written novel, was reviewed on the front page of the *New York Times Book Review*; this was indeed a great and important honour for a writer who makes her home in the country north of the United States.

f) Atwood was fascinated by the experiences of an early settler which were written about and by Susanna Moodie, *ipso facto* one of the earliest people to have been a writer in Canada, and in the year of our Lord 1970 Atwood published a book containing poems with Moodie as their subject.

2. When you have finished, go over the sentences again to see if you can get rid of even more words while retaining the original meaning.

3. When you cannot cut another word, turn to the Suggested Answers to compare responses.

Exercise Four

1. You and your partner read and rewrite this paragraph according to the instructions following it.

Signing Her Name to Her Books

During the year of 1969, while Ms. Margaret Atwood was attending a session in which she signed her John Henry in copies of her initial effort at long fiction, which she had titled *The Edible Woman*, she purveyed only two books. The gathering took place in the area set aside for the sale of knitted foot coverings to male humans, located in that emporium at The Bay in the metropolis of Edmonton. Twelve years further down the road, while another autographing session was going on in a store located in Hogtown where books were sold, the numbers of people were so great that they formed a line three times into themselves surrounding the store. What happened to Atwood is an illustration in extremely graphic terms of the popularity of books written in this country of Canada.

2. Tighten the paragraph as much as possible, but before you start trimming, note these categories of words that can usually be eliminated.

a) jargon, such as *waste the enemy*;

b) foreign words and phrases, such as *persona non grata*;

c) dead metaphors, such as *the straw that broke the camel's back*;

d) unnecessary descriptive words, such as *terribly*;

e) superfluous verbs, such as *I await your instructions and will act accordingly*;

f) unnecessary use of *to be* and *which*;

g) unnecessary compound prepositions, such as *in reference to*;

h) padding and pompous language, such as *It may be presumed that the fundamental position of ideology is that all reality can be construed as an expression of psychoanalytical thought.*

3. Start at the title of the paragraph and take out all unnecessary words; as well, replace complicated words with words that are easily understood.

4. When you have tightened the paragraph, turn to the Suggested Answers to see another response.

Exercise Five

Are you aware that many of our most frequently used words are mono-syllabic? Here are a few such words:

life, hate, death, kiss, sing, cry, wealth, weep, lie, cheat, war, care, food, sin, fool, peace, bad.

1. You and your partner continue the list, adding at least ten monosyllabic words.

2. Read this short paragraph:

Fame through Hope

Her fame has grown since she first came on the scene, but she was known from the start for her lean, sharp view of life. She wrote of men and how they brought out both love and hate from those near and dear to them. Their heads and hearts were at war. Hope was lost, then gained back in spite of pain. Her work has made those who read it see and feel in a new way.

3. Did you notice that each word is monosyllabic? What is the effect? Do you find the writing immature? Why or why not?

4. Do you see that writing a monosyllabic paragraph might be helpful if you suffer from wordiness? In what way?

5. Write a short monosyllabic paragraph about yourself.

6. Give it to your partner to check that you have included no words containing more than one syllable.

Special Writing Activity

Write a paragraph of 100 monosyllabic words for your partner on a topic that you think will interest him/her. When your partner edits your writing have him/her check for two things:

a) an unnecessary word. If a word can be omitted and the sense is not affected, you are in error.

b) a word that is not monosyllabic. If any word has more than one syllable, you are in error. (Read the model below.)

Last Words

The next time you write, remember Roger Garrison's words in *How a Writer Works*.

Words

We are too rich in words, and hence we tend to waste them. Long words tempt us, since they seem to show that we know more than we do. But short words do not let us hide what we do not know. These are words we use each day to tell us how we feel or what we think. When we love, we want to hug or kiss or say soft things. If we feel joy, we may sing or dance. If we feel hate, our words are harsh and we may curse. Short words tell what we are: they are strong and say what is real.

Activity **13** Punctuation

Background

Writers use punctuation marks for the purpose of communicating their thoughts more clearly to their audience.

Punctuation is discussed throughout *The Writer's Workshop*, but in this activity you and your partner can take the opportunity to check the main functions of all the end and internal punctuation marks.

"Don't worry about my punctuation. I'll be here at exactly nine o'clock every morning."

Exercise One

Note the three punctuation marks that can be used at the end of a sentence.

1. The *period* is used at the end of a statement.

A Canadian is a North American who does not owe allegiance to the United States or Mexico.   *George Woodcock*

The period is also used at the end of a command.

Have something to say. Say it. Shut up. Sit down.   *A.L. Horton*

2. The *question mark* is used at the end of a question.

Where is the old mailed fist? Has it gone down the drain? *A.D. McPhillips*

Note: the period is used at the end of an indirect question.

The poet Rubert Brooke once asked what one could say about Toronto.

3. The *exclamation point* is used at the end of an exclamation or an emotional command.

A premier of Manitoba should be able to kick manure off tractor wheels!
  Walter Weir

Widows rarely choose unwisely! *Arnold Haultain*

Note: a *single* exclamation point is sufficient.

Game One

How to End

Rules

a) You and your partner each find a newspaper or magazine article in which all three kinds of end punctuation have been used.
b) Paint out the end punctuation marks. Keep a record of which marks you painted out.
c) Exchange articles, put in end punctuation marks, return articles, correct, and compare results.
d) The object of the game is to see who puts in more correct punctuation marks.
e) Repeat the game as often as you need to.

Exercise Two

Of all the internal punctuation marks, the *comma* is the most common. It is the least emphatic way of indicating that the reader should pause.

There are a great number of uses of the comma, but the following eight are perhaps the most useful. You and your partner should discuss each one.

1. Generally, use a comma to separate two independent clauses joined by a co-ordinating conjunction: *and, but, or, for, so, yet.*

Call me anything you like, but don't call me a lady. *Charlotte Whitton*

J'aime mon Dieu, et j'aime mon Pays. *Sir Louis-Hippolyte Lafontaine*

When two independent clauses are short and closely related, the comma is not necessary:

I always wanted to make this trip and now I have. *Nathan T. Boya*

2. Use a comma to separate *all* parts of a series of three or more single words, phrases, or clauses.

My profession was robbing banks, knocking off payrolls, and kidnapping rich men. *Alvin Karpis*

3. Use a comma if two or more adjectives modify a noun individually.

Something strange, nameless, and profound moves in Canada today.
Bruce Hutchinson

Hint: you need a comma if you can replace it with *and*.

Something strange *and* nameless *and* profound moves in Canada today.

Notice that an *and* would make no sense between the adjectives in this sentence; hence, no comma is necessary.

There are two things that are not desirable for Canada, extreme economic nationalism and abject political colonialism. *John W. Dafoe*

Note: you could not put an *and* between *extreme/economic* or between *abject/political*.

4. Use a comma after a long introductory dependent clause or phrase.

Dependent Clause

If there's one phrase in the national vocabulary which stands out as being typically Canadian, that's it. Typically Canadian, I mean. *Pat Barclay*

Verbal Phrase

Sitting on a train going West across the repetitive prairies, a writer of our acquaintance finally burst out savagely, "This country could do with a great deal of editing!" *Derek Patmore*

5. Use a comma to set off absolutes no matter where they appear in the sentence.

To go into teaching was a matter of sheer necessity, *my education fitting me for nothing except to pass it on to the other people. Stephen Leacock*

6. Use a comma to prevent any misreading.

Literature, we said, is conscious mythology. *Northrop Frye*

7. Use a comma when a clause or phrase breaks the continuity of the sentence by offering additional but incidental information.

Non-Essential Clause

If a man must die, he has the right to die in peace, *as he would prefer to do if asked. Wilder Penfield*

Non-Essential Phrase

On his political success, John Diefenbaker said, "Everyone is against me but the people."

Hint: if the sentence makes complete sense *without* the clause or phrase, it is non-essential; hence, commas are required. Without their non-essential elements, the above sentences make sense:

If a man must die, he has the right to die in peace.
John Diefenbaker said, "Everyone is against me but the people."

Notice, though, commas are not required around essential clauses and phrases. They are necessary to the independent clause, which makes no sense without them.

Essential Clause

A good man *who does wrong* is just a bad man *who has been found out.*
   Bob Edwards

Note: "A good man is just a bad man" makes no sense.

Essential Phrase

No one should ever visit Toronto *for the first time.*   Allan Lamport

Note: "for the first time" is needed for the complete sense of the sentence.

8.   Use commas to set off parenthetical expressions and mild interjections, appositives, or adjective and adverb clusters.

Parenthetical Expression

We are here to add what we can to, *not to get what we can from,* life.
   Sir William Osler

Mild Interjections

Oh, no, it is not always winter in Canada.   William P. Greenough

Appositive

Last night I was listening to a radio celebration of Flaherty, *author of Nanook of the North.*   Wyndham Lewis

Adjective Cluster

Tawdry and romantic, bourgeois and impatient at once, Vancouver is where the small ambitions flourish and the large dreams move furtively.
   Donald Cameron

9.   When you look at the above examples one at a time, they make sense. But too many commas may strangle your meaning. Every comma in the following sentence can be justified. Which ones should be omitted?

You should use commas sparingly, but, to avoid misreading, you should, occasionally, include one.

Game Two   Commas Galore

Rules

Present your partner with one prepared sentence at a time, saying, "For one point, add a comma, omit a comma, or leave it the way it is."

Example

"A" presents "B" with: "The only thing(,) that really matters in broadcasting(,) is program content."

"B" answers, "The only thing( ) that really matters in broadcasting( ) is program content." Because everything is correct, "B" earns one point.

"B" presents "A" with: "What is the difference between a cat and a comma?

The answer is that a cat has claws at the end of his paws(,) but a comma is a pause at the end of a clause."
Continue the game.

Exercise Three

Review point 8 in Exercise Two before proceeding.

If the parenthetical expression, interjection, or appositive is a strong interruption, you might use a *pair of dashes* instead of commas.

Strong Parenthetical Expression

For some reason – *I really don't know why* – they've decided to name this magnificent body of water after me. *Joey Smallwood*

Strong Interjection

Canada looks like a rich, magnificent country – naturally – but there are not enough men to till the soil. *Thomas Wolfe*

Strong Appositive

I have heard that there is someone – not a human being but a spirit – in the moon. *Pitseolak*

If the parenthetical expression, interjection, or appositive is quite remote, you might use *parentheses*.

Remote Parenthetical Expression

There were four buildings on this corner – Government House itself, Upper Canada College, a church, and a saloon (to use the venerable term). *Vincent Massey*

Remote Interjection

Canada is a great school (I should know, all my training was in Canada) but it is in danger of remaining a school. *Jon Vickers*

Remote Appositive

Canada ("the land God gave to Cain," according to Jacques Cartier) still has areas where few people wish to live.

Game Three

Commas, Dashes, Parentheses?

Follow the rules in Game One. Find sentences which have interruptions, paint out the punctuation marks, and see if your partner knows whether to fill the spaces with commas, dashes, or parentheses.

In your writing, you might find occasion to use a single *dash*. Think before you use it. A comma, colon, semicolon, or even a period may be better. Overuse of the single dash can take away emphasis from your writing.

1. Use a dash to stress a word or words at the beginning or end of a sentence.

Popular, successful, prolific – these words and more can be used to describe Pierre Berton. *Barbara-Anne Eddy*

Montreal is wide-open – but honest. *Camilien Houde*

(Notice the difference between the hyphen ("wide-open") and the dash ("open – but")

2. Use a dash to set off a summary or even a conclusion to an involved sentence.

To me, the apex of life is to have dinner with a beautiful woman – my wife, preferably.   *Arthur Hailey*

3. Use a dash to mark an interruption in dialogue.

"I was shot at – "   *Tim Buck*
(He spoke these words while testifying at a trial. The rest of his testimony was not allowed into the record.)

Exercise Four

The *semicolon* is perhaps the most incorrectly used internal punctuation mark. Most people know that its function is somewhere between that of a comma and a period; however, its actual use in writing so bewilders beginners that they will write strings of simple sentences, or join all their sentences with "ands" and "buts," rather than take a chance and use a semicolon.

The main thing to remember about using the semicolon is that it separates elements of equal and substantial rank.

1. Use a semicolon to join common, independent clauses.

Modern Canadian life has not grown out of us; it has been imposed on us by technology.   *Hugh Maclennan*

As you have already seen (Exercise Two, point 1), if independent clauses are joined by a co-ordinating conjunction, you usually place a comma before the conjunction.

Modern Canadian life has not grown out of us, but it has been imposed on us by technology.

Some writers, for emphasis, include the semicolon before a co-ordinate conjunction.

Nature is great; but man is greater still.   *Anarulunguaq*

Do you see why the semicolon in the Anarulunguaq sentence works, but the semicolon in the following one does not?

Modern Canadian life has not grown out of us; but it has been imposed on us by technology.

2. When you join independent clauses with conjunctive adverbs such as *therefore, nevertheless, hence, however, moreover,* and so on, you should precede the conjunctive adverb with a semicolon and follow it with a comma.

I won't win the Leacock Medal for Humour; however, I console myself by remembering that Leacock never won the award either.
Max Braithwaite

Notice the punctuation when the conjunctive adverb moves within the clause.

I won't win the Leacock Medal for Humour; I console myself, however, by remembering that Leacock never won the award either.

You and your partner rewrite the sentence in at least three different ways, each time moving the *however*. Remember to retain the semicolon.

3. Use a semicolon when you use specifying words like *for example*, *that is*, and *namely*. (Instead of the Latin abbreviations *e.g.*, *i.e.*, and *viz.*, use their English equivalents above.)

Toronto has been frequently insulted by outsiders; for example, Bob Hope said of it, "You're going to have a great town here if you ever get it finished."

Foster Hewitt created in 1933 the most famous exclamation in Canadian sports; namely, "He shoots! He scores!"

4. Use a semicolon to separate a longer series which contains commas.

His outfit consisted of a red, white, and blue stocking cap with a tassel; a hand-knit, peppermint-striped, waist-length jacket; knee-length knickers; and long, thin, cross-country skis.

The reader would confuse the commas which separate each item in the series with the commas that are *within* each part of the series. Can you make sense of the following sentence?

His outfit consisted of a red, white, and blue stocking cap with a tassel, a hand-knit, peppermint-striped, waist-length jacket, knee-length knickers, and long, thin, cross-country skis.

Game Four

Semicolon Confusion

Follow the same rules as Game One. To make the game more difficult, but more helpful, find sentences which have long dependent clauses with either commas or semicolons joining them. Paint out the commas and semicolons.

Example
"A" presents "B" with: "In Canada we talk a lot about cultural protectionism(;) we don't do it much." *Robert Fulford*
"B" says "The semicolon is correct" for one point. Then "B" presents "A" with "Charles de Gaulle made a momentous announcement from the balcony of the Montreal City Hall(;) namely, 'Vive le Québec! Vive le Québec libre! Vive le Canada français! Vive la France!'"
Continue the game.

Exercise Five   You probably use a colon after *Gentlemen* in your business letters and to separate hours from minutes when you write *12:45*, but beyond that, the colon has several other uses.

1. Use a colon when you are writing a special, balanced sentence with two independent clauses. If your second clause is a more detailed explanation of your first, separate the clauses with a colon.

The reason is very simple: they wanted to put the prison outside the town rather than the town inside the prison.   *François Lemaître*

Do you see how the second clause merely provides a more detailed explanation of the first?

It might be appropriate at this point to note the difference between the colon and the semicolon: a semicolon indicates to the readers that they are at a stop sign; a colon tells them they are at a green light.   Never use a semicolon as a colon: its effect is exactly opposite.

2. Use a colon to separate a list from the rest of the sentence.

Recipe for living: equal amounts of work, play, love, and philosophy.
    Pauline Elizabeth Rhind

Do you see that this quotation is a non-sentence fragment?

3. Use a colon to add a dramatic touch to a sentence before you introduce a single word or phrase.

My political action, or my theory – insomuch as I can be said to have one – can be expressed very simply: create counterweights.   *Pierre Trudeau*

Why are there dashes here?

Game Five   **Colon or Otherwise**

Follow the same rules as Game Four, painting out the colons and semicolons.

Exercise Six   *Brackets*, [   ], not to be confused with parentheses, (   ), are used when you write research essays.

1. If you use a quotation that does not fit exactly into your own prose, and you have to introduce a word to make it fit, you must put brackets around that word to tell the reader that *you* added it.

"Oh, he [Henrik Ibsen] may be a very decent fellow for all I know," he exclaimed, "but his plays are far too disturbing for Canadians."
    Fred Jacobs

2. Use [sic] when you quote correctly something that might be thought to be incorrect.

"You are out of the way to Japon [sic], for this is not it."   *Luke Foxe*

Exercise Seven

Ellipses (three dots) indicate omission. Like brackets, ellipses are used with quotations in research essays.

1. If you wish to omit one or more words from a quotation, you use ellipses.

"In Canada we ... use English for literature, Scotch for sermons, and American for conversations." *Stephen Leacock*

2. Sometimes you may introduce ellipses when you omit words at the end of a sentence which could be easily supplied by your reader.

O Canada, we stand... *Stanley Weir*

3. Fiction writers use ellipses to indicate pauses and suspense.

Jack could be behind a chair or couch ...maybe behind the registration desk ...waiting for her to come down.... . *Stephen King*

Use this kind of ellipses judiciously; overuse ruins the effect.

Exercise Eight

Quotation marks have many uses. You and your partner discuss the differences between each of the sections in this exercise.

1. When you introduce dialogue or a short quotation into a passage of prose, use *double* quotation marks.

I once asked a Christmas Eve group of children if they believed in Santa Claus. The very smallest ones answered without hesitation, "Why, of course!" ... One future scientist asserted boldly, "I know who it is" and a little make-strong with his eye on gain said, "I believe it all; I can believe in anything." That boy, I realized, would one day be a bishop.
Stephen Leacock

He [Alfred, Lord Tennyson, the speaker's father] watched Canada to the last with great interest ... and may Canada be ever that "True North."
Lord Tennyson

Perhaps the question is not "Who are we?" but "What are we going to make of ourselves?" *Alden Nowlan*

The correct motto of the Force is not "Get your Man"; it is "Maintain the Right." *Sir James H. MacBrien*

Did Pierre Trudeau really ask, "Where's Biafra?"?

a) Do not let the exact position of quotation marks confuse you. Place quotation marks after periods and commas. (From the above quotations, you and your partner find all the places where a quotation mark comes after a period or comma.)

b) Place quotation marks before colons and semicolons. (Find one illustration.)

c) Place quotation marks before or after question marks and exclamation points depending on whether they are punctuating only the quotation or the entire sentence. (Find all the examples and discuss the reason for the position of the punctuation.)

d) Explain to each other the exact use of ellipses and brackets in the above quotations.

2. When you introduce dialogue within dialogue or a quotation within a quotation, you use *single* quotation marks in order to avoid confusion.

Douglas Marshall wrote: "John Porter said that the 1950s marked 'the high tide of post-war affluence'."

"Larry Mann, the actor who finally reluctantly moved to Hollywood in 1965, put it this way to me in an interview in 1964: 'You can be a full-time garbage collector in Toronto and you'll be accepted as such. Nobody says, "If he were any good he'd be collecting garbage in New York!" ... You're not expected to prove how good you are by moving away to practice medicine or law or accounting in Hollywood or London.' " *Alex Barris*

In order to make sure you and your partner understand the use of single and double quotation marks, answer these questions: What does Alex Barris say? What does Larry Mann say? Who says "If he were any good he'd be collecting garbage in New York!" and why are there double quotation marks around it? Why do the quotations end differently, ('.") ('.' ")? What do the ellipses indicate?

3. Use double quotation marks to enclose terms or expressions that seem out of harmony with the general tone of the writing.

No "think" gags. When the audience is thinking they can't be laughing.
Mack Sennett

Care is needed when using quotation marks to create emphasis. Why?

4. Use double quotation marks to enclose a word or phrase that you are using in a special sense.

I had created enough stars, if I may use the word "create" modestly, to fill the Hollywood skies.   *Jack L. Warner*

(You could use italics or underlining in place of double quotation marks.)

5. Use double quotation marks to enclose titles of poems, stories, chapters, essays, or articles appearing in a larger work.

"Bicultural Angela," by Hugh Hood, appears in Alan Dawe's *Portrait of a Nation*.

6. Use double quotation marks only at the beginning of each paragraph (rather than at the end of each) when dialogue extends over several paragraphs. This usage makes clear that until the closing quotation marks appear, the original speaker is still speaking.

To show your partner an example of this, check a novel that you are reading.

Game Six

Double or One

Follow the same rules as in Game Four. Find examples of double and single quotation marks which involve other punctuation marks. The correct order of the quotation marks with the other punctuation marks will determine whether the player wins a point.

Special Writing Activity

Write a short essay for your partner on a topic that you think will interest him/her in which you use at least one example of each of these punctuation marks:

. , ; : " " ' ' ( ) ! ? — ... [ ]

During your partner's editing, discuss the effectiveness of your use of *each* punctuation mark.

Last Words

Remember that the purpose of punctuation is to help your audience understand what you want to say. One way to determine whether you have punctuated correctly is to read your paper aloud. If you pause as you read, you should insert a punctuation mark. But do not punctuate if you do not know why. The adage, "When in doubt, leave it out," should be your guide as you learn how to punctuate properly.

Activity **14** Word Punctuation

Background

Well-trained writers, when they think of punctuation, consider not only internal and end punctuation within sentences and paragraphs, but also punctuation within words.

Some word punctuation is necessary; some is added by the writer for the purpose of bringing a word or words to the audience's attention.

Word punctuation involves the hyphen, the apostrophe, the period for abbreviations, underlining or italics, capital letters, and the slash.

Exercise One

The *hyphen* is essentially a combining mark. If you trace the derivation of many English compound words, you will find that at one time they were two words, then they became hyphenated words, and finally compound words. When you come to such a word in your writing, consult a current dictionary to see if it lists the word as two words, a hyphenated word, or a compound word.

You and your partner read these rules, then make up a sentence according to the instructions following each rule.

1. Use hyphens with two or more words acting as one adjective.

Example

For many musicians, receiving a gold record for selling a million copies of a single is a *once-in-a-lifetime* experience. For some, it does not happen even once in a lifetime.

(Note that *once-in-a-lifetime* is considered a single word describing "experience", while *once in a lifetime* are four separate words.)

Make up sentences using *high school* and *high-school*, *make work* and *make-work*, *once in a year* and *once-in-a-year*.

2. Use hyphens with a very long phrase used as a single adjective.

Example

Walt Grealis, the godfather of Canadian pop music, referred to record production in Canada in the Sixties as a "*fly-by-the-seat-of-your-pants* sort of thing."

Make up a sentence using the phrase "*butter-wouldn't-melt-in-her-mouth*."

3. Use hyphens with compound adjectives containing a prepositional phrase.

Example

Johnny Cash has frequently sung with the Carter Family, a group founded by his *mother-in-law.*
Make up a sentence with *fly-by-night* and *jack-in-the-box.*

4. Use hyphens between parts of a compound title used as an adjective.

Example

There is no such thing as a *Governor-General's* award for pop music.
Make up sentences with *Lieutenant* and *Governor* as well as *Secretary* and *Treasurer.*

5. Use hyphens to separate prefixes ending with a vowel from root words beginning with a vowel. (Running the prefix and root word together can cause confusion in pronouncing the word.)

Example

The presentation of the Juno awards each year is a *co-operative* effort by musicians, producers, and other members of the music industry.
Make up sentences with *pre* and *eminent, co* and *existence,* as well as *anti* and *establishment.*

6. Use hyphens to separate prefixes from capitalized words.

Example

People who promoted Canadian music only a few years ago were accused of becoming *anti-American*; they said they were *pro-Canadian.*
Make up a sentence with *ex* and *President* as well as *neo* and *Nazi.*

7. Use hyphens with compound adjectives and nouns containing *self.*

Example

Doug and the Slugs' Doug Bennett is not a *self-effacing* performer.
Make up a sentence with *self* as well as *doubt* and *self* as well as *serving.*

8. Use hyphens in compound words consisting of a verb and a preposition. In some words, however, the hyphen is no longer used. Check the dictionary if you are in doubt.

Example

Few Canadian bands have followed the example of the rock group KISS in wearing outrageous *make-up* on stage.
Make up sentences with *shut* and *in, follow* and *up* as well as *send* and *off.*

9. Use hyphens between compound numbers under 100 and between fractions used as adjectives.

Example

Thirty-three and *one-third* percent of records played on AM radio in Canada must have Canadian content; therefore, *one third* of the music played is Canadian.

10. Use hyphens to avoid confusion between adjectives and adverbs.

Example

Ritchie Yorke is a *hard-working* Canadian rock music columnist. (*Hard* is an adverb modifying *working*, rather than an adjective modifying *columnist*.)
Make up a sentence with *well* and *known* as well as *blue* and *eyed*.

11. Use hyphens to avoid confusion between two words, such as *recreation* and *re-creation*.

Example

Canadian-content regulations of the CRTC fostered a virtual *re-creation* of the Canadian music scene.
Make up sentences using *reform* and *re-form*, as well as *resign* and *re-sign*.

12. Use hyphens to divide words that do not fit at the end of a line. The rule for hyphenating at such a time is to make sure you place a hyphen between syllables or between double letters. The hyphen is always placed after the final syllable on the first line.

Example

The success of many Canadian musicians is the result of Pierre Juneau's foresight and his support of Canadian-content laws.
Where would you place a hyphen if these words did not fit the end of the line: *Canadian, musician, result, Pierre, support, laws*? (Which word/s would you not be able to hyphenate? Why?)

Game One

The Hyphen

Play this and the following games with your partner, using the rules outlined in Activity 16.

Example

"A" says, "In the sentence 'I am well known in the school,' is *well known* two words, a hyphenated word, or a compound word?"

"B" answers, "*Well known* is two words," for one point. Then asks, "In the sentence 'He has a pet inchworm,' is *inchworm* two words, a hyphenated word, or a compound word?"

Continue the game. If each of you prepares a list of words, from a dictionary, prior to the game, you will speed it up.

Exercise Two

The *apostrophe* functions either as a mark of omission or a sign of possession. You should be aware that contractions are often inappropriate in formal writing; therefore, you are advised to check the rules of your audience before you use them.

You and your partner read these sentences, noting particularly which letters have been omitted and replaced by apostrophes.

"Which Way You Goin', Billy?" was the first big hit for the Poppy Family. Most Canadians don't distinguish between Canadian rock musicians and those from other countries. They'd say, "I couldn't care less about their nationality."

The apostrophe also shows possession. Look over some of the more familiar rules concerning possession.

1. Most inanimate objects use an *of* phrase rather than an apostrophe.
   Most teenagers are concerned about the quality of their records.
   (It would be wrong to say, "Most teenagers are concerned about their records' quality.")

2. An apostrophe is used in everyday references to time and measurement:
   a week's holiday, their money's worth, three years' experience

3. An apostrophe would also be used to personify an inanimate object:
   death's knock, the semester's reading list

4. Most other nouns take apostrophes to show possession.
   a) Both singular and plural nouns which do not end in *s* take an apostrophe plus an *s*:
      woman's voice, John's guitar, the child's singing, his son-in-law's band, the ox's lowing
      women's voices, men's guitars, children's singing, his sons-in-law's band, oxen's lowing

   b) Singular nouns which end in *s* take an apostrophe plus an *s*:
      the bus's musical horn, James's piano, the actress's sing

      But plural nouns ending in *s* add only an apostrophe:
      the busses' musical horns, the Jameses' pianos, actresses' singing

   c) If two or more people possess something jointly, only the last person in the list needs an apostrophe:
      Frank and Dave's band, Joe and his father's company, Mike, Dani, and Sheila's accompanist

      (If you were to write "Frank's and Dave's band," your reader may wonder if you mean that they both have a band. It would be better to indicate this to the reader by writing "Frank's and Dave's bands.")

Rewrite the other two items so that Joe and his father have separate companies, and the three musicians have separate accompanists.

d) Note the subtlety of possession in these examples:

Paul McCartney's music, John Lennon's music
Lennon's and McCartney's music
Lennon and McCartney's music
The Beatles' music

Which two possessives are plural?

5. Very few pronouns take an apostrophe to show possession.

a) Personal pronouns never use apostrophes to show possession:

my voice, its howling, your harmony, our band
The band is theirs, not ours.

(If you ever see or use an apostrophe with a personal pronoun, it signifies a contraction, not possession.)

he's playing = he is playing
it's howling = it is howling

b) Relative pronouns follow the same rule as personal pronouns:

whose band = possession
who's playing in the band? = Who is playing in the band?
The Who's band = possession because the band is associated with the group *The Who.*

c) Indefinite pronouns take apostrophes in the same way as nouns do:

one's opinion, somebody's microphone, the other's decision

But an indefinite pronoun can be used with a contraction, so be careful.

Everyone's singing. = Everyone is singing.
Everyone's singing was a disappointment. = The singing of each person was a disappointment.

6. If you want to show possession using one or more nouns with a personal pronoun, the nouns must use an apostrophe, and the pronouns must use the possessive form.

Frank's and my band, yours and your mother's books, the twins' and our instruments
The Osmonds' recording studio is their own.

7. *No* other part of speech, other than nouns and indefinite pronouns, uses the apostrophe to show possession; therefore, an apostrophe used correctly in other parts of speech indicates a *contraction*, not possession.

he's = *he is* or *he has*
there's = *there is* or *there has*

it's = *it is* or *it has*

its' = nothing (there is no such word)

My guitar *make's* a good sound. = nonsense (Verbs cannot show possession and there is no such expression as *make is*.)

8. Some writers use apostrophes to indicate the plurals of numbers and letters; for example, *100's, B's, 1980's*. But to avoid confusion with the apostrophes used to indicate possession or contractions, many writers use *100s, Bs, 1980s*. Notice how the use of the apostrophe avoids any misreading in this sentence:

What will happen to the 1970s' music in the 1980s is anyone's guess.

Game Two | To Apostrophe or Not To Apostrophe

Example

"A" hands "B" a piece of paper with this sentence: "XTC's popularity among lovers of rock and roll is based on its hard-driving sound." Then "A" says, "Is there any mistake in the use of the apostrophe?"

"B" says, "Nothing is wrong" for one point, then presents "A" with: "Its difficult to discover how Canadians' tastes in music differ from Americans'."

"A" replies, "*Its* should be *it's* because it is a contraction," for one point. Then "A" presents "Ian's and Sylvia's success as a duo came to an end when they divorced."

Continue the game.

Exercise Three

Abbreviations are perfectly appropriate in certain situations and formats: condensing material, writing a memo, writing a personal letter.

1. Even in more formal contexts you may use certain conventional abbreviations, including: *Mr., Mrs., Ms., Dr., Jr., A.D., B.C., M.D., et al.*

You would write "I visited Dr. Jones."

You would write "I visited my doctor."

You would not write "I visited my Dr."

Make up a sentence with *St.* and *saint* as well as *Rev.* and *reverend*.

2. Some accepted abbreviations do not require periods: CBC, TNT, FBI, OED (Oxford English Dictionary), OPEC. Make up a sentence using an abbreviation which does not require periods.

3. Most of the time, though, you should not use abbreviations in formal writing. For example, you should say *and so forth* instead of *etc.* and *for example* instead of *e.g.* What other abbreviations should you not use in formal writing?

Exercise Four

Italics call attention to a word or words. This is done by underlining the word/s when you write by hand or type. When printed, words are set in italic type. You and your partner note the difference between these pairs of sentences:

1. *Typed*

   One of Gordon Lightfoot's most popular albums has been <u>Sit Down Young Stranger.</u>

   In Print

   One of Gordon Lightfoot's most popular albums has been *Sit Down Young Stranger.*

   (By the way, titles of cuts from the album would not be underlined or printed in italic; they would be put into quotation marks.)

2. *Typed*

   The <u>chansonniers</u> such as Gilles Vigneault have made Québécois music popular at home and abroad.

   In Print

   The *chansonniers* such as Gilles Vigneault have made Québécois music popular at home and abroad.

   (Italics indicate a non-English word that has not been assimilated into English.)

3. *Typed*

   <u>RPM</u> magazine was a pioneer in the promotion of Canadian musical talent.

   In Print

   RPM magazine was a pioneer in the promotion of Canadian musical talent.

   (Italicize titles of books and publications, but put quotation marks around parts of published works: essays, poems, short stories, and so on.)

4. *Typed*

   The Beatles were <u>the</u> musical group of the 1960s and 1970s.

   In Print

   The Beatles were *the* musical group of the 1960s and 1970s.

   (Italicize to indicate the importance of a word, letter, or number. Do not, however, overuse this method of gaining an emphatic effect.)

Exercise Five

End punctuation followed by *capitalization* tells the reader when a new sentence begins. Words within a sentence can also begin with capital letters. An initial capital letter indicates that a word is a proper noun or a proper adjective. You and your partner read these sentences, paying particular attention to capitalization.

1. Healey Willan, though he is virtually unknown, was one of Canada's foremost classical composers. (The proper nouns require capital letters.)

2. The West has displaced the East as the centre of Canadian pop music. (Capitalizing *West* and *East* makes them specific geographical areas.)
3. In her concerts, Indian singer Buffy Sainte-Marie plays native instruments. (The proper adjective *Indian* requires a capital letter.)

Game Three

Punc Words

On separate pieces of paper, write a predetermined number of sentences with up to three word-punctuation mistakes in each sentence.

Example

"A" gives "B" this sentence: "Roger Doucet's bilingual rendition of O Canada became popular through it's use at Montreal Canadiens hockey games."

"B" says, "*O Canada* should be underlined, *its* should not have an apostrophe, and everything else looks right." "A" points out that *Canadiens* should be *Canadiens'*. "B" makes two points; "A" makes one point.

"B" then gives "A": "The so called "supergroup" Lighthouse, an eleven piece band, made its mark on Canadian music in the 70s."

"A" says, "*So called* and *eleven piece* should both have a hyphen; *70s* should be *70's*." "B" points out that *70s* does not show possession; therefore, it should not have an apostrophe. Thus, "A" gets two points; "B" gets one.

"A" gives "B": "Burton Cummings, whose former group was the Guess Who, is a multi talented Canadian musician and composer."

Continue the game.

Exercise Six

The *slash* (also called an oblique stroke) is a little-used punctuation mark that is making a comeback. The need to refer to both men and women in advertisements, instructions, and elsewhere has made the use of *his/her*, meaning *his and her* or *his or her*, popular. Though its use in this way in formal writing is not yet acceptable, the slash, like the apostrophe in contractions, is finding its way into other sorts of writing.

1. Use the slash judiciously to separate two words that you wish to use interchangeably.

   Lyricists, like writers, struggle to fill blanks with an appropriate word/s.

   (Technically this should read "... an appropriate word or words.")

   Before buying a Chopin record as a birthday gift for a friend, first determine whether he/she likes to listen to classical music.

2. Use a slash to separate opposites that you want to use in the same context.

   Either you do/don't like rock and roll.
   Answer true/false to the music quiz.

3. Do not use *and/or.* It's too inconclusive. With your partner, discuss the meanings of these sentences.

The band leader said men and/or women should apply.
The band leader said men and women should apply.
The band leader said men or women should apply.
The band leader said men/women should apply.

4. The following was taken from a band's advertisement. What sort of songs do you think they play?

The BBs can play jazz and/or rock and classical music and/or show tunes.

Special Writing Activity

Write a paragraph on a topic that you think will interest your partner. Include a hyphen, an apostrophe, an abbreviation, underlining, capitalization of a word within a sentence, and a slash. Also include these words: *its, 100s,* and *1950's.* During editing, your partner should pay particular attention to word punctuation.

Last Words

Remember, word punctuation should be used to help your audience. Omitting necessary word punctuation is as confusing for a reader as is overusing it for emphasis.

Activity 15 Usage

Background

We all have various "languages" – levels of usage – that we adapt for different occasions. Language that is appropriate in one situation may not be appropriate in another.

Choosing the most suitable language for a particular audience and purpose is one of the most difficult and challenging tasks facing writers and speakers.

Exercise One

Words can be classified according to levels: *formal*, *standard* (informal), and *substandard* (colloquial or slang). For example:

Formal	Standard	Substandard
gentleman	man	guy
domicile	house	pad

1. Here is a list of standard words. See if you or your partner can come up with a formal and substandard counterpart.

child, home, dance, meet, small, large, round

Example
woman: lady (formal), chick (substandard)

2. Not all words can be labelled with these terms, but you may find it useful to discuss with your partner under what circumstances you would choose each of the words in parentheses.

I (ran, fled, split, took to my heels, flew the coop).

He (sleeps, slumbers, rests in the arms of Morpheus, dozes, naps, catches a wink, sleeps like a log, sleeps like the dead, saws wood, gets some shut-eye, gets some sack time, kips, hibernates.)

Which of the verbs would you use in a formal research essay, in a persuasive essay, in a conversation with a friend?

Exercise Two

1. Separately, you and your partner should write three drafts of the following sample sentence, using the word choices in parentheses. Think about levels of word choice before you write. (Normally you should avoid mixing word levels.) Also consider the writing variables. Draft one should be to a very good friend of both you and the deceased. Draft two should be for a cheap paperback thriller. Draft three should be for the deceased's minister.

When (Uncle Edward, Uncle Eddie, my old man's brother, dear old Ed, the apple of my grandmother's eye) (succumbed, expired, departed, shuffled off this mortal coil, gave up the ghost, went the way of all flesh, popped off, slipped his cable, bought it) (this morning, this morn, this matin, sometime today, this grey-eyed morn, this A.M., at sun up, at the crack of dawn, this forenoon), he (disposed of, gave away, donated, willed and bequeathed, wrote into his will, dropped) (riches, resources, his worth, material assets, his loot, his fortune, pretty near every penny, his wad, piles of moola) to (the poor, the have-nots, the down-and-outs, the underprivileged, the urban poor, welfare families, the wretched of the earth, paupers, the impoverished) and not to (me, yours truly, the writer of this sentence).

2. After you have written the three drafts of the above sentence, you and your partner should compare your sentences and discuss the type of audience who would appreciate each sentence. Also, you should discuss the type of person who would have written each version.

Exercise Three

Standard English is usually defined as word usage that is widely recognized and accepted. With the exception of letters to close friends, or diary or journal entries, most of your writing should be in standard English.

You may ask, "Why do I have to use only accepted combinations of words? What's wrong with being original?" The simple answer is that much of your writing will be read by informed people. Your lack of correctness will give the impression that you are uninformed. Your word usage may even cost you a job, or prevent you from being considered for a promotion.

In order to master standard word usage, you should read and listen to informed people, people who are the leaders in the use of language – editorial writers, public figures, professional writers. To keep up with current usage, you should listen to news broadcasts, watch documentaries, and pay attention to popular speakers. Occasionally, even they may use words improperly, but you will generally profit if you follow their example.

1. Make up some sentences using these words: *accept, except, among, between, amount of, number of, as, like, because of, due to, can, may, compare to, compare with, lie, lay, sit, set.*

2. Discuss the correctness of your word usage with your partner. You may both need to consult a dictionary or reference book, if you do not *know* whether you are correct.

Exercise Four

Often, particular combinations of words no longer make literal sense, but they continue to be used nonetheless. These combinations of words, which no longer make literal sense, are known as *idioms*.

People rarely think about common idiomatic expressions; they simply use them. But when you hear speakers whose first language is not English misusing them, you become aware that idioms are illogical; for example, a Scandinavian might say to a girl, "May I follow you home?" instead of the idiom, "May I walk you home?"

1. Discuss with your partner the literal meanings or illogicality of these common idioms: "How do you do?" "Look up a word." "I'm fed up." "Got the picture?" "Now you're going to town." "You're pulling my leg." "Run for office." "Take a bath." "Bring up a subject."

2. Each of you think of five similar idiomatic expressions, then discuss the literal meanings or illogicality of each of them.

3. Discuss in what situations idioms would be appropriate or inappropriate.

Exercise Five

When you are with your friends, you likely use words and expressions that people of another generation, or from another country, would not understand. These colourful *slang* expressions are quite appropriate in casual conversation, but are usually considered too informal for written communication.

1. Here is an example of Cockney slang. Would you know what the speaker is talking about?

My skin and blister was cash and carried Saturday by the Garden Gate.

If you know what each of these means, you must appreciate rhyming slang. *Skin and blister* is *sister, cash and carried* is *married, Garden Gate* is *magistrate.*

2. Here are a few other examples of Cockney rhyming slang.

bucket and pail – jail	cuts and scratches – matches
loaf of bread – head	biscuits and cheese – knees
April showers – flowers	cat and mouse – house
army and navy – gravy	ding dong – song
bacon and eggs – legs	field of wheat – street

Now have a chat with your partner on any topic, trying to use as many of the above examples of rhyming slang as you can.

3. A variation of slang that you may have used as a child is pig Latin.
Sound these out to each other to see if you can discover the pattern, and thus, the meaning.

Ow-hay ong-lay an-cay oo-yay eak-spay ig-pay atin-lay?
Iting-wray is-ay I-may avorite-fay astime-pay.
Ock-ray and-ay oll-ray is-ay ere-hay oo-tay ay-stay.

Young people usually enjoy speaking pig Latin because they are using language other groups do not understand. After you and your partner crack the code, see if you can carry on a chat for five minutes using only pig Latin.

4. With your partner, make a list of slang expressions used in your group, and discuss their meanings.

Exercise Six

All groups of people have their own special words that they use among their friends. Similarly, there are special words that people use in various professional situations. Language used in a special sense (by and for members of a particular audience) is called *jargon*.

1. Here is an example of sports jargon:

Paopao hands off the ball to White, who takes it at his own twenty, gets a couple of key blocks from the guards, dipsy-doodles through the defence, and is finally clotheslined by Fennell on the Eskimos' forty-five.

What sport is being talked about? Can you explain to your partner the meaning of the jargon used?

2. Write a similar piece on another sport for which you know the jargon. Give it to your partner to see if he or she knows what you are talking about.

3. List five examples of jargon that you would use legitimately in one of your specialized subjects: chemistry, home economics, typing, and so on. For example, with what subject would you associate *floppy disk*, *byte*, *time sharing*, *stand-alone*, and *cursor*?

Does your partner understand what your examples mean? When is technical jargon legitimate?

Jargon has a purpose in sports and technical reports. It has a place among your close circle of friends. But in ordinary writing, jargon may confuse your reader. So reserve technical language for technical uses and current expressions for conversations with your friends.

Special Writing Activity

Write a short paragraph for your partner that you think your teacher or parents would not understand. In other words, use slang or jargon that you think only your partner would appreciate.

In the evaluation, discuss the effectiveness of your slang or jargon and how well your partner understands and appreciates your paragraph. In order to see if you are totally successful, perhaps you might show your paragraph to your teacher and parents to see if, indeed, they fail to understand what you have written.

Last Words

If you keep in mind your purpose and audience as you write, you should be able to choose the correct words for your topic. There is no better way to learn word usage than by hearing and reading words properly used.

Activity 16 Vocabulary

Background

You have learned that the most important step in writing is to have an idea worth expressing. However, the more extensive your vocabulary, the more effectively you will be able to express your ideas. This does not mean that you must use big words in order to communicate your ideas. Much of the time a smaller word may be more appropriate. The key is to find the words that best communicate your intended meaning.

I THINK THE, ER, WHOSEE'S, GONE ASKEW ON THE WHATCHAMACALLIT, OR MAYBE IT'S THE, YOU KNOW, WHATSIT, ON THE THINGME.

Exercise One

There are many ways to build your vocabulary; the next few two-way games will give you practice. Use the games that you enjoy most to begin building an extensive vocabulary. Decide with your partner, before you play, what the general rules will be and how you will keep score.

Scoring and general rules

a) Take turns providing one answer at a time. The one who cannot come up with a correct response loses.

   OR

   Write your responses separately on a piece of paper. The one who has the greater number of correct responses wins.

b) It is assumed that you know the meanings of the words you use in the game; however, you may bluff and use a word whose meaning you are not sure of. If your partner challenges a word, you must explain its meaning. Check the meaning in a dictionary. If, on the challenge, you are right, you gain a point; if you are wrong, you lose one.

c) Reference books (dictionaries and thesauri) can be used during the game only in the event of a challenge. They can also, of course, be used to prepare for a game.

d) To make each game fair, take turns in choosing which game to play and with which "word" to begin each game.

Game One

Roots

A root (or stem) is that part of a word which contains the core of its meaning: *aster* (meaning *star*) is the root of such words as *aster*isk, *astro*nomy, and dis*aster*.

Rules

Alternate announcing a root and its meaning. Then follow either method of scoring.

Example

Partner "B" begins the game by saying the root word *fin* (meaning "boundary").

"A" says *finish*;

"B" says *finite*;

"A" says *infinity*;

"B" says *definite*;

"A" cannot think of another word with *fin* in it. The score is tied unless "B" can come up with a word.

   If you want to follow this method, continue with *fin*.

   If you are following the second scoring method, write independently on your own pieces of paper all the words that have *fin* in them. Whoever produces the higher number of correct responses wins.

To get you started, here are some roots you might use: *chronos* ("time"), *therme* ("heat"), *algia* ("sickness"), *phonos* ("sound"), *equ* ("equal, just"), *voc, vok* ("to call").

Game Two — Prefixes

Rules

The rules are exactly as in Game One except that you use prefixes.

Example

The prefix *ab* means "from, away from" as in *abnormal*, *abduct*, and *absent*. Continue the game with *ab*.

Here are a few prefixes to get you started with Game Two: *ambi* ("both"), *ante* ("before"), *bi* ("two, twice"), *bene* ("good, well"), *circum* ("around"), *tele* ("far off"), *epi* ("upon"), *dia* ("through"), *peri* ("around").

Game Three — Suffixes

Rules

The rules are exactly the same except that you use suffixes.

Example

The suffix *dom* means "condition" as in *kingdom*, *freedom*, and *wisdom*. Continue the game with *dom*.

Here are a few suffixes to get you started with Game Three: *fold* ("number, quantity"), *less* ("lacking, wanting"), *ward* ("in the direction of"), *wise* ("way, manner").

Game Four — Family Words

Rules

"A" says a word; "B" provides a family word; "A" provides another family word and the game continues.

Example

"A" says *satire*.
"B" says *satirize*.
"A" says *satiric*.
"B" continues.

Here are a few words to get you started with Game Four: *admit, strange, straw, omit, personal, fertile, liquid, thick, solid.*

Game Five

Synonyms

Rules

"A" says a word; "B" provides a synonym of that word and uses it correctly in a sentence; "A" does the same thing and the game continues.

Example

"A" says *stop*.

"B" says, *"Halt* in the name of the law."

"A" says, "My progress in the game was *arrested*."

"B" challenges the use of *arrested*.

"A" explains that *arrested* means *stopped*, checks the dictionary to discover if the definition is correct, and wins an extra point.

"B" continues.

Here are some words to get you started with Game Five: *level, quaint, harmony, freedom, catch.*

Game Six

Antonyms

Rules

Take turns giving each other words. The other must provide the antonym, used correctly in a sentence.

Example

"A" says *rough*.

"B" says, "My chin is *smooth*."

"B" says, *complicated*.

"A" says "The directions were *simple*.", and gives "B" *intelligent*.

The game continues.

Use the words from Game Five to get you started with Game Six.

Game Seven

Plurals

Rules

Take turns giving each other singular nouns. The other must furnish the plural.

Example

"A" gives *datum*.

"B" answers *data*, then gives *ox*.

"A" answers *oxen*, then gives *mongoose*.

"B" continues.

Here is a list to get you going with Game Seven: *deer, Siamese, agendum, city, alumnus, alumna, buffalo, census, basis.* (If you want to include a Spelling Challenge in your rules, this would be an appropriate place. Also, you can reverse this game by providing the plural and requiring a singular answer.)

Game Eight

Degrees

Rules

Take turns giving each other adjectives or adverbs. The other must supply the comparative and the superlative degree.

Example

"A" gives *bad.*

"B" answers *worse, worst,* then gives *good.*

"A" answers *better, best* , then gives *tiny.*

"B" continues.

    Here is a list to get you going with Game Eight: *wise, great, careful, carefully, far, late, much, old, serene, handsome.* (You may bluff by giving a word that has no degrees, such as *unique, infinite, empty, dead, absolutely, certainly.* Furthermore, you may vary the game by providing downgraded comparisons and superlatives, such as *less agreeably, least agreeably; less strong, least strong.*)

Exercise Two

If you really want to build your vocabulary, make a word calendar for each other. Learning a new word each day can be a painless way of building your vocabulary.

Example

Prepare a list of words for each day in a month. Exchange the list with your partner. Each list should look something like this:

October 1	tantamount
2	anathema
3	fulsome
4	tenacious
5	rapacious

    If you already know the meaning of the word that your partner has chosen, you can have the day off. If you are unfamiliar with the word, look up its meaning and try to use it throughout the day. See if the adage "Use a word ten times and it's yours" is true.

Exercise Three

Words are used both for their dictionary meanings and for their appeal to the reader's emotions. The dictionary meaning of the word is termed the *denotative meaning*; the emotional appeal of the word is termed the *connotative meaning*.

    Words can have either positive or negative connotations. The word *determined*, for example, has a positive connotation; the word *stubborn* a negative one.

1. For each of the words from the following list, suggest a similar term with a negative connotation: *doctor, corpse, anti-feminist, baby, obese, demonstration, television set, stomach, afraid, teenager, pimple, father, decay*

2. For each word below, suggest a similar term with a positive connotation: *conceited, pushy, blunt, rich, jock, brain, skinny, lie, short, mousy, smell*

Exercise Four

You may have heard of poets who jot down dozens of words to fit into a single position in their poems. After much agonizing, they finally decide on one word that fits both the subject and the rhythm. The process is rather like the out-takes of a television show or a movie. For one scene that the audience sees, perhaps as many as fifty scenes wind up on the film editor's floor.

1. You and your partner fill in each blank with a word that fits the poem's rhythm, metre, tone, rhyme scheme, purpose, and meaning.

Blow, Bugle, Blow

> The splendour falls on _____ walls
> And _____ summits old in story:
> The long light _____ across the lakes,
> And the wild _____ leaps in glory.
> Blow, bugle, blow, set the wild echoes _____ .
> Blow, bugle; answer, echoes, dying, dying, dying.

Discuss each other's word choices. For interest, see if your word choice matches Tennyson's version in the Suggested Answers.

2. Each of you find a poem. Duplicate it but leave a few key words out. Exchange duplicated poems and each try to fill in the blanks with appropriate vocabulary. Afterwards, discuss the choices.

Exercise Five

Prose writers, too, must always take into account both the connotative and denotative meanings of the words they use, the level and appropriateness of the words, and the effect they wish to achieve by their word choice. A thesaurus and dictionary will help you find words, but if you do not take into account the *full* meaning of the word you choose, your audience may misinterpret what you write.

1. You and your partner try to supply a suitable word for some of Francis Bacon's famous sentences. If you want to compare your words with his, you will find the lines in the Suggested Answers.

   a) Men fear Death, as children fear to go in the _____ .
   b) Revenge is a kind of wild _____ .

c) _____ amongst thoughts are like bats amongst birds, they ever fly by twilight.

d) Studies serve for _____, for _____, and for _____.

e) Some books are to be tasted, others to be _____, and some few to be _____ and _____: that is, some books are to be read only in parts; others to be read but not curiously; and some few to be read wholly, and with diligence and attention ... Reading maketh a _____ man; conference a _____ man; and writing an _____ man.

f) It is as natural to die as to be _____; and to a little infant, perhaps, the one is as _____ as the other.

2. Choose a prose author and prepare a similar exercise for your partner. After each of you has completed the other's exercise, discuss your vocabulary choices. Then, for interest, compare your choices with the author's.

Exercise Six

1. New words are continually being coined to add to the 800,000 English words we now have. These blended words, for example, have caught on:

chuckle + snort = chortle,
cranberry + apple = cranapple
lunch + breakfast = brunch.

What two words have been blended to produce *jazzercise, smog, flurry, rollerthon, blooper, participaction*? You and your partner each coin five new words. Exchange your sentences and see if you can discover their meanings.

2. In the 1930s and 1940s Tom Swift was the hero of a series of boys' books. One feature of these books is the way the author uses descriptive words: Tom and other characters always say things *quietly, abruptly,* or *emphatically.*

"Tom Swifties" use this feature and carry it one step further: they show a punning relationship between the descriptive word and the quotation.

Examples

"I couldn't get the horse to stop," Tom said woefully.

"I don't want to prepare the cheese for this macaroni dish," complained Mike gratingly.

"This suit is the wrong size," Ted moaned fitfully.

"Choreographing the equestrian team has given me laryngitis," whispered Susan hoarsely.

You and your partner make up three "Tom Swifties" for each other.

3. In a wonderful play by Richard Sheridan, the character of Mrs. Malaprop appears. Examine her choice of words.

Mrs. Malaprop:

You are very good and very considerate, captain. I am sure I have done everything in my power since I *exploded* the affair; long ago I laid my positive *conjunctions* on her, never to think on the fellow again; – I have since laid Sir Anthony's *preposition* before her; but, I am sorry to say, she seems resolved to decline every *particle* that I *enjoin* her.

Absolute.

It must be very distressing, indeed, ma'am.

Mrs. Malaprop:

Oh! it gives me the *hydrostatics* to such a degree. – I thought she had *persisted* from corresponding with him; but, behold, this very day, I have *interceded* another letter from the fellow; I believe I have it in my pocket ... . [After reading some passages from the letter:] There, sir, an attack upon my language! what do you think of that? – an aspersion upon my parts of speech! Was ever such a brute? Sure, if I *reprehend* any thing in this world it is the use of my *oracular* tongue, and a nice *derangement* of *epitaphs*!

Malapropism is the term now given to words that have a sound similar to, but a meaning different from, the intended word. For example:

I have laid Sir Anthony's *preposition* before her.

(A *preposition* is a part of speech. The intended word is *proposition*, or offer.)

Can you and your partner understand Mrs. Malaprop's "derangement of epitaphs"? Re-read the exchange substituting new words for the malapropisms. Check the Suggested Answers.

Special Writing Activity

Ask your partner to give you five words that you do not understand. Your task is to write a paragraph in which you use the five words correctly and effectively. You also must create a unified and coherent piece of writing that makes sense.

Last Words

An extensive vocabulary is an asset to a writer, but do not use a big word if a smaller one suits your purpose just as well.

Activity **17** Spelling

Background

Some word processing systems have a built-in 50,000-word spelling memory, which means that when you complete an essay on the machine, all you have to do is push the *spell* key and it will check for misspellings. The word processor does not, however, correct your spelling; it just brings to your attention words that do not agree with its memory. You must correct the misspelled words yourself.

A remarkable invention, the spelling memory not only saves valuable time but reduces spelling to a mechanical chore, its rightful place in the writing process.

On the other hand, it may be a long time before everyone has a word processor. In the meantime, spelling will continue to be the bane of many a student. No matter how interesting the topic, how honourable the purpose, or how apt the format, audiences are prone to discount a piece of writing if the writer cannot spell. There is only one safe rule about spelling: when in doubt, check the dictionary, where every word is spelled correctly.

Exercise One

There are rules in spelling that can be learned; it's the exceptions to these rules that confuse poor spellers.

1. One-syllable words *usually* double the final consonant when a suffix beginning with a vowel is added.

Examples: slap, slapping   hop, hopping

2. Words of two or more syllables *usually* double the final consonant when a suffix beginning with a vowel is added to an accented final syllable.

Examples: refer, referring   occur, occurrence

3. Words that end with a doubled consonant *usually* keep both when a suffix is added.

Examples: impress, impression   embarrass, embarrassment

4. When the same consonant ends the prefix and begins the root word, both consonants are kept.

Examples: natural, unnatural   spell, misspell

5. Similarly, when the same consonant ends the root word and begins the suffix, both consonants are kept.

Examples: total, totally   open, openness

6. Words that end with a silent "e" *usually* drop the "e" before a suffix beginning with a vowel.

Examples: hope, hoping   believe, believing

7. But the "e" is *usually* kept before a suffix beginning with a consonant.

Examples: rare, rarely   hope, hopeful

8. A final silent "e" preceded by "c" or "g" is kept before a suffix beginning with "a" or "o."

Examples: enforce, enforceable   manage, manageable

9. Words that end in "y" preceded by a consonant *usually* change the "y" to "i" before a suffix.

Examples: justify, justification   risky, riskier

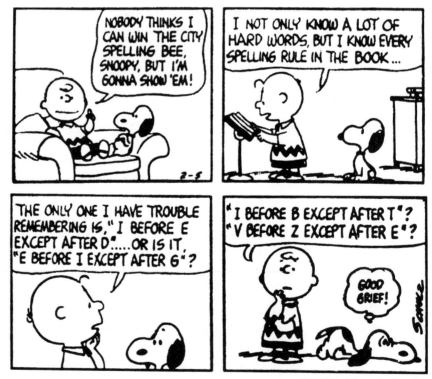

©1966 United Feature Syndicate, Inc.

10. Words that end in "y" preceded by a vowel *usually* keep the "y" before a suffix.

Examples: employ, employing   play, player

11. Words ending in "c" add "k" before adding suffixes that start with "e," "i," or "y."

Examples: picnic, picnicking   traffic, trafficker

12. The "ei" or "ie" rule needs special attention:

a) *Usually* "e" follows "i."

   Examples: relieve   siege

b) But "i" follows "e" and "c" and whenever it is pronounced like a long "a."

   Examples: receive   freight

13. Learning four words will make the "ceed/cede" rule easy.
Supersede is the only English word that ends in "sede."
Exceed, *proceed*, and *succeed* are the only English words that end in "ceed."
All other words having the same sound end in "cede."

Examples: precede   recede

14. There are some words that you just have to learn how to spell. They follow no rules.

Examples: rhyme, unnecessary, psychiatry, phlegm.

Game One   Rules or Exceptions

For this and subsequent spelling games, follow the rules outlined in Activity 16, Exercise One.

After you and your partner have decided which of the nine spelling games you want to play, each of you should prepare a list of words to use. This will speed up your game.

Examples

"A" says, "*courageous* is spelled correctly. Which rule does it follow, or is it an exception to a rule?"

"B" says, "*courageous* follows Rule Eight" for one point, then says, "*seize* is spelled correctly. Which rule does it follow, or is it an exception to a rule?"

"A" says "*seize* is an exception to Rule Twelve a" for one point, and says, "*cynicism* is spelled correctly. Which rule does it follow, or is it an exception to a rule?"

"B" continues.

15. There are many rules for spelling plurals.

a) Nouns *usually* form plurals by adding an "s" to the singular.

   Examples: flower, flowers   girl, girls

b) If the plural will make another syllable, "es" should be added.

   Examples: kiss, kisses   patch, patches

c) Nouns ending in "o" preceded by a vowel form plurals by adding "s."

   Examples: radio, radios   cameo, cameos

d) Nouns ending in "o" preceded by a consonant form plurals by adding "s" or sometimes "es."

   Examples: solo, solos   hero, heroes

e) Nouns ending in "f" or "fe" *usually* change the "f" to "ve" and add "s."

   Examples: thief, thieves   wife, wives

f) Nouns ending in "y" preceded by a consonant change the "y" to "i" and add "es."

   Examples: pity, pities   flurry, flurries

g) Nouns ending in "y" preceded by a vowel add "s" to form plurals.

   Examples: monkey, monkeys   boy, boys

h) Nouns borrowed from other languages may retain their original plurals or may use the same forms as similar English words.

   Examples: datum, data   alumna, alumnae or alumnas

i) Compound nouns form plurals by making the most important part of the word plural.

   Examples: brothers-in-law   step-sisters

j) Several nouns have their own unique way of forming plurals. If you are in doubt, check the dictionary.

   Examples: foot, feet   mouse, mice   basis, bases

Game Two

Plurals

Example

"A" says, "Spell the plural of *secretary-general*. Which rule should you follow?"

"B" spells *"secretaries-general"* for two points and says, "It follows *Rule 15 i*" for one point. Then "B" says, "Spell the plural of *soprano*. Which rule should you follow?"

"A" continues.

Game Three

Frequently Misspelled Words

Perhaps you and your partner could each make up (or find) a short list of frequently misspelled words and plan to dictate them to each other at predetermined intervals (each week or every two weeks).

Decide if you want the words to come as a surprise or whether to exchange them the day before you dictate them. Also, decide on scoring procedures.

Here is a typical list:

immediately	occasionally	business
exaggerate	development	conscious
embarrass	privilege	separate
all right	beginning	convenience
equipment	grateful	occurrence
existence	beneficial	fascinate
environment	recommend	humorous
parallel	quiet	loose

Exercise Two

If you know how to pronounce a word properly, you stand a better chance of spelling the word correctly.

If there are words that you regularly misspell, check your dictionary to see how they are pronounced. For example, *pronunciation* is pronounced prə nun sē ā′ shən; hence you would not put an "o" before the "u."

If you do not understand how to interpret the pronunciation instructions, check the pronunciation key in your dictionary.

In English, however, many words have letters that do not make any sound (*knight*), that have one sound for two letters (*stopping*), or that sound nothing like what you would expect (*phylum*).

Game Four

Pronunciation Only

Example
"A" hands "B" a piece of paper with the word *hyperbole* written on it.
"B" pronounces it (hī ′per′ bə lē) for one point, then hands "A" the word
 nuclear.
"A" continues.

Game Five

> ### The Silent Letter
>
> *Example*
>
> "A" says, "What is the silent letter in *writing*?"
>
> "B" answers, "The *w*" for one point, then spells it for two points. Then says, what is the silent letter in *hopeful*?"
>
> "A" continues.

Game Six

> ### Double or One?
>
> *Example*
>
> "A" says, "Is there a double *t* in *omitting* or is there only one?"
>
> "B" says, "Double" for one point, then spells it for two points. Then "B" says, "Is there a double *m* in *accommodating*?"
>
> "A" continues.

Game Seven

> ### Sounds Familiar
>
> *Example*
>
> "A" says, "Spell *phial*. Hint: the *f* sound is spelled *ph*."
>
> "B" spells "*p-h-i-a-l*" for two points. If it is spelled incorrectly the first time, try again for one point. Then "B" says, "Spell *rough*. Hint: the *f* sound is spelled *gh*."
>
> "A" continues.

Game Eight

> ### Homonyms
>
> *Example*
>
> "A" says, "Spell the homonym for *t-h-e-r-e*." (Spell the word. Do not pronounce it.)
>
> "B" says, "*t-h-e-r-e* is pronounced *there*" for one point, and says "its homonym is *t-h-e-i-r*" for two points. Then "B" says, "Spell the homonym for *h-a-r-e*."
>
> "A" continues.

Exercise Three

One way to learn how to spell difficult words is to link them to something else. Such a memory association technique is called *mnemonics* (pronounced (ne mon' iks) from the Greek, "to remember."

1. *Examples of mnemonics using sight spelling techniques*

Sergeant equals *serge* plus *ant*.
There is *sin* in business.
A *counsellor sells*.
You *hear* at a *rehearsal*.
You *lop* the final "e" in *develop*.

2. *Examples of mnemonics using sound spelling techniques*
Many words are spelled exactly as they sound. So if you are having trouble spelling a word, break it into syllables. You may find that the word is spelled exactly as you say it, providing you pronounce it carefully and correctly.

Examples
grat i tude
pen in su la
cam a rad e rie

Game Nine

Sound Mnemonics

Example
"A" says, "Break *melodic* into syllables before you spell it."
"B" says "*me lod ic*" for one point and spells it for two. Then "B" says
    "Break *mellifluous* into syllables before you spell it."
"A" continues.

Last Words

Never put yourself in a position where you do not use a word because you cannot spell it. Have a dictionary handy.

The games in this activity can be played anywhere, any time. So, if you have a couple of minutes to spare, play a spelling game.

Activity **18** Slant

Background

The term *slant* is used to describe the way in which a writer may, consciously or unconsciously, convey attitudes or feelings to the reader. As a result of the writer's purpose or attitude, his or her material may have a *positive* or *negative* slant.

Exercise One

We are often unaware of the slant in our own material. This exercise will help you to appreciate how your presentation changes, depending on your audience.

1. Recall the last time you were out with someone. Think about what kind of a time you had. Write down several key words that honestly describe your experience; for example, *choice, the pits, great, foolish, terrific, O.K.* and so on. These words are for your eyes only.

2. Now, imagine telling the person you were out with about the time you had. Write down the words you would use. Compare the original list with the new list. Which of the original words would you not use? What words would you use instead? (For example, if you had used *terrible* to describe the occasion, you might not want to use that word to your companion. You might use *not bad* instead.) What thoughts might you leave unsaid?

3. Next, imagine telling one of your parents (new audience) about the time you had. Which words in the previous lists would you not use? Which words would you use instead? Which details about the experience would you leave out of your account?

4. Now, in the classroom (new situation) tell your partner (new audience) about the time you had. How many of the original key words did you not use?

Exercise Two

Your presentation is also affected by your attitude towards your subject.

1. With your partner, choose a subject (for example, an activity, a person, or a location) that one of you likes and one dislikes.

2. Each of you write a description of your subject. Do not state how you feel about your subject, but merely describe it.

3. Compare your descriptions. Discuss the differences in word choices, facts, and so on.

Exercise Three

There are three ways that writing may be slanted in either a positive or negative manner:

a) *Words*

Words with positive connotations will cause your reader to feel good about your subject and possibly about you; words with negative connotations will cause your reader to react against your subject and possibly against you as well. Which of the following sentences use words with positive connotations? negative connotations? Which sentences merely state the facts?

The team members flew into position on the court.
The so-called team members stumbled to their spots on the battlefield.
The team quickly took their positions on the gym floor.
The man laughs a lot with his friends.
The dope giggles his head off with his buddies.
The fellow chuckles a great deal with his pals.

b) *Comparisons*

If you literally or figuratively compare your subject with something pleasant, your reader will know you approve of your subject; if you use unpleasant comparisons, your reader will know you disapprove of it. With your partner, discuss which of the following common comparisons are positive and which are negative.

He eats like a bird.
He eats like a pig.
She has a voice like a nightingale.
She has a voice like a crow.

Now, make up three positive comparisons, and three negative comparisons.

c) *Details*

You can influence your reader by the specific facts or details that you choose to report about your subject. If you choose only favourable details or facts, and ignore unfavourable ones, you are slanting your material in a positive manner. Discuss which of the following statements have positive or negative slant.

Wars are good for the economy.
Microcomputers are simply a modern form of home entertainment: everyone who owns one has a stack of video games.
Cars are a menace: they kill people all the time.
Compared with hard drugs, marijuana is harmless.
Jogging can give you shin splints; it's better to stick to weightlifting.
Proper English may be only a convention, but using it will make communication more effective.

Exercise Four

Words can have no slant, positive slant, or negative slant. For example:

Positive	No Slant	Negative
physician	doctor	pill pusher
mansion	house	shack

1. Draw a diagram similar to the one above. Choose five of the words from the list below, or five words of your own, and write them in the *No Slant* column, then write words for the positive and negative columns that mean almost the same thing as your original word.

policeman, child, muscular, sleeps, eats, small, large, round, money, prison, party, angry, language

2. Remember that because a word is in a particular space, it does not mean that it must forever remain there. The word "girls," for example, was acceptable when applied to women of all ages ten or fifteen years ago. Today, many women object to this term, as it implies a condescending or patronizing attitude.

The context in which a word is used will also affect its meaning. If an angry patient rushes into the doctor's office and yells, "Now you look here, Doc!", the word "doc" will have a negative slant.

3. Within the positive and negative categories, there will be degrees of slant. For each term, you could have several words, each one a little more positive or negative than another. This fact makes your search for "just that right word" a challenge.

4. When you have completed this activity, go over your lists with your activity partner. It might be an interesting exercise for you both to choose at least one word that is the same, work on it separately, then compare your responses.

Exercise Five

A writer may use slant unintentionally, as a result of his or her feelings about a certain subject; or intentionally, to create a specific effect on the reader. The intentional use of slant is widespread. We are inundated by examples of both negative and positive slant in newspapers, magazines, and direct mail, and on radio, television, and billboards. Advertisers want us to buy their products; politicians urge us to support their platforms; government agencies encourage us to start exercising.

1. Choose ten advertisements from the print media that illustrate either positive or negative slant. Look at the names of the products: *Quik, Dynamo, Magic Touch*. Also discuss words that are used to describe the product. (Most advertisements will have positive slant. Why? In what ways might they use negative slant?)

2. Exchange advertisements with your partner to see if you both can find the negative and positive slant in each other's collection. Discuss your findings.

Exercise Six

Propaganda usually provides excellent examples of slant. Notice the use of negative and positive slant in the following sentences:

The Americans are storing weapons to be able to protect the democratic system of government from total destruction while the Commies are stockpiling them in order to enslave the rest of the world.

The Union of Soviet Socialist Republics, with its impressive increase of weapons, is enlarging its sphere of socialist influence on other countries in order to save them from the Yanks and their imperialist bombs.

1. Can you pick out examples of each kind of slant? The language has been carefully chosen to appeal to the reader's emotions. An intelligent reader soon realizes that propaganda arouses the emotions, but does not satisfy the intellect, for it provides little information.

The sentence below is a rewrite of the propaganda piece. Notice that it contains information with no emotional slant:

The main difference between the American and Soviet arms build-up is that the American purpose is defensive while the Soviet purpose is offensive.

2. Write a short piece of propaganda telling why your school is better or worse than another. Then, rewrite your piece so that it is objective, without negative or positive slant.

3. Discuss your pieces with your partner.

Exercise Seven

Read the following model, then discuss it with your partner.

The Thirties

Farm life is not always the idyllic existence many city dwellers fantasize. On the Manitoba farm where I grew up during the Depression, summers were insect-ridden and winters godforsaken.

In spring and summer, our sparse grain fields were always at the mercy of unpredictable weather. If sneaking late frosts didn't nip the heads off seedlings, or scorching winds didn't burn weak stems, ruthless hailstones would crush the grain just before we could harvest it. If by some stroke of luck the capricious weather took a year off to devastate another unsuspecting farmer's crop, hungry grasshoppers munched their way across our fields while gophers, mice, and crows devoured the remaining kernels.

Summers like these do not see families through bitter winters. Every winter, searching for work far from home, my father left my mother, sister, and me to fend for ourselves. Blizzards smothered our two-room tar-papered shack with impenetrable snowdrifts. We had to dig tunnels to feed the starving livestock in their barns. I remember one three-month stint when we never did see the sky. That year when the thaws finally came, emaciated wolves ravaged the countryside. Scrawny though we were, we must have smelled like tender tidbits. Many an April night we were huddled around our potbelly stove with shotguns aimed at our front door while we listened to them snarling and clawing on the other side. When spring finally did come, my father returned and the whole rigmarole started all over again.

No wonder, when World War II began, my father and many of his neighbours gave up the pastoral life to fight the Axis while we traded our farm for bustling Winnipeg. Anything looked better than our barren homestead – Il Duce's chin, the Führer's moustache, even Portage and Main.

1. In general, would you say that this selection has positive or negative slant?

2. What words or expressions contribute to the emotional impact of the selection?

3. What details has the writer included about his topic? What other details might he have included to give an opposite slant to his material?

4. Discuss the meaning of the allusions: "Il Duce's chin, the Führer's moustache, even Portage and Main." How do these contribute to the slant of the selection?

Special Writing Activity

1. Find a piece you have already composed that has a strong point of view. If you do not have such a piece available, compose one, using words, comparisons and details to give your selection positive or negative slant.

2. Ask your partner to discuss the effectiveness of your slant. Does it help to achieve your purpose, or does it leave him or her unconvinced and mistrustful?

Last Words

Before you use slant in what you write, ask yourself: "Do I want negative or positive slant in my writing? Or do I want a mixture of positive and negative slant because I have two points of view and want to support one thing and reject another? Always consider your writing variables when making these decisions.

Activity **19** Style

Background

Everyday things that you encounter have style: clothes, make-up, music, teachers, telephones, stores, and so on. Writing also has style – qualities and characteristics that distinguish the work of one writer from that of another.

Most beginning writers consider a personal writing style difficult to define and impossible to achieve. They believe only the professionals – the Shakespeares, the Hemingways, the Huxleys – capable of creating a writing style.

This activity attempts to disprove this myth and shows you how to identify your own unique writing style.

Exercise One

1. You and your partner bring to class the weekend coloured comics.
2. Determine which is the most formal comic strip. Support your answers by saying two or three specific things about each of the following: the cartooning technique, the subject, the story line, and the dialogue of the characters.

Example
"Prince Valiant" is formal. The creator, Hal Foster, presents realistic pictures instead of cartoons; the subjects are appropriately coloured; the story line continues from week to week; and the dialogue is not placed in balloons. (Much more can be said about this comic strip.)

3. When you have discussed all the specific things about each comic strip, choose a word to describe each overall style. This word should take into account all the specifics.

Example
The style of "Prince Valiant" is *dignified*.

Exercise Two

1. At home, find a comic strip from a newspaper that is a few weeks old (so your partner will not remember it). Cut out the words in all the balloons and bring the comic strip to class.
2. Give each other the blank comic strips in order to fill each balloon with *formal* dialogue that fits the characters and the situation. When finished, discuss the appropriateness of the dialogue to the comic strip. The dialogue may be unsuitable because the cartooning style is *informal*.

3. Now each of you fill each balloon with appropriate *informal* dialogue. Determine its appropriateness. Does the dialogue fit the cartooning?

4. Now each of you fill each balloon with the dialogue that you think the creator of the comic strip wrote. When finished, compare yours with the original. How close were you? Were the styles of yours and the creator's close? Which word would you use to describe the overall style of the original comic strip?

5. Provide appropriate dialogue for this cartoon:

Exercise Three

1. Each of you bring an entire newspaper and a pair of scissors to class.

2. Cut out photos that you think are the most serious, the most comic, and the most sensational.

3. Exchange photos. Label your partner's photos *serious*, *comic*, and *sensational*. Then think of five reasons for your choices.

4. Discuss your reasons with your partner.

5. Each of you cut out ads that you think are the most *dignified*, the most *confusing*, and the most *sensational*. Exchange ads and follow points 3 and 4 once again.

6. Each of you cut out two headlines: one that you think is sensationally misleading and the other, completely factual. Exchange headlines with their accompanying articles. After reading the article, rewrite each headline so that you change its style.

Example

From the sensationally misleading MILLIONS WILL STARVE to the completely factual WHEAT SHORTAGE FEARED.

7. Each of you cut out several letters to the editor. Your task is to arrange them in order from the most cautiously written to the most aggressively written. When finished, discuss your arrangement with your partner, giving specific reasons.

8. Each of you cut out articles that you think are written in a formal style, a standard style, and a substandard style. (See Activity 15, Exercise One if you do not understand these terms.) Exchange articles and discuss the reasons for your choices.

Exercise Four

1. Bring to class at least three different articles that deal with exactly the same topic. One can be from your daily newspaper, one from your weekly newspaper, and one from a magazine.

2. Exchange articles with your partner.

3. Read the articles, carefully noting the similarities and differences. Jot down the differences in order to determine the style of the article. Take into account these fundamentals:

    a) A writer's vocabulary contributes to style. Words can be classed as formal, standard, and substandard.

    b) A writer's attitude contributes to style. A writer can take a positive or negative approach to the topic. A sincere, direct piece is quite different from a comically satiric piece.

    c) The length of sentences can also contribute to style. Entire selections can be written with short, direct sentences (under ten words), with long, contrived ones (over thirty words), or with a combination of short, long, and in-between sentences.

    d) A writer can develop the main claim in specific, concrete ways or in subtle, abstract ways.

    e) If a writer uses a number of rhetorical devices, the style may seem contrived, as opposed to natural.

    f) Some writers use many figurative comparisons (even lengthy analogies); others use no imagery.

    g) The writer's point of view affects the style. Sometimes the writer's personality shows; sometimes a persona is used.

4. Talk in detail with your partner about each of your articles. Use the items in point 3 in order to discuss the stylistic differences. You may both like to practise on the following three articles and the accompanying questions before you work on the three articles that you have found.

Example One

VATICAN CITY – Pope John Paul II was shot three times in the abdomen today by a man believed to be a Turkish fugitive who had vowed to kill him.

The attack came as the pontiff rode into St. Peter's Square for a general audience before an estimated 15,000 people.

Vatican radio said no vital organ was struck; two bullets were removed and surgery was continued to remove the third.

Example Two
A raw-edged day yesterday, all murky and dreary, as the bright colors of life ran together and made another puddle of gun-metal grey.

The madmen of the world have augmented the shooting of presidents in the U.S. and each other in Ireland and have taken their guns into the Vatican to shoot holy men. The gentle Pope John Paul II, the reaching-out, touching-hands spiritual father of the world's Catholics, is proved to have earthly guts, mortal enough to bleed, tough enough to absorb bullets from a gun wielded by yet another mind-bent assassin.   *Denny Boyd*

Example Three
He was an intense, youngish man with his left hand jammed into the pocket of his beige jacket, and when he presented his ticket to the forward section of a sunlit St. Peter's Square to attend Pope John Paul II's weekly audience from close up, the guard didn't even look twice. He soon wished that he had. In a blurred moment of ferocity, Mehmet Ali Agca, a Turkish terrorist whose road to Rome began 18 months ago when he made up his mind to slay the pontiff, abruptly struck at the object of his obsession ... with a burst of fire from a 9 mm Browning pistol. The slim, unblinking gunman's bullets failed to kill the most popular Pope in modern times. But he may well have torn the heart out of John Paul's remarkable papacy by permanently damaging his rugged constitution.   *Peter Lewis*

Questions
(Answer the questions with your partner so that you both are in agreement.)
  a) Which of the three articles is easiest to read? Why?
  b) Which one mixes levels of vocabulary? Provide examples.
  c) Which one appeared on the front page of a newspaper?
  d) Which one contains the longest sentence?
  e) Which is developed in the most specific, concrete way?
  f) Which is developed in the most subtle, abstract way?
  g) Which piece is designed to appeal to the reader's emotions?
  h) Which one contains satire? Provide an example.
  i) Which uses the most inventive adjectives? Provide two or three examples.
  j) Which contains figurative language? Provide examples.
  k) Which writer is closest to the reader?
  l) Which is the most personal? impersonal?
  m) Which is the most emotional? objective? Provide examples.
  n) Which word would you use to describe the overall style of each article? Use the list of words in Exercise Five.
     (If necessary, turn to the Suggested Answers for further help.)

Exercise Five

Being able to recognize style in something you read is useful, but it is more important to acquire your own unique writing style. Your background has a definite influence on your writing style: your age, education, experiences, sex, travel, amount and kind of reading, interests, opportunities, and on and on. You should not think of your writing style as better or worse than someone else's style – it's just different. Perhaps you never thought that you had a writing style. Well, think again.

1. To prove that you have style, you and your partner apply the seven fundamentals outlined in Exercise Four to your last writing assignment. As you discuss each idea, find specific details in your writing to support your statements. End the exercise by using one of these terms to describe your style:

serious	humorous
sincere	ironic
objective	subjective
formal	informal
concrete	abstract
impersonal	personal
consistent	uneven
stiff	conversational
direct	ambiguous
straightforward	rambling

2. Now, reverse the exercise by analyzing your partner's latest piece of writing.

Exercise Six

Most of what you will write will be from your own personal point of view. It is possible for you, however, to pretend that you are someone else and write with a new personality (*persona*) in order to fulfil a different purpose for a particular piece of writing.

Have you ever talked to someone about a personal problem and pretended that it was somebody else's problem? If so, you have already used a persona.

1. You and your partner read these two pieces by the same writer.

Persona One

Zig Zag is a program on the CBC on Saturday mornings. This week *Zig Zag* had a story about a captain and his tugboat. Today the captain tells us how he drives his tugboat without even steering it! A man called the "engineer" has a really tough job; he has to make sure everything is tied down in the right place.

The hardest job on the boat is tying ropes to posts. The man who does this job has to wear big gloves because it is a "dirty job." Not only does he tie ropes to posts, he also unties them.

The captain's job is not simple either. He does more than steer his boat; he also checks for other boats so he does not run into them. When the captain is not dodging other boats, he tells other men what to do, because he needs help to do all these difficult things.

When I grow up I want to be a tugboat driver and make $25,000 a year, just like the captain does.   *Ricardo Mancebo, student*

Persona Two

Zig Zag, a television series evidently designed for children, presents a mendacious outlook on life for the young. Among others, a sapient captain and his intrepid crew, who brave the ominous Burrard Inlet with their tugboat, appeared on this program. The captain demonstrated proper steering methods; by steering in a neutral direction, he has less chance of colliding with other boats in the same inlet. This generates a large amount of idle time for the captain and his crew.

The true test of "captainship" appears in the captain's ability to delegate tasks to his obstreperous crew. The engineer on deck performs various duties that require considerable expertise, such as ensuring that everything is tied down in its proper place. The education required for his job is no less than a university degree!

The skill involved in rope tying was apparently never before recognized until shown on television. One can identify the worker who does this job by the large gloves he wears. The responsibility of the "rope tier" is to "make ends meet" in such a way that the rest of the crew should never have to concern themselves about falling cargo or toppling containers.

Perhaps the most difficult occupation on the entire tugboat is withstanding the prolixities of the pedantic captain.

2. You and your partner should agree on the answers to these questions:

a) It's rather hard to believe that these two pieces were written by the same student writer, but indeed they were. In the first piece the writer chooses the persona of a young boy in order to comment ironically on the program; for example, look at what he says about the captain's ability to steer his boat. Can you find other examples of irony?

b) In the second piece he chooses the persona of a philosopher-critic in order to comment, again ironically, on the same show; for example, he says that the captain's proper steering methods "generate a large amount of idle time for the captain and his crew." Can you find other examples of irony?

c) Obviously both personae have the same attitudes about the show. What are they? Had the writer used his own authentic voice, would his attitude be the same as those of his personae?

d) Test how well he uses his personae. Can you find any examples of language that either persona would not logically use?

3. Tell your partner what you felt about watching a recent movie, TV show, or sports event.

4. Restate your opinion, but this time assume the persona of someone of the opposite sex.

5. Now assume the persona of someone who did not like the performance.

6. Now assume the persona of a visitor from another planet who is bewildered by the antics of human beings.

By assuming a persona, you will be able to use irony. Your audience will often forget that the opinions expressed in the piece are yours rather than the persona's.

7. In *Gulliver's Travels*, Jonathan Swift assumes the persona of an adventurous young doctor. Harper Lee assumes the persona of Scout, a young girl, to narrate *To Kill a Mockingbird*. Can you think of other writers who have assumed a persona?

Exercise Seven

You and your partner say at least five specific things about the style of each of these selections. Use the items in Exercise Four to get you thinking. (If you are stuck, turn to the Suggested Answers for help.) Then choose one word to describe the overall style of each selection.

1.
Lemons
by Mary-Lou Gazely

Lemons were used by Elizabethans to cleanse their teeth and to lighten the skin. You can make a hair rinse from lemon juice that will remove every last trace of shampoo and add shine. Use the juice of half a lemon, strained and diluted in a glass of water, then follow with a rinse of cool, clear water.

2.
Energy Myths
by Ralph Hedlin

Myth: Canadians consume about the same amount of energy as other industrialized countries.

Fact: Wrong! Canadians consume *more* energy per person than people in any other developed country!

We may think we have good reasons for this. Our country is big. Our climate is cold. But other countries have these characteristics, too. The fact is, we use a lot of energy because it has been relatively cheap here. Higher prices have encouraged other nations to use less.

The problem is that at the present time Canada only produces 80% of its crude oil needs. The other 20% is imported from other countries. Political instability in some of these countries means our supply sources are unreliable. Also, imported oil is becoming more expensive as time goes on.

Since taxes help pay the bill for imported oil, it makes sense to use less of it. We can do this by conserving, and by finding more oil here in Canada.

3.   Camaro

by Bob Ottum

Cale [Yarborough]'s Camaro weighs 2,351 pounds and has a 350-cubic-inch engine that's been bored out to 393 cubic inches, and it'll pound out 600 horsepower. The body sits on an "outlaw" frame; that is, a 108-inch chassis designed for small, backwoods U.S. racetracks – and that's the trick that has gotten it into Le Mans in its GTO category, right in there with the BMWs and other good stuff, all of which come up to about the door handles of Cale's car. It's a real stock car, and the only things on it that ever saw a Camaro production line are the taillights.

4.   Awards Banquet

by Erma Bombeck

Probably the most blatant contradiction between what a child is at home and what he is at school manifests itself at the annual Athletic Banquet.

Next time you attend an athletic awards banquet, catch the look on the faces of mothers as the accomplishments of their sons and daughters are revealed. It is as if they are talking about a different person with the same name as your youngster.

By intense concentration, you can sometimes read the parents' thoughts, as the coaches pay them homage.

"Mark is probably one of the best sprinters I've had in my entire career here at So. High. Hang onto your hats, people. Mark ran the hundred-yard dash in nine point nine!"

(Had to be nine days and nine hours. I once asked him to run out the garbage and it sat by the sink until it turned into a bookend.)

"I don't know what the baseball team would do without Charlie. We've had chatterers on the team before who get the guys whipped up, but Charlie is the all-time chatterer. There isn't a moment when he isn't saying something to spark the team."

(Charlie speaks six words to me in a week. "When you going to the store?")

"For those of you who don't really understand field events, I want to explain about the shot-put. It's a ball weighing eight pounds that was thrown a hundred feet by an outstanding athlete here at So. ...Wesley Whip."

(That's funny. Wesley looks like the same boy who delivers my paper and can't heave a six-ounce Saturday edition all the way from his bike to my porch.)

"Wolf Man Gus will go down in football annals as one of the all-time greats here at So. High. In the game with Central, Gus scored the winning touchdown despite a chipped bone in his ankle, a dislocated shoulder and a fever of a hundred and two."

(So how come Wolf Man Gus stays home from school every time he has his teeth cleaned?)

"I don't suppose anyone has better reflexes in this entire state than our outstanding basketball rebounder, Tim Rim. When the Good Lord passed out coordination, Tim was first in line."

(Tim is seventeen years old and I can still only pour him a half-glass of milk because that's all I want to clean up.)

"Tennis is a gentleman's game. This year's recipient of the Court Courtesy award is none other than So. High's Goodwill Ambassador, Stevie Cool."

(He's certainly come a long way since he tried to break his brother's face last week when he took a record album without asking.)

"The swimming team would never have made it this year without our plucky little manager, Paul Franswarth. Paul picks up those wet towels off the floor, hangs up the suits to dry, and is responsible for putting all the gear back where it belongs."

(Let's go home, Ed. I feel sick.)

5. Borderline Shows about to Take Off

by Peter Wilson

The following series are under consideration for the season.

BLOCK BROTHERS (situation comedy): Raymond Burr stars in the dual role of twin real estate salesman Ray and Burr Smith who sell properties just across the international border from one another. Ray lives in White Rock, B.C., and his office is a mere block away from Burr, who resides in the lovely border town of Blaine, Wash. It's a laugh riot in the first episode as Ray and Burr ponder the effect of 34-per-cent mortgage interest rates on their business and are reduced to sharing a single black suit between themselves. The boffo line, "Tell them Mr. Smith sent you" never fails to get a laugh.

FAIR TRADE (situation comedy): Bill Cosby and Lorne Greene star. Cosby plays an American black comedian who has to fly to Toronto every month or so to make commercials for the Coca-Cola company. In these commercials he talks with Canadians about how Coke outsells all its other rivals including the dreaded Pepsi-Cola. Greene plays a Canadian actor and newscaster who pushes

Alpo dog food and hospitalization insurance for the elderly on U.S. television. In each episode Cosby and Greene team up to prevent British actors from working in either Canada or the U.S.

Exercise Eight

This exercise is exactly the same as Exercise Seven except that there is no help in the Suggested Answers. You and your partner are on your own. What makes each of these models different? How would you describe the style of each?

Autobiography of a Tumbleweed

by John McLean, student

Born of the Earth, sheared from my umbilical stalk by the wind's sharp knife, I begin my journey. Gathering momentum and scraps of debris to round and fill my personality, I'm suddenly trapped by a barbed wire fence. The struggle for freedom only causes more misery from the twisted, devilish barbs. Finally, after gaining freedom, I wearily roll down the hill to spin lazily in the ditch; I cross the road only to be struck by a car, then land in the opposite ditch. Fences, roads, cars, hills – all are the obstacles of my life. Again, my courage must be found to fight and escape, my will steeled to overcome mental and physical barriers. When all goes well, open fields and good rolling are mine, but a house, fence, or rusting farm equipment may lie waiting. At worst a farmer's son can set a match to me; then, I go up in a puff of smoke. So ends my existence, my life as a tumbleweed.

1 Corinthians 13

Love is patient and kind; love is not jealous or boastful; it is not arrogant or rude. Love does not insist on its own way; it is not irritable or resentful; it does not rejoice at wrong, but rejoices in the right. Love bears all things, believes all things, hopes all things, endures all things.

Love never ends; as for prophecy, it will pass away; as for tongues, they will cease; as for knowledge, it will pass away. For our knowledge is imperfect and our prophecy is imperfect; but when the perfect comes, the imperfect will pass away. When I was a child, I spoke like a child, I thought like a child, I reasoned like a child; when I became a man, I gave up childish ways. For now we see in a mirror dimly, but then face to face. Now I know in part; then I shall understand fully, even as I have been fully understood. So faith, hope, love abide, these three; but the greatest of these is love.

How our Country Got its Name

by Ainslie Manson

On Aug. 10, 1534, Jacques Cartier arrived at a gulf leading into a very large river on the east coast of our country. To honor Saint Lawrence, whose feast day it was, he named this gulf the Gulf of St. Lawrence.

Cartier recorded the event in his journal, so we know exactly how that particular name was chosen. Unfortunately, however, the origins of a lot of Canadian names aren't quite so easy to trace. There are many different opinions, for example, as to how the name Canada originated.

After thoroughly exploring the Gulf of St. Lawrence, Cartier proceeded up the river with Indian guides and he named the river the Canada River. If his guides were Iroquois, Cartier may have adapted their word, "Kanata" to name the river. This word means village or dwellings and could have referred to the settlements along the shores.

But we have no definite proof that the guides were Iroquois. They may have been Algonquins, and their word, "Canada," means welcome. It is quite possible that they greeted Cartier with this word on his arrival in the new world. We would hope that the name of our country did not come from the Cree word, "Konata" ...because this word means without purpose, reason or design; for nothing!

Another possibility is that the Spaniards were actually the first to discover this land. They were searching for gold and they were very disappointed in our eastern coast. "Aca nada" they said, "here is nothing."

The Basques of northern Spain and the Portuguese were great sailors and travelled far in those early days. They both have a word "Canada" which means narrow passage. They could easily have entered the Gulf of St. Lawrence and viewed the river as a narrow passage leading into a new land.

Canada – it is a fine sounding name! No wonder so many countries would like to feel that they are the ones responsible for its origin. First, it was the name of the great river that drew explorers into the land, then it became the name of the surrounding territory and finally in 1867, it became the official name of our country.

Though we feel the name is as solid and permanent as the ground we walk on, oddly at the time of Confederation at least 13 other names were suggested as possibilities: Albertsland, Albionora, Borealia, Britannia, Cabotia, Colonia, Efisga, Hochelaga, Norland, Superior, Transatlantic, Tuponia and Victorialand. Do you think we chose the best name?

from *Willows Revisited*

by Paul Hiebert

...This chapter which was entitled "Willows Revisited," after John Swivel's poem by that name, was most appropriately prefaced by a hitherto unpublished poem entitled "Spring" written by Sarah Binks herself. Concerning this poem at least, there has never been any dispute as to its authorship, since it was actually signed by Sarah. It was discovered by sheer chance in a desk in the office of *The Horsebreeder's Gazette* by one of two tax auditors who happened to be examining the desk at the time, and it was at once recognized as having literary value. Apparently it had been submitted by Sarah two years before her death and had been accepted for publication, since it bears the stamp, "Paid, June 15th, 1925." Such manuscripts, according to the editor of the *Gazette*, were kept for filler and were used as occasion arose. But this particular poem had been completely forgotten, since it had been pushed to the back of the drawer because of his secretary's habit of keeping both her lunch as well as his in front. The editor, however, was quite willing to trade Sarah's "Spring" for a copy of Joyce Kilmer's "Trees" of which he had never heard and which on examination he declared to be "just about the same length."

In "Spring" Sarah's natural exuberance takes over without any stress upon the more solemn political spirit which characterizes "Moonlight on Wascana Lake" and it is therefore more appropriate as an introduction devoted to poetry and culture of Saskatchewan. In "Spring" Sarah simply bubbles with joy. She catches that fleeting movement in which the seasons in Saskatchewan change from the dead of winter to the heat of summer. For spring in Saskatchewan is never a season, it is an event. It is a day like Christmas Day or Fair Day except that it never comes by the calendar, it comes as a complete surprise. No one in Saskatchewan ever *expects* spring; he hopes for it. Spring there is a matter of faith, not science, but faith there is always justified, however late. Saskatchewan would be only too glad to celebrate the arrival of spring on a certain day much as the ancient Druids celebrated the arrival of the vernal equinox, if they only knew when it would arrive. But Sarah catches it on the fly:

Spring

by Sarah Binks

It's spring again! Who doubts the day's arrival.
Peeks not the thistle from the garden bed?
And shrieks the robin not the glad survival
Of cut-worm lifting up its vernal head?

In swelling chords, full-throated to the weather,
And strong of lung, once more spring voices sway –
Alto and bass, the cow and calf together,
Spring, spring is here, peal out its passing day!

I know of nothing that can so elicit,
Such great relief as spring, I know no boon,
That's half as welcome as the annual visit,
Of spring between the equinox and June,

Let voices then lift up in high endeavour,
To greet this day – the robin and the kine,
And add the wind at sixty for full measure,
And one shrill note which happens to be mine.

Sarah is always the true artist. There is something positively Wagnerian in her adding her own voice, the "one shrill note," to all that noise with which spring announces itself.

(Hint: For his satire of Saskatchewan, Hiebert assumes the persona of a literary critic who dotes on every word of Sarah Binks, another Hiebert persona.)

Special Writing Activity

Choose not only a topic but also a persona that you think will interest your partner and write a selection in a distinctive style. Concentrate on unifying the content, tone, word choice, and sentence structure. Once you have chosen a persona, do not be afraid to put yourself entirely into your persona's position. If your persona takes a stance, write firmly and courageously, using the style of the persona.

Ask your partner to point out instances where you could add greater unity to your style by adding, subtracting, or substituting.

Last Words

When you write, no matter what the format, strive to acquire a consistent style that is appropriate for you, your topic, your audience, and your purpose.

Activity **20** Satire

Background

To *satirize* is to ridicule a social ill or an aspect of the human condition.

Of all the styles of writing, you will perhaps find satire the most difficult, even though it is easy to talk about and usually easy to see in other people's writing. Before you use satire in any format (from a serious expository essay to a humorous friendly letter), you should decide whether the purpose and topic warrant a satiric treatment, and whether your audience would appreciate it.

Exercise One

1. You and your partner make a list of ten things that are wrong with today's society.

Example
People are starving.

Which item from your list would you find easiest to satirize? How would you satirize it?

Example
In "A Modest Proposal" Jonathan Swift suggested that the starving Irish fatten their babies and sell them to the English for their Sunday dinners.

2. You and your partner make a list of ten things that are part of the human condition. Try to think of some of those silly, human things you do that seem serious at the time, but you laugh about afterwards.

Example
When you discover a blemish on your face, you think everyone notices.

Which item from your list would you find easiest to satirize? How would you satirize it?

Example
When I noticed my first ... oh I can't say the word ... but when I noticed *it*, I knew I would have to go into hiding until my face cleared up.

Exercise Two
In most evening newspapers you can see satire at work. The editorial page is usually emblazoned with a political cartoon depicting the latest antics of civic, provincial, federal, or world leaders. No one is safe from the cartoonist's mocking eye.

1. Bring two satiric cartoons to class. Exchange them with your partner. Discuss what is being satirized. Study the cartoon carefully to see the overall effect as well as the details. Point out to each other the reason why it is or is not effective satire.

2. Write new satiric lines or captions for your two cartoons even if they already have lines or captions. Discuss the effect of your lines with your partner.

Reprinted with permission — the Toronto Star.

Reprinted with permission – Toronto Star Syndicate

Exercise Three

Many daily, weekly, and monthly columnists satirize society's ills. Of the many specific kinds of satire they could use, they seem to delight in airing their insults in *sardonic* (biting, contemptuous, often hilarious) ways.

1. Find a column that uses sardonic satire and exchange it with your partner. See if you can find examples of satire in each other's column. Then answer these three questions:
  a) What exactly does the columnist want changed?
  b) How does the columnist suggest it might be changed?
  c) In what ways is the satire sardonic?

Example
The television screen, surely the most sadly used invention in man's reach for perfection, dispenses bullets as regularly as deodorants. Violence is the currency of a television age that ended a war in Vietnam by the simple fact that it grew *bored* with it.   *Allan Fotheringham*

Analysis
   a) Fotheringham does not want violence on TV.
   b) The viewers may grow bored with it.
   c) By comparing the regular use of bullets and the constant advertising of deodorants, and talking about a war that ended because of boredom rather than because of its horrors, he shows sardonic satire.

   In order to write a piece of sardonic satire, you must understand your topic very well, feel strongly about it, want to bring about change, and have a great deal of courage.

2. Working together with your partner, compose an example of sardonic satire that you could drop into one of the columns you have been analyzing. It can be a word, phrase, or complete sentence. In the following example, the new piece of sardonic satire is in brackets.

Example
The television screen, surely the most sadly used invention in man's reach for
   perfection, dispenses bullets as regularly as deodorants. [Every Saturday
   morning kiddies watch unconcerned as cartoon characters get squashed,
   hammered, blown-up, or murdered.] Violence is the currency of a television age that ended a war in Vietnam by the simple fact that it grew
   bored with it.

3. Test to see that *your* piece of satire does not jar the tone of the original. If you read the column aloud, with your part included, it should read smoothly.

Exercise Four

Reviewers and critics are sometimes unkind. They will often pour out satiri-cal invective as they write a critique of a book, play, movie, or event.
1. Find an example of a critic's satire and exchange it with your partner.
   a) What has displeased the critic?
   b) Can you see what the critic is trying to say?
   c) Do you think the critic is justified in using invective?
   d) Could the satiric passage be written another way?
   e) Would it be as effective?

Example
The orchestra ... was, of course, out of sight in the pit, but the curious
   sounds that wafted forth from that bunker-like refuge gave the impression that much of the score was being played on jugs and bottles, combs
   and toilet tissue, and, possibly, kazoos. Perhaps it was only the effect of
   the wind or the hearty competition provided by the nesting birds and the
   restless animals in the nearby zoo. One must, after all, make allowances.
[The] director ... has clearly done his best to make it all hang together, but
   unfortunately his idea of keeping the show moving seems to be to keep
   everybody jumping about as if they had ants in their pants. If only somebody, *anybody*, would stand still, just for a minute.   *Christopher Dafoe*

Analysis
a) Dafoe was displeased with the quality of the music and dancing.
b) Simply saying "The orchestra did not play well" would not create the impact of this review. Nor would it be suggestive of how badly the critic feels it actually played. If the production was truly bad and people would waste their money by buying tickets, the sarcasm may be justified.

2. Add a single example of invective satire which can be dropped into one of your reviews. Does it fit in well with the tone of the critic? In the following example, ellipses are used because only portions of the review are quoted. Note that the words in brackets have been added and are not the critic's.

Example
...but unfortunately his idea of keeping the show moving seems to be to keep everybody jumping about as if they had ants in their pants. [Never have so many moved around so much to so little effect.] If only somebody ...

Exercise Five

On television and stage you often see an impressionist who satirizes well-known celebrities, politicians, or movie stars. The impressionist obviously has studied the subjects very well in order to *parody* them (imitate them through exaggeration).

1. Talk about parodists with your partner. Do you have a favourite? Rich Little and Craig Russell are popular Canadian impressionists who are international stars. What techniques does a parodist use to bring the subject to the stage so that the audience recognizes who is being parodied?

2. If you imitate another writer, you are parodying. You can do this by imitating the writer's style and tone or by using words from the original piece.

Many school songs are parodies. You and your partner write a new song for your school. Use many of the original words as well as the original rhythm and tune. To make this task easier, write out the original and see which words you need to change to fit your school. Although a parody can contain invective, keep yours good-natured.

Example
The original:
> From the halls of Montezuma
> To the shores of Tripoli
> We will fight our country's battles
> On the land as on the sea.
> First to fight for right and freedom
> And to keep our honour clean;
> We are proud to claim the title
> Of United States Marines.

The parody:
> From the halls of mathematics
> To the shelves of history
> There is joy in lads and lasses
> For they know they'll soon be free.
> The end of June is coming,
> Cry the boys and girls with glee,
> From the books and from the classrooms,
> Summertime will make us free.

3. Here are three famous and often-parodied quotations from Shakespeare. You and your lab partner, working separately, compose a parody of each. (In the speech from *Hamlet*, key words have been italicized and the first line of a parody has been started to help you.)

a) from *Hamlet:*
> To *be*, or not to *be*, that is *the question:*
> Whether 'tis *nobler* in the *mind* to suffer
> The *slings* and *arrows* of outrageous *fortune*,
> Or to take *arms* against a sea of troubles,
> And by *opposing, end them.*

> Sample first line of parody:
> To pass, or not to pass, that is my problem.

b) from *Romeo and Juliet:*
> O Romeo, Romeo, wherefore art thou Romeo?
> Deny thy father and refuse thy name;
> Or, if thou wilt not, be but sworn my love,
> And I'll no longer be a Capulet.

c) from *Macbeth:*
> Tomorrow, and tomorrow, and tomorrow,
> Creeps in this petty pace from day to day,
> To the last syllable of recorded time;
> And all our yesterdays have lighted fools
> The way to dusty death.

Exercise Six

A popular kind of satire is a *travesty* where you take as your subject some lofty, illustrious, distinguished, outstanding, prominent subject and treat it in trivial, frivolous, even degrading terms. For example, Monty Python's *Life of Brian* is a travesty on the life of Jesus. Although many people found it highly amusing, *Life of Brian* outraged many religious groups.

You and your partner talk about a travesty that you have seen or read. What was being satirized? How did you feel about it? (You usually either laugh or become outraged at travesties.)

Exercise Seven

Irony may be used to achieve satire. Irony is a figure of speech in which the words express a meaning that is often the direct opposite of the intended meaning. For example, if someone says to you, "Lovely weather, eh?" when there is a sub-zero blizzard, that person would be either grossly out of touch with reality or would be ironically satirizing the bad weather.

Do not get irony mixed up with sarcasm, a low form of satire. Sarcasm is usually found in speech where intonation can make a biting taunt more noticeable. For example, "Too bad you weren't around when brains were handed out."

1. You and your partner work *separately* on a very short piece of irony. Assume a persona. Exchange to see if you both have succeeded in satirizing an aspect of the human condition or a social problem.

You might like to have your persona spout pretentious, absurd ideas as if you were a philosopher, scientist, or professor. Again, to bring out the irony, you should let your reader know that your persona always *knows* that he/she is deliberately exaggerating. For example, to satirize the need for nuclear power, you might write:

"I know that we would only lose one and a half billion people by entering a nuclear war, but think of all the wonderful space the rest of us would be able to enjoy. And there would be so much oil available, that every family could be a 'three-car' family."

2. By writing with a persona you may find that it is easier to introduce an ironic tone into any topic.

You might like to use a persona that pleads ignorance all the time. To bring out the irony, you should let your reader know that your persona always *knows* the answers to any questions, but is using understatement as an ironic device. For example, to satirize the "correct" way to eat, you might write:

"I do not understand why you have so many knives, forks, and spoons surrounding each table setting. It seems to me that only one utensil would be sufficient to eat with."

Exercise Eight

Read the following models of satire with your partner. What is being satirized in each? If you get stuck, turn to the Suggested Answers for some ideas.

1. Write Right, Right?

by Dave Kowan, student

Overly cultured newsmen, reporters, and journalists often use a great variety of clever sentence patterns in order to enhance their shallow, sparsely documented works. Nonverbal adjectables, subclausative profixes, and redundant pre-clausables – all litter the pages of present-day periodicals. Writers (clever, persuading devils that they are) can, and often do, make "See Spot run" a major occurrence on which the fate of civilization rests. But the blue-collar workers of this country want something they can sink their teeth into, get drunk over, and fight about. So how about it, guys? Give us some news and hold the Shakespeare.

2. Your Friendly Flight Attendant

"...smoking is not permitted in the aisles or the lavatories. If you are caught smoking in the bathroom, not only will your potty privileges be taken away but you will be asked to leave this airplane immediately. ... and in the unlikely event of a water landing, you may use your seat cushion as a flotation device. There will be no lifeguard on duty and women with long hair will be required to wear bathing caps."

3. A New England Morning

by Mark Twain

It was a crisp and spicy New England morning in early October. The lilacs and laburnums, lit with the glory fires of autumn, hung burning and flashing in the brilliant air, a bridge provided by kind Nature for the wingless wild things that have their home in the treetops and would visit together. The larch and the pomegranate flung their purple and yellow flames in broad splashes along the slanted westward sweep of the woodland; and the sensuous fragrance of innumerable deciduous flowers rose upon the atmosphere in a swoon of incense. Far in the empty sky, a solitary pharynx slept among the empyrean on motionless wing. And everywhere brooded stillness, serenity, and the peace of God.

4. The Somers of our Discontent
by Peter Wilson

My worries are over.

For about six months now I have been concerned about Suzanne Somers. I have spent many a sleepless night worried whether she and husband-agent-manager Hamel (once described by Somers as Canada's Johnny Carson) would settle their differences with ABC.

Some days I have been almost totally preoccupied with the future of *Three's Company*. Would Suzanne be back? Wouldn't she? Had she asked for too much money as a bluff only to have ABC take her seriously? Would her dramatic career be destroyed because of a few measly dollars in an industry known for its immense salaries and even bigger profits?

There were interviews and magazine covers and almost daily reports. Gosh, wasn't it enough that Somers had to go through all those old shoplifting charges and relive her days as a Playboy model without this? I remember pounding my desk one day in rage and screaming: "No more, please, no more."

5. A Kiss for Leia – Trouble for Luke
from the Vancouver Sun

There's good news and bad news for fans of our Star Wars comic strip.

The bad news is that this week's color strip arrived too late, because of postal problems. The good news is that we're going to tell you what happened in this week's episode.

The story so far ... When we left, our heroes, Luke, Tanith, Artoo Detoo and Cee Threepio had crashed on a distant world. But they survived.

Meanwhile, in the Millennium Falcon, Han and Princess Leia were trying to dodge Imperial pursuers. This week, the Falcon reaches the neutral outworld Kabal. And then Leia stomps off.

"She can't abandon us like we're just delivery boys, Chewie," says Han. "Leia! Stop right there!"

"Han, I ordered you to return to base," Leia replies. "My duties here don't require..."

"You feel guilty because lowering your guard with me sent Luke off on that spy mission," Han says.

"I feel personal matters are starting to interfere with the rebellion, and I won't allow that," Leia responds. "Now go home!"

"Okay, Your Worship," says Han. "But first ...you're gonna learn what you're missin'."

And he gives her a big kiss while Chewbacca looks on.

Meanwhile dawn breaks on another world – a world where Luke Skywalker has crashed.

"Tanith! Threepio! Artoo!" he shouts. "There's something in the distance – coming our way!"

6.

HERMAN

"Members of the jury, have you reached a verdict?"

Special Writing Activity

To write a piece of satire is not easy, but if you investigate your present surroundings, you will probably see something you can satirize for your partner.

A word of caution about satire: you cannot suddenly drop a single example of irony, parody, and so on, into your straightforward, logical prose. Your *entire* piece of writing must have a satiric tone.

When your partner has finished reading your piece, discuss the method of satire you used and any satirical points that your partner missed.

Last Words

The next time you have to write something, consider if your topic could be treated satirically. If satire would fulfil your purpose and suit your audience, decide which kind(s) of satire you could introduce into your format. Nearly every format *could* be written with a satiric tone.

Activity **21** Research Skills

Background Not only does a library have the kind of books you read for enjoyment from cover to cover, it also has the ones you use to find facts. In this activity, you will concentrate on the latter, the library's reference books. This activity deals with methods of researching as well as setting up footnotes and bibliographies.

Before you begin any of the exercises in this activity, you and your partner should take a library tour, noting the following areas:

The Catalogue
Some catalogues are on cards classified by subjects, titles, and authors, and some are wholly or partly on microfiche.

No matter what system your library uses, you should learn how to find the call numbers of particular books. These call numbers are based either on the Library of Congress or the Dewey Decimal System, and allow you to locate the section in the library in which a particular book is to be found.

The Reference Area

This area contains important research books – dictionaries, encyclopedias, cumulative book indexes, concordances, and so on. These reference books are usually not allowed out of the library. This means that the books will always be available. You will soon get to know where specific reference books are stored.

The Periodical Area

Most well-stocked libraries subscribe to current magazines and newspapers. Back issues are bound in hard covers or put on microfilm. If you suspect that something you are researching is in a magazine, you should look through one of the guides to periodicals under the proper subject area. The well-known periodical indexes such as *Reader's Guide to Periodical Literature* and *Canadian Periodical Index* provide easy-to-follow instructions for their use. A librarian will be happy to introduce you to them.

The Media Area

Many libraries contain collections of tapes, records, slides, and films. The department has its own catalogue system. You should familiarize yourself with this important area and plan to spend a few hours there when you can. To sit at a tape-recorder with a Mozart concerto or a Shakespeare play filling your ears is a wonderful experience. Perhaps your media library has tapes and slides on basic spelling and grammar that might clear up problems. Also you may be able to borrow a film or set of slides to help you with a special presentation you have to make.

The File Drawers

Often, near the catalogue area or in the periodical section, the library has clipping files. In these files you can find articles and pamphlets on many topics.

The Librarian

Unquestionably the librarian is your most important resource. The librarian can not only provide information about the location of a book or the documentation of a fact, but can also offer inspiration in what may seem a fruitless search. Most librarians have a knowledge of and a love for their collections, and are only too glad to encourage you to get to know the contents of the library. So if you have not already done so, make yourself known to your local librarian.

Exercise One

As you and your partner go on your library tour, answer these questions together.

1. Does your library use a card catalogue or a microfiche?

2. Are the books in the library organized by subject, title, or author?

3. Does the library use call numbers based on the Library of Congress or the Dewey Decimal System?

4. Go to the Reference Area.
 a) What is the title of the smallest dictionary? The biggest dictionary? Besides size, what are the main differences between the two dictionaries? (Compare a single entry; for example, read what each dictionary says about the word *set*.)
 b) Which set of encyclopedias would you find most useful? Why?
 c) Name one cumulative book index. What would you use it for?
 d) Look for a concordance. What is it used for? Find another concordance.
 e) What is a variorum? For what would one be used?
 f) Name one reference work that you would use if you were writing an essay on art history, mythology, Canadian history, a British poet, music, religion, science, and mathematics.
 g) What would you use a book review index for? What is the title of a book review index?
 h) What is the name of the best atlas in the reference section?

5. Name two current magazines in your library.

6. Name one newspaper to which it subscribes.

7. Look at all of the library's guides to periodicals. For the year 1980, how many articles in magazines could you find on the subject of "Canadian Demolition Derbies"?

8. If your library has a media area, what audio-visual material – tapes, films, slides – does it contain?

9. What do you find in the file drawers under the subject of "Horses"?

10. Answer "a" or "b."
 a) For the Library of Congress classification, what books would be in the "D," "R," and "M" sections?
 b) For the Dewey Decimal System, what books are numbered 600, 200, 900?

11. If your library does not have a book that you want, find out how you could get it.

Exercise Two

With your partner, plan to go on a library search. You are going to make up questions for each other as though you are preparing for a treasure hunt.

How to make up questions

1. Beforehand, each of you should prepare three questions to ask each other. This means that you have to go to the library to find the questions *and* the answers. Make sure you record your sources for the answers.

2. Write each of the questions on separate index cards. Each answer must be found in the library, where the research is to take place, in a secondary source (a reference book), or a primary source (a poem, short story, essay, novel, or play). Set up a question like this:

> *Where is Canada's Tropical Valley ?*

3. Here are sample questions that you might ask your partner:

a) The musical group Blood, Sweat, and Tears takes its name from a quotation by a politician. What is the exact quotation, who said it, when was it said, and under what conditions?

b) From what play is this taken?
   For Brutus is an honourable man,
   So are they all, all honourable men.
   Provide act, scene, line, and speaker. Who are "they"?

c) Would I be able to use the word "prejudism" in a literary essay on "The Hockey Sweater"(Assignment 10)?

d) Which actors and actresses mentioned in Activity 9 were not born in Canada?

e) Name Pierre Berton's first and most recently published books.

f) Name two Greek plays in which Oedipus is a character. Who wrote them? When were they written?

g) What is acid rain? Name the acid and tell how it gets into the rain, where it is most prevalent, and what it does to the environment.

h) When was the National Hockey League founded, what leagues joined to form it, and what were the names of the original teams?

4. Choose a time to meet your partner in the library when you can exchange questions.

How to find the answers

1. Go to the library with your three questions and a dozen blank index cards.

2. Exchange questions with your partner and plan to meet in one hour with all three answers.

3. To find the answers, take some time to plan your strategy. Begin at the Catalogue Area. The object is to find the book, magazine, or file that has the answer.

4. When you find an answer, write it on another index card. The answer should be either a direct quote with quotation marks or a summary of the author's original words. Make sure you include the author's name and the page number where you found the answer. Your answer should look like this:

> *Colombo, p. 271*
>
> *"A legendary valley ... in the southwestern corner of the Northwest Territories ..."*

5. On another card place the bibliographical information for the source. Set up your card like this:

Call number	*398.20971*
	C 71c
Author's name	*Colombo, John Robert*
Title	*Colombo's Book of Marvels*
Facts of publication	*Toronto: N C Press Ltd., 1979*

6. If you have had to use another book in order to refer you to your answer, you should make up a bibliographic card for that book too.

7. At the end of the hour exchange cards to see if the answers are correct. It might be interesting to see if you both used the same sources to find the answers.

Exercise Three

When you have to write a research report, you will probably need to spend a few hours in the library, gathering facts. Here are a few ideas to make your research easier.

Details of the exercise

1. For practice, you and your partner make up a research essay topic for each other. Here are some general topics you could use:
   a) Foreign aid
   b) Horseshoe-pitching as a sport
   c) Cross-country skiing
   d) Medieval mystery plays
   e) The forest industry
   f) Amnesia

2. You will need to provide information for each of the following on index cards. When you write a research paper, you should write *one* note to a card so that you can organize your cards in any order.

a) On the first index card provide a direct quote that you would use if you were to write an essay on your partner's topic.
b) On the second card, provide bibliographical information on the book you used.
c) On the third card, give a summary of something that you would like to use, if you were to write the essay. If your summary takes up two or more index cards, indicate at the top of each card: 1st of 3, 2nd of 3, and 3rd of 3. This will help keep your cards organized.
d) Give all cards to your partner so that the entries can be checked against the suggestions below.

Suggestions and examples

1. If you plan to use any portion of a book, the first thing you should do is to make up a separate bibliography card. This card should look something like this:

Call number 971 M 134c
Author's name McDevitt, Daniel J., Angus F. Scully, and Carl F. Smith
Title Canada Today
Facts of publication Scarborough, Ontario: Prentice-Hall of Canada Ltd., 1979

2. Any time you use an author's words, make sure you quote exactly, placing quotation marks around the words. Forgetting to use quotation marks may result in unintentional plagiarism. At the top of the card write a subject heading to help you organize and find the card quickly. Identify the source of your quotation by listing the author's last name and the page number of the quotation. Your card should look like this:

> Foreign aid
>
> Mc Devitt et al, p. 468
>
> "Since 1945, Canada has played a major role in helping poor countries. Our help comes from two sources: the government and private charities."

3. Wherever possible summarize what you read. This way you can select and extract what is important to your purpose. Too many quotations in a research report give your reader the feeling that *you* did not write it, but merely strung together statements made by others. When you do summarize long portions, you still should identify the source and subject title in the usual way.

> Suggestions
>
> Mc Devitt et al, p. 472
> Some suggestions for helping poor nations :
> · Give to CARE or some other organization at Christmas
> · Become a Foster Parent alone or with others at school
> · Write to politicians
> · Collect money or old clothing

4. When you have both completed the exercise, discuss with your partner the thoroughness and accuracy of your research.

Exercise Four

In this exercise, you and your partner can learn about footnoting. To prepare for this exercise, each provide a copy of six different books or magazines, with an indication of a specific page to be footnoted. The object of the exercise is to set up footnotes using each of the six as a footnote source. First, read over the following general instructions on how to set up a footnote.

1. Footnotes are used primarily to acknowledge borrowed material and to identify the source of statements or quotations. Raised figures following the statement are used as a cross reference to the footnote.

"Since 1945, Canada has played a major role in helping poor countries. Our help comes from two sources: the government and private charities."[1]

The footnote itself is identified by a corresponding figure.

    [1]McDevitt et al., Canada Today (Toronto: Prentice-Hall, 1979), p. 468.

2. Footnotes are placed at the bottom of the page on which the statement or quotation appears. A two-inch line and small space should separate the footnotes from the text. Alternatively, all the notes may be placed on a separate page at the end of an essay. (For this activity, place all your notes on one page.) It is a good idea to provide a loose, duplicate copy of your endnotes for your reader to refer to; the constant flipping to notes at the end of an essay can be tedious and distracting.

3. Each footnote must be numbered consecutively with a raised number. Do not leave a space between the number and the first word of the footnote.

4. Only the first line of a footnote is indented.

5. Study the following specific footnotes:

A book by one author

    [1]M.C. Bradbrook, Themes and Conventions of Elizabethan Tragedy (London: Cambridge University Press, 1966), p. 101.

A book by more than one author

    [2]Anne Collins and Prue Hemelrijk, eds. You Asked Us (Toronto: Fitzhenry and Whiteside, 1978), p. 71.

An essay found in a collection

    [3]M.C. Bradbrook, "Shakespeare and his Collaborators," in Shakespeare 1971: Proceedings of the World Shakespeare Congress, Vancouver, August 1971, ed. Clifford Leech and J.M.R. Margeson (Toronto: University of Toronto Press, 1972), p. 21.

An article in a magazine

    [4]Ida Burns, "In an Octopus's Garden," Westworld, November 1981, p. 44.

An article in a journal

    [5]Howard Klein, "Lifelong Reading: Dream and Reality," Reading-Canada-Lecture 1 (April 1981): 44.

A book or pamphlet in which the author is not named
     [6]Consumers Association of Canada, Buying Guide 1981 (Ottawa: Consumers Association of Canada, 1981), p. 270.

A signed encyclopedia article
     [7]Encyclopedia Canadiana, 3d ed., s.v. "salmon," by A.L. Pritchard.

An unsigned encyclopedia article
     [8]Encyclopedia Canadiana, 3d ed., s.v. "Simon Fraser University."

A dictionary citation
     [9]Gage Canadian Dictionary, rev. ed. (1983), s.v. "Bluenose."

5. In a longer work you may quote several times from the same source.

a) Customarily, the expression *ibid.* (from the Latin *ibidem*, "the same") is used for a footnote that is identical to the preceding footnote; if an identical footnote does not *directly* follow its look-alike, the author's name is followed by *op. cit.* (from Latin *opere citato*, "in the work cited.")

> [5]Ibid., p. 56.
> [8]Collins and Hemelrijk, op. cit., p. 22.

b) Nowadays, though, most writers do away with *ibid.* and *op. cit.* and write their identical footnotes this way:

> [5]Burns, p. 56.
> [8]Collins and Hemelrijk, p. 22.

c) If you quote from more than one work by the same author, you should write in each footnote the author's name *and* enough of the title to make it clear which work is referred to.

> [5]Bradbrook, "Themes and Conventions," p. 56.
> [7]Bradbrook, "Shakespeare," p. 13.

6. When you have completed your six footnote entries, give them to your partner. Discuss any errors.

Exercise Five

In this exercise you and your partner can learn about setting up a bibliography. For this exercise, use the same six books and magazines that you used in the previous exercise. The object of the exercise is to set up a bibliography listing all six publications. First, read over the following general instructions on how to set up a bibliography:

1. Entries should be listed alphabetically by the author's or editor's last name or by the name of the body responsible for the work; if neither of these appears, the entry should be listed alphabetically by title.

2. Notice that the spacing of a bibliography entry is the reverse of a footnote entry; for example, the works cited in the list of footnotes appearing in Exercise Four would appear in a bibliography as follows:

Bibliography

Bradbrook, M.C. "Shakespeare and his Collaborators." In Shakespeare 1971: Proceedings of the World Shakespeare Congress, Vancouver, August 1971, pp. 19–27. Edited by Clifford Leech and J.M.R. Margeson. Toronto: University of Toronto Press, 1972.

_____ . Themes and Conventions of Elizabethan Tragedy. London: Cambridge University Press, 1966.

Burns, Ida. "In an Octopus's Garden." Westworld, November 1981, pp. 43–47.

Collins, Anne, and Hemelrijk, Prue, eds. You Asked Us. Toronto: Fitzhenry and Whiteside, 1978.

Consumers Association of Canada. Buying Guide 1981. Ottawa: Consumers Association of Canada, 1981.

Encyclopedia Canadiana, 3d ed. S.v. "salmon," by A.L. Pritchard, and "Simon Fraser University."

Gage Canadian Dictionary, rev. ed. (1983). S.v. "Bluenose."

Klein, Howard. "Lifelong Reading: Dream and Reality." Reading-Canada-Lecture 1 (April 1981): 43–51.

3. After you have compared the bibliography with the footnote entries, discuss the differences between them. Notice the differences in punctuation. Which entries do not need a page reference? What does the "_____" in the second entry mean?

4. When you have completed the bibliography of the six books and magazines, discuss your scholarship with your partner.

Last Words

A researcher must be thorough. When you research, you must present the facts honestly. Avoid any distortion or omission; this breeds distrust in your reader.

Use the latest reference material. You do not want your reader telling you that your research is several years out of date.

Suggested Answers

Activity 1

Exercise Four

1.
a) exposition
b) description
c) exposition
d) narration
e) description
f) exposition
g) narration
h) description
i) exposition
j) narration

Activity 3

Exercise Three

1.
a) After negotiations were successfully completed with Native Peoples, Quebec began the vast James Bay hydro-electric project.
b) Churchill Falls in Labrador furnishes power to nearby Quebec; moreover, it exports excess capacity to New York State.
c) The Ark was built in Prince Edward Island, and it has become world-famous because it uses energy efficiently.
d) Canada's energy policy stresses the ownership of Canadian resources by Canadians: first, Petro-Canada purchased Philips Petroleum; then it purchased Petrofina; in the future, it may purchase other foreign-owned oil companies.
e) Since Nova Scotia has no hydro-electric generating capacity, it must purchase expensive foreign oil to provide electricity; therefore, its citizens pay the highest electricity rates in Canada.

2. Nuclear power can be dangerous; you never know when there might be an accident at a power plant. There was, for example, an accident at Three

Mile Island in Pennsylvania. Many people from nearby Middletown were evacuated by the US National Guard and the Pennsylvania state authorities, because they were afraid the radioactive core of the reactor would melt. Though there were no casualties at Three Mile Island, the movie *The China Syndrome* dramatized a disastrous accident at a plant like it. Moreover, people should be more concerned about problems like the disposal of radioactive waste. If thousands of people protest, authorities may listen.

(Why was "A near-disaster occurred in Mississauga, Ontario" left out?)

Activity 5

Exercise Three

b) First, perform all dives in deep water to avoid injuries. Stand on the edge of the pool deck with feet shoulder-width apart and toes curled over the edge. Place arms directly above the head. Maintain this position throughout the dive. Second, bend knees and upper body forward. After adopting this position, fall forward, kicking the feet behind. Follow these directions to master this dive in a few tries.

Exercise Five: Sentence Work

a) If you want to go to Yellowknife, North West Territories, the most convenient way you can travel is by plane. (Or use *she* twice.)

b) When I moved to Vancouver, I discovered that I was able to live quite contentedly without snow. (*One* is acceptable, but *I* is better.)

c) The government of Alberta has made a historic site of its first oil well, Imperial Leduc Number one; it's not far from the Trans-Canada Highway.

d) If one wants to give credit for the discovery of Saskatchewan, it should go to Henry Kelsey.

Exercise Six

a) Indubitably, the province of Manitoba, being in the geographical centre of the country, is well located to obtain goods and services from the East and West.

b) If you have to do hard time in a federal prison in Ontario, chances are you'll find yourself in Kingston, where several penitentiaries are located.

c) A stone wall surrounds the older section of Quebec City, and some of the streets are made of stone too.

d) Legally, Moncton should be spelled with a "k," since it was given its name in honour of General Monck.

e) Halifax has been and continues to be one of the most important (or largest) seaports in North America.

(If you and your partner have had difficulty with any of the exercises in Activity 5, find a practical handbook and do a few basic exercises on consistency.)

Activity 6

Paraphrase of *A Political Manager is Born*
Joe Clark's Youth

Joe Clark's parents were political opposites; his father was Conservative and his mother a Liberal who supported Mackenzie King. Almost everyone else in High River supported the Social Credit party; his parents and aunt were among the few members of the old-line political parties.

Clark says that his neighbours' view of him as a serious child who always wanted to become prime minister is unfair. He says he knew when he was in high school that he wouldn't grow up to be a rodeo performer or a rancher, and that people expected great things of him, though he points out that people have expected great things of other people who have ended up as insurance salesmen.

Memories of his parents and friends occasionally differ, but most people remember him as a serious child, old for his years, who liked to talk to older people, a stubborn young man who went his own way and excelled in studies rather than sports. A friend describes him as an awkward teenager who tried to impress his teachers with his vocabulary. His parents recall that he wanted to be a sportswriter and broadcaster, and that he memorized the *Encyclopedia of Sports* and played a good deal of baseball.

Précis in Author's words

Joe Clark's Boyhood

Joe Clark's household was politically ambidextrous; his father was a Conservative, his mother Liberal. Yet High River was predominantly Social Credit.

The Conservative leader considers the perception of him as a serious youngster as overblown. "The feeling that I started at age two," he says, "is just not true." He admits that he was not cut out to be a rancher or rodeo rider.

The memories of parents and friends seem to conflict, yet there emerges a picture of a serious, mature youngster fond of talking to older people, a determined, individualistic youth given more to debating than athletics. His friend, fertilizer dealer Jim Howie, describes him as "not well co-ordinated" and "trying to tie teachers in knots with big words." His parents recall that he had an ambition to be a sports broadcaster; he played a lot of baseball and memorized the *Encyclopedia of Sports*.

Précis of paraphrase

Joe's Youth

Joe Clark's parents were political opposites: his father Conservative, his mother Liberal. His parents and his aunt were among the few members of old-line parties; almost everyone else in town was Social Credit.

Clark says his neighbours' view of him as a serious child is unfair. He knew in high school that he wouldn't be a rancher or a rodeo performer. People expected great things of him, but they had expected great things of other people who ended up as insurance salesmen.

Most people remember him as a serious, mature child who liked to talk with older people, a stubborn, scholarly youth who went his own way. He was an awkward teenager who tried to impress with his vocabulary and wanted to be a sportswriter and broadcaster; he played baseball and memorized the *Encyclopedia of Sports*.

Exercise Seven

Précis of excerpt from *The War Within Greenpeace*

Saving the Whales

In June 1975, we finally came upon a fleet of Russian whalers off California. We roared into the line of fire between a harpooner and his prey in our high-speed rubber boats; one boat, with cameras focused on the action, stayed off to the side. We got spectacular footage of a harpoon exploding in the body of a whale. In San Francisco, we released the film to TV, notably to Walter Cronkite, and from that moment we had a reputation as the world's most macho environmentalists.

We had rewritten *Moby Dick* for the TV-watching masses, with the whale no longer Leviathan and the hunter no longer Captain Ahab. From that moment, humanity's image of whales was altered and essentially our job of consciousness transformation was done.

Précis of a paraphrase

A Whale of a Job

We finally met the Russian whaling fleet in June 1975. We launched our high-speed rubber boats; one containing a film crew, stayed off to the side to record everything on film, while the rest of us moved between the whales and the harpooners. Despite the ordeal, we got spectacular film of the harpoons flying over our boats, hitting a whale, and blowing up inside it. Proceeding to

San Francisco, we gave the film to the TV networks, and, with Walter Cronkite's help, we became known as the world's most daring environmentalists.

For the first time the TV audiences saw Russian whaling ships hunting every whale, even undersized ones. Whaling was no longer the huge whale against the courageous man, as *Moby Dick* had portrayed. We changed the way people thought about whales, and, though we didn't know it then, our real job was over.

Exercise Eight

Paraphrase of excerpt from *The Last Chance Energy Book*

Here Comes the Sun!

As we look for new sources of energy, we naturally are turning to the sun. To supply large amounts of energy some time in the future, the sun is the obvious choice, though in the United States at the present time little has been done to explore the possibilities of solar energy. In Western Australia, for example, many houses have solar collectors on their roofs. But Australia, unlike America, has no oil and few other energy sources; on the other hand, it has a generally sunny climate, making the use of solar panels practical.

Can the United States do what Australia has done? It probably will in the future, as other fuels become more expensive and solar technology improves. But not everyone can install solar panels; they are not practical on apartment houses, hotels, and condominiums, or in areas where there is little sunshine during the winter. Solar panels on American homes will only supplement another heat source for some people.

Is there any way solar collectors can be used on a large scale? Possibly not. Covering desert areas with solar collectors would not only anger local residents, but might also destroy the desert's delicate environmental balance. It would also be a very costly procedure, since large storage systems or a back-up system using other fuels would be needed when the sun is not shining. So it would seem that solar power could produce some needed energy, but would not be the whole answer.

Précis in author's words

From *The Last Chance Energy Book*

Solar energy is almost certainly a long-term answer in the search for new energy sources. But the United States has been behind countries such as Australia in developing solar power. That part of the world is energy poor, but because of its generally sunny climate, solar panels can provide plenty of heat and hot water. Can the United States use the same method?

No doubt it can, as domestic solar panels become more economical and the prices of alternative fuels rise. But solar panels are not for everyone. They are not practical for apartment houses, hotels, and condominiums, or in areas of the country where the sun shines only intermittently in winter. Domestic solar collectors may realistically provide sufficient energy for a relatively few people and be a valuable supplement for others.

The long-term answer could be to cover the desert with solar collectors to generate power. But, though New Englanders might not mind, Arizonans might not be enthusiastic about having their desert covered with solar collectors. In addition, the fragile desert ecology might not survive large solar farms. Furthermore, there are enormous capital costs for storage and back-up facilities to be used at night and during cloudy periods. Solar power from the deserts may be a partial solution, but is probably not the whole solution.

Précis of a paraphrase

Energy from the Sun

The sun is a source of energy which we are now considering more seriously. Up to now other countries such as Australia have made more use of solar power than has the United States. In Western Australia, where there are few other sources of energy but where sunshine is abundant, solar collectors are widely used.

Can the United States follow suit? Certainly. But would domestic solar collectors be practical? Apartment houses, hotels, and condominiums could not use them, nor could people in areas where winter sunshine is scarce. Probably domestic solar panels could only supplement a few persons' heat supply.

Can solar collectors be used on a large scale? Probably not. Putting them in the desert would upset both the local inhabitants and the fragile desert ecology. It would also be very expensive, since a storage facility and a back-up system would be needed at night and during cloudy periods. All things considered, solar power is probably a partial, not a complete, answer to energy needs.

Summary

Solar Energy Prospects

Owen Phillips says that the United States has not done as much in the field of exploiting solar energy as countries such as Australia. He contends that domestic solar collectors may be impractical for most people because of the types of buildings they live in and the part of the country they inhabit. And he points out that large-scale solar energy farms, in the deserts of Arizona, for example, would be objectionable to the local people and hazardous to the desert ecology, as well as being very expensive. All in all, he says solar energy is a partial, not a complete, solution to future energy needs.

Outline

Prospects for Solar Energy

I. Domestic use in Western Australia
  A. Few other energy sources
  B. Large amount of sunshine
II. Possible domestic use in U.S.
  A. As solar technology costs decrease
  B. As cost of other fuels increases
  C. Not practical in some buildings
  D. Not practical in some climates
III. Possible commercial use in U.S.
  A. Effect on local inhabitants
  B. Effect on desert ecology
  C. Cost
IV. Conclusion
  Partial, not complete, solution

Main Claim

Solar energy, whether generated for individual homes or on a large scale, is probably a partial, not a complete, solution of the United States' future energy needs.

Activity 7

Exercise Eight

a) Wilfrid Laurier, Canada's prime minister at the beginning of the century, is famous for his statement that the twentieth century was Canada's.
b) The "Just Society" was Pierre Trudeau's anti-poverty program of the late '60s; the "Great Society" was the brainchild of U.S. president Lyndon Johnson in the early '60s.
c) You would only appreciate how appropriate the headline was if you knew McLuhan's most famous quote, "The medium is the message."
d) "Guru" is the Hindi word for a teacher, especially of religious subjects; the term is now used for any widely followed and respected person in a particular field.
e) This is a parody of the phrase "wolf in sheep's clothing," describing people who plot to deceive others by appearing innocent.

f) There are two allusions here: one to Mark Anthony's remark about Brutus' stab wound of Julius Caesar in Shakespeare's play, "This was the most unkindest cut of all," and to the musical term "change of pitch." (There may also be a pun on "pitch" as "a speech designed to sell something.")

g) This alludes to the title of Steven Spielberg's remarkable film, *Close Encounters of the Third Kind*.

h) In Greek mythology, for offending the gods, Sisyphus was condemned to try forever to roll a stone up a steep hill, only to have the stone slide down again just before he reached the top.

i) This alludes to a quote from the Old Testament of the Bible: "The Lord giveth and the Lord taketh away; blessed be the name of the Lord."

j) Near the end of Shakespeare's *Macbeth*, the despairing king says:
Life's but a walking shadow, a poor player
That struts and frets his hour upon the stage
And then is heard no more.

Obviously the book reviewer feels that Hodgins' characters are so feeble that they will be "heard no more."

The reference at the beginning of Exercise Eight alludes to Paul's blinding. Once he comprehended, he was cured of his blindness, changed his name from Saul to Paul, and became the most famous of early Christian missionaries.

Activity 8 **Exercise Nine**

a) Canadians hear "Participaction" spreading its message through radio and TV, encouraging them to exercise.

b) Jacqueline Gareau won the women's division of the Boston Marathon in 1980, after Rosie Ruiz was disqualified.

c) James F. Fixx is the author of the best-selling book, *The Complete Book of Running*.

d) Magazines such as *Runner's World*, published in Mountain View, California, contain articles of interest to runners.

e) Terry Fox became Canada's best-known runner when he ran halfway across Canada on one leg.

f) Recent research indicates that women who run long distances may not become pregnant.

g) People who find running too strenuous often turn to walking. Senior citizens are especially fond of it.

h) Everyone who wants to lead a healthy life should benefit from physical fitness.

Activity 9   Exercise Two

alliteration	slim, strong, sleek
exaggeration	thousands of helpful representatives
non-sentence fragment	Hey, guys and gals!
allusion	satisfaction guaranteed or money refunded (slogan of Eaton's)
pun	pining for a willowy figure ... off your trunk ... no need to be stumped ... numerous branches
rhyme	Use your head! Think ahead!
rhetorical question	Who doesn't want to look great?
word punctuation	do ... now
climactic parallelism	sentence starting "Everyone can find..."
opposites	Some people visit "The Shape of Things to Come" to shrink their bodies; others go there to enlarge them.
analogy	having a figure like that of a tree: *willowy, whittle, trunk, branches* (as well as *pining* and *stumped*)

Activity 11   Exercise Six

1. a) Timothy Findley's fascinating book, *The Wars*, has become a film, directed by Robin Phillips and starring Brent Carver.
   b) One of Farley Mowat's books, *A Whale for the Killing*, tells of the inhabitants of a Newfoundland village who kill a beached animal.
   c) Bruce Hutchison, best known as a political commentator, recently wrote *Uncle Percy's Wonderful Town*, his first work of fiction.
   d) Peter Newman wrote *Renegade in Power*, describing John Diefenbaker in unflattering terms.
   e) His military career having made him aware of international intrigue, Richard Rohmer has used his knowledge in such novels as *Exxoneration* and *Patton's Gap*.
   f) Vancouver author Keith Maillard has recently published his third novel, *The Knife in My Hands*.
   g) Sheila Fischman has translated the works of such Québécois authors as Roch Carrier.
   h) In latter years Margaret Atwood brought Canadian literature to greater world prominence than Margaret Laurence.

Exercise Seven

The Twenties vs. the Thirties

The stock market crash of 1929 became one of the worst days for the citizens of Canada. The depression, soon worldwide, began from this day. The value of Ford stock, one of the richest companies in Canada, went down fifty per cent. Losses of over sixty-two million dollars in less than two months, however, marked only the beginning. The drought on the Prairies, soon to follow, transformed once fertile land, with valuable fields of wheat, into a barren desert, its precious topsoil swept away with every gust of wind. The Maritimes, also in bad shape, and with no natural resources to support them, asked the government for assistance. The inhabitants of the Prairies and the Maritimes turned to a program set up to help desperate people during the Depression. Proud Canadian citizens became victims of relief programs.

Activity 12

Exercise Three

a) Margaret Atwood is a well-known Canadian novelist, poet, and critic.

b) She first gained fame with books of poetry such as *The Circle Game* and *The Animals in That Country.*

c) Atwood is the author of several novels, all of them best sellers.

d) In *Survival: A Thematic Guide to Canadian Literature*, Atwood discusses her so-called "victim-theory."

e) A recent novel, *Life Before Man*, was reviewed on the front page of the *New York Times Book Review*, a significant honour for a Canadian.

f) Fascinated by the experiences of pioneer Susanna Moodie, one of Canada's earliest writers, Atwood published a book of poems about her in 1970.

Exercise Four

Autographing

In 1969, during an autographing session for Margaret Atwood's first novel, *The Edible Woman*, in the men's socks department of The Bay in Edmonton, she sold two copies. In 1981, for an autographing session for her most recent novel, *Bodily Harm*, crowds were lined up three deep around a Toronto book store. Atwood's experience is a graphic illustration of how popular Canadian books have become.

Activity 16   Exercise Four

1. **Blow, Bugle, Blow** by Tennyson

> The splendour falls on *castle* walls
>   And *snowy* summits old in story:
> The long light *shakes* across the lakes,
>   And the wild *cataract* leaps in glory.
> Blow, bugle, blow, set the wild echoes *flying*.
> Blow, bugle; answer, echoes, dying, dying, dying.

Exercise Five

1.
a) Men fear Death, as children fear to go in the *dark*.
b) Revenge is a kind of wild *justice*.
c) *Suspicions* amongst thoughts are like bats amongst birds, they ever fly by twilight.
d) Studies serve for *delight*, for *ornament*, and for *ability*.
e) Some books are to be tasted, others to be *swallowed*, and some few to be *chewed* and *digested:* that is, some books are to be read only in parts; others to be read but not curiously; and some few to be read wholly, and with diligence and attention ... Reading maketh a *full* man; conference a *ready* man; and writing an *exact* man.
f) It is as natural to die as to be *born*; and to a little infant, perhaps, the one is as *painful* as the other.

Exercise Six

3. exploded – exposed
   conjunctions – injunctions
   preposition – proposition
   particle – article
   enjoin – entreat
   hydrostatics – hysterics
   persisted – desisted
   interceded – intercepted
   reprehend – comprehend
   oracular – auricular
   derangement – arrangement
   epitaphs – epithets

Activity 19 Exercise Four

4. a) One – simple vocabulary, straightforward style – "just the facts."

   b) Three – "blurred moment of ferocity," "torn the heart out"

   c) One

   d) Three – "In a blurred moment ... Browning pistol."

   e) One

   f) Two

   g) Two

   h) Two – "the shooting of presidents in the U.S. and each other in Ireland"

   i) Two – "raw-edged," "gun-metal," "touching-hands spiritual"

   j) Two and Three – "the bright colours of life ran together," "he may well have torn the heart out of John Paul's remarkable papacy"

   k) Two

   l) Two, One

   m) Two – aggressive: "the madmen of the world," "another mind-bent assassin";

     One – cautious: "a man believed to be a Turkish fugitive," "no vital organ was struck"

   n) One – straightforward

     Two – moving

     Three – journalistic

Exercise Seven

These answers are provided to serve as discussion points.

1. "Lemons"

a) Standard word choice.

b) "You" point of view, sentences are written commands with "you" understood.

c) Easy to read.

d) The main claim is developed through specific instructions.

e) The writer is not close to the reader.

style: informative

2. "Energy Myths"

a) Informal: use of exclamation points, non-sentence fragments, short words (though some longer words, especially in paragraph 4, because of the subject)

b) Slant is definitely negative.

c) Mainly abstract.

d) Parallel structure is used several times for emphasis.
e) This is the author speaking, not a persona, and he uses "we" to establish closeness with his readers.

style: conversational

3. "Camaro"
a) This piece is technically oriented to a specific group of people. The vocabulary is informal, even slangy (*pound out, good stuff*).
b) It has a definite positive slant.
c) Despite its informal vocabulary, the sentences are longer than usual. (One is fifty-six words long!)
d) This is very concrete, replete with technical detail.
e) This piece certainly qualifies as aggressive.

style: aggressive

4. "Awards Banquet"
a) This is a comic piece by a well-known columnist.
b) Bombeck uses the persona of a mother attending a banquet for her son's team. As well, she writes part of the piece as the master of ceremonies presenting awards to several team members.
c) Irony is provided by the comments in parentheses after each award, contrasting the "ideal" boy who is receiving the award with his real personality as his mother sees it.
d) The examples of behaviour are concrete: spilled milk, rude treatment of a player's brother, and so on.
e) The names of the players refer ironically to either their sport or their award; for example, Tim Rim, the basketball player.

style: comic

5. "Borderline Shows about to Take Off"
a) This is a satiric piece by a television critic.
b) He uses the plot outlines of two imaginary shows to criticize programs currently on the air.
c) He uses a number of allusions; for example, the title of the first program, *Block Brothers*, refers to a real-estate company for which Raymond Burr is the spokesman.
d) He also puns on the title: the show is about twin brothers who live a block from each other.
e) In *Fair Trade,* he uses sardonic satire: the show portrays attempts by its stars to prevent fair trade by barring British actors.

style: ironic

Activity 20

Exercise Eight

1. Dave Kowan, in "Write Right, Right?" is using parody to mock the pretensions of some news reporters. Notice his take-off of grammatical terms. Can you find examples where he mocks reporters and grammatical terms?

2. "Your Friendly Flight Attendant"

Those of you who have heard the standard announcement at the beginning of a flight will enjoy this article. Can you tell where the normal announcement ends and the parody of it begins? A flight attendant in the U.S. actually uses this and similar announcements to get passengers' attention. Is the device effective?

3. "A New England Morning."

Mark Twain wrote the satiric spoof about a New England morning for a young would-be writer. He is sending up romantic writers who use an overblown descriptive style. His readers would know that lilacs bloom only in the early spring, laburnums and pomegranates do not grow in New England, larches are bluish-green and pomegranates orange-red, and a pharynx is found in the throat, not the sky. What other bits of nonsense has he used? Which verbs refer to actions which could not possibly happen? For example, how do plants "hang in air"? How do you "fling a flame that splashes"? Do serenity and stillness "brood"?

4. "The Somers of our Discontent"

Peter Wilson is satirizing the publicity churned out by press agents about TV and movie stars. He asks questions that seem to indicate his concern, but by the tone of the article you can tell that, by the time he starts to pound his desk, he really does not care about discovering the answers. Give other examples of his ironic tone.

5. It's hard to tell whether "A Kiss for Leia – Trouble for Luke" is written with tongue in cheek or not. It seems at first glance to convey information straightforwardly. But the use of phrases like "good news and bad news," or "our heroes," and "gives her a big kiss" may have ironic significance too. Can you find other examples which will put this article firmly in the category of satire?

6. Jim Unger, in this *Herman* cartoon, is satirizing the legal system. The jury members are supposed to consider the facts calmly and objectively, but the cartoon shows they are far from calm and objective. In the cartoon they obviously have not come to a decision, so when the judge asks if they have reached a verdict, he is being ironic.

Laboratory
Section

About the Labs

Professional writers bring variety to their work by using all possible combinations of eight different word groups: independent clauses, dependent clauses, prepositional phrases, verbal phrases, absolute phrases, adjective clusters, adverb clusters, and appositives. The labs are designed to help you master these word groups so that you can express yourself with clarity and variety. As in any activity, practice is necessary to achieve results. Eventually, however, you should reach the point in your writing where you can use these word groups automatically; in other words, you should develop a habit of good writing.

Introduction

These labs have been designed for individualized instruction. Unlike the Assignment Section, which needs peer and teacher/editor feedback, and the Activity Section, which involves you and a partner, the Laboratory Section is for you to work on alone.

You should work through the labs at your own pace. It is not really necessary for you to involve anyone else, although your teacher may work on a particular lab with your entire class. When you work on a lab by yourself and there is something you do not understand, there are three things you should do before you ask your teacher for help:

1. Reread the section of the lab slowly, noting every word, every example. You may have missed something significant.

2. Go to a handbook and look up the problem. Another author may have presented the problem from a different point of view. The Laboratory Section approaches writing from a positive viewpoint. It does not stress error; rather, it explains how to write correct, emphatic sentences through a variety of sentence-combining techniques.

3. Ask one of your activity partners to help you. If your partner is able to supply a satisfactory answer to your question, he/she will have gained something, too. Not only has your partner helped you, but he/she – through teaching – has probably learned a great deal. Keep asking, "Why?" until your partner has cleared up your confusion.

If you have tried all the above suggestions and still cannot understand a point, then ask your teacher for assistance. You must remember, though, that your teacher is the editor for the entire class; conducting one-to-one feedback sessions is time-consuming. Do not take your teacher/editor from this important task until you have tried all the other routes.

How to Work in the Laboratory Section

Before you begin to work in the Laboratory Section, spend ten minutes determining what it contains. Let the labs fulfil *your* needs. Begin with Lab 1, which takes you through some basic terminology, and Lab 2, which examines all the word groups. From there you can let your teacher or your own requirements be your guide.

Each lab contains a short Introduction and the following sections:`

1. Explanation

Read this section with care, rewrite useful examples, and copy out techniques you would like to master. You should not continue in the lab if you do not fully understand the basic points of the explanation. If you are confused, reread the Introduction and Explanation carefully and go over the examples and techniques again.

2. Sentence Work

You might want to write these sentences in a notebook one at a time, checking the Suggested Answers as you go; or you might do them all at once and check the answers after you have finished.

3. Suggested Answers

Suggested answers are provided for all labs; however, don't worry if your response differs from one in the Suggested Answers. The English language is in constant flux: "formal" spelling changes, "bad" grammar becomes acceptable, and "correct" punctuation seems unimportant. The answers given are correct but are not necessarily the *only* answers. If you feel, therefore, that *your* sentence is equally effective, you should follow the procedures outlined in the Introduction above.

4. Paragraph Work

As a step between assigned sentence-combining exercises and using special word groups in your own writing, you can complete or rewrite the specially constructed paragraphs in your notebook. Then check your paragraph with the completed one in the Suggested Answers.

To ensure that you truly understand and appreciate the writing techniques discussed in each lab, begin to use them in your own writing. Test your knowledge by writing a short paragraph in your journal (Appendix A), where you *use* what you have learned in the lab. These short paragraphs may become useful for your future writing: some as parts of larger works, others as the basis of an entire essay.

Lab **1** Learning the Basics

Introduction

"Why do I have to know about nouns and verbs?"
"Why should I have to know what a dangling modifier is?"
"Why should I know the difference between a clause and a phrase?"

Students have been asking these questions for years. The simple answer to each one is that knowledge of terms will not make you a better writer. Nevertheless, this knowledge will be useful when you and your readers discuss, evaluate, and edit your drafts. In other words, you and your readers need a common language.

If you spend a little time to become familiar with some basic writing terms, you will be able to enjoy and appreciate both the Laboratory Section of this textbook and the comments of those who read your work. But remember, the purpose of this lab is to help you become a more concise and emphatic writer.

Explanation

In this lab you will be able to look at the eight parts of speech and two word groups that make up the English language. The eight parts of speech are *verb*, *noun*, *pronoun*, *adjective*, *adverb*, *preposition*, *conjunction* and *interjection*. The two word groups are *clauses* and *phrases*.

A. Clauses

There are two kinds of clauses: *independent* and *dependent*. Both contain subjects and verbs.

1. Independent Clauses

An *independent clause* may stand alone as a grammatically complete sentence. It is a word group with at least one subject, either understood or expressed, and one verb.

Because a single verb may convey a complete thought, it can form an independent clause. Hence, some single verbs can be complete sentences:

Come. Jump. Stop.

(These are all complete sentences with *you* as an understood subject.)

Similarly, the following are independent clauses:

subject	verb
Terry Fox	ran.
The Canadian Cancer Society	profited.
He	will be remembered.

Notice that the last sentence has a *verb phrase*, "will be remembered," made up of the *helping* or *auxiliary* verbs "will be" plus the *main* verb "remembered."

To add more information for the reader, a writer may compound either the subject or the verb.

subject	verb
Women, men, and children	cheered.
Everyone	cheered and applauded.

Writers also enrich their main subjects and verbs by adding any number of clauses, phrases, and single words. But no matter how long an independent clause is, it can be divided into two sections: the *complete subject* and the *complete predicate*. All words that are associated with the main subject are known as the complete subject, just as all words associated with the verb are the complete predicate. (In the examples below, the main subjects and main verbs are in italic; the remaining words add details. Notice that the sentences would make no sense without the main subject and the main verb, although they make a certain amount of sense without one or more of the other words.)

complete subject	complete predicate
Nearly every *Canadian*	*knows* about Terry Fox.
Terry	*was born* in Winnipeg on July 28, 1958.
The *family*	*moved* to Port Coquitlam, B.C.
He	*died* in New Westminster on June 28, 1981.
Fox	*ran* across half of Canada.
The *victory*	*was* ultimately his.

Summary

The *main subject* does the action or has the experience.
The *main verb* reveals what the action or the experience is.

All the main subjects that have been used so far in the sample sentences have been *nouns* (names of persons, animals, plants, places, things, actions, substances, qualities, ideas, or states) or *pronouns* (words that take the place of nouns). The nouns were *Terry Fox, Canadian Cancer Society, women, men, children, Canadian, family, Fox,* and *victory.* The pronouns were *you, he,* and *everyone.*

In addition to the main subjects, there were other nouns and pronouns in the sentences. Which of these are nouns and which are pronouns?

Winnipeg, July, Port Coquitlam, half, Canada, hero, his.

Throughout the labs, there are similar questions for you to answer. If you cannot answer one, get into the habit of re-reading the material until you understand it. If you are absolutely stumped, ask someone for help. Do not continue the lab if there is something you do not understand.

2. Dependent Clauses

A *dependent clause*, which also contains a complete subject and complete predicate, cannot stand alone as a sentence. It *depends* on something else to make complete sense.

These two sentences are independent clauses. They can stand alone. They are both acceptable sentences.

The Marathon of Hope began quietly.
The Marathon of Hope gained Terry worldwide attention.

These two independent clauses can be combined by making the first one dependent on the second. The italicized part of the new sentence is the dependent clause.

The Marathon of Hope, *which began quietly*, gained Terry worldwide attention.

The same sentence-combining technique is used in the following two examples.

From
He stubbornly fought the disease.
The disease had cost him his leg.
To
He stubbornly fought the disease *that had cost him his leg*.

From
His family gave him support and encouragement.
His family loved him.

To

His family gave him support and encouragement *because they loved him.*

The above sentences will now be divided into separate word groups so that you can see the function of each part.

First, notice that a dependent clause is part of either the complete subject or the complete predicate, depending on how it relates to each.

Second, notice that each clause is presented separately: the **main subject** and **main verb** of the independent clauses are in heavy type; the *main subject* and *main verb* of the dependent clauses are in italics.

complete subject	complete predicate
a) The Marathon of Hope, which began quietly,	gained Terry worldwide attention.
The **Marathon of Hope**	**gained** Terry worldwide attention.
which	*began* quietly
b) He	stubbornly fought the disease that had cost him his leg.
He	stubbornly **fought** the disease
that	*had cost* him his leg.
c) His family	gave him support and encouragement because they loved him.
His **family**	**gave** him support and encouragement
because *they*	*loved* him.

Notice that all the independent clauses are able to stand alone as sentences, while the dependent clauses are unable to stand alone as sentences.

The first dependent clause is "which began quietly." What are the two other dependent clauses?

Here are a few sentences that have more than one dependent clause. You will notice that some of the verbs in the independent clauses need a dependent clause to make complete sense.

From

He was not very tall.

Terry was determined to become a fine college basketball player.

He became a fine college basketball player.

To

Although he was not very tall, Terry's determination ensured that he became a fine college basketball player.

complete subject	complete predicate
Although *he*	*was* not very tall
Terry's **determination**	**ensured**
that *he*	*became* a fine college basketball player.

From

His right leg was amputated in 1977.
He played wheelchair basketball with the Vancouver Cablecars.
The Vancouver Cablecars won the Canadian championship in 1980.

To

After his right leg was amputated in 1977, he played wheelchair basketball with the Vancouver Cablecars, who won the Canadian championship in 1980.

complete subject	complete predicate
After his right *leg*	*was amputated* in 1977
he	**played** wheelchair basketball with the Vancouver Cablecars
who	*won* the Canadian championship in 1980.

From

He ran hundreds of kilometres in training before his Marathon of Hope.
He embarked on his Marathon of Hope.
He started his Marathon of Hope on April 12, 1980.

To

He ran hundreds of kilometres in training before he embarked on his Marathon of Hope, which he started on April 12, 1980.

complete subject	complete predicate
He	**ran** hundreds of kilometres in training
before *he*	*embarked* on his Marathon of Hope
which *he*	*started* on April 12, 1980.

From

He started to cross the country.
Terry's run gained momentum.
At the beginning few people realized its significance.
At the end the momentum was tremendous.

To

What few people realized at the beginning was the tremendous momentum that Terry's run would gain as he crossed the country.

complete subject	complete predicate
What few people realized at the beginning	**was** the tremendous momentum
[What few *people*	*realized* at the beginning]
that Terry's *run*	*would gain*
as *he*	*crossed* the country

The main subject of the verb "was" is an entire dependent clause. Can you distinguish the independent from the dependent clauses? To show that you understand clauses, write a sentence that contains both an independent and a dependent clause. If you are unsure about your sentence, ask one of your activity partners for an opinion.

B. Modifiers

Both independent and dependent clauses can contain *modifiers* to enrich the nouns, pronouns, and verbs. Modifiers are either *adjectives* or *adverbs*.

1. Adjectives

Adjectives (including the articles *a*, *an*, and *the*) describe nouns or pronouns. Which nouns or pronouns are being modified by the adjectives in italic?

He was *athletic* and always *interested* in sports.

Terry's distinctive hobbling gait became *a familiar* sight on *Canadian television* screens.

The famous artificial leg was repaired *several* times during *the strenuous* journey.

2. Adverbs

Adverbs (which explain where, when, why, or how) describe verbs, adjectives, or other adverbs. Which words do the adverbs in italic modify?

Terry *stubbornly* continued his run and manoeuvred *so skilfully* on his artificial leg that onlookers were *noticeably* impressed.

Acclaim came *slowly* but *steadily*, and as each day passed he had *usually* gained several hundred more supporters.

By the time his run ended *tragically* at Thunder Bay, most Canadians had become *truly* enthusiastic.

Add some adjectives and adverbs to these sentences:

Terry became a hero.
Thousands donated money.

Ask someone to check your sentences to see that you have used both adjectives and adverbs.

C. Phrases

The difference between phrases and clauses is that phrases do not have both complete subjects and complete predicates. As a result, a phrase can never stand alone as a sentence. There are three different kinds of phrases; all can be used within independent or dependent clauses.

1. Prepositional Phrases

The first kind of phrase begins with a *preposition* and modifies words in exactly the same way as adjectives and adverbs. This kind of phrase does not contain a subject or verb.

In order to make your writing more concise and emphatic, you can combine sentences by making one or more of either the independent or dependent clauses into *prepositional phrases*.

From
The Canadian Cancer Society has received millions of dollars so that it can continue its search.
The Marathon of Hope is the reason it received millions.
A cancer cure is what the Society is trying to find.
To
Because of the Marathon of Hope, the Canadian Cancer Society has received millions *of dollars* so that it can continue its search *for a cure for cancer*.

From
The Society works diligently.
Cancer patients receive help now.
Cancer patients will receive hope.
To
Through the diligent work of the Society, patients *with cancer* receive help *for the present* and hope *for the future*.

a) Which words in the above two combined sentences do the phrases in italic describe?

Without the phrases, the sentences would be:

The Canadian Cancer Society has received millions so that it can continue its search.

Patients receive help and hope.

b) Add some similar phrases to the above sentences. Make sure your phrases begin with prepositions like these:

in	of	through	by	beneath
above	below	because of	into	around
beyond	for	like	about	despite
over	behind	in spite of	in front of	with respect to
up	since	concerning	on account of	

2. Verbal Phrases

The second kind of phrase is one that has a *verbal*, or incomplete form of the verb, in it. Because it does not contain a complete verb or a subject, it is dependent on something else in the sentence to make complete sense.

Notice how sentences can be combined by using *verbal phrases*. In the sample sentences the *verbal* is in heavy type and the rest of the verbal phrase is in italic.

From

Terry faced a crippling infirmity.

He turned disaster into unqualified triumph.

To

Faced *with a crippling infirmity*, Terry turned disaster to unqualified triumph.

From

Terry did not want personal fame.

He wanted more research.

That was his purpose.

To

To gain *personal fame* was never Terry's purpose; rather, he wanted **to encourage** *research*.

From

Terry risked his life during his run.

He gained millions of admirers and friends.

To

Risking *his life during his run* gained Terry millions of admirers and friends.

Now, write a sentence that contains a *verbal phrase*. If you are not sure that your sentence is correct, ask one of your activity partners for an opinion.

3. Absolute Phrases

The third kind of phrase is one that has a *verbal* and a *subject*, but it cannot stand alone because it does not contain a complete verb. Like all the other phrases, this kind of phrase is dependent on something else in the sentence to make sense. This kind of phrase is known as an *absolute phrase* and acts as a modifier in the same way as an adjective.

Notice how sentences can be combined by using an absolute phrase.

From
Terry encouraged other cancer victims.
His determination was always apparent.
To
His determination being always apparent, Terry encouraged other cancer victims.

Do you see that "determination" is the subject and "being" is the verbal in the absolute phrase? The entire phrase describes "Terry." An interesting feature about absolutes is that you may often leave out the verbal.

His determination always apparent, Terry encouraged other cancer victims.

Which version of the absolute phrase do you like better? Why?

From
Terry's face sported a boyish grin.
He easily won over everyone he met.
To
His face sporting a boyish grin, Terry easily won over everyone he met.

Can you add one more absolute phrase to this sentence?

4. One interesting possibility of using phrases is that you will be able to place a complete dependent clause within a phrase. Being able to do this will enrich your writing immeasurably. Your sentence structure will become varied and emphatic.

Notice how the following sentences have been combined. The phrases are underlined and the dependent clause in each phrase is in italic.

From
Some people dream of Canadian unity. If you are one of them, think what Terry Fox accomplished in a few months of his life. He, like no other, united Canada from coast to coast.
To
For you *who dream of Canadian unity*, think about *what Terry Fox accomplished in a few months of his life*; he, like no other, united Canada from coast to coast.

From
He decided that he would run across Canada. Following his decision, he presented his plan to the director of the B.C. branch of the Cancer Society.
To
Having decided *that he would run across Canada*, he presented his plan to the director of the B.C. branch of the Cancer Society.

From

His run was halted when lung cancer struck. Terry was then showered with honours by governments and other groups. They wanted to show how much they admired him.

To

His run having halted *when lung cancer struck*, Terry was showered with honours, governments and other groups showing *how much they admired him*.

5. As well as being able to insert entire dependent clauses into a phrase, writers are able to bring more details to their sentences by inserting phrases within phrases. To understand this, read the following sentence:

His voice breaking, Terry Fox, forced to stop, vowed to complete his run.

To the main subject and main verb, "Terry Fox vowed," three phrases have been added:

"His voice breaking" is an absolute phrase,
"forced to stop" is a verbal phrase, and
"to complete his run" is a verbal phrase.

You can shape sentences in many ways by introducing new word groups.

Notice what happens when a phrase is added within each of the above phrases.

His voice breaking *with emotion*, Terry Fox, forced to stop *near Thunder Bay*, vowed to complete his run *at a later date*.

D. Specific Words

1. So far you have seen six of the eight parts of speech: noun, pronoun, verb, adjective, adverb, and preposition. The seventh is the *conjunction*. Conjunctions join single words or word groups, or even paragraphs.

See how conjunctions can be used to combine sentences.

From

The people of B.C. never want to forget Terry.
The British Columbia government renamed a mountain Mount Terry Fox.

To

Because the people of B.C. never wanted to forget Terry, the British Columbia government renamed a mountain Mount Terry Fox.

Do you see that the two clauses are joined by the conjunction "because"? Now, see if you can identify what is being joined by the conjunctions in italic in the following two examples.

From

The British Columbia government presented Terry with its highest civilian medal.

The Canadian government presented him with its highest civilian medal.

The Governor-General came to Port Coquitlam to present the Order of Canada to him.

To

Both the British Columbia *and* Canadian governments presented Terry with their highest civilian medals; *moreover*, the Governor-General came to Port Coquitlam to present the Order of Canada to him.

From

A specially commissioned painting of Terry has been done.

Prints of the painting with his signature were sold.

The proceeds were donated to cancer research.

To

Not only has a specially commissioned painting of Terry been done, *but* prints of the painting with his signature were *also* sold *and* the proceeds donated to cancer research.

Now, write a sentence using a conjunction. Ask a partner to edit it.

2. The eighth and final part of speech is the *interjection* or exclamation. An interjection has little or no grammatical function.

Wow! Terry Fox was a remarkable human being.

Summary

Sentences can be divided into *independent* and *dependent* clauses, each of which is made up of a *complete subject* and a *complete predicate*. Clauses can be constructed by using eight different parts of speech: *noun, pronoun, verb, adjective, adverb, preposition, conjunction,* and *interjection*. Clauses may also contain three different kinds of phrases: *prepositional, verbal,* and *absolute*. Moreover, to make writing richer and more interesting, *dependent clauses* can be made a part of any of the three kinds of phrases.

Your grammar lesson is over. In future labs you will find various refinements to the facts that you have learned in this lab. Now, see how much you remember by testing yourself with the Sentence Work.

Sentence Work

The purpose of these exercises is to see if you can identify your writing tools. Later labs deal with sentence combining.

1. Identify the words in italic as an *independent clause* or *dependent clause*.

a) *Canada has many other heroes besides Terry Fox.*

b) Many people consider Louis Riel a hero, *though he was proclaimed a traitor.*

c) *Roy Brown became one of World War I's best-known fliers* when he shot down the Red Baron.

d) A Canadian *who gained great renown in China* was Doctor Norman Bethune.

e) Ken Taylor, who was Canada's ambassador to Iran, became a hero *when he sheltered American hostages.*

2. Identify the words in italic as one of the eight parts of speech: *noun, pronoun, verb, adjective, adverb, preposition, conjunction,* or *interjection.*

a) *Both* men *and* women have performed *heroic* deeds in Canadian history, as the *stories* of Dollard des Ormeaux and Madeleine de Verchères prove.

b) *Those* who believe that Canada has no heroes *should consider* the thousands of immigrants who endured *untold* hardships to build new *lives.*

c) Explorers such as Pierre de La Vérendrye and Alexander Mackenzie *fearlessly* explored *vast* parts *of* North America *previously* unknown to Europeans.

d) *Gracious!* The heroic *deeds* of Canadian soldiers *during* the two World Wars are recorded on *memorials* all over the world.

e) *Moreover,* no one should forget people *like* Doctors Banting and Best, whose *persistent research* resulted in the *discovery* of insulin.

3. Identify the words in italic as *phrases* or *clauses.*

a) By the time Terry Fox died, he had won the hearts of millions *throughout the world.* His statement, "Don't tell me *we can't raise $25,000,000.00!*" was a rallying cry. (two word groups)

b) Bob McGill, his high-school coach, delivered the eulogy *at his private funeral.* Memorial services were held all over Canada *to coincide with the time of his funeral.* (two word groups)

c) Canada's Postmaster-General, *breaking with tradition* and responding *to requests from thousands of Canadians,* announced on July 1, 1981 *that a stamp would be issued to honour Terry.* (three word groups)

d) Research *into the causes and treatments of cancer, helped by the millions of dollars raised through the Marathon of Hope,* may one day be successful *in finding a cure.* (four word groups)

e) *What all of us can do* to remember Terry Fox is *to continue the fight he started.* (two word groups)

(The answers to these exercises and subsequent lab work are at the end of the Laboratory Section. Use the answers as part of the process of becoming a better writer – during or after each exercise.)

Paragraph Work   Rewrite the following paragraph so that you change the carpentry analogy to another figurative comparison. Replace these key words, *carpenter's helper, hammer, saw, Phillips screwdriver, Robertson screwdriver, screwdriver, crisscross on the end, middle-sized square head,* with ones from another trade, profession, hobby, or interest that you know something about.

Your Tool Kit

This, more than any of the other labs in *The Writer's Workshop*, is your tool kit. In the same way as a carpenter's helper needs to know the difference between a hammer and a saw, you need to know the difference between a subject and a verb when your reader refers to one or the other. What a waste of time it would be if a carpenter had to ask, "Give me the screwdriver with the kind of funny criss-cross at the end," or "I want the one with the middle-sized square head." All the carpenter should need to say is, "Give me a Phillips screwdriver," or "I want a Robertson." When one of your readers says, "I think you should have used a phrase instead of a clause," you have to know what he/she is talking about. Words and word groups are a writer's tools. Learn to identify them.

If you were to choose a medical analogy, the first three words you might use would be *nurse* or *physician*, *scalpel*, and *stethoscope*. If you were to choose a sewing analogy, you might use *seamstress* or *tailor*, *needle*, and *thimble*.

Now, choose your own analogy and complete the paragraph. If you need further assistance, turn to the Suggested Answers at the end of the labs.

This, more than any of the other labs in *The Writer's Workshop*, is your tool kit. In the same way as a ( ) needs to know the difference between a ( ) and a ( ), you need to know the difference between a subject and a verb when your reader refers to one or the other of them. What a waste of time it would be if a ( ) had to ask, "Give me the ( ) with the kind of funny ( )," or "I want the one with the ( )." All the ( ) should need to say is, "Give me a ( )," or "I want the ( )." When one of your readers says, "I think you should have used a phrase instead of a clause," you have to know what he/she is talking about. Words and word groups are a writer's tools. Learn to identify them.

Lab **2** A Look at Sentence Patterns

Introduction

This lab presents the total scope of the word groups that go into creating sentence patterns. Knowledge of the patterns will enhance your sensitivity to all the choices at your disposal. The patterns are discussed separately and in more detail in subsequent labs. (Lab references are given after each sentence pattern is introduced.)

Explanation

1. The most common word group is the simple, *independent clause* (Lab 3). Canada is an energy-rich country.

2. If you combine two or more independent clauses, the new sentence pattern is a *compound sentence* (Lab 4). Notice that the independent clauses are joined by the conjunction *and*.

From
Water power is abundant.
Oil has been found in the East, West, and North.
Natural gas reserves are potentially greater than both of these.
To
Water power is abundant; oil has been found in the East, West, and North; *and* natural gas reserves are potentially greater than both of these.

3. By combining an independent clause with one or more dependent clauses, you will have a *complex sentence* (Lab 5). The dependent clauses below are in italic.

From
Canada's energy potential makes her the envy of many countries.
Oil must still be imported.
The Maritimes lack an energy supply.
To
Canada's energy potential makes her the envy of many countries, *though oil must still be imported because the Maritimes lack an energy supply.*

From

Oil is important in North America.

It has kept vehicles and businesses running throughout the twentieth century.

To

Oil is *what has kept North America's vehicles and businesses running throughout the twentieth century.*

4. If you add one or more dependent clauses to two or more independent clauses, you will create a *compound-complex* sentence pattern (Lab 6). The dependent clause in the sentence below is in italic. Do you see the independent clauses?

From

Canada's first oil well was drilled in Ontario in 1857.

Oil was discovered in Alberta in the 1940s.

Alberta quickly became Canada's chief oil supplier.

To

Canada's first oil well was drilled in Ontario in 1857, but Alberta quickly became Canada's chief oil supplier *after oil was discovered there in the 1940s.*

All the other word groups that are going to be introduced can be added to any of the above sentence patterns to enrich them. But in order for you to see the function of each word group clearly, each has been added to an independent clause.

5. By adding a *prepositional phrase*, you are able to elaborate on a particular point, and thus create a new sentence pattern (Lab 7).

From

British Columbia exports natural gas.

The United States receives British Columbia natural gas.

To

Natural gas *from British Columbia* is exported *to the United States.*

From

Some Canadians have strong opinions.

They feel Canada should use these exported supplies itself.

To

In the opinion of some Canadians, these exported supplies should be reserved *for Canada's own use.*

Read the preceding sentences without the prepositional phrases in italic to see what details have been added to the independent clauses.

6. By adding a *verbal phrase,* you can create a new sentence pattern (Lab 8). Notice how the three different kinds of verbal phrases below affect the independent clauses. The verbal phrases are in italic.

From

Since the late 1970s, the Canadian government has had a policy.

It bought foreign-owned oil companies.

To

Since the late 1970s, *buying foreign-owned oil companies* has been a policy of the Canadian government.

From

Canada's oil and gas industry was controlled for many years by non-Canadians.

Canada's oil and gas industry is slowly reversing the trend.

To

Controlled for many years by non-Canadians, Canada's oil and gas industry is slowly reversing the trend.

From

Petro-Canada was established for a good reason.

A Canadian-owned oil company would have a more powerful influence in world markets.

To

Petro-Canada was established *to give a Canadian-owned oil company a more powerful influence in world markets.*

7. Professional writers like to use the sentence pattern that includes an *absolute phrase* (Lab 9). Notice how extra detail is added with the absolute phrase in italic.

From

The Athabasca tar sands may be an important source of petroleum by the end of this century.

Their value is not yet fully known.

To

The Athabasca tar sands, *their value not yet fully known,* may be an important source of petroleum by the end of this century.

8. You can create an interesting sentence pattern by using two word groups side by side (a) that refer to the same thing and (b) that can be substituted for each other (Lab 10). Notice that the subject of this sentence and the word group in italic refer to the same person and can be substituted for each other. The second word group is *in apposition* to the first, and is called an *appositive.*

From

In the 1980s, the premier of Alberta led the fight of the provinces to control their energy resources.

The premier of Alberta was Peter Lougheed.

To

In the 1980s, the premier of Alberta, *Peter Lougheed,* led the fight of the provinces to control their energy resources.

Notice that you could leave either "the premier of Alberta" or "Peter Lougheed" out of the sentence and it would still make sense. This feature is characteristic of appositives.

9. You can achieve a useful sentence pattern by clustering a few adjectives somewhere in the sentence (Lab 11). The *adjective cluster* is in italic.

From

Western Canada's oil and natural gas have been the main subject of argument.

The oil and natural gas are abundant.

They are easy to get at.

The supply is extremely valuable.

To

Western Canada's oil and natural gas, *abundant, accessible, and invaluable*, have been the main subject of argument.

10. You can develop another pattern by clustering adverbs (Lab 12). The *adverb cluster* is in italic.

From

In the view of some Westerners, the federal government acted illegally in 1980 when it charged tax on resource revenue.

The act was also considered immoral.

Many people thought it was unjust as well.

To

In the view of some Westerners, the federal government acted *illegally, immorally, and unjustly* in 1980 when it charged tax on resource revenue.

11. Finally, you can create a sentence pattern by adding a single, *emphatic word* to a sentence (Lab 13).

From

Ottawa proclaimed its right to tax exported gas and oil.

Ottawa was not bothered by anyone's reactions.

To

Unperturbed, Ottawa proclaimed its right to tax exported gas and oil.

From

Some Westerners became angry.

They talked of separating from Canada.

To

Angrily, some Westerners talked of separating from Canada.

As you move through the other labs, you will see that all the word groups can be placed before, after, or in the middle of independent or dependent clauses. This gives a writer sentence variety. The word groups are few, but the combinations are limitless.

Sentence Work

The purpose of this exercise is to identify word groups; later, you will be combining sentences.

Examine each of the word groups in italic. Try to match the pattern of each entire sentence with the models in the Explanation section of this lab. Then identify the sentence pattern using the corresponding numbers 1 to 11.

a) Many experts predict the *slow, sure, and inevitable* decline of the industrialized world as fossil fuels run out.
b) Other experts paint a rosier picture; they say *that new technology can produce all the power necessary for a good life.*
c) *In an age-old process,* cow dung is still used as fuel in India.
d) *Methane gas from garbage is a well-known source of heat,* yet *in North America it is scarcely used.*
e) *Living in underground houses* can save energy during cold winters.
f) *Coal is an important energy source.*
g) *Its impact still being debated,* the 1978 accident at Three Mile Island, Pennsylvania, convinced many people of the dangers of nuclear power.
h) Gasohol, *which consists of grain alcohol mixed with gasoline,* is now available in some parts of the United States.
i) *Cleanly, easily, but expensively,* solar cells can convert the sun's heat to storable energy.
j) William Blake, *the English poet,* called energy "eternal delight."
k) *Unfortunately,* we in the twentieth century have greatly misused this delight.

When you finish, check to see that you have used all the numbers from 1 to 11 once. Then, check your answers with the Suggested Answers at the end of the labs.

Paragraph Work

Complete the paragraph below by rewriting the sentences in the brackets with suitable word groups so that they fit into the existing sentences.

Example
Energy conservation continues [It is an important concern.] for everyone.
Satisfactory combining
Energy conservation continues to be an important concern for everyone.

Since there are many different kinds of energy, [We may wonder about something.] how there can be an energy crisis. The reason is [North America has used only a few energy sources]. These have been mainly coal and oil. If we can learn [There are other fuel sources that we can use.] – solar power, wind power, and biomass – our energy crisis will soon be over.

Lab 3 Simple Sentences

Introduction
A simple sentence contains *only one* independent clause. Though the simple sentence can be a most useful writing tool, its over-use can be monotonous. In this lab you will look at the ways to bring variety to the *simple sentence*.

Explanation
Examine these simple sentences.
1. Simple sentence with *you* as an understood subject:

Look.   Go.   Push.

2. Simple sentence with a single subject and a single verb (or verb phrase):

Alexander Graham Bell invented the telephone.

3. Simple sentence with descriptive words:

The much-honoured Bell *later* founded the *world-famous* National Geographic Society.

4. Simple sentence with a compound subject:

Doctors Alan Brown, *T.G.H. Drake*, and *F.F. Tisdall* created Pablum baby food.

5. Simple sentence with a compound verb:

John McIntosh *developed* and *improved* the McIntosh apple.

6. Simple sentence with a compound subject and a compound verb:

Americans and *Canadians invented* and *patented* many labour-saving devices.

(Can you find the subjects and verbs?)

7. Simple sentence with an appositive:

Thomas Edison, *the wizard of Menlo Park*, developed the first functioning motion picture camera.

8. Simple sentence with prepositional phrases:

Anton van Leuwenhoek is credited *with the invention of the microscope*.

9. Simple sentences with verbal phrases:

Unknown in his own country, Canadian Reginald Fessenden is considered the father of radio.

Charles Saunders grew dozens of wheat plants *to find one suitable for the Prairies.*

By *inventing the self-propelled combine*, Thomas Carroll revolutionized wheat farming.

10. Simple sentence with an absolute phrase:

His fame obscured by that of the American Clarence Bidseye, Dr. Archibald Huntsman remains unrecognized for his pioneering work with frozen food.

11. Simple sentence with a single emphatic word:

Truly, inventors are remarkable people.

12. Notice how two or more simple sentences can be joined to make one, more detailed simple sentence. As long as you add only single words or phrases to the independent clause, you will still have a simple sentence.

From
Sir Thomas Crapper is credited with improving the flush toilet.
He lived during the time of Charles II.
To
Sir Thomas Crapper is credited with improving the flush toilet during the time of Charles II.

From
Thomas J. Ryan lived in Toronto.
He developed a popular sport.
The sport is five-pin bowling.
To
Thomas J. Ryan, a Torontonian, developed the popular sport of five-pin bowling.

From
Thomas Willson discovered a process.
He could make cheap acetylene gas.
It could be used in lamps.
It could be used in welding torches.
To
Thomas Willson discovered a process for making cheap acetylene gas to be used in lamps and welding torches.

From
A Vancouver inventor developed a handle for cardboard beer cartons.
The handle collapses into the carton.

To

A Vancouver inventor developed a collapsible handle for cardboard beer cartons.

Sentence Work

Combine each of the groups of simple sentences into a single, more detailed simple sentence. Vary the methods of sentence combining by using the different patterns outlined in sections 3 to 11 of the Explanation.

a) Norman Breakey worked in Toronto in 1940.
   He invented the paint roller.
   It was truly remarkable.
   It revolutionized the painting industry.

b) Benjamin Franklin invented several things.
   One of them was bifocal glasses.
   Many older people wear bifocals.
   They help them to read better.

c) Doctor John Hayward is from the University of Victoria.
   Doctors Martin Collis and John Eckerson are from the same university.
   They developed a jacket.
   With this jacket people are able to survive in cold water.

d) Quebec has cold winters.
   Arthur Sicard had an idea.
   He invented a machine to blow snow away.

e) Samuel F. B. Morse made a contribution to the development of the West.
   His code made long-distance communication possible.

Paragraph Work

Rewrite what is in brackets in the following paragraph so that each sentence remains a simple sentence.

Example
The first match like those of today was made by John Walker, [He was a pharmacist from England].

Sentence combining
The first match like those of today was made by John Walker, an English pharmacist.

The E.B. Eddy Company, [which is one of the world's largest matchmaking operations,] was established in Hull, Quebec in 1851 by Ezra Butler Eddy. Over the years, friction matches were merchandised under different names. [The names were *Telegraph*, *Parlour*, and *Eddy Matches*.] The name *Telegraph* was used [because it suggested speedy ignition]. The name *Parlour* was used [because it suggested use of the matches in the parlour]. The name *Eddy Matches* was used [because the company wished to honour the founder]. The company, [which includes widespread lumbering interests] introduced the book match into Canada in 1928.

Lab 4 Compound Sentences

Introduction

In this lab you will examine ways to combine simple sentences. When you have two or more simple sentences with thoughts of equal (co-ordinate) importance, you should put them into the same sentence. This method of sentence combining is known as *co-ordination*, and the type of sentence produced is a *compound sentence*.

Explanation

You can combine simple sentences in six ways:

1. By using a *semicolon*

From
The Inuit are Canada's original settlers.
They migrated from Asia at an undetermined time thousands of years ago.
To
The Inuit are Canada's original settlers; they migrated from Asia at an undetermined time thousands of years ago.

Many inexperienced writers avoid using semicolons because they are afraid of making punctuation mistakes. When you use a semicolon, you must make sure your two independent clauses are equally important and are closely related. (If, by the way, you had used a comma to join the two simple sentences above, you would have created a *comma splice*; if you had used no punctuation mark, you would have produced a *run-on sentence*. In your writing, avoid both the comma splice and the run-on sentence either by leaving the simple sentences as they are or by joining them with a semicolon.)

2. By using a *co-ordinating conjunction*
a) When you join two simple sentences by a co-ordinating conjunction, you use a comma before the conjunction.

From
The word "Eskimo" is a Cree term meaning "eaters of raw meat."
Most Inuit do not use it.

To

The word "Eskimo" is a Cree term meaning "eaters of raw meat," *and* most Inuit do not use it.

b) If the simple sentences to be combined are short and very close together in content, you may not require the comma:

From

There are only a few thousand Inuit.

They occupy a vast area.

To

There are only a few thousand Inuit *but* they occupy a vast area.

The following are the co-ordinating conjunctions:

but,   so,   nor,   or,   yet,   for,   and.

3. By using a *correlative conjunction*

From

The Inuit live in northern Canada.

They inhabit Alaska, Siberia, and Greenland as well.

To

Not only do the Inuit live in northern Canada, *but* they *also* inhabit Alaska, Siberia, and Greenland.

From

Their nomadic lifestyle was based on following the caribou herds.

They also hunted the polar bear and walrus.

To

Their nomadic lifestyle was based *both* on following the caribou herds *and* hunting the polar bear and the walrus.

When you use a correlative conjunction, you will be able to stress the equality of two parts of your sentence.

Refer to this list of correlative conjunctions when you need to stress something in your sentences:

both ... and	either ... or	so ... as
neither ... nor	not only ... but (also)	whether ... or

4. By using a *conjunctive adverb*

From

Some Inuit have moved south for medical or other reasons.

Most of them remain in the North.

To

Some Inuit have moved south for medical or other reasons; *however*, most of them remain in the North.

Some Inuit have moved south for medical or other reasons; most of them, *however*, remain in the North.

Some Inuit have moved south for medical or other reasons; most of them remain in the North, *however*.

Note how the punctuation changes when the conjunctive adverb "however" is moved. All three examples show sentence combining through co-ordination. Here are some other conjunctive adverbs:

accordingly	hence	nevertheless	additionally
however	in fact	no	also
on the contrary	indeed	at any rate	in other words
on the other hand	anyway	in short	still
besides	likewise	then	consequently
moreover	therefore	furthermore	namely
yes	especially	notably	yet

5. By using a *colon*

From

The writer James Houston has greatly influenced modern Inuit life.
He discovered the Inuit talent for print making and carving.
He brought their work to the attention of collectors.
He helped the Inuit to form co-operatives to market their work.

To

The writer James Houston has greatly influenced modern Inuit life: he discovered the Inuit talent for print making and carving, he brought their work to the attention of collectors, and he helped the Inuit to form co-operatives to market their work.

You use a colon when a second independent clause is a more detailed explanation of the first independent clause. Do you see that the three final clauses in the above example are a more detailed explanation of the first clause?

Now omit the word "he" from the final two clauses in the combined sentence. What is the effect?

Notice the effect of rewriting the sentence with co-ordinating conjunctions:

The writer James Houston has greatly influenced modern Inuit life, *for* he discovered the Inuit talent for print making and carving, brought their work to the attention of collectors, and helped the Inuit to form co-operatives to market their work.

If you were to use conjunctive adverbs in the last three clauses, you would make the sentence clearer:

The writer James Houston has greatly influenced modern Inuit life: *first*, he discovered the Inuit talent for print making and carving; *then*, he brought their work to the attention of collectors; *finally*, he helped the Inuit to form co-operatives to market their work.

Even though these sentences are very long, they are still easy to understand. Why? Which of the different versions do you like best? Why?

6. By using *parallel structure*

You can achieve a special kind of co-ordination by making parts of one independent clause parallel to another independent clause.

From

The Inuit claim a large area of northern Canada as their aboriginal land.
The Dene Indians claim other parts of the North as their aboriginal land.

To

The Inuit claim a large area of northern Canada as their aboriginal land; the Dene Indians claim other parts of the North.

In what ways is the second independent clause parallel to the first? Because both clauses are balanced, this kind of sentence is often referred to as a *balanced sentence*.

It is possible to omit even more words from the second clause in order to avoid unnecessary repetition. The following sentence is still considered to be balanced:

The Inuit claim a large area of northern Canada as their aboriginal land; the Dene Indians, other parts of the North.

Summary

The combined sentences in this lab have used:

semicolons
co-ordinating conjunctions
correlative conjunctions
conjunctive adverbs
colons, or
parallel structure

The term *compound sentence* refers to every combined sentence in this lab. When you want to write a compound sentence, remember the six different ways to co-ordinate your sentence.

Sentence Work

Combine each of the groups of simple sentences using *three* different *co-ordinating* methods; then, decide which is the best. Try to vary your techniques so that you practise using all six methods of co-ordination.

   a) The people of the North learned to live with their harsh climate.
      Their bodies grew extra layers of fat.
      They wore several layers of well-made fur clothing.
      Their high-protein diet provided large amounts of energy.
   b) Weather in the North may sometimes be unpleasant.
      Montreal receives more snow in an average winter than some parts of Northern Canada.
   c) Anthony Thrasher was a talented Inuit artist.
      He died alone and unhappy.
   d) In the old days the Inuit used dogsleds to move across snow and ice.
      Nowadays the Inuit use snowmobiles to move across snow and ice.
   e) Northern peoples want to benefit from the development of their land.
      They want money for the use of the land.
      They want jobs on the pipelines and oil rigs.
      They want guarantees of the preservation of their hunting and fishing rights.

Paragraph Work

In the paragraph below, provide an appropriate word or punctuation mark to join the independent clauses. Fill in the parentheses with:

, and	, but	, for	, yet
;	:	; however,	; moreover,
both ... and	not only ... but also	neither ... nor	either ... or

Most people in southern Canada ( ) have little knowledge of the North ( ) have little interest in it. This is an unfortunate attitude ( ) Northern Canada is a land of almost unlimited opportunity ( ) it is not simply a barren expanse of ice and snow ( ) a bewitchingly beautiful place.

Lab **5** Complex Sentences

Introduction   In this lab you will examine ways to combine important and less important ideas in the same sentence. This is accomplished by putting the less important ideas into dependent clauses. The technique is called *subordination*, and a sentence that has one or more dependent clauses combined with an independent clause is a *complex* sentence.

Explanation   A *dependent clause* is a group of words, containing a subject and a verb, which depends on some other word or words in another clause for its meaning. It is always joined to the other clause by a special connecting word, either a *relative pronoun* or a *subordinating conjunction*.

Relative Pronouns
that   who   whom   where   what   which   whoever   whichever

Subordinating Conjunctions

   Time: as, as long as, as soon as, often, before, since, till (until), when, while

   Reason or Cause: as, because, inasmuch as, since, why, although, though, if, unless, whether ... or

   Purpose: in order that, so, that, lest

   Comparison: than, as

There are three ways to subordinate through sentence combining:

1. Put the information into a dependent clause that acts like a single adjective. (Remember, adjectives modify nouns or pronouns.)

From
Bruce McConachy is eighteen years old.
He comes from West Vancouver.
He balanced 170 coins on the side of a penny.
To
Eighteen-year-old Bruce McConachy, *who comes from West Vancouver*, balanced 170 coins on the side of a penny.

The dependent clause modifies the noun "Bruce McConachy." Note that it has commas around it because it is not essential to the sentence; if it were left out, the sentence would still make sense.

From

Sudbury houses the world's biggest coin.
It stands just over nine metres high.
It is only a nickel.

To

Sudbury houses the world's biggest coin, *which stands just over nine metres high* but *which is only a nickel.*

Which noun do both dependent clauses modify? They are both non-essential to the sentence; hence a comma is needed.

From

James Warnock was a man from Cantley, Quebec.
He built a sixty-one-storey house of cards.
He achieved a world record.

To

The man *who built a sixty-one-storey house of cards for a world record* was James Warnock of Cantley, Quebec.

Which noun does the dependent clause modify? Because it is essential to the sentence, no commas are required. To test if a dependent clause is essential, leave it out and see if the meaning of the sentence is changed. Does "The man was James Warnock of Cantley, Quebec" have the same meaning as the original?

From

Barbara-Anne Eddy is from Vancouver.
She won the largest untaxed television prize.
She won $128,000.00 in 1979.

To

The person *who won the largest untaxed television prize* is Barbara-Anne Eddy of Vancouver, *who won $128,000.00 in 1979.*

Why does the first dependent clause not have commas around it?

All the dependent clauses are placed as near as possible to the nouns they modify. This is essential when you subordinate with clauses that function as adjectives. Why? If you cannot answer this question, try to move the dependent clauses elsewhere in their sentences. Do they still make sense?

2. Put the information into a dependent clause that acts like a single adverb. (Remember, adverbs modify verbs, adjectives, or other adverbs.)

From

Most people go to Niagara Falls to see the waterfalls.
The city contains the world's largest floral clock.

To

Though most people go to Niagara Falls to see the waterfalls, the city also contains
the world's largest floral clock.

The dependent clause in italic works quite differently from those in number 1. It can be moved to at least two other positions in the sentence. Try to move it and see the effect, but wherever you move it, remember to set it off from the independent clause with commas.

Another feature of this kind of dependent clause is that you may choose to reverse the emphasis in the sentences by subordinating the independent clause and making the dependent clause your main one.

Though the city contains the world's largest floral clock, most people go to Niagara
Falls to see the waterfalls.

Which sentence do you think is better? Why?

From

The people of Vegreville, Alberta, built the world's largest Easter egg as a
tribute to their heritage.
Many of its citizens are of Ukrainian origin.
Ukrainians are famous for producing beautifully decorated eggs.

To

Because Ukrainians are famous for producing beautifully decorated eggs, and
because many of its citizens are of Ukrainian origin, the people of Vegreville,
Alberta, built the world's largest Easter egg as a tribute to their heritage.

Could you move the two dependent clauses to other positions? Is it necessary to repeat the subordinating conjunction *because*? What word do both the dependent clauses modify? If you were to try to subordinate the independent clause, the new sentence would not make sense. ("Because the people of Vegreville, Alberta, built the world's largest Easter egg as a tribute to their heritage, Ukrainians are...") Such an error is known as *faulty subordination.*

3. Put the information into a dependent clause that acts like a noun or pronoun. (A noun or pronoun can do many things in a sentence, so a clause that functions as a noun or pronoun is extremely versatile.)

From

You might want to visit the world's smallest church.
You should go to Drumheller, Alberta.

To

Whoever wants to visit the world's smallest church should go to Drumheller,
  Alberta.

The dependent clause in italic functions as the subject of the verb *should
go* in the same way as the pronoun *you* in the preceding sentence. It begins
with the relative pronoun *whoever.*

From

The world's largest frog is found in the museum in Fredericton, N.B.
John Fisher's *Complete Cross-Canada Quiz and Game Book* states this.

To

John Fisher's *Complete Cross-Canada Quiz and Game Book* states *that the
  world's largest frog is found in the museum in Fredericton, N.B.*

Which single noun or pronoun could replace the dependent clause?

From

Alert Bay is a town in British Columbia.
The world's tallest totem pole stands there, according to the *Guinness Book of
  World Records.*

To

Alert Bay, B.C., is *where the world's tallest totem pole stands,* according to the
  Guinness Book of World Records.

Notice that in the dependent clause the subject is "totem pole" and the
verb is "stands." If you were to rewrite this sentence without a dependent
clause, you would write something like this: "Alert Bay is the site of the
world's tallest totem pole, according to the *Guinness Book of World Records.*"
Now the sentence is a simple sentence with only one subject, "Alert Bay"
and one verb "is."

From

John Fisher's book says that the world's tallest totem pole is in Victoria.
Other information in this lab comes from that book.

To

John Fisher's book, from *which other information in this lab comes,* says *that the
  world's tallest totem pole is in Victoria.*

Name the subject and verb in the dependent clauses in italic. Name the
subject and verb in the independent clause. Can you think of another way of
combining the same information into a single sentence?

Sentence Work

Although there are a number of ways to combine sentences, in this lab you should do so by producing one single independent clause and one or more dependent clauses. Your dependent clauses should begin with either a relative pronoun or a subordinating conjunction. Think your sentences through carefully so you do not have any faulty subordination. Your sentences must make complete sense.

a) Vancouver hosted the world's largest tea party on July 29, 1981.
   The city wanted to celebrate Prince Charles's wedding.

b) The largest number of championships in log rolling was won by Jubiel Wickheim.
   Log rolling is a popular sport all over North America.

c) Louis Cyr pitted his strength against horses and steam engines.
   He astonished everyone.
   He was called "the strongest man in the world."

d) In 1975 Paul Mears smoked thirty-five full-sized cigars at once.
   This fact may not be worth much.

e) People talk about Canada-U.S. relations.
   They mention with pride the world's longest undefended border.
   It stretches almost 6500 km from coast to coast.

Paragraph Work

Convert these independent clauses into dependent clauses and place them in the appropriate spaces in the paragraph.

People should be interested in conserving energy.
Some people are interested in alternate energy sources.
The Bay of Fundy tides are the highest in the world.
New Brunswick is exploring these tides as a source of future power.

[dependent clause], they should look to the sea. Specifically, [dependent clause] should know about the tides in the Bay of Fundy. These tides, [dependent clause], are [dependent clause].

Lab **6** Compound-Complex Sentences

Introduction

This lab is merely a combination of the two previous labs. Do not continue with this lab unless you have completed them.

If you write a sentence with at least two independent clauses and at least one dependent clause, you will have a *compound-complex* sentence. This kind of sentence is very useful for including a great deal of information within a single sentence.

Explanation

1.   When you create a compound-complex sentence, you must make sure you punctuate it so that your reader will not become confused. You must follow the rules for both compound and complex sentences. So, as you go through this lab, pay particular attention to the punctuation.

From
The Canadian National Exhibition is an annual event.
It has been held in Toronto since 1879.
It is the world's largest fair.
People come from all over the world to participate in it.
To
The Canadian National Exhibition, which is the world's largest fair, *has been held in Toronto since 1879*, and *people come from all over the world to participate in it.*

Notice the various parts of the compound-complex sentence. The two independent clauses are in italic. What is the subject and verb of each of them? What conjunction joins them? What is the dependent clause? What is its subject and verb?

So that you can see clearly the different sentences that went into the previous compound-complex sentence, notice the effect when some of the simple sentences are combined separately. Which clause is removed from each?

Compound sentence

The Canadian National Exhibition has been held in Toronto since 1879, and people come from all over the world to participate in it.

Complex sentence

The Canadian National Exhibition, which is the world's largest fair, has been held in Toronto since 1879.

The compound sentence has two independent clauses; the complex sentence has one independent and one dependent clause.

2. Now examine how the following sentences have been combined to make a compound-complex sentence.

Simple sentence

Boating is a popular sport in Canada.

Compound sentence

Regattas are held in many parts of the country; St. John's and Kelowna host two of the best-known regattas.

Compound-complex sentence

Because boating is a popular sport in Canada, *regattas are held in many parts of the country; St. John's and Kelowna host two of the best-known regattas.*

In which other way could you combine the previous sentences so that you would still have a compound-complex sentence?

Compound sentence

The Calgary Stampede is justly famous; it is the largest show of its kind in Canada.

Simple sentence

A parade, a rodeo, and street dancing are all big attractions.

Simple sentence

The chuckwagon race is the most popular event.

Compound-complex sentence

The Calgary Stampede is justly famous as the largest show of its kind in Canada; though a parade, a rodeo, and street dancing are all big attractions, *the chuckwagon race is the most popular event.*

Complex sentence

When the Dutch royal family had to flee their home during World War II, Canada welcomed them.

Complex sentence

In gratitude, each year the people of the Netherlands give Canada millions of tulip bulbs, which bloom in Ottawa during the Tulip Festival.

Compound-complex sentence
When the Dutch royal family had to flee their home during World War II, *Canada welcomed them,* and *in gratitude, each year the people of the Netherlands give Canada millions of tulip bulbs,* which bloom in Ottawa during the Tulip Festival.

There are two dependent and two independent clauses in the previous sentence. Pick out the subject and verb from each.

Compound sentence
The days of the Klondike gold rush are long over, but Edmonton nostalgically celebrates its past during Klondike Days.
Simple sentences
Stores are decorated.
People wear Victorian clothes and sing old-time songs.
Pubs become saloons.
Compound-complex sentence
The days of the Klondike gold rush are long over, but *Edmonton nostalgically celebrates its past during Klondike Days*, when stores are decorated, pubs become saloons, and people wear Victorian clothes and sing old-time songs.

Besides having two independent clauses, the previous sentence has a long dependent clause. In order for the various parts of the dependent clause to be clear to the reader, they are arranged in a logical order. Can you think of another order?

Sentence Work

Combine the sentences in each group to create a compound-complex sentence. Make sure each sentence has at least two independent clauses and one dependent clause. Watch your punctuation.

a) Bonhomme Carnaval, a giant animated snowman, presides over Quebec City's annual winter carnival.
   Ice sculptors and canoe racers vie for top honours.
   Revellers crowd the city from dawn to midnight.

b) When the Okanagan peaches are ripe, visitors flock to Penticton's Peach Festival.
   They can take part in street dancing or watch the Square Dance Jamboree.

c) Many residents of Kitchener are of Swiss-German descent.
   Each year they celebrate Oktoberfest.
   This is a German harvest festival where a great deal of sauerkraut, sausage, and beer is consumed.

d) Tossing the caber is an old Celtic sport.
It involves throwing a long pole as far as possible.
Many people attend Nova Scotia's Highland Games to see the caber tossing, but few will try it.

e) The Banff School of Fine Arts provides courses in painting, ballet, music, and theatre.
It is also the home of the annual Festival of Arts.
The talents of its students are displayed there.

Paragraph Work

Rework these sentences so that they fit into the paragraph. When you finish, you should have two compound-complex sentences.

You can go anywhere in Canada.
Tourists flock to enjoy them.
The Maritimes have their maple-syrup breakfasts.

[dependent clause], someone will be celebrating something: Nanaimo has its bathtub races; [independent clause]; Stratford, its Shakespeare Festival; and Saskatoon, its Pioneer Days. Canadians break up the yearly calendar with festivals, fairs, and shows that spring from a spirit of good fun and a sense of national pride; [independent clause].

Lab 7 Prepositional Phrases

Introduction In this lab you will examine ways to pare down a dependent clause or independent clause into a *prepositional phrase*. This is another useful way to combine sentences.

Explanation 1. A *prepositional phrase*, whether it is short or long, functions as a single adjective or adverb. Like dependent clauses, prepositional phrases can be essential or non-essential to a sentence. Remember, essential phrases are not separated by commas, whereas non-essential ones are. Read these examples:

From
Canada shares the world's longest undefended border.
The United States shares the world's longest undefended border.
To
Canada shares the world's longest undefended border *with the United States*.

The phrase in italic acts as an adverb, modifying and describing "shares." Depending on where you wish to place the emphasis, the sentence could be reworded.

The United States shares the world's longest undefended border *with Canada*.

2. You use prepositional phrases in exactly the same way as dependent clauses. A prepositional phrase that functions as an adjective should be near the noun or pronoun it modifies; a prepositional phrase that functions like an adverb may be placed anywhere in the sentence, for emphasis.

Notice how the following sentences are concisely combined through the use of prepositional phrases:

From
There has been peace between Canada and the U.S.
This peace has lasted 150 years.
To
There has been peace *for 150 years between Canada and the U.S.*
For 150 years there has been peace *between Canada and the U.S.*

From

We Canadians use the symbol of the maple leaf.

Americans use the symbol of the stars and stripes.

We declare ourselves "children of a common mother."

To

We *of the maple leaf* and they *of the stars and stripes* declare ourselves "children *of a common mother*."

From

U.S.-Canadian trade is the world's largest.

It is worth over 60 billion dollars a year.

To

Because of its value of over 60 billion dollars a year, the U.S.-Canadian trade is the world's largest.

Where else could you move the above prepositional phrases? Are your sentences more emphatic when the phrases are relocated? As you read the following combined sentences, try to move the phrases into various positions.

3. If you find that you can get rid of a clause by using a prepositional phrase and *keeping the original sense*, then do so. Study the following pairs of sentences. Decide which is more effective.

Compound sentence

The Canadian and American governments have worked together on large projects; one of these projects has been the St. Lawrence Seaway.

Tightened by using a prepositional phrase

The Canadian and American governments have worked together on large projects, *like the St. Lawrence Seaway project*.

Complex sentence

While they watch one American TV program after another, Canadians unconsciously absorb American attitudes.

Tightened by using a prepositional phrase

By watching one American TV program after another, Canadians unconsciously absorb American attitudes.

Compound-complex sentence

The Mounties, who have symbolized Canada all over the world, have been especially popular in the U.S.; Pierre Berton makes this point in his book, *Hollywood's Canada*.

Tightened by using a prepositional phrase

The Mounties, who have symbolized Canada all over the world, have been especially popular in the U.S., *according to statements Pierre Berton made in his book, **Hollywood's Canada**.*

Notice that in the last three combined sentences, the prepositional phrases have been separated from the rest of the sentence by a comma. Why?

Remember, a prepositional phrase always begins with a preposition; it can contain a dependent clause or a verbal phrase. Which of the previous sentences contains a dependent clause? A verbal phrase?

Including clauses and verbal phrases in your prepositional phrases will give your writing variety; you will be able to use the various word groups in endless combinations.

Sentence Work

Use prepositional phrases to join or restructure these sentences.

a) The United States is smaller than Canada.
   It covers less land area.
b) Some people say that Canada has a "branch-plant" economy.
   Many American companies have subsidiaries in Canada.
c) American troops burned Toronto.
   This was while the War of 1812 was going on.
d) Even though they know they should not, Canadians enjoy the more violent American TV shows.
e) Few people know that Canada introduced North American football to the U.S.
f) More than twenty American universities offer courses that deal with Canadian affairs.
g) The CBC was created in 1936 because many talented performers had left for the U.S.; its series and specials have been exported all over the world.
h) Only 40 per cent of Canadians who are over twenty-one years old have completed high school; 65 per cent of Americans who are over twenty-one have done so.

Paragraph Work

Use these sentences to complete the paragraph below.

Canada has been conscious about its identity for the last ten years.
Canadians insist on staying separate from the U.S.
Canadians and Americans have many things that are common to both of them.
In the years that have passed since 1900 both countries have influenced each other.
Canada has linguistic and cultural ties with the U.S.
This makes people who live in each country comfortable in dealing with the people of the other country.

For each set of brackets in the paragraph, complete the prepositional phrase; the preposition is provided for you.

Canadians have become more conscious about their separate identity [within]. Americans are sometimes annoyed at Canadians [because of] [on]. Nonetheless, Canadians and Americans have many things [in]. [During] both countries have increased their influence further than their boundaries. Linguistic and cultural ties [between] have made the natives [of] comfortable [with].

Lab **8** Verbal Phrases

Introduction

In this lab you will examine ways to pare down a dependent clause or even an independent clause into a verbal phrase. This will be useful when you wish to combine sentences because a verbal phrase allows you to be brief and emphatic.

Explanation I

1. A *verbal* has the qualities of a verb in all respects except one: a verbal cannot stand alone as a sentence.

Verbs
Run. Conquer. Live. (*You* is the understood subject of each verb.)
Verbals
Running. Conquered. To live. (Adding *you* would not make sense.)

A verbal requires additional words for it to make sense.

Running was both a sport and a much-needed skill for many Indians.
The North American Indians became a conquered people.
For centuries, they managed to live in harmony with nature.

2. Like a verb, a verbal can take modifiers (single words, phrases, or clauses), and in some cases a verbal can even take a subject. A verbal and its related words are called a *verbal phrase*, but even a verbal phrase cannot stand alone. It always requires a word in the rest of the sentence to make complete sense.

Verbal phrases
moving throughout North America wherever they wanted to
to leap as high as my shoulder
Sitting Bull's coming to Canada
on leaving the reserve

All the preceding verbal phrases are fragments. They cannot stand alone, but require other words to make sense:

Moving throughout North America wherever they wanted to, the Indians were the freest of people.

Add more words to the other three verbal phrases so that you make sense of them. The words can come *before* or *after* the verbal phrase.

3. When a verbal or verbal phrase is within a complete sentence, you can see how the other half of its dual personality functions. A verbal or verbal phrase *always* relates to a word in the rest of the sentence. It may function as an adjective or adverb and modify, or it may function as a noun or pronoun and connect itself to a verb or a preposition. The verbal, then, is extremely versatile.

The dual personality of verbals

$$\text{verbal} = \begin{cases} \text{verb \& adjective or adverb} \\ \\ \text{verb \& noun or pronoun} \end{cases}$$

4. Following are examples of verbals and verbal phrases that act as modifiers.

a) *Verbals that modify as adjectives or adverbs:*

From
Indian youths took part in religious rituals.
They chanted.
They danced.
To
Chanting and *dancing* Indian youths took part in religious rituals.

From
The warrior who endured the Sun Dance was courageous indeed.
He was starved.
He became exhausted.
To
Starved and *exhausted*, the warrior who endured the Sun Dance was courageous indeed.

From
The tribes took part in sun-worshipping rituals.
They feasted and danced first.
To
Having feasted and *danced*, the tribes took part in sun-worshipping rituals.

The above verbals are called *participles*.

From
The West Coast Indians went miles out to sea.
They hunted in the sea.
To
The West Coast Indians went miles out to sea *to hunt*.

From

A large canoe is carved.

It might take months before it is completed.

To

A large canoe might take months *to carve.*

The above verbals are called *infinitives.*

b) *Verbal phrases that modify as adjectives or adverbs:*

From

West Coast Indian boys celebrated their coming of age.

They swam in icy waters.

They were then ritually beaten.

To

Celebrating their coming of age, West Coast Indian boys swam in icy waters and then were ritually beaten.

From

Indian men danced the Sun Dance.

Leather thongs were secured through their chest muscles to the sacred Sun Lodge.

They danced until they tore free or until they fainted.

To

Secured to the sacred Sun Lodge by leather thongs through their chest muscles, Indian men danced the Sun Dance until they tore free or until they fainted.

From

After he had proved he was a courageous warrior, a man who survived the Sun Dance ritual was honoured among his people.

To

Having proved himself a courageous warrior, a man who survived the Sun Dance ritual was honoured among his people.

From

Indians believed in the principle of "a life for a life."

They sought revenge for slain warriors.

To

Believing in the principle of "a life for a life," Indians sought revenge for slain warriors.

The verbal phrases used above are called *participial phrases.*

From

The West Coast Indians made beautiful canoes.

They used them on the hunt.

To

The West Coast Indians made beautiful canoes *to use on the hunt.*

From

A Nootka chieftain went into isolation for a day of prayer. This would ensure successful fishing.

To

To ensure successful fishing, the Nootka chieftain went into isolation for a day of prayer.

The above verbal phrases are called *infinitive phrases*.

5.   When you use a verbal phrase that modifies, you must make sure that it comes next to the word that it describes and that it is set off by commas. If it does not come near the word it describes, it will probably confuse the reader. Such a verbal or verbal phrase is called a *misplaced modifier*. If it appears in a sentence where there is no word for it to modify, it's called a *dangling modifier*.

a) Which word do each of the verbals or verbal phrases in italic in "4a" and "4b" modify?

b) The following verbal phrases are dangling. There is no word that they modify in the sentence.

Dangling verbal phrase

Hoping for the Great Spirit's favour, a trance was induced. (A *trance* cannot *hope*.)

Correct use of verbal phrase

Hoping for the Great Spirit's favour, warriors induced trances through fasting and chanting. (*Warriors* can *hope*.)

Corrected by changing the verbal phrase to a dependent clause

Since they hoped for the Great Spirit's favour, warriors induced trances through fasting and chanting. (*They* can *hope*.)

Dangling verbal phrase

Prepared for a religious experience, a dream would appear. (*A dream* cannot *prepare*.)

Correct use of verbal phrase

Prepared for a religious experience, the men would dream of their future. (*Men* can *prepare*.)

Corrected by changing the verbal phrase to a dependent clause

After they had prepared for a religious experience, the men would dream of their future. (*They* can *prepare*.)

Dangling verbal phrase

To take part in a whaling expedition, fasting for a week was thought necessary. (*Fasting* cannot *take part*.)

Correct use of verbal phrase

To take part in a whaling expedition, a man had to fast for a week. (*A man* can *take part*.)

Corrected by changing the verbal phrase to a dependent clause
If a man wanted to take part in a whaling expedition, he had to fast for a week.
(*A man* can *want*.)

6. To avoid a dangling verbal phrase, use active voice rather than passive voice. When the doer of the action is the subject of the verb, the voice is active; when the doer is not even in the sentence, the voice is passive. The verbs *was induced, would appear,* and *was thought* are all passive.

Misplaced verbal phrase
The Hurons, *having become deadly enemies*, and Iroquois attacked each other throughout the seventeenth century.
Correct placement of verbal phrase
Having become deadly enemies, the Hurons and Iroquois attacked each other throughout the seventeenth century.

Misplaced verbal phrase
The members of West Coast tribes frequently, *to demonstrate their personal wealth and that of their clan*, held potlatches.
Correct placement of verbal phrase
To demonstrate their personal wealth and that of their clan, the members of West Coast tribes frequently held potlatches.

Can you think of one other position where the verbal phrases in the sentences above could be correctly placed?

Sentence Work I

1. Tighten or combine these sentences by using verbals or verbal phrases that modify. Hints are given after each item. You are to begin your verbals with the words that are in parentheses. Make sure you place each verbal or verbal phrase near the word it describes, and set each apart from the rest of the sentence by using commas.
   a) The hosts of a potlatch would use it as a means of paying back previous hosts. They would also gain the right of an invitation to future potlatches. (to pay, to gain, to be)
   b) Though they varied a great deal in ritual and dogma, all religions of all Indian tribes shared a belief in the spirits of nature. (varying)
   c) Religion was the life-force of the Indians.
      It was present in everything they did. (being)
   d) The spirits set the sun and moon in the sky, controlled their courses, and caused the change of season; they were part of everything and everyone. (setting, controlling, causing)
   e) Once a spirit that was able to guide had been discovered, it would be called on in time of need. (once discovered, guiding)

f) The tribal rituals showed the Indians their spiritual heritage.
They were fervently observed and carefully practised. (fervently observed, carefully practised)

Before you continue with the next portion of this exercise, make sure you have combined or tightened the above sentences correctly. Check your responses with the ones in the Suggested Answers.

2. The following verbals or verbal phrases are either misplaced or dangling. Decide the best way to rewrite the sentence.
  a) The Ojibway held ceremonies of apology for the death of a friend, having killed a bear.
  b) Skilled in dealing with spirits, charms were prepared to keep away sickness and evil.
  c) Dancing and singing, the intimacy with the spirit was felt in every part of an Indian's being.
  d) To record their clan's history and achievements, chief's houses had totem poles in front of them.
  e) To see authentic Haida totem poles, a visit to the Queen Charlotte Islands is recommended.
  f) To ensure the survival of this art form, the traditional carving methods have been taught.

Explanation II

1. Verbals and verbal phrases can also function as nouns.

  a) Verbals that end in "ing" and function as nouns are called *gerunds*.

From
The main occupations of most tribesmen on the plains was hunting.
They also fought a great deal.
To
Hunting and *fighting* were the main occupations of most tribesmen on the plains.
The main occupations of most tribesmen on the plains were *hunting* and *fighting*.

  b) The *infinitive* is the most versatile of the verbals. It can function as an adjective, an adverb, or a noun.

From
The skilful hunters seldom missed their prey.
They chased and caught their prey.
To
The skilful hunters seldom missed their prey; *to chase* was *to catch*.

  c) Verbal phrases that contain a gerund and function as nouns are called *gerundial phrases*.

Simple sentence
They hunted buffalo.
The buffalo was vital to the survival of the tribe.
Sentence combining with a verbal phrase
Hunting buffalo was vital to the survival of the tribe.

Complex sentence
When a hunter killed one buffalo, it gave his family food, clothing, and shelter.
Changed by using a verbal phrase
A hunter's killing of one buffalo gave his family food, clothing, and shelter.

Complex sentence
After the hunt, they enjoyed a feast of fresh buffalo meat.
Changing of emphasis by using one verbal or one verbal phrase
After *hunting*, they enjoyed *feasting on fresh buffalo meat.*

Complex sentence
As the Plains Indians' lifestyle was nomadic, the length of their stay in one
    place depended on whether they could find game.
Reconstructed by using a verbal phrase
As the Plains Indians' lifestyle was nomadic, the length of their stay in one
    place depended on *their finding game.*
As the Plains Indians' lifestyle was nomadic, the length of their stay in one
    place depended on how successful they were in *finding game.*

   d) The *infinitive phrases* below also function as nouns.

Complex sentence
When it burned blankets, distributed jewellery and killed slaves, a group
    showed how abundant its possessions were.
Changed by using four verbal phrases
To burn blankets, distribute jewellery, and *kill slaves* was *to show how abundant a*
    group's possessions were.

Complex sentence
When people prepared for a potlatch, they spent many weeks in which they
    assembled the gifts, while food was gathered and stored.
Tightened by using three verbal phrases
To prepare a potlatch took many weeks; time was needed *to assemble the gifts*
    and *to gather and store the food.*

    Did you notice that the above verbals and verbal phrases in italic generally have no commas to set them off from the rest of the sentence? The reason for this is that they do not modify; they function as nouns. They are either directly connected to the verb or to a preposition. Because you would not put a comma before or after *was* in this sentence:

The animal was a buffalo.

you should not put a comma before or after *was* in this sentence:

To kill a buffalo from a galloping horse was *to show courage beyond belief.*

2. When a verbal phrase immediately follows a preposition, the entire phrase functions as a modifier and not as a noun; therefore:
- a) it needs a comma to set it off from the rest of the sentence,
- b) it needs to be near the word it modifies, and
- c) it can quite easily dangle when there is no word for it to modify.

Dangling verbal phrase
By *living in easily portable tepees*, moving quickly from place to place was possible. (*Moving* cannot *live*.)
Correct use of preposition plus a verbal phrase
By *living in easily portable tepees*, the Plains Indians found it possible to move quickly from place to place. (*Plains Indians* can *live*.)

Dangling verbal phrase
In *acquiring the horse*, a powerful weapon for survival was gained. (*Weapons* cannot *acquire*.)
Correct use of preposition plus a verbal phrase
In *acquiring the horse*, they gained a powerful weapon for their survival. (*They* can *acquire*.)

Sentence Work II

Here is an exercise in verbals and verbal phrases that function as nouns.

1. Combine, tighten, or change each item by using a verbal or verbal phrase so that it functions as a noun. Watch your punctuation. (Words are provided in parentheses to get you started.)
- a) When the Spanish conquistadors brought the horse to the New World, the Indians' lifestyle was changed. (the Spanish conquistadors' bringing)
- b) A brave could chase game across the plains for hours, and his pony would not stumble. (without his pony's stumbling)
- c) If a brave joined one of the tribal military societies, he would be allowed certain privileges; for example, he would receive the best food. (joining, receiving)
- d) There was one method to become a member of a military society that was commonly used. That was to buy society symbols from older members. (of becoming, to buy)

e) During the early 1800s a Blackfoot warrior could gain glory if he joined either a horse-stealing party or a war party. (by joining)
f) Gifts could be given as compensation for an injury done to someone. (to compensate)
g) If someone was hurt without receiving an offer of compensation, this was a grievous insult to him. (to hurt, to insult)

Do not continue with the second part of this exercise until you have checked your answers with the suggested ones.

2. These verbal phrases are dangling. Rewrite them.

a) By stealing the horse of a renowned warrior, much prestige could be gained.
b) By touching an enemy with his feathered coup-stick during an attack, humiliation would result.
c) When fighting, an arrow could be shot fairly accurately from under the horse's belly.

A wonderful substitute for dependent clauses, verbals encourage you to be brief and emphatic. The benefits of using verbals far outweigh the few difficulties that you can run into when using them.

Paragraph Work

Rewrite this short paragraph, making it more emphatic by using verbals and verbal phrases.

This lab only scratches the surface of Indian culture. It does, however, give many facts about Canada's Indians. Their culture was varied and it was fascinating too. Why not learn more about them? You can do this if you ask your librarian for some reading material. If you use a book such as Fraser Symington's *The Canadian Indian*, it will give you background information. You might then go on and read more because it will whet your appetite for books on modern Indian life.

Lab 9 — Absolute Phrases

Introduction

In this lab you will examine ways to add a descriptive or a narrative detail to a sentence by introducing an *absolute phrase*. Used regularly by professional writers, the absolute phrase is often shunned by beginning writers. Once you have mastered the absolute phrase, your writing will take on a new and interesting dimension.

Explanation

1. Instead of trying to learn how to define an absolute phrase, you should learn the several ways of constructing absolute phrases so that you will be able to use them with confidence and purpose. First examine the sentences below. The absolute phrases are in italic. Notice that they add details to a word in the rest of the sentence and are always set off from the rest of the sentence by commas.

Gordon Lightfoot, *his career one of the most successful in Canadian popular music*, performs to sell-out audiences throughout North America.

His eyes twinkling gently, his fingers moving briskly on his fiddle, Don Messer won the hearts of millions of Canadians.

The Dionne quintuplets, *their pictures and names world famous*, starred in several movies.

Now, take a look at each absolute phrase so you can learn to recognize one. First of all, it has a subject. The subjects in the above absolute phrases are: "career, eyes, fingers," and "pictures and names." Absolute phrases do not have full verbs; that is why they are phrases, not clauses. Some have verbals; some have no verbs. In the above absolute phrases the verbals are "twinkling" and "moving." Two absolute phrases have no verbals. By supplying a verb or part of a verb to each absolute phrase, you can create a full independent clause; for example:

His career *was* one of the most successful in Canadian popular music.

His eyes *were* twinkling gently.

His eyes *twinkled* gently.

His fingers *were* moving briskly on his fiddle.

His fingers *moved* briskly on his fiddle.
Their pictures and names *were* world famous.

You can create an absolute phrase by reversing the procedure: in some cases remove the verb from an independent clause; in other cases change the verb to a verbal. The absolute phrases function exactly like adjectives, adding a descriptive or narrative detail to a noun.

2. Notice how to combine sentences by using absolute phrases:

From
Rich Little was born in Ottawa.
His imitations of American presidents are well known.
To
Rich Little, *his imitations of American presidents well known*, was born in Ottawa.

From
Wayne and Shuster began their long television career in 1954.
Their work on CBC radio had been very popular.
To
Their work on CBC radio having been very popular, Wayne and Shuster began their long television career in 1954.

How have the above two absolute phrases been created? What verbs have been deleted or changed?

3. Now examine how to tighten longer sentences by changing dependent clauses to absolute phrases.

Complex sentence
A number of Canadian ballet dancers, of whom Karen Kain is the most famous, have become internationally known.
Tightened by using an absolute phrase
A number of Canadian ballet dancers, *Karen Kain being the most famous*, have become internationally known.
Tightened further by removing the verbal from the absolute phrase
A number of Canadian ballet dancers, *Karen Kain the most famous*, have become internationally known.

4. By including several absolute phrases in a single sentence, you can be more concise than by including the details in several sentences or clauses.
Also, notice the effect of moving a cluster of absolute phrases:

Absolute phrases at the beginning of a sentence
Their eyes shining, their hearts palpitating, their voices screaming his name, fans all over the world worshipped American singer and movie star Elvis Presley.
Absolute phrases at the end of a sentence
Fans all over the world worshipped American singer and movie star Elvis Presley, *their eyes shining, their hearts palpitating, their voices screaming his name.*

For practice in making up absolute phrases, change Elvis's name to that of your favourite singer and continue the sentence by filling in the blanks:

... their voices screaming his name, their arms _____, their ears _____, their stomachs _____, their psyches _____, their toenails _____.

Do you see that you can create absolute phrases by subdividing the subject, in this case, *fans*, into an incredible number of parts?

5. Besides adding several absolute phrases to a sentence, you can add other word groups to your absolute phrases.

Simple sentences
Doug Henning was born in Winnipeg.
He performs remarkable feats.
His skilful magic makes tigers and elephants disappear.
He astounds theatre, nightclub, and television audiences.
He is also thrilling movie fans.

Notice how the sentences have been combined by using an absolute phrase and two verbal phrases:

Sentence combining
Astounding theatre, nightclub, and television audiences as well as thrilling movie fans, Winnipegger Doug Henning performs remarkable feats, his skilful magic making tigers and elephants disappear.

Simple sentences
Anne Murray is familiar to millions.
She has short, blonde, neatly styled hair.
She has a friendly smile.
She is an all-Canadian girl.

Notice how the sentences have been combined by using two absolute phrases and an appositive:

Sentence combining
Anne Murray is familiar to millions, her short blonde hair neatly styled, her smile friendly — an all-Canadian girl.

6. Besides merely adding details, absolute phrases can suggest relationships of cause and effect.

Simple sentences

Montreal-born William Shatner was the logical choice to play Captain Kirk in *Star Trek – The Motion Picture*.

The television show of *Star Trek* has been syndicated all over the world.

William Shatner's face and exploits are known to thousands of devoted "Trekkies."

A natural cause-and-effect relationship is established using dependent clauses.

Sentence combining

Because his television show has been syndicated all over the world and because his face and exploits are known to thousands of devoted "Trekkies," Montreal-born William Shatner was the logical choice to play Captain Kirk in *Star Trek – The Motion Picture*.

But notice the conciseness of the cause-and-effect relationship when absolute phrases are used.

Sentence combining

His television show syndicated all over the world, his face and exploits known to thousands of devoted "Trekkies," Montreal-born William Shatner was the logical choice to play Captain Kirk in *Star Trek – The Motion Picture*.

7. In addition to absolute phrases, there are other absolute constructions less closely related to the main sentence in which they appear. On first glance, these absolutes appear to modify the entire sentence.

All things considered, many Canadian entertainers have been quite successful.

To be honest, I think that Canadians like jazz singer Salome Bey deserve more recognition.

If you were to convert these absolutes to full clauses, they would be extremely wordy.

When I consider all things, many Canadian entertainers ... .

I am being honest when I say that Canadians like jazz singer ... .

Sentence Work

Rewrite or combine these sentences by using absolute phrases or other absolutes.

 a) Ronald Reagan has gained one of the world's highest offices – President of the United States.
   His career as an actor began in the 1930s.
 b) I am telling the truth when I say that no one knows why one talented performer becomes a star and another does not.

c) David Steinberg is a popular guest host of *The Tonight Show.*
His humour is always irreverent and intelligent.
d) Canadian women have written a number of folk-rock hits.
Joni Mitchell has composed "Both Sides Now."
Buffy Sainte-Marie has composed "Indian Cowboy."
e) His thatch of white hair gleamed.
His voice rang out from centre ice at the Montreal Forum.
Roger Doucet sang national anthems for both NHL and international hockey.
f) René Simard had made a name for himself in Quebec.
CBC producers decided to star the teenage singer in his own national TV show in the 1970s.
g) His records sell in the millions.
His appearances in Las Vegas and elsewhere are always well attended.
His songs are performed by singers like Frank Sinatra and Tom Jones.
Ottawa-born Paul Anka can truly be called an international celebrity.

Paragraph Work

Use any ideas in these sentences to add absolute phrases to the paragraph below. Expand upon the suggestions in the brackets.

Bruce Lee is remembered for a few movies.
They still live in his fans' minds.
His face did not smile in his movies.
His hands and feet flew on the screen.
His fans' hearts thrilled to his unbelievable antics.
His fans' minds wish that he were still alive to make more movies.
My mind is always exploring possibilities.

Bruce Lee, [the memory], lives on as a cult figure. Lee, [his face], [his hands and feet], was *the* hero of martial-arts movies during his lifetime. Now that he is dead, fans still flock to his movies, [their hearts], [their minds]. [My mind], I wonder if he would still be popular had he not died.

Lab 10 Appositives

Introduction   The word group discussed in this lab has four significant characteristics.

1. It always comes next to the word it refers to.
2. It is always separated from the word by punctuation.
3. It can easily be exchanged with the word or word group it refers to.
4. It can easily be left out or substituted for the word group it refers to.

If you would like to provide details in a single sentence *without* using adjectives, phrases, or clauses, consider using an *appositive*.

Explanation   **A.** An appositive is an extremely useful word group for emphasizing or tightening a part of a sentence.

Single sentences
The first immigrants to Canada were the ancestors of today's Indians.
They may have come from Asia.

Sentence combining
The first immigrants to Canada, who were the ancestors of today's Indians, may have come from Asia.

Tighter sentence combining
The first immigrants to Canada, *the ancestors of today's Indians*, may have come from Asia.

Notice how this last sentence follows each of the four characteristics outlined in the Introduction:

1. The appositive, *the ancestors of today's Indians*, comes next to the words it refers to, *the first immigrants to Canada*.
2. The appositive is separated from the rest of the sentence by commas.
3. The sentence would read just as well if written:

The ancestors of today's Indians, the first immigrants to Canada, may have come from Asia.

4. The sentence *without* the appositive makes sense:

The first immigrants to Canada may have come from Asia.

It would also make sense to use the appositive as the subject:

The ancestors of today's Indians may have come from Asia.

Try to apply the four characteristics to these longer appositives:

Viking explorers, *the first Europeans to try to settle permanently in Canada*, called the country "Vinland."

The fur trade, *the industry which was the source of New France's wealth*, also prompted exploration of all parts of North America.

B. The appositive may be used in various ways. Notice the effect of the following appositives.

1. An appositive can come first:

A remarkable Scotsman, Lord Selkirk invested his own money to bring settlers to what is now Winnipeg.

2. A short appositive at the end can be particularly strong:

Those who fought hardest against immigration to the West were those with the most to lose – *buffalo hunters and fur traders*.

(The dash, a stronger form of punctuation, shows more emphasis than the comma.)

3. Appositives can be longer than the main sentence:

Susanna Moodie, *a remarkable woman who wrote of her experiences as a pioneer in* **Roughing It in the Bush**, deserves to be better known.

4. Notice the effective repetition connected with this appositive:

The potato famine in Ireland during the 1840s – *the famine portrayed in Cecil Woodham-Smith's* **The Great Hunger** – forced many people to emigrate to North America.

C. There are two ways to set appositives apart from the rest of the sentence: with a comma, or a dash. The comma is more matter-of-fact, the dash more emphatic. Notice the different effects of these two sentences.

At the end of the nineteenth century, immigrants from Britain were so disliked that some farmers hung signs on their gates, "No Englishmen or dogs allowed."

At the end of the nineteenth century, immigrants from Britain were so disliked that some farmers hung signs on their gates – "No Englishmen or dogs allowed."

Sentence Work

Combine each group of sentences into a single sentence by using an appositive:

Example

The Mennonites were promised freedom from military service when they came to Canada. The Mennonites are devoutly religious. They are of German origin.

Combined sentence

The Mennonites, *devoutly religious people of German origin*, were promised freedom from military service when they came to Canada.

a) Sharon Pollock wrote a play called *The Komagata Maru Incident*.
It has caused a great deal of controversy.
The play describes the Canadian government's refusal to accept a boat-load of East Indian immigrants.

b) Vancouver is a point of entry for many immigrants from Asia.
Vancouver is a city which has the second-largest Chinese population in North America.

c) The internment of Japanese Canadians during World War II has been the subject of books by several former prisoners.
The internment is not an incident to be proud of.

d) The settlement of thousands of immigrants on the Prairies assisted in Canada's becoming one of the world's leading agricultural nations.
The settlement was helped a great deal by the building of the CPR.

e) Victims of persecution have come to this country in large numbers.
The victims have included the Asians of Uganda.
Other victims have included the Chinese of Vietnam.

Paragraph Work

Read over these pairs of sentences. Combine them so that there is an appositive in each sentence. Then join the sentences into a unified, coherent paragraph.

We are the people of Canada.
We have welcomed immigrants from all over the world.

People work and save to come to our country.
They say it is the land of opportunity.

Some of us are immigrants; some, natives.
We should all strive to make this the best country in the world.

Lab 11   Clusters of Adjectives

Introduction

By grouping a few adjectives together and placing them before or after the noun they modify, you will be able to add special emphasis to a sentence. Clusters of adjectives, however, can be repetitive and ineffective if used in sentence after sentence, so be careful when you use them.

Explanation

1. Notice the effect of putting the cluster of adjectives in two different positions:

Before the noun
Huge, mysterious, and terrifying monsters can, according to legends, be found all over the world.

After the noun
Monsters – *huge, mysterious, and terrifying* – can, according to legends, be found all over the world.

2. Notice the position and punctuation of these clusters of adjectives.

At the beginning of a sentence
Bearlike, gigantic, menacing, the Yeti or Abominable Snowman stalks the Himalayas.

At the end of a sentence
The Himalayas are stalked by the Yeti or Abominable Snowman – *bearlike, gigantic, menacing*.

Although you could use a comma to separate the cluster, the dash makes the word group more emphatic. Can you think of one other position for the adjective cluster in this sentence?

3. A blend of adjectives, participial verbals, and prepositional phrases can add an effective touch to a long sentence. Arrange all adjective clusters in some kind of order (climactic, spatial, structural, and so on). When you are introducing phrases, watch for parallelism in addition to order.

Example

Eager for thrills, searching for evidence, or hungering for fame, crackpots and
   scientists haunt the shores of Loch Ness for a glimpse of its famous monster.

4. Now see how to combine sentences by using adjective clusters.

Two sentences

Photographs that are allegedly of "Nessie" (the Loch Ness monster) show a
   creature with a large, snakelike body and a small head.
   For some reason the creature seems to have a strange appeal.

Combined sentence

Photographs that are allegedly of "Nessie" show a *large-bodied, small-headed,
   snakelike, but somehow appealing* creature.

Three complex sentences

Ancient legends told of ferocious monsters which had some human characteristics.
People thought they were in danger from these creatures.
Nowadays we have discovered that we are in danger from a ferocious creature
   who is fully human – our fellow man.

Combined sentence

Ancient legends told of *ferocious, part-human, dangerous* monsters; nowadays
   we fear a *ferocious, fully human, and much more dangerous* monster – our
   fellow man.

Simple sentences

Lake Manitoba's Manipogo has been sighted since 1909.
It moves quickly through the water.
It upsets the fish.
It terrifies the local residents.

Combined sentence using clusters of verbal phrases

Lake Manitoba's Manipogo, *speeding through the water, upsetting the fish, and
   terrifying the local residents*, has been sighted since 1909.

Simple sentences

Igopogo inhabits Lake Simcoe in Ontario.
Its face is like a dog's.
It has a neck like a stovepipe.

Combined sentence using clusters of prepositional phrases

With a face like a dog and a neck like a stovepipe, Igopogo inhabits Lake
   Simcoe in Ontario.

Simple sentences

A nineteenth-century monster named Jacko had a body like a man's.

Its coarse black hair gleamed.

Its arms extended below its knees like a gorilla's.

It was considered a type of Sasquatch.

Combined sentence using clusters of absolute phrases

Its body resembling a man's, its coarse black hair gleaming, its arms extending gorilla-like below its knees, a nineteenth-century monster named Jacko was considered a type of Sasquatch.

Simple sentences

The lake monster Ponik is humped like a camel.

It is sinuous, as a serpent is.

It is as good-natured as a puppy.

It appeared as a centennial symbol for a Quebec town.

Combined sentence using clusters of adjectives and prepositional phrases

The lake monster Ponik, *humped like a camel and sinuous like a serpent*, but *good-natured like a puppy*, appeared as a centennial symbol for a Quebec town.

Sentence Work

Tighten each sentence by using clusters of adjectives, verbal phrases, or prepositional adjective phrases:

a) British Columbia boasts several monsters. One of them is an ancient creature, resembling a serpent, which inhabits Okanagan Lake. He is known as Ogopogo. He has proved extremely hard to catch.

b) The Sasquatch of British Columbia, the Giant Hairy Ape of Washington, and Bigfoot of California are different names for the same beast. Though it dates from prehistoric times, it is supposed to be alive and well today.

c) Cadborosaurus is affectionately known as "Caddy." He has a large body. He has an eager manner. He has an intelligent appearance.

d) Bigfoot is a manlike beast found in Oregon and California. Many people claim to have seen him. He is huge and covered with hair. He is known for his ferocity.

e) Stenwyken, the "wild man of the woods," has often been seen by the Shuswap Indians. It fishes at the mouths of creeks. It runs through the woods. It has even abducted an Indian girl.

Paragraph Work

Place clusters of adjectives, prepositional adjective phrases, verbals, or absolutes into the brackets. Use these sentences for material.

King Kong was ferocious.

He terrified audiences.

But he had dignity.

Frankenstein's monster dominated the movie industry.

He was ugly but kind-hearted.

Movies about the devil showed beautiful children with monsters' hearts.

Werewolves were doctors who worked hard, teenagers who were industrious,
    Americans who visited London.

Things from outer space slithered, pulsated, and erupted.

In modern movies faces become hideous, hands turn into claws, bodies burst
    veins, and even heads explode.

Audiences were struck with terror and screamed when they first saw Godzilla.

Film directors have created many monsters that have become myths. King Kong – [   ] – strode through two film epics. Grotesque characters have always dominated the movie industry [from] [to]. Werewolves, also, were of many types: [   ]. Things came from outer space – [   ]. Recent movies have become a technician's dream. [With], actors in horror movies must sit for hours while make-up artists perform miracles. Movie fans expect more from each new monster movie they see. Today's audience would snicker if Godzilla were to walk across the screen. But do you remember when that Japanese monster first made its appearance to a [   ] audience?

Lab **12** Clusters of Adverbs

Introduction

Like adjectives, clusters of adverbs can be placed before or after the word they modify. Adverb clusters should be used appropriately, economically, and judiciously.

Explanation

Because the principles of using adverb clusters are similar to those for adjective clusters, this lab is a short one. Refer to Lab 11 if you are confused at any stage during the explanation of how to use *adverb clusters*.

1. Notice the different effect of the two positions of the cluster of adverbs.

Before the verb
Wayne Gretzky *swiftly, skilfully, and effortlessly* carries a puck from one end of a hockey rink to the other.

After the verb
Wayne Gretzky carries a puck *swiftly, skilfully, and effortlessly* from one end of a hockey rink to the other.

Can you place the cluster of adverbs in two other positions?

2. Notice the effect of these two positions of the cluster of adverbs.

At the beginning of the sentence
Confidently and unerringly, he directs the puck either to his waiting teammates or into the opponents' net.

At the end of the sentence
He directs the puck either to his waiting teammates or into the opponents' net, *confidently and unerringly.*

Can you place the cluster of adverbs in two other positions?

3. Generally, you should use commas or dashes to set off a cluster of adverbs that disturbs the normal flow of your sentence.

Example

Edmonton Oilers' fans greet "The Great Gretzky" – *enthusiastically, boisterously, and unashamedly* – every time he sets foot on the ice.

Where else could you place the cluster? Would you still use dashes around it?

4. Prepositional adverb phrases can add an effective touch to a long sentence. You should always arrange the adverbs in your clusters in some kind of order (climactic, quality, and so on). When you are using phrases, watch for parallelism (Lab 14) as well as order.

The following prepositional adverb phrases work on the same principle as adverbs; they modify the verb *has made*.

By scoring fifty goals in thirty-nine games, by gaining more than 200 points in a single season, by becoming the first hockey player to win the 1981 Sporting News athlete of the year award, Wayne Gretzky has made sports history.

Where else could you place the cluster of prepositional adverb phrases?

5. Now see how to combine sentences by using adverb clusters.

Simple sentences
Gretzky is a humble young man.
He is not a selfish person.
His words are sincere.
He shares his success with his teammates.

Combined sentence
Humbly, unselfishly, and sincerely, Gretzky shares his success with his teammates.

Complex sentence
Because his passes are deadly accurate and his shots are uncommonly precise, Number 99 has shattered goal and assist records.

Recombined sentence
With deadly accurate passes and *with uncommonly precise shots,* Number 99 has shattered goal and assist records.

Sentence Work   Combine or tighten each of the following sentences by including clusters of adverbs or prepositional adverb phrases in one sentence. Vary the position of your clusters.

a) His brothers still practise at every opportunity.
They are diligent workers.
They practise on the backyard rink in Brantford, Ontario, where Wayne learned to play.

b) Gretzky appears in commercials.

He puts his name on hockey sweaters and T-shirts.

He talks to high-school students.

He has become known to more North Americans than any other hockey player.

c) His $21 million contract has made him the world's richest hockey player.

There is no question about this.

No player deserves the honour more.

d) He will patiently sign autographs for young fans.

He has a deliberate manner.

He will sign autographs, without tiring, for hours after a practice or a game.

e) On February 24, 1982, Wayne Gretzky scored his record-breaking 77th goal.

He appeared on *Good Morning America*.

President Ronald Reagan phoned him.

He became an American sports superstar.

Paragraph Work

Add to the following paragraph by including within the brackets either adverb or prepositional adverb phrase clusters. Use these sentences for material for your clusters.

Sports experts all agree that Gretzky is the world's current hockey star.

They are enthusiastic in their agreement.

Even at a young age, Gretzky was calm and quiet in his approach to breaking scoring records.

He deliberately set out to be the greatest.

He will continue to amaze people because he is still young, has enormous skill, and has luckily avoided injury.

Sports experts [   ] agree that Wayne Gretzky is currently the world's greatest hockey player. Since he was nine years old, he has [   ] gone about the business of breaking scoring records. [   ], this twenty-one-year-old marvel will probably continue to amaze both peers and fans for many years to come.

Lab **13** Emphasis

Introduction

In this lab you explore the possibilities of paring down a clause or a phrase to a single word. As a writer you should always attempt to be precise, concise, and emphatic.

Explanation

1. The strongest positions in a sentence are the beginning and the end. To place a single word or a short phrase in either position – especially if it is set apart by a comma or a dash – will make it emphatic.

The 1968 election produced Canada's sixteenth prime minister – *Pierre Elliott Trudeau.*

As host and guest, Trudeau has been involved in many conferences of world leaders.

2. Single words or short phrases can also be effective in mid-sentence; sometimes they are set off by punctuation, and sometimes not.

Trudeau, *undoubtedly*, has been one of Canada's most influential politicians.
Trudeau has *undoubtedly* been one of Canada's most influential politicians.

3. An existing single word or phrase can often be re-positioned for greater emphasis.

His three sons – Justin, Sasha, and Michel – *frequently* accompany him on foreign trips.

Frequently, his three sons – Justin, Sasha, and Michel – accompany him on foreign trips.

Where else could you place *frequently* and *undoubtedly* (from point 2) so that they would be in emphatic positions?

4. Repositioning an existing word or phrase may not only give it greater emphasis, but may change the meaning of the sentence.

Only Trudeau * has * been * elected * prime minister * five times.

Move *only* to the position of each asterisk. How does each move change the meaning of the sentence? Which is the most correct and emphatic?

5. The occasional coined word or phrase, which may or may not be set in quotation marks, can also be emphatic.

His "*fuddle-duddle*" in the House of Commons became a household word.
Before his 1968 election, the first signs of *Trudeaumania* appeared.

6. When you combine or condense sentences, you may often find that you can substitute a short, emphatic word or phrase for a longer word group. Are the words in italic in the most emphatic position?

Complex sentence
A prime minister who speaks English and French fluently, Trudeau has been compared with Sir Wilfrid Laurier.
Single phrase emphasis
Fluently bilingual, Trudeau has been compared with Sir Wilfrid Laurier.

A wordy sentence
One can be sorry that many Westerners have not been fond of some of Trudeau's policies.
Single word emphasis
Alas, many Westerners have not been fond of some of Trudeau's policies.

7. You might notice as you revise your sentences that some part can be pared down to a single word or phrase which is emphatic in itself regardless of its position.

Simple sentences
Trudeau is Canada's leader.
He has served one of the longest terms as prime minister.
Single word emphasis
Trudeau is one of Canada's *longest-serving* prime ministers.

Simple sentences
Women flocked around him in large groups.
Women begged for a hug or a kiss.
Single phrase emphasis
Mobs of women begged for hugs or kisses.

Simple sentences
Over the years Trudeau has become an international spokesman.
He pleads the cause of the world's less-developed countries.
Single phrase emphasis
Over the years Trudeau has become an international spokesman for *Third World* countries.

Sentence Work

Move the word or phrase in italic to a more emphatic position.

a) Trudeau has, *to say the least*, stressed the importance of a strong central government.

b) He has *only* dealt with five U.S. presidents: Johnson, Nixon, Ford, Carter, and Reagan.

c) The dialogues between the wealthy nations of the Northern Hemisphere and the poorer nations of the Southern Hemisphere have *recently* become very important to Trudeau.

d) Often heavily criticized in Canada, *internationally*, Trudeau has always had great stature as a leader.

Combine each group of sentences into a single sentence which contains at least one emphatic word or phrase.

e) George Radwanski wrote a fascinating biography. It was called *Trudeau*.

f) Richard Gwyn wrote a book called *The Northern Magus*. He says in it that Trudeau is stylish but that there is no substance to him.

g) Out of Quebec and into federal politics came Pierre Trudeau, Jean Marchand, and Gérard Pelletier. They were nicknamed "the three wise men."

h) Trudeau fought for his constitutional plan. This brought him into conflict with the provincial premiers. They were just as stubborn as he was.

Paragraph Work

Rewrite this paragraph, moving or changing portions of it so that you have several examples of emphasis.

There is no doubt about it – Pierre Elliott Trudeau is an enigma; some people support him; a number of other people oppose him. Trudeau is, without question, the Canadian prime minister who has intrigued the largest number of people. There is no doubt that he loves Canada, and travelling throughout the world, he has made Canada more prominent. Wherever he travels, his lifestyle, that is not like that of other people, inspires headlines throughout the world. Through what he does and says, the other countries of the world are often given a favourable impression of Canada. But at home, Trudeau has irritated many Canadians. He often gives an impression that he is arrogant, though he claims to be a meek person. He demands to have privacy, yet he takes his children on worldwide tours. Trudeau is surely a puzzling person.

Lab 14 Parallelism

Introduction

Consider parallelism in the world around you. An orchard is filled with trees that are all the same distance apart. Why? A well-manicured lawn on one side of a sidewalk shows up an unkempt lawn on the other side. In what way?

Although faulty parallelism in writing may not have disastrous consequences, it may cause members of your reading audience to become derailed and miss the point you are trying to make.

To master parallelism is to add strength and control to your writing. Parallelism, perhaps more than any other method of grouping words, helps not only to structure ideas, but also to clarify relationships among these ideas.

Explanation

A. If you want to include several ideas in a single sentence, use *parallelism* to organize the ideas and to express the relationship among them. Even when there are only two elements in a sentence, you can use parallelism.

There may be parallelism between words, phrases, or clauses: noun matched with noun, adjective with adjective, verbal phrase with verbal phrase, and so on.

Sometimes the parallelism is so natural as to require no effort by the writer and is almost unnoticed by the reader; sometimes it is elaborate and striking.

1. Study the following examples of parallel structure:

a) *Nouns*
   Television and *radio* are two of the twentieth century's most influential inventions.
b) *Verbs*
   They have *revolutionized* communication and *improved* our knowledge of other parts of the world.
c) *Adjectives*
   Immediate, visual, on-the-spot coverage of all sorts of news events is now commonplace.

d) *Verbal phrases*

Millions of viewers and listeners, *working in factories* and *relaxing at home*, rely on radio and television. (Do you see two other instances of parallelism?)

e) *Prepositional phrases*

Television has changed the course *of politics*, *of education*, and even *of history*.

f) *Dependent clauses*

We can scarcely imagine a world *where we could not listen to radio* or *where we could not watch television.*

The previous sentences contain parallel elements that are all linked by co-ordinate or correlative conjunctions.

2. If a writer joins grammatically *unlike* elements, his or her sentence contains faulty parallelism.

Weak parallelism

Canadian Reginald Fessenden, one of the pioneers of radio, has gained acclaim abroad, but his own countrymen have neglected him.

There are two ways of making the elements parallel:

Parallel

Canadian Reginald Fessenden, one of the pioneers of radio, has been *acclaimed abroad* but *neglected at home.*

Parallel

People abroad have acclaimed Reginald Fessenden, one of the pioneers of radio, but *his own countrymen have neglected him.*

Faulty parallelism

Dr. Abraham Gesner was a physician and an inventor, and he also wrote poetry.

Parallel

Dr. Abraham Gesner was a *physician, inventor, and poet.*

Do you see how the elements in the previous sentences have been made parallel?

3. Now, notice how to combine sentences by using parallelism.

Separate sentences

Torontonian Tommy Ryan invented five-pin bowling.

He did not patent his invention.

He made no profit from it.

Parallel sentence

Torontonian Tommy Ryan invented five-pin bowling, but he did not *patent his invention* or *make a profit from it.*

Separate sentences

Thomas "Carbide" Willson was an inventor and scientist.

He was a brilliant man.

He had a great deal of influence on the scientific community.

Parallel sentence

Thomas "Carbide" Willson was both *a brilliant inventor* and *an influential scientist*.

B. The *balanced sentence*, a special kind of parallelism, is discussed briefly in Lab 4. The balanced sentence gives your writing precision; it allows no part of the thought to get lost.

1. Look at these two balanced sentences:

Oil spills can destroy beaches and harm fish, but "Slicklickers" can absorb oil and prevent damage.

McIntosh apples grow in the Annapolis Valley of Nova Scotia; they also flourish in the Okanagan Valley of British Columbia.

They have four things in common:

a) They are composed of two independent clauses.

b) They use parallel structure.

c) They rely on identical or closely similar words.

d) They have approximately the same number of words in each clause.

2. When you write a balanced sentence with similar ideas, make each clause parallel:

George Eastman developed the Kodak camera, and Edwin Land developed the Polaroid camera.

Then see if you can take out any unnecessary words. Your sentence will still be balanced:

George Eastman developed the Kodak camera, and Edwin Land, the Polaroid camera.

3. There are two main ways of writing a balanced sentence.

a) To show *similar* relationships between its parts, use a comma plus *and*:

King Gillette invented the safety razor, and Jacob Schick, the electric razor.

Or use a semicolon:

King Gillette invented the safety razor; Jacob Schick, the electric razor.

b) To show *opposite* relationships between its parts, use a comma plus *but*:

Armand Bombardier first developed the snowmobile as a working vehicle, but most people now use it as a recreational vehicle.

Or use a semicolon:

Armand Bombardier first developed the snowmobile as a working vehicle; most people now use it as a recreational vehicle.

4. When you want to make a balanced sentence memorable, try using reversals:

Not only is necessity the mother of invention, but with modern advertising, invention has become the mother of necessity. (What two words have been reversed?)

5. It is not only possible, but effective, to balance three ideas:

Scotsman Andrew Meikle invented the threshing machine in 1786, American Cyrus McCormick, the reaping machine in 1831, and Canadian Thomas Carroll, the self-propelled combine in 1938.

The first wristwatch was made in Switzerland in 1790, the first self-winding wristwatch, in England in 1924, and the first electronic wristwatch, in the United States in 1961.

What three things are balanced in each of the previous sentences?

6. You can balance dependent as well as independent clauses within sentences, but then only part of the sentence will be balanced. After you have written the main part of a sentence, you can balance independent clauses, dependent clauses, or phrases.

Sentence with balanced independent clauses

Canadians have become involved in garbage recycling: *Johann Sollinger has invented a method of making edible products out of sewage*, and *Richard Keefer, a method of making energy out of carbohydrates*.

What verb is understood in the second balanced clause?

Sentence with balanced dependent clauses

Since small receivers can be built and *since inefficient vacuum tubes can be eliminated*, the invention of the transistor has greatly changed modern communications.

Sentence with balanced dependent clauses

Leonardo da Vinci has gained fame not only *because he painted the "Mona Lisa"* but also *because he invented the parachute*.

Sentence with balanced phrases

Leonardo da Vinci has gained fame not only *for painting the "Mona Lisa"* but also *for inventing the parachute*.

When you balance portions of a sentence, you should follow the same guidelines as you would for a perfectly balanced sentence. (See points 1 and 3.) Look over the sentence models in point 6. Point out the characteristics of the balanced parts according to point 1; notice if the parts are similar or opposite according to point 3.

Sentence Work

Combine these sentences by using parallelism. Create a balanced sentence where appropriate.

a) Basketball was invented by a Canadian.
   It is played throughout the world.
b) Jacques Cousteau developed the aqualung, which made him famous.
   He hosted a television series, which is another of his claims to fame.
c) The electronic calculator is a phenomenon of the twentieth century.
   The ancient Chinese abacus is also a calculator.
d) The flush toilet was invented by Sir John Harington.
   It was improved by Sir Thomas Crapper.
e) Thomas Edison was a remarkable man.
   He invented the electric light bulb.
   He developed a recording device.
   He worked on motion pictures.

Paragraph Work

Rewrite this paragraph. Wherever possible, make use of parallelism and balanced sentences. If you see any faulty parallelism, correct it.

There is a saying, "Build a better mousetrap and the world will beat a path to your door." Most inventors, though, have been shunned instead of being cheered. For every Canadian who has succeeded, there are dozens who have failed. Lack of interest has plagued inventors. So has lack of money. The government encourages inventions. Private sources should help inventors.

Lab 15 Loose and Periodic Sentences

Introduction   In your writing, you will usually use loose sentences because they correspond more closely to normal speech rhythms and patterns; you will, nonetheless, find many opportunities to write a periodic sentence.

Explanation   The meaning in a *loose sentence* is disclosed to the reader near the beginning of the sentence. The reader of a *periodic sentence* does not know the full meaning of the sentence until near the period.

1. Notice the two ways you can combine these simple sentences.

Simple sentences
Canada is certainly a less violent place than the United States.
In the U.S. a violent crime is committed every thirty-one seconds.
In Canada a violent crime is committed every four minutes.

Combined as a loose sentence
Canada is certainly a less violent place than the United States, since in the U.S. a violent crime is committed every thirty-one seconds, compared with one every four minutes in Canada.

Combined as a periodic sentence
Since in the U.S. a violent crime is committed every thirty-one seconds, compared with one every four minutes in Canada, Canada is certainly a less violent place than the United States.

Do you see that there is a natural built-in suspense in periodic sentences because the topic is withheld until the last moment? When would you most likely use periodic sentences?

2. In order to create a good periodic sentence you need to know how to subordinate using dependent clauses, prepositional phrases, verbal phrases, and absolute phrases. A periodic sentence should end with what you consider the most important item from an independent clause and begin with all the other information which is presented in subordinate constructions.

Simple sentences

Roger Caron became a celebrity overnight.

His book, *Go-Boy*, won the Governor-General's Award for nonfiction.

It describes a major portion of his life.

He spent this portion behind bars.

Sentence combining with dependent clauses

When his book *Go-Boy*, which describes in detail the major portion of his life that he has spent behind bars, won the Governor-General's Award for nonfiction, Roger Caron became an overnight celebrity.

Sentence combining with a variety of subordination

Describing in detail the major portion of his life spent behind bars, Roger Caron's book, *Go-Boy*, not only won the Governor-General's Award for nonfiction, but also made Caron an overnight celebrity.

Can you subordinate this periodic sentence in a different way?

3. When you write a periodic sentence, you must decide which piece of information to withhold from your reader by putting it at the end of the sentence. Read these different versions.

Making "escaped" the period word

Montreal gangster and narcotics overlord Lucien Rivard, given permission during a warm spell to water the outdoor skating rink at the supposedly secure jail where he was being held, caused a scandal when he climbed over the jail wall and escaped.

Making "scandal" the period word

Montreal gangster and narcotics overlord Lucien Rivard, who was given permission during a warm spell to water the outdoor skating rink at the supposedly secure jail where he was being held, not only escaped by climbing over the jail wall, but also caused a scandal.

Practise writing a periodic sentence by making "jail" the period word.

4. When parallel structure is added to a periodic sentence, the suspense becomes more intense.

Simple sentences

N. William Kennedy cut the mooring lines of the S.S. *Orient Trader*.

He let the vessel drift toward a nearby tug.

He boarded the *Orient Trader*.

He sailed for Spain.

He had carried out the theft of the largest object ever stolen by a single person.

Sentence combining with parallel dependent clauses

When N. William Kennedy cut the mooring lines of the S.S. *Orient Trader*, let the vessel drift to a waiting tug, boarded the *Orient Trader*, and sailed for Spain, he carried out the theft of the largest object ever stolen by a single person.

Sentence combining with parallel verbal phrases

Cutting the mooring lines of the S.S. *Orient Trader*, letting the vessel drift to a waiting tug, boarding the *Orient Trader*, and sailing for Spain, N. William Kennedy carried out the theft of the largest object ever stolen by a single person.

Sentence Work

Combine the simple sentences into periodic sentences, using the suggested hints.

a) The British Columbia Penitentiary discharged its last prisoner in 1980.
Riots, hostage takings, and murders occurred behind its grim stone walls.
(Begin with *The British Columbia Penitentiary*; end with *1980.*)

b) The youngest person ever to appear at London's Old Bailey was an eleven-year-old girl.
She was charged with stealing a doughnut and a frosted bun.
She was acquitted by a jury.
(Begin with *Charged*; end with *girl.*)

c) Bill Miner was Canada's most famous train robber.
He led a double life as churchgoer and thief.
He originated the expression, "Hands up!"
(Begin with *Bill Miner*; end with *"Hands up!"*)

d) Albert Johnson was called "the mad trapper of Rat River."
He fled to the North after killing a Mountie.
He led the RCMP on the most spectacular manhunt in Canadian history.
He has become the subject of a film called *Death Hunt*.
The stars of the film are Lee Marvin and Charles Bronson.
(Begin with *Albert Johnson*; end with *Death Hunt.*)

e) Winnipeg police had been unable to find $57,000 in loot from a bank robbery.
Two eleven-year-olds and a twelve-year-old decided to play amateur detectives.
They found the money in a back lane.
(Begin with *Two eleven-year-olds and a twelve-year-old, deciding*; end with *back lane.*)

Paragraph Work

From these sentences write a single paragraph composed of three periodic sentences. Begin sentence one with *While* and end it with *paroled*. Begin sentence two with *Ten* and end with *parole*. And begin sentence three with *More Joy in Heaven* and end with *Ryan's story*.

Norman "Red" Ryan was sentenced to life imprisonment for bank robbery.
He was a model prisoner.
He persuaded a Catholic chaplain and the Toronto press that he was a changed man.
He was paroled.
He masterminded bank robberies while on parole.
He was killed ten months later while trying to rob a liquor store.
Morley Callaghan wrote the novel *More Joy in Heaven*.
The novel is based on Ryan's story.

Suggested Answers

Lab 1   Sentence Work

1. a) independent
   b) dependent
   c) independent
   d) dependent
   e) dependent

2. a) conjunction, conjunction, adjective, noun
   b) pronoun, verb phrase, adjective, noun
   c) adverb, adjective, preposition, adverb
   d) interjection, noun, preposition, noun
   e) conjunction, preposition, adjective, noun, noun

3. a) phrase, clause
   b) phrase, phrase
   c) phrase, phrase, clause
   d) phrase, phrase, phrase, phrase
   e) clause, phrase

Paragraph Work

This, more than any of the other labs in *The Writer's Workshop*, is your tool kit. In the same way as a (*caddy*) needs to know the difference between a (*club*) and a (*ball*), you need to know the difference between a subject and a verb when your reader refers to one or the other of them. What a waste of time it would be if a (*golfer*) had to ask, "Give me the (*club*) with the kind of funny (*thick, wooden head with the number 1 on it*)," or "I want the one with the (*thin, blade-like, straight-faced, iron head*)." All the (*golfer*) should need to say is, "Give me a (*driver*)," or "I want the (*putter*)." When one of your readers says, "I think you should have used a phrase instead of a clause," you have to know what he/she is talking about. Words and word groups are a writer's tools. Learn to identify them.

Lab 2 Sentence Work
a) 9
b) 4
c) 5
d) 2
e) 6
f) 1
g) 7
h) 3
i) 10
j) 8
k) 11

Paragraph Work

Since there are many different kinds of energy, [we may wonder] how there can be an energy crisis. The reason is [that North America has used only a few energy sources]. These have been mainly coal and oil. If we can learn [to use other fuel sources] – solar power, wind power, and biomass – our energy crisis will soon be over.

Lab 3 Sentence Work

If your responses differ from these, make sure that each of your sentences has only **one independent** clause. If your sentence has more than one clause, it may read perfectly well, but the assignment was to write only simple sentences. To help you check your answers, note that both the main subject and main verb of each sentence are in italic. Some sentences have compound main subjects and main verbs.

a) In Toronto in 1940, *Norman Breakey invented* the truly remarkable paint roller, revolutionizing the painting industry.
b) Among other things, *Benjamin Franklin invented* bifocal glasses, worn by many older people to help them to read better.
c) *Doctors John Hayward, Martin Collis, and John Eckerson* of the University of Victoria *developed* a jacket to help in cold water survival.
d) Quebec's cold *winters gave* Arthur Sicard the idea for the snowblower.
e) *Samuel F. B. Morse made* a contribution to the development of the West, his code making long-distance communication possible.

Paragraph Work

The Eddy Company, one of the world's largest matchmaking operations, was established in Hull, Quebec, in 1851 by Ezra Butler Eddy. Over the years the friction matches were merchandised under the names *Telegraph*, *Parlour*, and *Eddy Matches*. The name *Telegraph* was used to suggest speedy ignition. The name *Parlour* was used to suggest use of the matches in the parlour.

The name *Eddy Matches* was used to honour the founder. The company, with its widespread lumbering interests, introduced the book match into Canada in 1928.

Lab 4   Sentence Work

If any of your versions are not the same as the ones below, do not be concerned. They may be just as correct. So discuss your responses with your partner. Check carefully that you have used co-ordination and not subordination. The use of subordination would definitely be the wrong response for this lab, even if your sentences make perfect sense.

a) The people of the North adapted to their harsh climate: their bodies grew extra layers of fat, they wore several layers of well-made fur clothing, and their high-protein diet provided large amounts of energy.
b) Weather in the North may sometimes be unpleasant, but Montreal receives more snow in an average winter than some parts of northern Canada.
c) Anthony Thrasher was a talented Inuit artist, yet he died alone and unhappy.
d) In the old days the Inuit used dogsleds to move across snow and ice; nowadays they use snowmobiles.
e) Northern peoples want to benefit from the development of their land: first, they want money for the use of the land; then, they want jobs on the pipelines and oil rigs; finally, they want guarantees of the preservation of their hunting and fishing rights.

Paragraph Work

Most people in southern Canada (not only) have little knowledge of the North (but also) have little interest in it. This is an unfortunate attitude (, for) Northern Canada is a land of almost unlimited opportunity (; moreover,) it is not simply a barren expanse of ice and snow (, but) a bewitchingly beautiful place.

Lab 5   Sentence Work

a) *Because it wanted to celebrate Prince Charles's wedding,* Vancouver hosted the world's largest tea party on July 29, 1981.
b) The largest number of championships in log rolling, *which is a popular sport all over North America,* was won by Jubiel Wickheim.
c) *When Louis Cyr pitted his strength against horses and steam engines,* he so astonished everyone *that he was called "the strongest man in the world."*
d) For *what it's worth,* in 1975 Paul Mears smoked thirty-five full-size cigars at once. ("For" begins a prepositional phrase which contains a dependent clause that acts like a noun. Another answer would be – "*Although the fact*

may not be worth much, in 1975 Paul Mears smoked thirty-five full-size cigars at once." It's wordier but correct.)

e) *Whoever talks about Canada-U.S. relations* mentions with pride the world's largest undefended border, *which stretches almost 6500 km from coast to coast.*

Paragraph Work

[Because people should be interested in conserving energy], they should look to the sea. Specifically, [whoever is interested in alternate energy sources] should know about the tides in the Bay of Fundy. These tides, [which are the highest in the world], are [what New Brunswick is exploring as a source of future power].

Lab 6   Sentence Work

a) While Bonhomme Carnaval presides over Quebec City's annual winter carnival, *ice sculptors and canoe racers vie for top honours* and *revellers crowd Quebec City from dawn to midnight.*

b) When the Okanagan peaches are ripe, *visitors flock to Penticton's Peach Festival*; there, *they can take part in street dancing or watch the Square Dance Jamboree.*

c) *Many residents of Kitchener are of Swiss-German descent*; *each year they celebrate Oktoberfest*, where a great deal of sauerkraut, sausage, and beer is consumed.

d) *Tossing the caber is an old Celtic sport* which involves throwing a long pole as far as possible; *many people attend Nova Scotia's Highland Games to see the caber tossing*, but *few will try it.*

e) *The Banff School of Fine Arts provides courses in painting, ballet, music, and theatre*; *it is also the home of the annual Festival of Arts*, where the talents of its students are displayed.

Paragraph Work

[Wherever you go in Canada], someone will be celebrating something: Nanaimo has its bathtub races; [the Maritimes, their maple-syrup breakfasts]; Stratford, its Shakespeare Festival; and Saskatoon, its Pioneer Days. Canadians break up the yearly calendar with festivals, fairs, and shows that spring from a spirit of good fun and a sense of national pride; [tourists flock to enjoy them].

Lab 7   Sentence Work

a) The United States is smaller *in land area* than Canada.

b) Some people say that Canada has a "branch-plant" economy, *because of the many subsidiaries of American companies in Canada.*

c) American troops burned Toronto *during the War of 1812.*

d) *In spite of themselves*, Canadians enjoy the more violent American TV shows.

e) Few people know *of Canada's introduction of North American football to the U.S.*

f) More than twenty American universities offer courses *about Canada*.

g) The CBC was created in 1936 *on account of the departure of many talented performers for the U.S.*; its series and specials have been exported all over the world.

h) Only 40 per cent of Canadians *over twenty-one* have completed high school; 65 per cent of Americans *over twenty-one* have done so.

Paragraph Work

Canadians have become more conscious about their identity [within the last ten years]. Americans are sometimes annoyed at Canadians [because of their insistence] [on staying separate]. Nonetheless, Canadians and Americans have many things [in common]. [During the twentieth century] both countries have increased their influence further than their boundaries. Linguistic and cultural ties [between Canada and the United States] have made the natives [of each] comfortable [with the other].

Lab 8

Section "4a"

The answers include the verbals or verbal phrases plus the word they modify:

Chanting and *dancing*, youths
Starved and *exhausted*, warrior
Having feasted and *danced*, tribes
went *to hunt*
months *to carve*

Section "4b"

Celebrating their coming of age, boys
Secured to the sacred Sun Lodge by leather thongs through their chest muscles, Indian men
Having proved himself a courageous warrior, man
Believing in the principle of "a life for a life," Indians
made *to use on the hunt*
To ensure successful fishing, chieftain

Sentence Work I

1. a) The hosts of a potlatch would use it *to pay back previous hosts* and *to gain the right to be invited to future potlatches*.

   b) *Varying a great deal in ritual and dogma*, all religions of all Indian tribes shared a belief in the spirits of nature.

   c) *Being the life force of the Indians*, religion was present in everything they did.

d) *Setting the sun and moon in the sky*, *controlling their courses*, and *causing the change of seasons*, the spirits were part of everything and everyone.

e) *Once discovered*, a *guiding* spirit would be called on in time of need.

f) *Fervently observed* and *carefully practised*, the tribal rituals showed the Indians their spiritual heritage.

The portion of the exercise dealing with dangling modifiers provides one suggested answer for each. There would be at least one other. (Remember how to prevent creating a dangling modifier: use active, rather than passive, voice.)

2. a) The Ojibway, *having killed a bear*, held ceremonies of apology for the death of a friend.

b) *Because they were skilled in dealing with spirits*, medicine men prepared charms to keep away sickness and evil. (A dependent clause is used instead of a phrase.)

c) *Dancing and singing*, an Indian felt the intimacy with the spirit in every part of his being.

d) *To record their clan's history and achievements*, chiefs had totem poles put up in front of their houses.

e) *To see authentic Haida totem poles*, you should visit the Queen Charlotte Islands.

f) *In order that this art form will survive*, young carvers have learned the traditional carving methods. (Another dependent clause is used instead of a phrase.)

Sentence Work II

1. a) *The Spanish conquistadors' bringing of the horse to the New World* changed the Indians' lifestyle. (Can you explain why the *s'* is needed?)

b) A brave could chase game across the plains for hours, *without his pony's stumbling*.

c) *Joining one of the tribal military societies* allowed a warrior certain privileges, such as *receiving the best food*.

d) A common method of *becoming a member of a military society* was *to buy society symbols from older members*.

e) During the early 1800s a Blackfoot warrior could gain glory by *joining either a horse-stealing party or a war party*.

f) Gifts could be given to someone *to compensate for an injury*.

g) *To hurt someone without offering compensation* was *to insult him grievously*.

The portion of the exercise dealing with dangling modifiers provides one suggested answer for each. There would be at least one other.

2. a) By *stealing the horse of a renowned warrior*, an Indian could gain much prestige. (The verbal phrase is linked to *by*; therefore, the entire prepositional phrase which contains a verbal phrase, modifies *Indian*.)

b) If a warrior was touched by an enemy's feathered coup-stick during an attack, he would be humiliated. (A dependent clause is used instead of a verbal phrase.)

c) When *fighting*, a rider could shoot an arrow fairly accurately from under the horse's belly.

Paragraph Work

The verbals and verbal phrases are in italic. (Your paragraph may be quite different, but it should have several verbal phrases.)

This lab, while *giving many facts about Canada's Indians*, only scratches the surface of their *varied, fascinating* culture. *To learn more about them*, ask your librarian *to suggest material*. By *using a book such as Fraser Symington's **The Canadian Indian** to give you background information*, you may want *to go on, having had your appetite whetted*, to books on modern Indian life.

Lab 9 Sentence Work

a) *His career as an actor having begun in the 1930s*, Ronald Reagan has gained one of the world's highest offices - President of the United States.

b) *To tell the truth*, no one knows why one talented performer becomes a star and another does not.

c) *His humour always irreverent and intelligent*, David Steinberg is a popular guest host of *The Tonight Show*.

d) Canadian women have written a number of folk-rock hits, *Joni Mitchell having composed "Both Sides Now" and Buffy Sainte-Marie, "Indian Cowboy."*

e) *His thatch of white hair gleaming, his voice ringing out from centre ice at the Montreal Forum*, Roger Doucet sang national anthems for both NHL and international hockey games. (*Or* put the absolute phrases after *games.*)

f) *René Simard having made a name for himself in Quebec*, CBC producers decided to star the teenage singer in his own national TV show in the 1970s. *Or* CBC producers decided to star René Simard in his own national TV show in the 1970s, *the teenage singer having made a name for himself in Quebec.*

g) *His records selling in the millions, his appearances in Las Vegas and elsewhere always well attended, his songs performed by singers like Frank Sinatra and Tom Jones*, Ottawa-born Paul Anka can truly be called an international celebrity.

Paragraph Work

Bruce Lee, [the memory of his few movies still in fans' minds], lives on as a cult figure. Lee, [his face unsmiling], [his hands and feet flying], was *the* hero of martial-arts movies during his lifetime. Now that he is dead, fans still flock to his movies, [their hearts thrilling to his unbelievable antics], [their minds wishing that he were still alive to make more movies]. [My mind always exploring possibilities], I wonder if he would still be popular had he not died.

Lab 10 Sentence Work

Though your appositives may look quite different from the ones in italic, they very well may be fine. For your sentences that are different, apply the characteristics in the Introduction of Lab 10 or discuss your sentences with your partner.

a) *A play by Sharon Pollock which describes the Canadian government's refusal to accept a boatload of East Indian immigrants,* The Komagata Maru Incident has caused a great deal of controversy.

b) Vancouver, *a city with the second-largest Chinese population in North America,* is a point of entry for many immigrants from Asia.

c) *Not an incident to be proud of,* the internment of Japanese Canadians during World War II has been the subject of books by several former prisoners.

d) The settlement of thousands of immigrants on the Prairies – *a settlement helped a great deal by the building of the CPR* – contributed to Canada's becoming one of the world's leading agricultural nations.

e) Victims of persecution, *victims including Asians of Uganda and the Chinese of Vietnam,* have come to this country in large numbers.

Paragraph Work

We, *the people of Canada,* have welcomed immigrants from all over the world. People work and save to come to our country, *the land of opportunity.* We should all, *immigrants and natives,* strive to make this the best country in the world.

Lab 11 Sentence Work

a) British Columbia boasts several monsters: one, known as Ogopogo, is an *ancient, serpentlike, elusive* creature which inhabits Okanagan Lake.

b) The Sasquatch of British Columbia, the Giant Hairy Ape of Washington, and Bigfoot of California are different names for the same beast: a supposedly *living, breathing, prehistoric* creature.

c) Cadborosaurus *with his large body,* [*with his*] *eager manner, and* [*with his*] *intelligent appearance,* is affectionately known as "Caddy."

d) Many people claim to have seen Bigfoot – the *huge, hairy, ferocious, manlike* beast found in Oregon and California.

e) Stenwyken, the "wild man of the woods," has often been seen by the Shuswap Indians, *fishing at the mouths of creeks, running through the woods, even abducting an Indian girl.*

Paragraph Work

Film directors have created many monsters that have become myths. King Kong – [ferocious, terrifying, yet dignified] – strode through two film epics. Grotesque characters have always dominated the movie industry [from Frankenstein's ugly monster with a kind heart to the devil's beautiful children with monsters' hearts]. Werewolves, also, were of many types: [hard-working doctors, industrious teenagers, Americans visiting London]. Things came from outer space – [slithering, pulsating, erupting]. Recent movies have become a technician's dream. [With faces becoming hideous, hands turning into claws, bodies bursting veins, even heads exploding], actors in horror movies must sit for hours while make-up artists perform miracles. Movie fans expect more from each new monster movie they see. Today's audience would snicker if Godzilla were to walk across the screen. But do you remember when that Japanese monster first made its appearance to a [terror-stricken, screaming] audience?

Lab 12   Sentence Work

a) His brothers still practise *frequently and diligently* on the backyard rink in Brantford, Ontario, where Wayne learned to play.

b) *By appearing in commercials, by putting his name on hockey sweaters and T-shirts*, and *by talking to high-school students*, Gretzky has become known to more North Americans than any other hockey player.

c) His $21 million contract has made him *unquestionably and deservedly* the world's richest hockey player.

d) He will sign autographs for young fans – *patiently, deliberately, unstintingly* – for hours after a practice or a game.

e) On February 24, 1982, *with his record-breaking 77th goal, with his appearance on* Good Morning America and *with his phone call from President Ronald Reagan*, Wayne Gretzky became an American sports superstar.

Paragraph Work

Sports experts [unanimously and enthusiastically] agree that Wayne Gretzky is currently the world's greatest hockey player. Since he was nine years old, he has [calmly, quietly, and deliberately] gone about the business of breaking scoring records. [Because of his youth, his skill, and his ability to avoid injury], this twenty-one-year-old marvel will probably continue to amaze both peers and fans for many years to come. (Written in 1982.)

Lab 13   Sentence Work

a) *To say the least*, Trudeau has stressed the importance of a strong central government.

b) *Only* he has dealt with five U.S. Presidents: Johnson, Nixon, Ford, Carter, and Reagan.

c) The dialogues between the wealthy nations of the Northern Hemisphere and the poorer nations of the Southern Hemisphere have become very important to Trudeau *recently*. (You could also begin the sentence with *recently*.)

d) Often heavily criticized in Canada, Trudeau has always had great stature as a leader *internationally*.

e) George Radwanski wrote a fascinating biography, *Trudeau*.

f) Richard Gwyn's book, *The Northern Magus*, accused Trudeau of being *all style and no substance*.

g) Out of Quebec and into federal politics came Pierre Trudeau, Jean Marchand, and Gérard Pelletier – "*the three wise men*."

h) *Fighting* for his constitutional plan brought Trudeau into conflict with the *equally stubborn* provincial premiers.

Paragraph Work

Undoubtedly, Pierre Elliott Trudeau is an enigma; some people support him; *others* oppose him. Trudeau is *unquestionably* Canada's most *intriguing* prime minister. *Without doubt*, he loves Canada, and travelling throughout the world, he has made Canada more prominent. Wherever he travels, his *unconventional* lifestyle inspires *worldwide* headlines. *Through him*, the other countries of the world are often given a favourable impression of Canada. But at home, Trudeau has irritated many Canadians. Often he gives an impression *of arrogance*, though he claims to be meek. He *demands* privacy, yet takes his children on worldwide tours. Trudeau is surely a *puzzle*.

Lab 14

Sentence Work

a) A sport *invented by a Canadian* and *played throughout the world*, is basketball.

b) *Developing the aqualung* and *hosting a television series* are two of Jacques Cousteau's claims to fame.

c) *The electronic calculator is a phenomenon of the twentieth century*, but *the Chinese abacus is a calculator of ancient origin*.

d) *Sir John Harington invented the flush toilet; Sir Thomas Crapper improved it.*

e) The remarkable Thomas Edison not only *invented the electric light bulb*, but also *developed a recording device* and *worked on motion pictures*.

Paragraph Work

There is a saying, "Build a better mousetrap and the world will beat a path to your door." Most inventors, though, have been more shunned than cheered.

For every Canadian who has succeeded, dozens have failed. Lack of interest and lack of money have plagued inventors. The government encourages inventions, but private sources must help inventors.

Lab 15

Sentence Work

a) The British Columbia Penitentiary, behind whose grim stone walls occurred riots, hostage takings, and murders, discharged its last prisoner in 1980.

b) Charged with stealing a doughnut and a frosted bun, and acquitted by a jury, the youngest person ever to appear at London's Old Bailey was an eleven-year-old girl.

c) Bill Miner, Canada's most famous train robber, who led a double life as churchgoer and thief, originated the expression, "Hands up!"

d) Albert Johnson, "the mad trapper of Rat River," who fled to the North after killing a Mountie and led the RCMP on the most spectacular manhunt in Canadian history, has become the subject of a film starring Lee Marvin and Charles Bronson called *Death Hunt*.

e) Two eleven-year-olds and a twelve-year-old, deciding to play amateur detectives after Winnipeg police had been unable to find $57,000 in loot from a bank robbery, found the money in a back lane.

Paragraph Work

While he was serving a life sentence for bank robbery, Norman "Red" Ryan, after persuading a Catholic chaplain and the Toronto press that he was a changed man, was paroled. Ten months later, after Ryan had been killed trying to rob a liquor store, it was discovered that he had masterminded bank robberies while on parole. *More Joy in Heaven*, a novel by Morley Callaghan, was based on Ryan's story.

Introduction to the Appendices

Because of the usefulness of certain information, it has been placed in appendices for easy access.

Appendix A will help you in the prewriting process by giving you ideas on how to keep a journal.

Appendix B contains check lists to aid you in the editing of your own work. It also discusses the importance of feedback during the revising process, offering a number of specific techniques to help you and your peers conduct a feedback session.

Appendix C points out the need to proofread your paper before submitting it to your final reader. Ideas are provided to help you in your polishing process.

Appendix A Keeping a Journal

Introduction

As a young actor in Hollywood, Charlton Heston kept a journal. In 1978, he brought those otherwise unrecorded experiences together to create a fascinating best seller, *The Actor's Life*.

During her visits throughout the world, Lois Wilson, moderator of the United Church of Canada, kept a journal of her impressions. The result of her recording her emotions and concerns is the book, *Like a Mighty River*.

Popular children's novelist Judy Blume recently brought out a unique diary which contains no dates. Only the occasional quotation appears. Thus, she encourages the owners of her book to write down their own feelings, reactions, and sensations. She, in fact, encourages journal writing.

For ten minutes each day, in or out of class, write in your journal.

Consider these comments

What is a journal? A book in which you write about your feelings, thoughts, and experiences.

Who will read my journal? Only you. Or anyone to whom you care to show it. Journal writing allows you to explore thoughts and ideas, and experiment with language, without worrying about evaluation.

What is the point of writing in a journal? To get in touch with yourself. The more you can write about your feelings, thoughts, and experiences, and the more you can experiment with paragraphs, sentences, and words, the more comfortable you should be with all of your future writing assignments. As you continue your journal entries, you should become more adventurous and should stretch your writing in untried ways so that your journal becomes more and more valuable to you. Discover your strengths; develop your own unique way with words by experimenting in your journal. So you can find a particular piece of writing quickly, you should date and label or title each journal entry.

Why is it necessary to write in my journal every day? Your goal should be to create a habit of writing. If you want to swim well, for example, you have to get into the water and practise swimming. Your journal writing is one way to practise your writing skills every day.

May I use any of my journal writing for other assignments? Certainly. You will find that in future assignments you will be able to refer to your journal for an idea, a particular sentence, or even a turn of phrase.

What do I do with my journal at the end of the school term? That is up to you. If you have begun the habit of journal writing, you will probably keep it up long after term's end.

Suggested Journal Topics

Once you are in the habit of writing in your journal, it should not be difficult to identify something you want or need to write about. But here are some suggestions to get you started.

1. Start with one of these openings and write about *yourself*. Do not be concerned about how your piece will end — just write.

People always thought I was strong (weak).
I would rather not be a lender (borrower).
I am (not) a victim of others.
I do (not) intend to get married.
I often (seldom) become embarrassed.

Or you can create your own opening.

2. Describe yourself to an imaginary reader. Tell about the following:

your favourite song
your favourite singer
your favourite teacher
your least favourite person
your likes and dislikes
your ambitions

Add to the list.

3. Recall a past event and list all the details that you can remember:

an event from childhood
a highly emotional event
your last birthday
the most scary time of your life
a sad event

Add to the list.

4. Use your senses to describe the place where you are writing. Record everything you hear, see, feel, and smell. From time to time repeat this entry, but change your writing location.

5. Recall a recent newspaper headline or news item. What was your reaction?

6. Think about a familiar saying such as one of the following:

A bird in the hand is worth two in the bush.

Most people are nicer to total strangers than they are to their loved ones and to themselves.

You are what you eat.

Success is a journey, not a destination.

With ordinary talent, and extraordinary perseverance, all things are attainable.

Explain why you agree or disagree, or describe an incident that illustrates the saying.

7. Write a piece that concludes *logically* with one of the statements below, or make up your own concluding statement *before* you begin.

And the blind man said, "Life's been good to me."

There is no such thing as a well-adjusted slave.

No one can bring you peace but yourself.

But she (he) promised me she (he) would come through.

It's impossible to go back in time.

8. Write down one of the more important events of the human condition, such as, love, fear, death, greed, loneliness, or birth. Write the word over and over until something else comes into your mind, then continue writing about that thought. Plan to write non-stop for ten minutes. If you get stuck, go back to writing the original word again until something new comes into your mind.

9. What are your feelings about some of man's more profound theories, ideologies, religions, and so on? Start with a word like one of the following and then write: *monogamy, numerology, psychiatry, capitalism.*

10. You may also use your journal to practise sentence variety and sentence combining. If you would like to master a particular sentence pattern that you have studied in the Laboratory Section, rewrite any past journal entry using that sentence pattern as often as possible.

Appendix B Suggestions For Revising

Introduction

Revision is an ongoing process for every writer; in fact, you may often hear a writer say of a published book, "There are still a few things I'd like to change." This textbook has gone through several drafts. Every section has been revised, reformed, refined, and reshaped because the author clarified his thoughts while developing the manuscript and listened to feedback from teachers, editors, and students using pilot editions of the textbook. The result of their interest and concern is *The Writer's Workshop*.

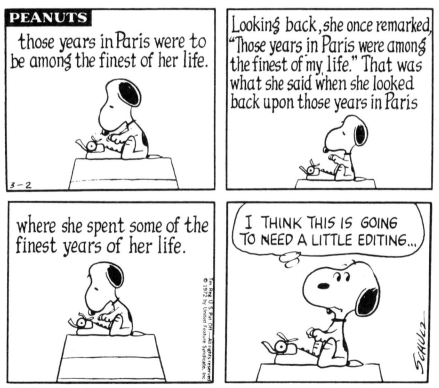

©1972 United Feature Syndicate, Inc.

Revising Your Own Work

This textbook advocates that when you have completed your final draft, you should ask your peer/editors and teacher/editor for their opinions before you submit your paper to its intended reader. Often, though, you will not have the time or opportunity for editorial feedback. At other times, you may not want to have your writing edited, but may want to give it directly to your intended reader without anyone else seeing it.

When you have completed your final draft, but *before* you give it to your editors or intended reader, you should examine your content, organization, style, and mechanics. Using the suggestions in the following four charts, judge your work as SUPERIOR, AVERAGE, or UNSATISFACTORY. Afterwards, if you are not satisfied with your paper, try to revise it to the standard you desire.

Content

Content involves the topic (subject, main claim, thesis) of the paper and its development.

SUPERIOR
1. The central idea is worth while: fresh, true, specific, and clear.
2. The idea is suitable for the length of the paper; therefore, it has been perfectly developed.
3. All the evidence has been fully presented through high-quality facts, reasons, details, examples, and so on.

AVERAGE
1. The central idea is apparent but unoriginal.
2. The development relies on common, everyday comments.
3. The idea and its development are of interest to only a small group of readers.
4. The development is often incomplete or repetitious as well as including unimportant, obvious, or irrelevant support.
5. There are some inconsistencies in the logical development of the idea.

UNSATISFACTORY
1. The central idea is either nonexistent or totally unimportant and trite.
2. There is no specific support of the idea.
3. The development does not clearly follow logical thought.
4. The idea and its development are inappropriate for the length of the assignment.

How would you judge your content: SUPERIOR, AVERAGE, or UNSATISFACTORY?

Organization

Organization involves the flow of a paper's development, the linking of each sentence within a paragraph, and how each paragraph logically follows the previous one.

SUPERIOR

1. The overall idea has been developed clearly and logically. It is obvious that a process of writing has been used and that the writing variables have been considered (Activity 1). The reader moves effortlessly from one section of the paper to the next.

2. The development has a specific, definite method of organization: comparison, cause/effect, spatial, chronological, climactic. Each piece of supporting evidence has been given just the right emphasis and is just the right length (Activity 2).

3. There is nothing irrelevant in the paper.

AVERAGE

1. The paper apparently has an organizational plan, but at times it gets off the point.

2. There is something wrong with the emphasis or order of some of the points; they are either over or under stressed, or in the wrong place.

3. Transitions (Activity 3) may be missing, or painfully overdone (for example: first, second, third, fourth, finally).

4. If the writer works on such a paper, he or she could produce a fairly good piece of writing. A bit of cutting, adding, and reshaping is needed. A close look at how finished papers have been organized would help (Activity 6).

UNSATISFACTORY

1. There is no clear organization.

2. The thoughts are either sketchy or redundant.

3. The paragraphs are not unified or coherent; transitions are insufficient or confusing.

4. Often, a new idea appears in a paragraph before the previous one has been developed fully.

How would you judge your organization: SUPERIOR, AVERAGE, or UNSATISFACTORY?

Style

Style involves not only the mode of expression but its effectiveness and appropriateness for each particular piece of writing (Activity 19).

SUPERIOR

1. The reader is always kept on track because the point of view is consistent (Activity 5).

2. Sentence variety is apparent throughout (Activity 8 and most of the labs). The mode of expression is as interesting as the thought it contains.

3. The word choice is clear and accurate, always appropriately linking the writer and the subject to the reader (Activity 15).

4. The level of language is consistent (Activities 15 and 18).

5. Effective figurative language has often been used (Activity 7).

6. The writer may include elements of satire (Activity 20).

7. The beginning and ending of the piece seem just right (Activity 4).

AVERAGE

1. The sentence structure is correct but lacks variety and emphasis. Some sentences may be wordy (Activity 12).

2. The writer often uses generalized rather than specific words; they are correct but not always apt.

3. Sometimes levels of language are mixed.

4. If figurative comparisons are used, they are sometimes strained, ineffective, or inappropriate.

UNSATISFACTORY

1. Sentences are confusing and monotonous.

2. Sentences lack emphasis, often because the verbs are weak and pronouns such as *it, this, which* are overused (Activity 11).

3. Word choice is limited and often ineffective or inappropriate (Activity 16).

4. Slang expressions, colloquialisms, and triteness fill the paper (Activities 15 and 18).

5. The writing is often unidiomatic, using non-English expressions or fracturing established modes of expression (Activity 15).

6. The point of view constantly shifts.

How would you judge your style: SUPERIOR, AVERAGE, or UNSATISFACTORY?

Mechanics

Mechanics deals with the nitty-gritty of writing: spelling, punctuation, grammar, and so on.

SUPERIOR

1. Grammar, punctuation, and spelling are generally accurate.

2. The paper is usually free of small mechanical errors, such as misuse of apostrophes, and hyphens (Activity 14).

3. Sentences are punctuated correctly, and show an understanding of the more complex punctuation marks: the semicolon, parentheses, dashes, as well as double and single quotation marks (Activity 13).

4. The writing contains no serious sentence errors, such as fragments and dangling modifiers.

5. The writing contains various methods of emphasis (Activity 9).

AVERAGE

1. Occasional mechanical errors creep into the writing.

2. The writing is often correct and careful, but to avoid making mechanical mistakes, the writer overuses the same words for fear of misspelling or misusing new ones; uses only commas and periods for fear of misusing semicolons; composes simple sentences for fear of creating misplaced modifiers. (To become a superior writer, you must take chances and learn from your mistakes.)

UNSATISFACTORY

1. The sense of sentences is often confused because mechanical errors abound. The writer has not come to terms with his or her writing problems, not knowing why he or she makes mistakes and not knowing how to correct them. The writer continues to shift tenses in mid-sentence, to run sentences together, and to let fragments stand as complete thoughts (Activity 10).

2. Punctuation marks are confusing.

3. Spelling errors are frequent.

How would you judge your mechanics: SUPERIOR, AVERAGE, or UNSATISFACTORY?

Revising Your Peers' Writing

Peer editing is so beneficial to the revision process that you and your peers should attempt to offer suggestions to each other on every assignment. Peer editing serves as an intermediate step between teacher-editing and self-editing. Through peer-feedback sessions with other students, friends, or relatives, you will be able to move toward becoming an independent, mature writer. Even professional writers have their editors, serving as an important part of their entire writing process.

Once you and your peer/editors become comfortable with editing each other's work, you will probably find that you will ask them for their comments before submitting anything you write to your intended reader.

What follows are some specific guidelines and suggestions for handling "feedback" sessions:

1. During a feedback session make sure that you and your peers comment on the writing variables. You should routinely ask questions like these:
   a) Is the topic worth while?
   b) Does the material fulfil its purpose: to persuade, to inform, to entertain, and so on?
   c) Is the writer's main idea or attitude toward the topic clear?
   d) Is the material suitable in content, level of language, and so on for its intended audience?
   e) Would the piece of writing be better in another format?

2. Every writer appreciates praise, so begin by pointing out the things that work well. Here are a few questions you might respond to after you have read one of your peers' papers:
   a) Which senses were stimulated?
   b) What part created the strongest impression?
   c) What part was the most genuine?
   d) Where did the paper divulge the most about the writer?
   e) What overall emotion will the intended audience be left with?

3. You should make suggestions about what to delete, add, substitute, or move; this applies to words, sentences, or paragraphs. In this part of the editing process you should consider the effectiveness of each sentence.

The more familiar you become with the Laboratory Section of this textbook, the more suggestions for revision you will be able to share during feedback sessions. Some of the most recent research refers to this step in the writing process as "reformation," where you, the writer, are encouraged to "reform" what you have written.

In essence, a feedback session should give you an impression of the effect that your writing will have on your intended audience, and provide ideas and suggestions on how to sharpen that effect.

4. A successful feedback session requires honesty and courage; you must be truthful, and the writer must be willing to accept your criticism. Thoughtfulness and thoroughness are also essential. When something is unsatisfactory, you should say so, pointing out what is wrong and making suggestions to improve the piece of writing.

5. Peer feedback takes time. It is very easy to say that everything someone writes is wonderful. This kind of statement saves a lot of talk, prevents any anxiety, and perhaps wins an immediate friend. But such a statement does not help a beginning writer. Treat your peer editing sessions as an essential part of your own writing process, and be prepared to spend time talking about a paper's main claim, organization, sentence variety, and word choice. If you, as a peer/editor, feel something in the paper is not working, even if you do not know exactly what is wrong, you should say so. A peer-feedback session is both a learning and a teaching time. When the members of your group learn to share knowledge with each other, you will all learn to write better.

6. All of the assignments in *The Writer's Workshop* have specific suggestions for peer-feedback sessions. If you are involved in peer editing with more than two people, make sure one of you takes on the duties of leader for that particular feedback session. The leader is responsible for keeping the discussion going and asking the questions contained in the Revising Suggestions in each assignment.

Your first attempts at editing may not be too successful, but research has shown that you can learn from your peers (often more effectively than from anyone else).

7. To make all your peer-feedback sessions profitable, you and your peers can choose from a variety of editing methods:

For pairs **Silent Reading**
   a) Exchange papers with your partner.
   b) As you read, prepare yourself to talk about what has been written, beginning with the strengths of the piece of writing, but not ignoring the weaknesses.
   c) Decide whether you will write directly on the piece of writing or make comments on a separate piece of paper.
   d) Do not talk until both papers have been read; then, discuss one paper at a time, using any of the suggestions above.

Read Aloud

a) Read your paper aloud. Your partner should be able to see what you are reading. This way he/she can hear your inflections while seeing your written words. Often your partner will see what you do not see. A writer often reads what he/she *thinks* is there, not what really *is* there.

b) Your partner should not interrupt your reading.

c) A discussion, using the suggestions above, should follow.

d) Repeat the procedure with your partner's paper.

For a three-member peer group

Numbers and Letters

a) Exchange papers.

b) Every time you see something that you would like to comment on, place a number in the margin near it.

c) Then on a separate piece of paper place the number and your favourable or unfavourable comment.

Example:

1. opening is very good
2. should appeal to the sense of smell
3. grammatical mistake

d) Then pass the piece of writing, with the numbers on it, to the next person to read. (DO NOT pass your comments. All the next person sees is the piece of writing with a series of numbers in the margin.)

e) The next person should repeat the same process, except he/she should use letters instead of numbers.

Example:

a) opening suspenseful
b) a run-on sentence
c) good image — I could really see it!

f) When the piece of writing has been seen twice, the owner should receive it with the two comment sheets.

g) Up to now, there should have been no talking, only reading and writing numbers/letters with comments. As you read, if any comments confuse you, ask your peers for clarification. This is the time to talk about your writing.

Read Aloud

a) Read your paper to the others in your group. No one should interrupt the reading, but one person should be able to see and follow what you have written as he or she listens. The other person should listen and make notes.

b) A discussion should follow the reading, beginning with the note-taker's comments. Start with praise.

c) When the group is satisfied that everything was said that should have been said, the next person reads his/her paper aloud, and the editing continues in the same way.

Duplicate
a) Give each member of your group a copy of your piece. Comments can be written directly on the paper, or on a separate piece of paper.
b) It is possible, using this method, for papers to be taken home in order to have more time to prepare for extensive editing. Class time can be spent on discussion rather than reading.
c) This method is ideal for longer essays and reports. It is also a more realistic approach when only one member of a group has something to be edited. In this case the duplicated essays can be given out the day before the feedback session.

For a peer group of three or more

Take-Home
a) Duplicate your paper and give a copy to the other members of your peer group to take home.
b) At home, they should write comments on your paper.
c) In class the *next* day, you read your paper aloud to your peer group. They may follow with their duplicated copy.
d) Using their comments, they should discuss how they felt, both as readers of and listeners to your paper. The discussion that follows can deal with ways you can improve your written paper.
e) Peers then give you their duplicated copy of your draft with their written suggestions.
f) You can incorporate into your final copy what you have heard in the discussion and what you read on copies of your drafts.

Fours and Twos
a) Divide your peer group into two pairs; then have each pair use any of the above methods to bring each paper up to a level that satisfies both writer and editor.
b) Then the pairs exchange papers. Each pair works together on the papers of the other pair. When the written critiques are complete, give the papers to their authors and discuss the critiques.
c) The discussion that follows will be quite different because both you and your partner will be able to talk about your paper. Remember, your partner helped you bring your paper up to a standard that satisfied him/her.
d) You should then revise *with* your partner, using or dismissing the suggestions made by the other pair in your peer group.

8. Once you have had your paper edited, you should prepare to write your final draft, using or rejecting the suggestions you have received from your group. In some cases your peers may suggest that you revise (reform) your paper completely and show them another draft at a later date.

Occasionally, your writing teacher may suggest that, for certain assignments, the revising process should end with you and your peer group. It is not necessary that your teacher/editor see *everything* you write. Your teacher may devise different methods of giving credit for the assignment; your peers, for example, could let your teacher/editor know that they think your piece of writing is ready for its intended reader. If this method of revision is used for a particular assignment, you should proceed directly to the Polishing Suggestions.

9. For most of your assignments, however, you will show your latest revised draft to your teacher/editor (who will not always be your intended reader). This one-to-one session will help you polish your writing for its intended audience. Remember, good writing should be written for a real audience and for a real purpose. Writing something just for the sake of writing usually produces bad results.

Are you becoming aware that it takes time to produce good writing? If a professional writer spends hours on revision and reformation, it is almost impossible for you, as a beginning writer, to dash off a 1000-word essay the evening before it is due, and finish with a high-quality product. Both you and your intended audience would suffer.

Appendix C Suggestions for Polishing

1. Professional proofreaders know that it is difficult to read a paper for its meaning and check it for mechanical errors at the same time. For this reason, many proofreaders read typeset copy backwards — so they will not become involved in the "story line," and miss errors in spelling, punctuation, and so on.

While you may not want to read your material backwards, you should take time to read it specifically for mechanical errors, once you are satisfied with its overall content and organization. You will likely discover errors that you or your peers have missed during the revision process.

2. Modern technology is already providing us with computers which scan essays for editing errors; therefore, checking for minor writing errors will eventually become the least important aspect of the writing process. But, until you have a word processor and a computer sitting on your desk, this part of the polishing process remains your responsibility. Do not let it overwhelm you; learn to use the writer's tools: the dictionary, the thesaurus, the handbook. They will help you strengthen your skill with words.

3. You should be able to answer yes to general questions like these concerning any particular piece of writing and its purpose and audience:

a) Are my sentences clear and varied?

b) Are my sentences grammatically correct?

c) Am I using the right words?

The Laboratory Section of *The Writer's Workshop* will help you with your sentence construction. You should find the sentence combining exercises particularly useful in bringing variety to your writing.

4. Use the "Mechanics" check list in Appendix B to help you in the proofreading process.

5. What you should try to accomplish in the polishing process is a publishable-looking paper with an appropriate title. "Publishable" simply means that, in your opinion, your work is ready to be presented to a final reader.

Index

492

Acknowledgments

Assignments

Text Credits:

"Pigs is Pigs" from *Pigs is Pigs* by Ellis Parker Butler. Used by permission of Harold Ober Associates Incorporated.

"Skalbania". Excerpt from THE ACQUISITORS by Peter Newman reprinted by permission of The Canadian Publishers, McClelland and Stewart Limited, Toronto.

"Drifting Home" from *Drifting Home* by Pierre Berton reprinted by permission of The Canadian Publishers, McClelland and Stewart Limited, Toronto.

"Never Cry Wolf" from *Never Cry Wolf* by Farley Mowat. © 1963 by Farley Mowat. By permission of Little, Brown and Company in association with the Atlantic Monthly Press; and reprinted by permission of The Canadian Publishers, McClelland and Stewart Limited, Toronto.

"The High Price of Soft-Sell" by Ken MacMillan. Used by permission of the author.

"Two Cities" from *Man: The Next Thirty Years* by Henry Still. Copyright © 1968 by Hawthorn Books, Inc. Reprinted by permission of the publisher, E.P. Dutton, Inc.

"Confessions of a Toe-Hanger" reprinted by permission of McIntosh & Otis, Inc. from *Confessions of a Toe-Hanger* by Christie Harris. © 1967 by Christie Harris.

"Prehistoric Drama: an Honest Bequest" by Marke Andrews © *The Vancouver Sun*, March 11, 1982. Used by permission.

"Hold Fast", review of *Hold Fast* by Irma McDonough from *In Review* — Canadian Books for Children, Summer 1978, published by the Provincial Library Service, Ministry of Culture and Recreation. Used by permission.

"The Hockey Sweater" by Roch Carrier, from *The Hockey Sweater and Other Stories*, translated by Sheila Fischman (Toronto: House of Anansi Press, 1979). Used by permission.

"Araby" from DUBLINERS by James Joyce. Originally published in 1916 by B.W. Huebsch. Definitive text Copyright © 1967 by the Estate of James Joyce. Reprinted by permission of Viking Penguin Inc.

"God Is Not a Fish Inspector" by W.D. Valgardson is reprinted from *God Is Not a Fish Inspector* by permission of Oberon Press.

"The Frisbee" and "How to Throw a Frisbee" are reprinted from MADE IN AMERICA by Murray Suid and Ron Harris, copyright © 1978, by permission of Addison-Wesley Publishing Company.

"Doing it With Style" from DOING IT WITH STYLE by Quentin Crisp and Donald Carroll. Copyright © 1981 by Carroll Regnier Associates, Inc. Used by permission of Franklin Watts, Inc.

"History Teacher's Comments" by Bonnie Sutherland. Used by permission of the author.

Student Writers:

Wun Yue Au, Conall Edward Barr, Melanie Boyle, David Brand, Michael Allan Chan, Judy E.M. Chapelsky, Linda Ann Danielson, Patricia Davies, Meldon Ellis, Shirleyanne Friesen, Steven J. Greenaway, Barbara Kaiser, Frankie Kirby, Carol Klassen, R. A. Klettke, John A. Lucas, Sherri Lynn McLennan, Chris Moffat, Gino Nasato, Chantal Phillips, Tracey Rockwell, Reg Romero, Charles Saramo, Lynn Stefonovich, Ivenie-Jean Thompson, Carol Vuch.

Activities

Text Credits:

"Pulling Your Own Strings." Specified excerpt (p. 13) from *Pulling Your Own Strings* by Dr. Wayne W. Dyer (Funk & Wagnalls). Copyright © 1978 by Wayne W. Dyer. Reprinted by permission of Harper & Row, Publishers, Inc.

"A Political Manager is Born". A selection from *Joe Clark - The Emerging Leader* by Michael Nolan, published and copyrighted by Fitzhenry & Whiteside, Toronto. Used by permission.

"The War Within Greenpeace" by Robert Hunter, used by permission of the author. First published in *Saturday Night*, October 1980.